VOYAGES AND VISIONS

D0878584

Critical Views

VOYAGES
AND VISIONS

Towards a Cultural History of Travel

Edited by
Jaś Elsner and Joan-Pau Rubiés

REAKTION BOOKS

ad amicitiam

Published by Reaktion Books Ltd
11 Rathbone Place, London W1P 1DE, UK

First published 1999

Copyright © Reaktion Books 1999

All rights reserved. No part of this publication
may be reproduced, stored in a retrieval system, or
transmitted, in any form or by any means, electronic,
mechanical, photocopying, recording or otherwise,
without the prior permission of the publishers.

Series design by Humphrey Stone
Printed and bound in Great Britain by
Biddles Ltd, Guildford and King's Lynn

British Library Cataloguing in Publication Data:

Voyages and visions : towards a cultural history of travel.
– (Critical views)
1. Travel 2. Voyages and travels
1. Elsner, Jas 11. Rubies, Joan-Pau
910

ISBN 1 86189 020 6

Contents

Notes on the Editors and Contributors

JAŚ ELSNER is Reader in the History of Art at the Courtauld Institute, University of London. He is author of *Art and the Roman Viewer* (1995) and *Imperial Rome and Christian Triumph* (1998). He edited *The Cultures of Collecting* (1994) with Roger Cardinal in this series.

JOAN-PAU RUBIÉS is Lecturer in History at the University of Reading. He has edited *Shifting Cultures: Interaction and Discourse in the Expansion of Europe* (1995). His book *Travel and Ethnology in the Renaissance: South India Through European Eyes, 1250–1625* is soon to be published.

KASIA BODDY is Lecturer in American Literature in the Department of English at University College, London. Her *Interviews with Contemporary American Writers* will be published soon.

MICHAEL T. BRAVO is University Research Fellow in the Department of Anthropology, University of Manchester. He is author of *The Accuracy of Ethnoscience* (1996) and is currently working on a historical anthropology of Inuit techniques of travel.

PETER BURKE is Professor of Cultural History at the University of Cambridge and Fellow of Emmanuel College. He has written many books on early modern cultural history, of which the most recent are *Varieties of Cultural History* (1997) and *The Fortunes of the Courtier* (1995).

MELISSA CALARESU is Fellow and Lecturer in History at Gonville and Caius College, Cambridge. She is a specialist in eighteenth-century intellectual history and is currently writing a book entitled *Enlightenment to Revolution in Naples: From Vico to Pagano*.

JESÚS CARRILLO is Lecturer in the History and Theory of Art at the Autonomous University of Madrid. He is currently writing a monograph on the representation of nature in the early chronicles of America.

PETER H. HANSEN is Associate Professor in History at Worcester Polytechnic Institute, Massachusetts. He has written widely on British mountaineering and imperial culture from the eighteenth century to the twentieth century.

EDWARD JAMES is Professor of History at the University of Reading. Besides his many books on medieval subjects, he has a passion for the history of science fiction. He is the editor of *Foundation: The International Review of Science Fiction* and author of *Science Fiction in the Twentieth Century* (1994).

NIGEL LEASK is Lecturer in English at the University of Cambridge and Fellow of Queens' College. He is an expert on Romanticism and is author, among other things, of *British Romantic Writers and the East: Anxieties of Empire* (1992).

WES WILLIAMS is Lecturer in French at New College, Oxford. He has recently published *'The Undiscovered Country': Pilgrimage and Narrative in the French Renaissance* (1998) and is currently writing a study on the representation of monsters in the Renaissance.

God between two angels presides over a 13th-century
T-O map of the world, with Jerusalem at the centre. British Library, London.

Introduction

JAŚ ELSNER AND JOAN-PAU RUBIÉS

TRAVEL AND THE PROBLEM OF MODERNITY

I may truly say that, of all the worshippers who clung weeping
to the curtain, or who pressed their beating hearts to the
stone, none felt for the moment a deeper emotion than did
the Haji from the far-north. It was as if the poetical legends
of the Arab spoke truth, and the waving wings of angels, not
the sweet breeze of morning, were agitating and swelling the
black covering of the shrine. But, to confess humbling truth,
theirs was the high feeling of religious enthusiasm, mine was
the ecstasy of gratified pride.

RICHARD BURTON[1]

This passage marks the culmination of a pilgrimage to Mecca made in
1853. The writer was not a Muslim, but an Englishman disguised as an
Arab, whose travels combined romantic exoticism, the attempt to map
unknown terrain in the interests of imperialist science, and the private
exploration of Oriental sexuality. All these different roles imply a conflict
with the act of pilgrimage as a religious experience. In his writing,
Richard Burton was clearly aware of the nature of his own pilgrimage of
pride (in heroically overcoming a cultural as well as geographical barrier,
and achieving what almost no non-Muslim had ever managed), by contrast
with the 'high feeling of religious enthusiasm' of the genuinely Muslim
Hajis.[2] What marks Burton as both modern and romantic is not simply
the cultural distance of European from Arab, or even the secular and
scientific from the religious, but his fascination with the depth of an
experience which for others may seem to evoke the 'waving wings of
angels'. Burton's claim to have progressed beyond the world of 'poetical
legends' is made significant by the fact that he is nostalgic for that world.
The claim to a universal scientific vision directing the progress of humankind is characteristically modern, implying a consciousness of historical
change as irreversible. However, beyond this lies the memory of a primeval

vision, which nineteenth-century Romantics would variously locate in pre-civilized, non-Western or pre-Enlightenment worlds. The world of poetical legends, in effect, represents the past of Burton's own European tradition and, in particular, a past of medieval quest and sacred vision which, paradoxically, makes possible his sceptical, even cynical, gaze.

In Burton's paean to 'beating hearts' and 'deep emotion', he and the genuine Hajis may seem briefly united at the goal of their journey. But, crucially, the Western traveller does not fulfil himself through a renunciation of identity in the face of a transcendent sacred reality. Rather he finds his pride gratified and his sense of a superior self affirmed through the accomplishment of a very different project. Burton's alternative project, at least in its public and rhetorical form, is proclaimed to the reader at the book's opening:

In the autumn of 1852, through the medium of my excellent friend, the late General Monteith, I offered my services to the Royal Geographical Society of London, for the purpose of removing that opprobrium to modern adventure, the huge white blot which in our maps still notes the Eastern and the Central regions of Arabia. (vol. I, p. 1)

This statement of intent, at the outset of Burton's book, with its double genuflection to military and scientific authority, defines a particular moment in the history of Western expansion, which has systematically combined imperialist claims with scientific and technological empiricism. The desire to map is never innocent.

In his description of the pilgrims' confrontation with the Kaaba in Mecca, Burton alternates between the high romanticism of the memory of angels' wings and a harder-edged scientific discourse. At times, the voice of science utterly replaces any hint of religious significance:

After thus reaching the stone, despite popular indignation testified by impatient shouts, we monopolised the use of it for at least ten minutes. Whilst kissing it and rubbing hands and forehead upon it, I narrowly observed it, and came away persuaded that it is an aërolite. It is curious that almost all travellers agree upon one point, namely, that the stone is volcanic. Ali Bey calls it 'mineralogically' a 'block of volcanic basalt, whose circumference is sprinkled with little crystals, pointed and straw-like, with rhombs of tile-red feldspath upon a dark background, like velvet or charcoal, except one of its protuberances, which is reddish'. Burckhardt thought it was 'a lava containing several extraneous particles of a whitish and of a yellowish substance'. (vol. II, p. 169)

Here Burton's 'narrow observation' is not just directed at an empirical examination of a reality irrelevant to the throng of worshippers. It is also, pointedly, a refutation of a series of earlier European writers who had preceded Burton by penetrating Mecca in disguise: 'Ali Bey' in 1807 and the Swiss John Burckhardt in 1814. 'Ali Bey' was in reality a Catalan called Domingo Badia, who travelled incognito in the service of the Spanish government from 1803 to 1808. His personality is illustrative of the tradition within which Burton fashioned his own *persona* as a man able to serve his own society while challenging its conventional moral values. Famous for the *Voyages d'Ali Bey*, published in Paris in 1815 and translated into English in 1816, Badia variously constructed himself throughout his career as enlightened reformer, scientific traveller and political spy.[3] Crucially, Burton's rhetorical attempt to claim authority as a direct observer – perhaps the fundamental literary mechanism of legitimation in the genre of travel literature – relies on his ability to supersede earlier writers in the scientific tradition.[4] Not only was Badia less knowledgeable, Burton claimed, but in his supposedly genuine narrative he constantly betrayed his origins as a European – suggesting that only Burton had learnt to disguise himself perfectly.

It would be possible to analyse Burton's journey to Mecca as the culmination of a tradition marked by curiosity and a desire for direct experience stretching back to Ludovico de Varthema from Bologna, who visited Mecca in 1503. In this perspective, what separates the Renaissance traveller, a freelance adventurer prompted by the discoveries of the Portuguese in India, from the Victorian traveller operating under the auspices of the British empire is the strengthening of the methods and structures of knowledge and domination; these frame the development of worldly curiosity by providing ever more detailed information, a system of cross-references to other sources, and hence the possibility for coherent criticism. The pioneer Varthema, who had no real models of travel for the sake of mere curiosity to refer to, is uncertain – for instance – as to whether his personal adventures in Mecca, Arab ritual customs or the two unicorns he claims to have seen were the more interesting objects of his description. Burton, by contrast, knows that precise geography, ethnography and classification are the real aims of his text, since – among other things – they allow him to distinguish an African antelope from a medieval fable.[5]

And yet this emphasis on scientific refinement impoverishes the cultural significance of Romantic travel. More interesting than the scholarly empiricism of Burton's text, and what perhaps separates him most clearly from his precursors, is its repeated turn to exoticism.[6] Burton's desire to see with his own eyes 'Moslem inner life in a really Mohammedan country' was opposed to his avowed tiredness of 'progress' and 'civilization'.[7] Of course, this cannot be separated from the scholarly, politically tainted Orientalism within which Burton's narrative of the East is inescapably caught.[8] As Edward Said wrote, referring to the Orient as a place of pilgrimage for Romantic travellers, 'Flaubert, Vigny, Nerval, Kinglake, Disraeli, Burton, all undertook their pilgrimages in order to dispel the mustiness of the pre-existing Orientalist archive'.[9] However, this Romanticism is no mere projection of Western desire upon the Oriental other for the sake of imperial dominance – or 'touring the realm of political will, political management and political definition', as Said puts it.[10] Burton's exotic East, like Walter Scott's Middle Ages and so much of Victorian medievalism, represents a nostalgia for something that modern Europe perceived itself as having lost. In this sense Romanticism fulfils a need within the history of European culture as perhaps the last bulwark of modernity against secularism. From Novalis in 1801 to Joseph Conrad in 1899, between Heinrich von Ofterdingen's allegorical search for a blue flower – seen originally in a dream – and Marlow's disquieting African journey into the dark heart of human nature, the progress of Romanticism reveals a disenchantment with the process of Western civilization and its most magnificent outward expressions. Secularism – which encompasses but is also larger than an empirical gaze – implies the condition of knowing that there was once a religious state of mind that was innocent.

We open this introduction with Burton in Mecca because he provides a hauntingly acute example of the condition of secular modernity. This book addresses the construction of modernity through a cultural history of travel. The literature of travel not only exemplifies the multiple facets of modern identity, but it is also one of the principal cultural mechanisms, even a key cause, for the development of modern identity since the Renaissance. A cultural history of travel invites us to examine the relationship between modern subjectivity and the ancient and medieval past from, and against, which the modern West has constructed its set of self-definitions.

Of course, much of the scholarly discussion of travel has revolved around issues of the encounter between different cultures (such as Englishmen and Arabs). There is, beyond the tradition of Western travel, also the theme of how other cultures write about and reflect upon their own travels; it would not be difficult, for instance, to contrast Richard Burton's views of Mecca with those described by genuine Muslim pilgrims.[11] Similarly, no history of cultural encounters can be complete without an assessment of how Europeans were seen by others, even by those who were conquered or defeated. However, the aim of this book – its introduction and the essays collected here – is to assess travel in the Western tradition in its full chronological span. This is perhaps a perspective missing from the now very rich and interdisciplinary field of the culture of travel. We do not propose to offer a diachronic or evolutionary account of how travel and travel writing developed. Rather we aim to focus on the crisis of secular modernity since the Renaissance – explored in its numerous ramifications in the different essays of the book – and to examine the conditions and causes of that crisis in this introduction, where we shall discuss travel in Antiquity and the Middle Ages.

In focusing on the period after the Renaissance, it would be a temptation simply to define the Western tradition as the opposition between a religious past and a secular present. However, what the different essays bear out, and indeed what the analysis of ancient and medieval travel suggests, is that we should not be talking about a linear development. Rather, the cultural history of travel is best seen as a dialectic of dominant paradigms between two poles, which we might define as the transcendental vision of pilgrimage and the open-ended process which typically characterizes modernity. By transcendental vision we mean the sense of spiritual fulfilment with which the traveller achieves a kind of completion at the goal of his journey – as is perhaps most eloquently exemplified in the theme of the quest for the Holy Grail, which derives its power from allegory and which ends with the most virtuous of the knights attaining the direct vision of a miraculous spiritual mystery. By contrast, we define as open-ended travel that process the fulfilment of which is always deferred because its achievements are relativized by the very act of travelling. As Susan Sontag has written:

The romantics construe the self as essentially a traveller – a questing, homeless self whose standards derive from, whose citizenship is of, a place that does not exist at all or yet, or no longer exists; one consciously understood as an ideal, opposed to something real. It is understood that the journey is unending, and the destination, therefore, negotiable. To travel becomes the very condition of modern consciousness, of a modern view of the world – the acting out of longing or dismay.[12]

Modern travel writing is a literature of disappointment. Because of the crisis of Christian mythology in the post-Renaissance West, the modern traveller, as questioner, is incapable of the spiritual fulfilment of the Arab Hajis in Burton's account, whose beating hearts are pressed against the sacred stone. Nonetheless, he or she may carry the desire for a sacred vision – a spiritual desire deeply embedded in the European tradition. In terms of the scientific paradigm of travel as exploration, the process of accumulating empirical knowledge and of perfecting maps ever more minutely implies an infinitely open-ended future of improvement. The positive mythology of this process is one that proclaims the triumph of progress; its negative face is futility.

The problem of modernity and its desire for a past in which the fragments inherited by the present were once available in an ideal wholeness is not confined to religious awareness. It also affects what we may term the desire for authenticity in cultural encounters. In one of the great travel books of the twentieth century, the French anthropologist Claude Lévi-Strauss puts the issue with an acute eloquence:

Insidiously, illusion began to lay its snares. I wished I had lived in the days of *real* journeys, when it was still possible to see the full splendour of a spectacle that had not yet been blighted, polluted and spoilt; I wished I had not trodden the ground as myself, but as Bernier, Tavernier or Manucci did [. . .] When was the best time to see India? At what period would the study of Brazilian savages have afforded the purest satisfaction, and revealed them in their least adulterated state? Would it have been better to arrive in Rio in the eighteenth century with Bougainville, or in the sixteenth with Léry and Thevet? For every five years I move back in time, I am able to save a custom, gain a ceremony or share in another belief. But I know the texts too well not to realize that, by going back a century, I am at the same time forgoing data and lines of inquiry which would offer intellectual enrichment. And so I am caught in a circle from which there is no escape [. . .] In short, I have only two possibilities: either I can be like some traveller of the olden days, who was faced with a stupendous spectacle, all, or almost all, of which eluded him, or worse still, filled him with scorn and disgust; or I can be a modern traveller, chasing after the vestiges of a vanished reality. I lose on both counts [. . .] A few hundred years hence, in this same place, another traveller, as despairing as myself, will mourn the disappearance of what I might have seen, but failed to see.[13]

Like Burton, the modern Lévi-Strauss plays with disguise, knowing that the '*real* journeys' belong to others, in the past. Like Burton, he is sensitive to the double-edged blade of scientific achievement: to discover is to supersede one's predecessors, but it is also, by the inexorable logic of history, to be surpassed in one's turn. Thus authenticity emerges as incompatible with modern historical consciousness. What is lost to the modern traveller is the 'stupendous spectacle' of the full vision, a reality once available but now vanished. This 'stupendous spectacle' is equivalent to Burton's 'waving wings of angels', which exotic others might still see, but not the Western visitor himself. What is gained is the knowledge ('the data and lines of enquiry') that the seeing, and the destroying, have brought. Lévi-Strauss's lost vision is ethnographic rather than sacral, but he shares with Burton the modern condition of sensing an absence – richer, fuller, more resplendent than the present. It is this, more perhaps than the practical goals of mapping, exploring and recording novelty, which constitutes the object of the traveller's desire.

Even while there may exist ideologies of modernity which proclaim a complete rejection of the past as the key to progress, this rejection entails an awareness of this past and can only function in the wider context of an appropriation of tradition (pure modernism is in this sense as utopian as the desire for detached observation, or the idea of civilizing the Other without leaving ugly scars). Because modernity is constituted in opposition to a past, for which there is also desire, a long-term view of the cultural significance of travel in history is as important as understanding the complexity of each separate moment. Although this book can only hope to sketch the complex and many-sided history of travel in the West – in any case, travel as a culturally significant event rather than as mere physical movement – the introduction and the essays together will attempt to do justice to these two dimensions. The essays explore the complex aspects of modernity's conflict between futility and progress, between desire and fulfilment. The introduction, however, traces a history of the fruition of the 'pilgrimage model', a mythical paradigm of the West which is broadly comparable to other cultural paradigms – such as the religious models of travel offered by Islam or China.[14] Although it is not our intention to go beyond the Western frame of reference, we are not really talking about 'pure' traditions: in Biblical and in Greek sources, for instance, there is a great deal of common ground between Western and Asian traditions.

This introduction will explore the genesis of the 'pilgrimage model' in European culture, beginning not with Christianity (as might be expected from its hegemonic status throughout the Middle Ages) but with the co-existence of sceptical and religious travel in Graeco-Roman Antiquity. After examining the apogee of the religious model of travel in the cultures of pilgrimage, crusade and chivalry in the Latin West, we will look at the crisis of this model in the late Middle Ages. It appears that scepticism was not born simply in the fifteenth century, nor was the 'pilgrimage model' entirely annihilated after the Renaissance. What we shall therefore do is set the dominant narratives of each period against the marginal (either emerging or peripheral) elements. We will also pay special attention to transitions which, although complex, are crucial to this story: transitions towards the Christian Middle Ages, the European Renaissance, the Enlightenment, Romanticism and Post-Modernity. Through these transitions the pattern of modernity emerges, in effect, as a series of attempts to reconstruct or relocate a mythical paradigm, followed by the repeated failures, or rejections, of those attempts at reconstruction.

'THE PILGRIMAGE MODEL': THE RISE AND DEMISE OF A CULTURAL PARADIGM

'Let us flee, then, to the beloved Fatherland' (*Iliad* 2.140) – this is the soundest counsel. But what is this flight? How are we to gain the open sea? For Odysseus is surely a parable to us when he commands the flight from the sorceries of Circe or Calypso – not content to linger for all the pleasure offered to his eyes and all the delight of sense filling his days. Our Fatherland is Thence whence we have come, and There is the Father. What then is our course, what the manner of our flight? This is not a journey for the feet: the feet bring us only from land to land. Nor need you think of coach or ship to carry you away; all this order of things you must set aside and refuse to see. You must close the eyes and call instead upon another vision which is to be waked within you, a vision, the birthright of all, which few turn to use.

Plotinus (AD 205–70), *Ennead* 1.6.8[15]

Since the literary creation of the *Odyssey* – whose portrait of a great journey home after the Trojan War was not only the very first major text in the European tradition (along with the *Iliad*) but also remains Antiquity's most famous book of travels – the theme of the voyager has been central to the Graeco-Roman tradition.[16] It is significant that the allegory of travel as a path to salvation within ancient philosophical writing (and particularly in the Neoplatonic school inaugurated by Plotinus) antedates the adoption of Christianity as the dominant religion of the Roman empire. It is significant, too, that a crucial aspect of this allegorical model of the spiritual journey towards an inner vision lay in casting a meditative reflection on the *Odyssey* as the ancient world's canonical literary narrative of travel.

In Neoplatonism, Odysseus – as the model for the wanderer who finally returns home through numerous adventures (military, sexual and magical) – is more than just a parable for everyman's potential flight from the world of the senses to the spiritual waking of the inner vision at the heart of Plotinus's philosophy. In the writings of Plotinus's close pupil and biographer Porphyry (*c.* AD 232–305), Odysseus figures as 'the symbol of man passing through the successive stages of becoming and is restored to his place among those beyond all wavecrash and beyond those who are "ignorant of the sea"'.[17] A number of early Christian writers, following this lead in the ancient philosophical tradition, presented Odysseus as a pre-Christian foreshadowing of wisdom striving for virtue.[18] Others focused on the hero as one who had escaped the siren-song of death and whose ship was piloted by the heavenly Logos itself, with the True Cross as the mast.[19]

All such readings, pagan and early Christian, look back with affection, but also with creative interpretation, on a thousand years of Graeco-Roman tradition. The Odysseus they create might not have been recognized by Homer himself or by the bulk of ancient Greeks and Romans. Indeed, since the sixth century BC Odysseus was the centre of a tradition of contrasting readings. In Greek tragedy, for instance, and in later Renaissance interpretations he serves the morally ambivalent role of the model of worldly wisdom. The allegorical Odysseus – the inner traveller who may serve as the paradigm of the pilgrim in the later Christian medieval tradition – was a creation of religiously-minded philosophical readers in Hellenistic times which came into its full flowering in late Antiquity. For Odysseus (and his numerous successors from Sir Perceval to John Bunyan's Christian in the *Pilgrim's Progress* of 1678) became the ideal model of a traveller whose journey brought inner as well as outer fulfilment, return to a spiritual plenitude lost in the travails of life, as well as success in the sense of worldly achievement.

It is no coincidence that this allegorical model (versions of which were always available throughout Classical Antiquity) should have reached a form both developed and relatively popular in the third century AD. Usually, this is regarded as a rather difficult time in the Roman empire – a period of crisis, civil war (especially in the half-century from AD 235 to 285), economic instability and political chaos.[20] However, it was also a crucial period for the rise of new religions (including Christianity) and the recasting of traditional philosophies and rituals in a more religious frame.[21] Whatever the actualities of life, the ideologies within the empire strove towards new forms of universalism which would be the bedrock for the universal and imperial Christianity established by Constantine and his successors in the fourth century.[22] A brief examination of travel literature reveals very clearly the genesis of this universalist, increasingly generalized and at the same time symbolic vision which was to culminate in the allegorical Odysseus.

In the second century AD, the Roman empire enjoyed a period of immense stability, in which the roads were safe and travel was frequent.[23] We possess a rich literature of travels which combined antiquarian, literary, even touristic interests with a strong emphasis on pilgrimage to oracles, healing sanctuaries and major temples. The Greek-speaking traveller Pausanias, who journeyed through mainland Greece in the AD 150s to the 170s, found a land enchanted with ancient myths, rituals and deities still inhabiting forgotten hamlets and half-ruined shrines.[24] The famous orator Aelius Aristides (AD 117–c. 185), burdened by health problems, became a devotee of the healing god Asclepius, whose shrines in Asia Minor he frequented for many years in a frenzy of ritual abstinences, ascetic acts and visions from dreaming of the god to purgation through enemas.[25] The Syrian-born essayist Lucian (c. AD 120–190), one of the sharpest and most elegant writers in Greek in all Antiquity, wrote with apparent piety of his pilgrimage to the Syrian sanctuary of Hierapolis and his worship of the Syrian goddess there.[26] Such travel texts reveal a culture of localism, in which the traveller's interest is directed to a deep immersion in a particular area. The geography explored is not just ethnographic or topographical, but also imaginative; it is directed to the cultivation of a particular deity in a series of sites (in the case of Aristides), to the careful unravelling of Syrian as opposed to Graeco-Roman identity (in the case of Lucian), to the evocation of ancient Greece in all her magical and mythic fullness within the modern world (in Pausanias). At stake in all these cases is both the traveller's own identity and that of the Graeco-Roman world within which he makes his journey but against whose far-away imperial centre his more parochial sacred geography may be defined. It is as if, in the assured domain of an empire hardly troubled by external foes or internal discord, it was possible to assert and to celebrate the parochial as a way of defining local identities and subjectivities not only within Roman dominion but also to some extent in opposition to it.[27]

The self-assurance of this culture can be evoked by looking briefly at two works by Lucian. In the *Anacharsis*, the Syrian-born author, writing in Greek, imagines the reactions of the legendary Anacharsis, a sixth-century Scythian (i.e. barbarian) who has come to Greece to learn wisdom.[28] By contrast with the Athenians whom he visits, Anacharsis is (in his own words, as written by Lucian) 'a nomad, a rover, who have lived my life on a wagon, visiting different lands at different seasons, and have never dwelt in a city or seen one until now'.[29] Lucian stages a conversation between Anacharsis and Solon, the great Athenian law-giver, in which the former comments with a combination of comic naivety and acute critical observation on a series of archetypal Greek cultural activities – gymnastics, the games, the lawcourts, the theatre. It marks a certain degree of cultural self-confidence when a system such as the Roman empire can not only incorporate 'foreigners' like the Gallic eunuch Favorinus or the Syrian 'barbarian' Lucian among its major Greek writers but can also give the 'other' a critical voice in commenting on its own customs and attitudes.[30]

By contrast, in his satirical novel *A True Story* – the ancestor of all the great travel fictions of the modern period, from *Gulliver's Travels* to science fiction – Lucian presents a wonderfully assured spoof of the traveller's tale. All travellers, he informs us, are liars, 'but my lying is more honest than theirs, for though I tell the truth in nothing else, I shall at least be truthful in saying that I am a liar'.[31] Lucian mocks equally the simultaneously empirical and antiquarian spirit of travel in the Roman world, the travel writer's persistent urge to tell his stories taller than they could possibly have been in reality, and a vast swathe of ancient literature (much of it now lost) into the bargain. Within only a few pages, Lucian's first-person narrator has arrived at the Moon, which he proceeds to describe in some detail, and by the end of the book he has passed through the underworld. In emphasizing the novelistic elements implicit in the recounting of travel (which had been, after all, a major trend in ancient travel writing since Homer) and effectively dividing them from actual travels, works such as Lucian's *A True Story* looked forward to a more ideological usage of the notion of the journey in ancient writing.

In the great pagan hagiography of the first-century holy man Apollonius of Tyana, written by Philostratus in the AD 220s or 230s for an audience at the imperial court, travel also plays a central role. Philostratus makes his sage visit the boundaries of the known world – India, Ethiopia and Western Spain – as well as travel to the major shrines of Greece and to Rome. The frame of travel serves not as an actual record of factual journeys but as a pervasive metaphor for Apollonius's religious supremacy. Not only does he go further than any other Greek (further even than Alexander the Great, with whom Philostratus compares him) in penetrating the edges of the known world, but Apollonius learns from and ultimately surpasses the holy men of India and Egypt in his wisdom and divine powers. His travels are rhetorically presented by Philostratus as a reflection of Apollonius' spiritual progress – their extent being a metaphor for the extent of his wisdom. On his return from his various journeys to the limits of Roman dominion and beyond, Apollonius becomes a kind of holy man to the Roman empire – correcting priests and wise men, putting right emperors and consuls, and not just confronting a tyrant like Domitian but actually defeating him in open court.[32]

The book ends with Apollonius' elevation into an object of pilgrimage at Olympia, the epicentre of Greek religion:

They all flocked to see him from the whole of Greece, and never did any such crowd flock to any Olympic festival as then, all full of enthusiasm and expectation. People came straight from Elis and Sparta, and from Corinth at the limits of the Isthmus; and the Athenians too...[33]

The traveller *par excellence* is elevated into one of the wonders which tourists and pilgrims travel the earth to see. We are told he was treated as a guest and an equal by the Boeotian oracular god Trophonius,[34] and that the Hellenes thought him divine, their response towards him coming 'near to that of actual worship'.[35] This attitude is confirmed by the fact that he is reported to have disappeared miraculously instead of dying – whether vanishing into a temple in Lindos or ascending into heaven in Crete.[36]

The hagiographic use of the topos of travel to underpin the spiritual progress of Apollonius and at the same time to present a universalizing picture of religious revival throughout the Roman empire is an important development from the 'real world' travel texts of the second century, focused on specific visits to sites with a local appeal. Apollonius, a rather obscure wonder-worker from the past, has become a paradigmatic holy man by being fictionalized. His travels – whatever their basis in dimly remembered and uncertainly recorded actuality – have become a mythical narrative simultaneously serving a didactic and literary purpose, rather like the travels of Sir Galahad and Sir Perceval in their quest for the Holy Grail. To create his hagiography, Philostratus drew on the centrality of the trope of travel to ancient fiction – especially in the erotic romances of Graeco-Roman Antiquity as well as in such texts as Lucian's *A True Story*.[37] In these novels, for example Achilles Tatius's *Leucippe and Clitophon* or Chariton's *Chaereas and Callirhoe* (both probably from the second century AD), the lovers are separated from each other and beset by numerous misfortunes, trials and disasters before finally being reunited. The action often spreads across continents, even venturing (like Apollonius himself) beyond the confines of the Roman empire. Even more significant, as a parallel (and perhaps even a source) for the kind of sacred biography written by Philostratus, are popular religious tracts produced by Christians – like the *Acts of the Apostles*, written towards the end of the first century AD by St Luke.[38] These were a form of fiction which mythologized Christian holy men – for example St Paul in the *Acts* – through the same rhetorical means (travel, miracles, appearances after death) as were used by the Gospel writers (including Luke himself) for Jesus Christ and by Philostratus for Apollonius.[39]

The difference between these fictions – romantic on the one hand and sacred on the other – and Philostratus's *Life of Apollonius* is that Philostratus was not simply writing popular romance for a general audience (though doubtless he would cheerfully have welcomed this readership for his hagiography), nor was he creating the sacred mythology of a highly marginal (and, in his time, socially insignificant) religious sect, as were Luke and the authors of the Christian novels. Rather, he brought the fictive features which characterized these genres into an elite text commissioned by the empress Julia Domna herself (at least according to Philostratus's own account)[40] and designed to inspire the Roman state with a Greek-led religious revival. Unlike the allegorical Odysseus embroidered at about the same time by the Neoplatonists, Apollonius was more than a fictional metaphor for human self-improvement through the image of travel. Rather, like Jesus Christ himself, he was a real man who had once lived, but who became a divine figure through the rhetorical elaborations of a sacred mythology. This explains why Christian theologians, such as Eusebius in the fourth century, were so uneasy about Apollonius – as if he were a potential rival for Christ – and felt the need to write refutations of Philostratus's account of his career as a holy man.[41] But it also suggests the significance of Apollonius as a model for Christian writers after the legal establishment of Christianity in AD 312. From the model of such pagan works as Philostratus's *Life*, Christianity was able to assimilate a view of travel as a universal and culturally cohesive mechanism (with sacred geography being essentially conceived as an empire-wide, and hence imperial, phenomenon), as well as to see it as a metaphor for the path to sainthood.

This portrayal of travel as simultaneously an inner and outer process, which – whether factual or fictive – is ultimately an allegory, is a particular heritage of late Antiquity. Whether the symbolism stood for a personal quest (as in the Neoplatonists' Odysseus) or for a universal religious revival within the context of empire (as in the case of Philostratus's Apollonius), it was to be at the root of what we have called the 'pilgrimage model' of travel as spiritual fulfilment in the Middle Ages.

It is one of the paradoxes of the ancient world that this idealist vision of travel should have developed within what was a long-held sceptical tradition based on ethnographic experience. As early as the pre-Socratic philosopher Xenophanes (who was born on the Greek-speaking coast of Asia Minor in the sixth century BC), we have a record of anthropological relativism born of the awareness of other cultures' customs. Among Xenophanes' sayings are the following: 'The Ethiopians say that their gods are snub-nosed and black, the Thracians that theirs have light eyes and red hair'.[42] And likewise:

But if cattle and horses or lions had hands, or were able to draw with their hands and do the works that men do, horses would draw the forms of the gods like horses, and cattle like cattle, and they would make their bodies such as they each had themselves.[43]

Such anthropological doubts about accepted lore went side by side with the tradition of a sceptical and worldly Odysseus, who escapes his various adventures by a variety of cunning deceits and mendacities, and who embroiders on his experiences in somewhat extravagant colours. Unlike Gilgamesh, the great Sumerian hero, for whom there is no evidence of a non-sacral reading of his epic travels (including a journey to the other world in a futile quest for immortality), there was a plurality of readings in Greek culture for even such especially canonical texts as the travels described by Homer.[44]

These kinds of inter-cultural awareness, the willingness to use other cultures in an implicit critique of, or at least as a means defining, Greek practice, and the scepticism potentially levelled at apparently tall tales, culminated in the classic text of Herodotus in the fifth century BC. Herodotus, whose book is a history of the wars between the Greeks and Persians, included much reportage of his own travels – claiming personal autopsy for the stories of other cultures which he retails (even when he says he disbelieves them). Among the other worlds mapped by Herodotus and used by him anthropologically to define Greekness by contrast with others were those of the Scythians, the Persians and the Egyptians.[45] Yet, for all its significance as a text to be read and even imitated (for instance, by Lucian in his *Syrian Goddess*), Herodotus's *Histories* was frequently attacked as the work of a malicious, deceitful and wilfully misleading liar.[46] It is as if the sceptical voice of the author, judging between the like-lihood of the tales he is told, was turned upon himself by his readers over the centuries. Like all purveyors of knowledge in Antiquity, Herodotus was subjected to the typically Greek agonistic culture of criticism and competition for the authority that a depth of wisdom was perceived to bring.[47] Travellers in particular were received sceptically for the fanciful accounts in which they presented imaginative fictions as foreign actuali-ties; in his *Lover of Lies*, Lucian satirizes such tendencies ruthlessly in the person of the liar Eucrates with his tall stories of Egypt.[48]

The success of ancient ethnographers and travel writers – Strabo, for instance, in the early first century AD, or Pausanias – lay in treading a careful, scholarly path through the range of objections which a sceptical critic might raise.[49] The rise of natural history, as we have it in the work of Pliny the Elder,[50] with its scholarly referencing of earlier accounts (a game which, as we have seen, both Burton and Lévi-Strauss were still playing in the modern period), and the development of the kinds of careful empirical observation which Pausanias directs to works of art, to rituals and to myths which he encounters,[51] were authorial strategies of legitimation and protection from attack in the agonistic market-place of knowledge in the Graeco-Roman world.

The 'pilgrimage model' in its ancient form bypassed the demands of empiricism and the need to demonstrate truthfulness by making a virtue out of fiction in the interests of allegory. What is striking in the earliest Christian travel accounts (as we shall see) – of pilgrimages made to the Holy Land in the fourth century AD – is that the various ancient traditions of empirical localism, universalist imperialism and allegorical idealism were combined in the new faith's transformation of the pagan topographical terrain into a sanctified Christian realm. In effect, it must be emphasized that Antiquity was not just the engine that powered modernity's heady mix of rationality, empirical knowledge and imperialism, which has been so significant a fuel for Western expansion. Antiquity was also the mother of the Middle Ages. Just as the open-endedness which characterizes travel in modernity can be traced to the open-endedness of scientific inquiry, critical scepticism and anthropological speculation of the Graeco-Roman world, so the archetypally Christian pilgrimage model of the Middle Ages is rooted in the ancient myths of heroes such as Apollonius, who travelled himself into sainthood, or the allegorical Odysseus, whose journeys became a metaphor for the spiritual progress of his readers' lives.[52]

*   *   *

The legalization, establishment and rapid dominance of Christianity in the course of the fourth century proved – among many other changes – to involve a radical rearrangement of the geographical hierarchies of the Roman empire. While Rome remained a capital city (and the seat of the premier bishop), it was soon to be superseded by a new imperial capital at Constantinople (founded in AD 330). The spiritual centre of the Christian empire, however, was relocated to a spot of truly parochial insignificance on the eastern periphery: the Palestinian landscape in which Christ's life, miracles and passion had taken place. It is a mark of the importance of these three sites, Rome, Constantinople and the Holy Land, that Constantine himself sponsored major building programmes of churches there.

Gradually, but systematically, the terrain of pagan Antiquity (enchanted in its every spot and landmark by countless local deities and numerous polytheisms and sects) was transformed into a world sanctified by the exclusive Christian God and his saints.[53] This was not so much a creation of a sacred landscape as the redefinition of a series of existing landscapes as sacred in a specifically Christian way. In the case of the Holy Land, the Christians possessed a guidebook which they used to redefine the actual places and landmarks they found on the terrain in relation to their dominant mythology, namely the Old and New Testaments.[54] In AD 333, when Constantine was still on the imperial throne, a pilgrim from Bordeaux visited Palestine and left us with our earliest surviving description of Christian pilgrimage.[55] This account is anonymous and tantalizing. The land the pilgrim visits is only meaningful in relation to scripture, and its landmarks acquire their significance by being interpreted in the light of the Biblical text which is the pilgrim's principal resource. For example:

A mile from here (Mt Gerizim) is the place called Sychar, where the Samaritan woman went down to draw water, at the very place where Jacob dug the well, and our Lord Jesus Christ spoke with her. Some plane trees are there, planted by Jacob, and there is a bath which takes its water from this well.[56]

Here a simple well, a bath-house and a copse of trees – sites of minimal significance in the rural or urban landscape of the Roman empire – acquire an intensity of meaning through being interpreted according to Biblical history. The well becomes the memorial – a landmark serving as a living geographical witness – to one of the great episodes in St John's Gospel (4.5–30). But the bath and the trees are nowhere recorded in the Bible. Their importance to the pilgrim comes from their conjunction with the famous well – either through using its water (a spatial and functional connection) or through an oral tradition (doubtless reported to the pilgrim by local guides, but just possibly made up by him) that the trees were planted by Jacob when he dug the well. Whether this actual well really was the one mentioned in the Gospel (and there were certainly pre-Christian Jewish and Samaritan traditions of holy sites associated with the Prophets according to which this site may well have been believed to be

Jacob's well)[57] is not very significant. What matters is that the pilgrim believed it to be the well of Sychar, and that through the well he was able to find a direct – even a tangible – access in the present day to the scriptural world of both the Old and New Testaments. Even as early as AD 333, this text shows the translation of the contemporary landscape of Roman Palestine into a series of scriptural mementos which attested to a simultaneously spiritual and historical reality believed by Christians to be immanent in the contemporary material world.

With the establishment of Christianity, Palestine became primarily a scriptural territory, in which landscape, buildings and features of an actual topography were mapped out according to the Biblical narratives of Christ and the Prophets. In effect, the Holy Land became an imaginative geography in which pilgrims could roam through the world of scripture in three dimensions, as it were, with every site testifying to the truth of the text and recalling a Biblical tag or quotation. Just as the text justified the interpretation of any one site as worth visiting, so the site provided material proof of the actual setting and context of any particular scriptural event. By the time of Egeria, a noblewoman from Spain, whose account of her pilgrimage to Palestine in the AD 380s is one of the most vivid to survive from any period, this scriptural world had become enriched by a flowering of liturgy. The sacred sites – peopled by monks and adorned with churches, altars, roadside chapels and crosses – had become the settings for elaborate liturgical ceremonial which recalled the Gospel not only in the specific places of its occurrence but also as a narrative (recollected in readings, prayers and hymns) and hence as a history.[58]

The pattern of pilgrimage which developed in Palestine would remain the archetype of Christian travelling, just as it was to become the ancestor of the phenomenon of crusade; but it was also the exception. Only for the Holy Land was there an unassailably authoritative guidebook (in the form of the Bible) which could ensure the sanctity and the veracity of the holy places. Outside Palestine, with the notable exception of the tombs of Peter and Paul in Rome, there were no Christian sites even tangentially linked with the doings of Christ and his apostles. In response to this problem, and to what appears to have been a virtually insatiable demand, the bishops of the fourth century developed the cults of saints and of relics. The bones of the holy ones offered pilgrims a material link – situated in accessible topography – with the spiritual world of perfected Christian life and its heavenly rewards. By the end of the fourth century, the entire landscape of the Roman empire would be dotted with martyria, shrines and churches marking the specific spots where important saints had lived, the places where their bodies finally came to rest, and the location of significant artefacts associated with them, such as the True Cross.[59]

These sites, as much as the holy places of scripture, were Egeria's target when she went east:

In Isauria, only three staging-posts on from Tarsus, is the martyrium of the holy Thecla, and, since it was so close, we were very glad to be able to make the journey there [. . .] In God's name, I arrived at the martyrium, and we had a prayer there, and read the whole Acts of the holy Thecla; and I gave heartfelt thanks to God for his mercy in letting me fulfil all my desires so completely, despite all my unworthiness. For two days I stayed there, visiting all the holy monks and apotactites (or virgins), the men as well as the women; then, after praying and receiving communion, I went back to Tarsus to rejoin my route.[60]

Such tombs and holy places (Egeria goes on to see the martyrium of Euphemia at Chalcedon, the tombs of the apostles and other martyria in Constantinople, and expresses the wish to see the shrine of 'the holy blessed Apostle John' at Ephesus)[61] echo the scriptural sites as local points for pilgrimage. They attracted church buildings, a plethora of liturgical activity, and the repetition of sacred narratives – in the case of Thecla the reading of an apocryphal hagiography. Like the sites of Palestine, they offered not only much sacred action in the form of services and prayers but also the company of holy men and women, who are as much the goal of Egeria's travels as the holy places themselves.[62]

But the tombs of the saints offered something else which was largely absent from the sites of the Holy Land, despite all their scriptural interest. As Egeria puts it of the martyrium of St Thomas at Edessa, this is 'where his entire body is buried'.[63] The bodies of the saints provided a means of tangible access to the spiritual achievements of Christianity's superstars. Although a martyr or confessor may be less significant than the founder of the religion himself, Christ's resurrection had left no body – no material object capable of being seen and touched – like the bodies of his saints (in the later Middle Ages, Christ's Holy Foreskin was discovered, which having been removed at the time of the Circumcision, could be presented as having survived the Resurrection!). Moreover, everything which came into contact with those bodies (both in life and in death) carried the same allure of a direct link with the saint, a link of mediation which could be made even through dust collected by the side of a tomb. It would be the cult of material things – imbued and immanent with a spiritual power that made the relics of the saints direct mediators with the other world – which would provide the greatest impetus for Christian travel in the succeeding centuries. From the fictional quest for the Grail to the very specific journeys of pilgrims to the tombs of famous saints such as Martin of Tours or Thomas of Canterbury, it would be the direct vision of, and the chance to touch, those relics sanctified by their saintly provenance which offered the lure of sacred fulfilment in pilgrimage.

The explosion in the cult of relics and in the discovery of lost saints during the fourth and fifth centuries is the historical result of supply attempting (and hardly managing) to fulfil demand. Just as the objects, and the hallowed places where they were located, proved the focus of desire since they offered the potential for the plenitude of spiritual vision, so the journeys of earlier pilgrims became allegories for the successes and achievements of the 'pilgrimage model'. By the seventh century, the Galician monk Valerius could write a letter to his brethren at Vierzo praising 'the valorous achievements [. . .] of the most blessed Egeria, who by her courage outdid the men of any age whatever'.[64] For Valerius, the journey of Egeria (as preserved in the text of her description) becomes a metaphor for the difficulties of the monastic path:

Nothing could hold her back, whether it was the labour of travelling the whole world, the perils of seas and rivers, the dread crags and fearsome mountains, or the savage menaces of the heathen tribes, until with God's help and her own unconquerable bravery, she had fulfilled all her faithful desires.[65]

While the dangers of the journey and its landscapes are hardly the main impression made on a modern reader by Egeria's text, in Valerius they are raised to an allegorical level. He takes the actualities of Egeria's narrative (as vivid and local as those in Pausanias or Lucian, two centuries before her) and imbues them with a metaphorical Christian meaning which raises the virgin 'who transformed the weakness of her sex into iron strength that she might win the reward of eternal life'[66] from being a real person into becoming a mythical paradigm like the allegorical Odysseus or Philostratus's Apollonius.

Besides these two Mediterranean patterns of travel as pilgrimage – broadly the scriptural model of visiting the Holy Land and the corporeal model of venerating a saint's body, tomb or relics – Celtic Christianity in broadly the same period developed a wonderfully allegorical form of pilgrimage as travel simply for the sake of God, with no particular material object or goal to attain. The Anglo-Saxon Chronicle for 891 reports that 'three Scots came to King Alfred in a boat without any oars from Ireland, whence they stole away, because they would be in a state of pilgrimage for the love of God, they recked not where'.[67]

The most famous example of such a journey into the wilderness which combined the joint idea of finding oneself and finding God is the *Voyage of St Brendan*, composed anonymously in Latin in the ninth century and describing the travels of a sixth-century Irish saint. In the *Voyage*, Brendan and his followers follow St Barrind, an older monk, in 'sailing westwards towards the island which is called the promised land' (sections 1 and 2). After an odyssey of allegorical adventures and tests, the holy Brendan returns to his community to die as a saint.[68] Arguably, this northern European tradition was the purest expression of the early medieval pilgrimage ideal.

It is the process of mythologizing – admittedly borrowed from pre-Christian late Antiquity – which brought the 'pilgrimage model' to its fruition. For – whether applied by Christians to pagan figures, like Virgil's Aeneas,[69] or to saints and other holy characters, like Egeria – the hagiographic myth of a spiritual journey through material difficulties to the attainment of divine grace would become a paradigm of travel to haunt posterity. In the Middle Ages it represented an always potentially attainable model for any pilgrim who chose to tread the path to Canterbury, Rome or Compostela: it served both to put a pilgrim's spiritual achievements into perspective (by contrast with the ideal) and to spur him or her onwards by promising the ideal as the ultimate goal. In the post-medieval world, it served as that purely mythic and always unachievable paradigm located in our historical memory, by contrast with which all human travelling – whatever its achievements and successes – can never transcend the abysm of futility.

PILGRIMAGE, CRUSADE AND CHIVALRY IN THE LATIN MIDDLE AGES

I shall state quickly my subject: the full greatness of the Work of God, all the miracles and all the signs of power that God has deigned to grant and accomplish in this world with His divine omnipotence, humiliating Himself for the salvation of mankind, lowering Himself to the point of adopting the form of a human body. All this appeared clearly to the venerable Willibald, through the testimony of his own eyes, of his feet, of his hands, of his whole body. Not only did he witness the miracles which are certified to us by the grace of the Gospel, but also saw the very places where, on earth, our God has wished to appear to us, by being born, by suffering and by resurrecting. . .[70]

Thus an eighth-century Anglo-Saxon nun introduced her narrative of the pilgrimage of the saintly monk Willibald, based on his own oral account.

It is significant how the life of the saint naturally merged with his actual pilgrimage, much as personal and bodily contact with the geography of the Incarnation brought the believer as close as possible to the miraculous power of God. If the Incarnation was the most significant of all Christian miracles, its meaning was no less accessible to the senses as geography than to the intellect as allegory. But Willibald's accomplishment was accentuated by the very difficulty of the journey to a now 'pagan' land. In effect, Christian pilgrimage remained the fundamental paradigm of travel in the Latin West – even during those centuries when the possibility of actual travel to the Holy Land was compromised by the rise of Islam, a situation marked by the fall of Jerusalem in 648 and the invasion of Spain in 711. The history of travel as a religious ideal is therefore, for much of the Latin Middle Ages, a history of loss – one which was met with guilt, hope and nostalgia.

The world of the Latin West, which survived both culturally and politically around an ecclesiastical and military core formed by the peculiar symbiosis of papal Rome and the Frankish empire, was for many centuries at the periphery of both religious geography and secular civilization. Certainly the nostalgia for the sacred spaces of Christianity was in part offset by the expansion of local cults, of which the most successful was that of Santiago (Saint James) of Compostela – a pilgrimage which emerged in the context of the Spanish reconquest and was consolidated after the eleventh-century collapse of the Caliphate of Cordoba. But the centrality of the Holy Land as the site of the Incarnation was irreplaceable in a society dominated by an elite of violent knights and literate monks who anxiously awaited the Last Judgement and, above all else, hoped for eternal salvation. For Willibald, as for many other travellers who followed him, pilgrimage was the supreme act of piety because it expressed the central fact that human life at its best was no more than a Christian journey towards God.

The fact that the year 1000 did not (as many expected) bring about the end of the world as described in the Apocalypse hardly dampened the sources of faith, but rather strengthened the transition towards a more human-centred and militant form of Christianity. Emerging from a frail economy of sheer survival towards a position of increasing, even if still largely fragmented, military might, with a more internationalized monastic network and new possibilities of learning, eleventh-century Latin Christians increasingly embraced pilgrimage as a penitential act. They now sometimes travelled in groups of thousands.[71] At the same time, the theological emphasis shifted from the contemplation of a message of divine power and majesty to the need for understanding the peculiar mythology of Christianity, and especially the mystery of the Incarnation, as a means for salvation. Did not Christ proclaim that he was the only way to salvation? What did it mean, then, that he – God – had become man to save mankind? This intellectual quest is exemplified by the *Cur Deus Homo* of Anselm of Canterbury at the end of the eleventh century. The humanity of Christ implied his historicity, and no site for pilgrimage other than the Holy Land, and especially the tomb from which Jesus Christ emerged resurrected, could fully guarantee the literalness of the experience of sacral power associated with this central mystery. Thus travel became a necessity. It was the desire for a literal, physical encounter as support for the allegorical meditation on the spiritual significance of the Christian mystery which characterized Latin piety, and with particular poignancy in the transition from the other-worldly Romanesque to the Gothic vision, with its emphasis on the humanity of Christ crucified.[72]

The emphasis on shrines as dynamic centres from which divine power emerged, and which therefore needed visiting, explains the popularity of pilgrimage and the belief that it was a meritorious act.[73] Although the practice of writing personal accounts of journeys to Jerusalem was quite limited until the late Middle Ages, the actual numbers of travellers were always considerable. Muslim domination, because of its principles of tolerance towards Christianity, was not a real obstacle to pilgrimage, even if it caused some difficulties at given periods.[74] The Christian belief in the literalness of the events of sacred history, and especially those concerning the Incarnation, eventually transformed the role of Jerusalem from an allegorical centre of the world into a literal one. This was expressed in sacred cartography. The Christian fathers had imposed a symbolic T-O structure upon classical maps of the world, with Jerusalem at the centre dividing the world in three parts: Asia occupied the top half of a schematic circle, with Europe and Africa sharing the two bottom quarters (see frontis.). After the eleventh century, Christian maps increasingly used this symbolic structure as the basis for a more elaborate empirical vision, so that Jerusalem remained an allegorical centre but became also an empirical one.[75] Pilgrims in Jerusalem were shown a hole within the Church of the Holy Sepulchre which was literally taken to be the navel of the world. As the twelfth-century German pilgrim John of Würzburg wrote to his fellow priest Dietrich on his return from Jerusalem:

In the Middle of the priest's choir and not far from the place of the skull is a marble table [. . .] under it there are slabs in the pavement with circles inside them. They say that the navel of the world is marked there, according to the passage 'Thou hast worked salvation in the centre of the earth' (Ps.74. 12). In that place after the resurrection the Lord is said to have appeared to blessed Mary Magdalene. . .[76]

Literal pilgrimage naturally had its limitations. For example, John understood that the reading of his account could help his friend to 'have a greater love' of the sacred places and meditate upon their holiness even if he was unable to visit them personally. More generally, the multiplication of local cults ensured the accessibility of holy sites well beyond those defined in the story of the Incarnation. Nonetheless, the almost obsessive concern with a centre, and with its literalness, stands out as a mark of medieval religious Christian culture. The importance of this ideal of religious travel could not but have an impact upon actual travellers' desires, expectations and experiences.

In effect the Western nostalgia for the centre to a sacred geography mirrored the nostagia for a Roman imperial universalism. Unlike Constantinople, which despite its losses remained both a political and a sacred centre for Greek-speaking Christendom, papal Rome could only hope to fulfil a guiding role in a fragmented political landscape. Muslim and Greek civilizations, however ambiguously perceived as moral forces, were clearly superior to the West in wealth and learning. In the tenth century a Western traveller to Constantinople such as the Lombard Liudprand of Cremona, an ambassador for Emperor Otto of Saxony, was mainly concerned with rationalizing, by recourse to systematic cultural criticism, the appalling treatment he received from his master's Greek rival and would-be ally. The ultimate point of this diatribe against the Greek court was to claim for the German emperor the true political leadership of Christianity.[77] This kind of criticism of Greek moral shortcomings – however justified in the circumstances – was essentially a manifestation of the economic and cultural peripherality of the West. Unlike the majority of empires with universalizing aspirations, which incorporated within their borders the fundamental myths of sacral power by re-creating a symbolic geography, Latin Christians were committed to a view of the world in which its real centre was specifically located elsewhere. In these conditions, and given the existence of a profound moral tension within the lay elite between military practice and religious ideals, it is not surprising that pilgrimage evolved into crusade. In this way the Middle Ages transformed ascetic travel into travel for conquest – a legacy that would permeate the cultures of travel in the West long after the religious idealism had been abandoned.

There was no doubt to those concerned that the crusade proclaimed by Pope Urban II in 1095 was a collective pilgrimage, a religious *peregrinatio*. However, it was a pilgrimage specifically addressed to the armed knights of Latin Christendom, with the idea of freeing from infidel abuse the Holy Land – which, according to some accounts, Urban II specifically referred to as the centre of the world.[78] The idea of crusade was welcomed enthusiastically by a pious laity, not because they stood to gain materially (for the majority a very dubious proposition) but rather because it allowed them to seek salvation without abandoning their military way of life.[79] With the subsequent creation of the military Orders, monastic life would become fully integrated with the military ethos. This issue was clearly understood by such contemporaries as Abbot Guibert of Nogent:

in our time God instituted holy warfare so that the knights [*ordo equestris*] and the wandering people [*vulgus oberrans*], who – like their ancient pagan model – were engaged in mutual slaughter, should find a new way of attaining salvation; so that they might not be obliged to abandon the world completely, as used to be the case, by adopting the monastic way of life or any other form of professed calling, but might obtain God's grace while enjoying to some extent their customary freedom and garb, in a way consistent with their station.[80]

For centuries to come Europeans were to cling to the image of the providential success of this first expedition of 1097–9. Through the sublimated pilgrimage of the crusades the idea of reconstituting a lost sacred centre created a new actuality, the Latin kingdom of Outremer with its capital at Jerusalem, as a peculiar manifestation of the military power of the Franks against both their Greek allies and their Muslim enemies. This Latin kingdom, of course, guaranteed easier and safer access to European pilgrims. Although in the long term its continuity proved to be an impossible enterprise, the crusades remained nonetheless the fundamental myth of the Latin Middle Ages and came to mediate rather aggressively the relationship of Europeans with other cultures. The idea of crusade certainly lost much of its prestige as it was repeatedly proclaimed and abused by the popes – against Muslims in Spain, against pagans in the Baltic, against heretics in Languedoc, and even against Catholic enemies of the Holy See. However, the papacy's very reliance on a crusading ideology also reveals its general appeal. Crusades remained fundamental to the identity of Latin Christendom and inspired a political vision of profound influence over many centuries, up until the wars against the Turks in the sixteenth century.

Crusaders shared with unarmed pilgrims a remarkable lack of ethnographic curiosity for the 'other' encountered in their travels. It was only with the development of missions to pagans or in the exceptional cases of writers thoroughly influenced by Latin literature – such men as William of Tyre (1130–86) or Gerald of Wales (1145–1223), who had personal experience of living with a mixed ethnic heritage in a frontier society – that curiosity for alien customs occasionally appeared within the twelfth-century genres of history and travel writing. These rare examples of ethnographic curiosity would however multiply in the thirteenth century, as the problem of dialogue with Muslims and pagans became part of a more sophisticated missionary programme. But this in itself was only a reflection of the basic failure of the crusades. During a brief period of less than a century, between the Latin conquest of Jerusalem in 1099 and the recapture of the city by Saladin in 1187, the possibility of controlling the centre of the world seemed real. The fall of Jerusalem to the Muslims and the repeated failure to recover it would unleash a profound crisis in Latin Christendom in the following centuries, one which had multiple and far-reaching effects, not least in the literature of travel.

Politically, the crisis found expression in the sack of Constantinople during the Fourth Crusade, a much-deplored incident engineered by a combination of Venetian greed, Byzantine internal politics and the financial needs of the crusaders, but which nevertheless perfectly expressed the fatal mixture of envy and contempt which traditionally marked the relationship between Franks and Greeks. Pope Innocent III, keen as he was to direct crusades, discovered (as other popes would later) that it was easier to offer indulgences than to control armies. The fact is that the crusades were losing moral direction as a form of Christian pilgrimage. As a result, the providentialist narrative which the crusaders attached to their previous victories and which for a century had dominated the epic chronicles of crusade was also now potentially in crisis. William of Tyre, Latin historian of the crusades born in Outremer (his real journey was to Europe, where he was educated), when reflecting upon the recent success of Saladin could not help but believe that moral decline was at the root of the problem:

In the place of our parents, who were religious men and fearful of God, have been born sons of perdition [. . .] it is only according to justice and their sins that the Lord, as if provoked to anger, withdraws His Grace. These are the men of the current century, and especially from the orient. Anyone who attempted to trace their habits with a diligent pen, or rather to portray the monstrosity of their vices, would succumb under the immensity of the material and would turn to satire rather than persist in the writing of history.[81]

A number of developments can be identified as following, directly or indirectly, from this crisis. All dealt with the failure of travel as crusade by transferring the object of real and imaginary voyages from access to, and control of, the centre of the world – that meeting-place of history, locality and transcendence – to other, more attainable objects. Whether chivalric, poetic, scientific or plain imperialist, these objects articulated new cultural forms of travel. The highest ideal could only be sublimated or substituted. Perhaps the most clear and immediate example of this substitution is the development of the chivalric theme of quest at the turn of the twelfth century.

The emergence of an Arthurian mythology was based on the Latin prose fiction of the British cleric Geoffrey of Monmouth, the *Historia Regum Britanniae* (1135) – as so often in the Middle Ages, a skilful pseudo-historical fabrication motivated by patriotic aims. It was however in France, and in particular at the refined feudal courts of Eleanor of Aquitaine and of her daughter Marie of Champagne, that between 1150 and 1180 the theme found its most influential development in the vernacular genre of the *roman* – in effect a novel written in verse. In the *Perceval* or *Conte du Graal* (c. 1182), the last work written by the most creative of the romance writers, Chrétien de Troyes, the sublimation of the crusading impulse into a chivalric ideal found its most far-reaching expression. The quest for the Holy Grail was originally no more than an intriguing theme in a story of chivalric self-discovery. Perceval, the young Welsh hero, leaves his home in the forest as a complete ignoramus, prompted by an overriding desire – one intrinsic to his inner nature – for the profession of knighthood. He embarks upon a long process of learning through experience which will fulfil his destiny to become 'the best knight in the world'. In a number of encounters he learns to fight and to love. However, his fundamental test, one which he initially fails, is the interpretation of the mysterious events which take place in the castle of the maimed fisherking, who is (as we later learn) in reality his own cousin. Perceval, tainted by the sin of ignorance, fails to ask about the significance of a strange procession of young men and women carrying precious objects – a white lance oozing fresh blood, two candelabras, a golden grail and a silver carving-dish.[82]

Chrétien never finished this *roman* and its significance remains ambiguous.[83] However, a plausible interpretation of this obviously allegorical story relates it to the context of the victories of Saladin in Outremer. Chrétien's patron for this work was not (as with his previous *romans*) Marie of Champagne, but Philip of Flanders, who in 1177 had failed to provide much-needed leadership in the Holy Land by refusing to accept the regency of the Latin kingdom from the weak king Baldwin IV, his sick cousin, and by aborting a Christian expedition to Egypt. Perceval stood to redeem his own failing and become the best knight in the world much in the same way that Philip of Flanders stood to regain his role as leader of the crusade (as he actually attempted to do in 1188, in the context of the Third Crusade, although he died in 1191 without managing to recover Jerusalem). The Holy Grail stood in this way as symbol of an ideal crusading destiny – one able to ensure the continuity of the Christian Eucharist in Jerusalem. Like Perceval, the Christian knight needed to learn to recognize and accept this destiny.[84]

Perhaps more significant than this, or any other alternative interpretation, is the dynamic pattern of allegorical development and literary re-creation which the theme of the quest for the Holy Grail, as a feudal paradigm for travel, underwent between its first appearance in Chrétien's work and the consolidation of a standard Arthurian prose cycle in the 1220s. The history of these adoptions and transformations is revealing of the fact that the knight-errant, with his stereotyped military encounters and erotic explorations, was in fact the focus for a redefinition of chivalric values and identities, one eagerly sought by writers with very different agendas. Not only were there a number of continuations of the *Perceval* (of limited merit) from 1200, but already in 1190 Robert of Boron produced his *Roman de l'estoire dou Graal*, in which the Christian and crusader themes suggested by Chrétien appeared more forcefully with the Grail transformed into the cup of the Last Supper, used by Joseph of Arimathea to collect the last drops of Christ's blood after his body was removed from the cross. Another lay poet, the Bavarian knight Wolfram von Eschenbach, also created his own version in the *Parzival*, one imbued with such 'orientalist' themes as the virtuous Saracen knight (probably inspired by Saladin) and which played up the other-worldly and magical traits of the Grail. This German Grail was still an object of redemption from sin, and the quest a process of learning, but the ethos of virtue and the vague mysticism of this poem stood very far from the dogmatic use of the crusades by Pope Innocent III. Certainly, Wolfram's pagan heroes challenged the spirit, if not the letter, of the decisions of the Lateran

Council of 1215, which established firmly the principle that 'no man can be saved outside the Church' (*extra ecclesia nullus omnino salvatur*).

In stark opposition to these lay poetic versions emerged the prose novels which, inspired by the work of Robert of Boron, adopted the Arthurian mythology within a clerical discourse. Glastonbury Abbey, which was quick to claim and exploit a historical association with 'Avalon', a key setting of the Arthurian cycle, sponsored an allegorical and spiritual view of the Grail in the early thirteenth-century novel *Perlesvaus*. More influential still was the *Queste del Saint Graal*, which was part of a comprehensive Arthurian cycle written by a team of Cistercian monks between 1215 and 1230. This was marked by a strong moral and ascetic emphasis and was modelled upon the idea of the subjection of the lay seeker to the wise hermit. Here Perceval stood as a man uniquely touched by grace, well above the fallen, adulterous Lancelot, but not yet as perfect as the novel's new hero, Galaad, Lancelot's son, who alone combined the virtues of moral effort and divine grace and thus alone was able fully to comprehend the mystery of the Grail – now a purely mystical vision.[85]

Thus the chivalric paradigm of travel as quest was contested ground. Between the open-ended moral explorations of courtly romance, placed ambiguously between secular desire and mystic piety, and the successful religious appropriation – slightly heterodox for its fanaticism – of these creations, stood the early thirteenth-century struggle between lay and clerical discourses for the control of the *Militia Christi*. Much of thirteenth-century culture would be conditioned by this tension, one which found a response in the ethos of poverty, preaching and secular engagement of the new mendicant Orders.

It was a tension which was also felt in the evolution of the Western idea of love. The figure of the knight-errant was only the most obvious response to the crisis of crusade, one which represented an abstract idealization of travel as knightly quest in order to make up for the deficiencies of travel as armed pilgrimage. No less significant was the direction taken by erotic poetry in the literature of courtly love, codified as an adulterous desire for an idealized married woman. The theme of courtly love had developed under the impact of Ovid's *ars amatoria* in the feudal courts of the twelfth century (Chrétien himself translated Ovid into French), but also went beyond its models.[86] The Provençal troubadour Jaufré Rudel expresses most clearly the fact that courtly love was a form of sublimated travel and an alternative to pilgrimage. Rudel's few surviving poems are marked by the theme of 'love from a distance' (*amor de lonh*), a desire for an inaccessible woman which leads from sexual frustration to religious fulfilment. The way this process substituted the ideology of crusade is made explicit in the thirteenth-century *Life* of the poet:

Jaufré Rudel of Blaia was a very noble man, the prince of Blaia. And he fell in love with the countess of Tripoli, without seeing her, because of the good things that he heard about her from the pilgrims coming from Antioch. And he composed many songs about her, with beautiful melodies and simple words. And in order to see her he took the cross and embarked, but an illness caught him in the ship. They took him to Tripoli, to a hostel, as a dead man. And they told the countess, and she went to his side by his bed, and took him in her arms. He knew it was the countess and recovered hearing and breath, and praised God because he had preserved his life until he saw her; and thus died in her arms. She had him honourably buried at the house of the Temple and afterwards, that very same day, she became a nun, on account of the pain of his death.[87]

Here the ideal woman stood as the real object of the pilgrims' accounts and of the crusader's desire. She was even more inaccessible than the Holy Land: the only real encounter with the beloved was, through death, in a spiritual realm. Biographies of poets were in themselves a novel genre (earlier biographies were reserved for saints, kings and military heroes, although in the twelfth century one also occasionally finds educated clerics, like Gerald of Wales or the unfortunate Abelard, who wrote auto-biographies). Their appearance marks a transition towards a legitimate form of poetic quest or spiritual travel which would gain recognition in the urbanized world of the following century, and which had its most famous and accomplished representative in Dante.

THE EMERGENCE OF A NATURALISTIC AND ETHNOGRAPHIC PARADIGM

With the failed crusades, the plague and the papal schism, the fourteenth century inaugurated a period of crisis for the feudal institutions of military, economic and ecclesiastical expansion. What characterizes the various manifestations of the theme of travel in the late Middle Ages was the necessity to respond to the problem of credibility of belief, a necessity which, as we shall see, could prompt lay writers to use the traditional form of the allegorical journey to explain theological dogma or to re-capture a religious vision. Ultimately, however, the most pervasive response was empiricism, and in this field the contribution of travel literature was not only significant at the level of symbolic expression, but also by its own development as a literary genre which offered an alternative source of narrative truth. What the Renaissance inherited from this period was, above all, the idea that there was a kind of truth about men and nature which was accessible to all, rather than just to a specialized religious elite, and which rested upon direct obervation rather than upon written authority. But this principle could grow only because traditional authorities were questionable. It was in the context of a crisis of traditional courtly codes of love and chivalry that ideologies of travel came to express new strategies to cope with the problem of religious belief and observance.[88]

Dante was, by reason of his exile from Florence, a wandering courtier forced to embrace a cosmopolitan identity. His attitude towards travel, as expressed in his *Divine Comedy* (*c.* 1315–20), exemplifies a tension between religious ideals and new forms of lay spirituality which manifested not only the increasing difficulty of the courtly themes of chivalry, love and pilgrimage after the thirteenth century, but also their continuing influence until the end of the Renaissance. In his great visionary poem Dante, as self-reflective poet, occupies centre stage in a quest where the erotic element is entirely subsumed within a theological vision. His journey from hell through purgatory to paradise is entirely allegorical and educational and was understood as such by Dante himself: after Beatrice's death, he had defined (in the last sonnet of the *New Life*) a 'new perception born of grieving love' which was to be the source for a 'spiritual pilgrimage', announcing in this way what would become the *Comedy*.[89] The journey, dominated by the desire for salvation, is therefore a positive action, and the idealized figures of both the pagan poet Virgil and the beloved woman Beatrice also play positive roles, since literature offers a path, while the beloved offers an image of purity. But Dante's capacity to recapture a strong image of Christian pilgrimage from the lay materials of poetry and erotic desire also requires a denial of an image of worldly travel which in the *Inferno* is represented by Ulysses (Odysseus). This Ulysses, unlike Homer's, never reaches Ithaca because he decides to sail towards the West, led by curiosity alone:

I and my companions were old and slow when we came to that narrow outlet where Hercules set up his landmarks so that men should not pass beyond. On my right hand I left Seville, on the other had already left Ceuta. 'O brothers', I said, 'who through a hundred thousand perils have reached the West, to this so brief a vigil of the senses that remains to us choose not to deny experience, in the sun's track, of the unpeopled world. Take thought of the seed from which you spring. You were not born to live as brutes, but to follow virtue and knowledge.'[90]

This journey could only lead to a futile vision. Ulysses reaches the shores of Mount Purgatory, but only to sink with his ship and crew. That truly successful travel had to be religious and canonical, few contemporaries could have questioned. There is however a paradox in the fact that Dante's early fourteenth-century denial of the worldly traveller co-existed with the growth of ethnographic literature in the Latin West, and that this period saw the development of overland travels to Asia and maritime exploration in the Atlantic.

In effect the late Middle Ages are characterized by the growth of ethnography within the related genres of geographical literature, ambassadorial reports, mission and even pilgrimage itself. It would be a mistake to see this ethnographic emphasis as a consequence of humanist education and the imitation of classical models: the missionary William Rubruck, the merchant Marco Polo, the imaginary pilgrim John Mandeville and many other travellers from the period between 1250 and 1450 responded to an entirely different impulse, one not primarily concerned with new educational ideals but rather with a number of more traditional concerns – sometimes the pursuit of practical knowledge, often the desire for entertainment, occasionally the ideological exploration of human cultural diversity within a traditional religious framework. What these separate developments within travel literature share is an empirical bent (a kind of 'realism'), which results not so much from a desire to challenge traditional religious ideologies as from the growth of naturalistic and historical narrative forms. This attention to the narration of observed experience, with special attention to human subjects, can in a general sense be seen as the ultimate relocation of the paradigm of travel from the ideal of pilgrimage to those of empirical curiosity and practical science. It results however from the growth and transformation, rather than the mere exhaustion, of the traditional ideologies of pilgrimage, crusade and chivalry under the impact of new religious, political and social concerns.[91]

The development of the missionary ideal is perhaps the most obvious expression of this shift of emphasis and helps us understand the extent to which the crisis of the traditional paradigms of pilgrimage and crusade led to rationalist ideologies and to historical narrative practices within what, essentially, were religious visions. We find, for instance, unprecedented ethnographic analysis in the narratives of the Mongol missions by the Franciscan friars John of Piano de Carpini (1245–7) and William of Rubruck (1252–5).[92] We are faced here with detailed narratives written in Latin by high-ranking missionaries imbued with the new Franciscan spirit but also acting as political agents – Carpini for Pope Innocent IV, Rubruck for King Louis IX of France. The attention devoted by the papacy and many European princes to the Mongols was related to their political importance, first as a direct threat to Christianity and afterwards as possible allies against common Muslim enemies in the Near East. The historical paradox is that these missions failed miserably in their primary concern to convert the Mongols, whilst succeeding in the creation of a new standard of ethnographic analysis for the sake of political and cultural espionage. As Rubruck declared in his preface to King Louis: 'You told me, when I left you, to put in writing for you everything I saw among the Tartars, and further urged me not to be afraid of writing to you at length. . .'[93] This he did with great competence, being aware that, among Mongols, he was entering *aliud seculum* (another world).[94]

In effect we find here the beginnings of a pattern that would be inherited by the missionary writers of the Counter-Reformation, especially by the Jesuits in Asia after the second half of the sixteenth century: not only was a historical analysis of human cultural diversity increasingly seen as a precondition for effective methods of evangelization, but in effect the impact of the missionaries as evangelizers could pale into insignificance when compared to their impact as political meddlers, empirical world historians and ethnologists. The Latin missionary, as traveller, became a figure with increasing importance from the thirteenth century onwards, often as colonial pioneer and information-gatherer in the late medieval and early modern expansion of Europe. However, despite their primarily religious aim, missionary activities actually stimulated the creation of an empirical, rather than a spiritual, travel literature. Ignatius of Loyola – the founder of the Jesuit Order – was, at a distance of three hundred years, an heir to Francis of Assisi who transformed his pilgrimage to Jerusalem into a worldly ministry to Christians and non-Christians. This, inevitably, required a worldly vision too – albeit one that was mystical and worldly at the same time.[95]

Throughout the late medieval period, mission and crusade were interrelated, rather than opposed to each other, as ideologies of religious travel. More often than not, a war against religious enemies was also seen as a prelude for conversion, and this outlook would be conveniently adopted by the explorers of Africa and the Atlantic in the fifteenth century. They could of course contemplate trade rather than conquest as a convenient option, and alliances with non-Christians were common, but the ideas of war against the infidel, of the conversion of pagans and of the ultimate crusade against Muslim-controlled Jerusalem (from the Atlantic as well as from the Mediterranean) always stood in the background and were crucial in shaping the imperial ideologies of the Spanish and Portuguese kings. However, crusade and mission obeyed two different impulses: if, as we have seen, crusade was originally understood as a form of pilgrimage, mission was an evangelical ideal particularly apt in the context of expanding geographical horizons. Certainly the idea of missions to Muslims was originally more relevant than the idea of missions to pagans on the edges of the known world (ranging from China to the Canary Islands), and many missions (like those to the Mongols or to the largely mythical Prester John of the Indies) were conceived as a way of helping the crusade. However, missions also increasingly responded to the consolidation of a more empirical geography, one created by such travellers as Marco Polo or Nicolò Conti. In this way the discovery of the New World by Christopher Columbus (which Columbus took to be Marco Polo's Indies) only completed a process of empirical re-orientation of the geographical imagination, and it is this wider focus which made the missionary ideal more apt than pilgrimage or crusade as a religious form of travel that could act as a corollary to trade and conquest. There was no longer an enemy to fight, but many to convert, in a world which still had a centre in Jerusalem but also vast new terrains to map, explore and describe for the sake of both profit and religion.

Mission also differed from pilgrimage and crusade in its rationalist bent. It implied preaching and, in any confrontation with alternative theologies, some kind of dialogue. The late medieval emphasis on empirical descriptions – which came to supersede the simple religious ritual of travel for salvation – also found expression in the increasing amount of attention devoted to understanding Islam and, after the sixteenth century, the gentile (non-Biblical) religions. These came to be seen as systems of belief that needed to be contradicted on a rational basis. This was in itself a result of the development of rationalism within Christian theology – that necessity to find arguments for faith which led in the twelfth and thirteenth centuries from Anselm of Canterbury's 'proofs' for the existence of God, through Abelard's advocacy of a rational, philosophical basis for Christian ethics, to the great thirteenth-century theological synthesis of the Dominican St Thomas Aquinas. It is significant, for instance, that important texts of Christian theology (e.g. Abelard's *Dialogus inter Philosophum, Iudaeum et Christianum* of *c.* 1141) were conceived as dialogues with Jews and Muslims, or presented (like Aquinas's *Summa contra gentiles* of 1256–64) as a tool for preaching in Spain. In its most extreme version, this desire for solid arguments – a desire that in effect expressed a deep insecurity – led to attempts to prove rationally the central mysteries of the Incarnation and the Trinity, which distinguished Christianity from other Biblical creeds.

The great visionary Ramon Llull (1232–1316), a Majorcan contemporary of Dante, organized a whole missionary programme for North Africa and beyond around this desire. In his cultural training he was a courtier imbued with chivalric ideals, a man who had composed poems in the tradition of courtly love. Like Dante, he saw the dangers of this worldly culture as a basis for lay piety but, whilst the Florentine sublimated love to make it divine, Llull threw himself into a missionary and writing career founded upon a religious and cosmological vision which he acquired, not through poetic labours, but through a direct mystical experience. Thus instead of composing a *Comedy* he wrote about his *Ars*, a vision of 'the best book in the world', which was both his understanding of the workings of God in nature and the key to his missionary method, since (he believed) it would allow him to convince intelligent Muslims and gentiles of the truth of Christianity. His *Book of the Gentile and the Three Wise Men* (c. 1275), presented as a peaceful religious dialogue, is based on this premise.

Although in the progress of Christian theology Llull's extreme faith in rational arguments was marginalized as the intellectually embarrassing excess of a freelancer and mystic, seen in its historical context what is striking is the way he effectively worked to recapture the image of the knight-errant as a religious figure. His own autobiography describing in some detail his visions, travels, works and trials – the *Vita coaetanea* of c. 1311 – was of course in the mould of a religious quest. A few months after dictating this, on his way to the Council of Vienne (where he was to advocate successfully the teaching of Oriental languages at the great European universities for the education of missionaries) he contrived to summarize it more concisely:

I was married and with children, reasonably well-off, licentious and worldly. All of this I willingly left in order to honour God, procure the public good, and exalt the Holy faith. I learned Arabic; several times I ventured forth to preach to the Saracens; and for the sake of the faith I was arrested, imprisoned and beaten. For forty-five years I have laboured to move the Church and Christian princes to act for the public good. Now I am old and poor, but my purpose is still the same and the same it will remain, if it so please God, until I die.[96]

His more influential works, those written in the vernacular, adopted the theme of travel as a pedagogical tool. An allegorical novel such as the *Felix or Book of Marvels* (c. 1288) was structured around the image of the innocent traveller who is led by the hermit (that fundamental figure in Chrétien's *Perceval*) through the marvels of the world, offering an excuse for an impressive exercise in Christian encyclopaedism. In this way, the traveller could still be, in the early fourteenth century, no more than a seeker and knower of God.[97]

In stark contrast to this persistence of allegory and religious idealism, no late medieval travel account exemplifies the emerging empirical bent as well as Marco Polo's almost contemporary *Divisament dou Monde* or *Description of the World* (*c.* 1298). The main difficulty with interpreting this text, with its extraordinary wealth of detail, is the lack of obvious models for it: Polo was certainly not dependent on the ethnographic analysis of such writers as Gerald of Wales, a sophisticated cleric writing in Latin in the twelfth century, for a book which was composed in an Italianate French with the help of a professional romance writer, Rustichello di Pisa.[98] The aim and audience were different altogether:

Emperors and kings, dukes and marquises, counts, knights, and townsfolk, and all people who wish to know the various races of men and the peculiarities of the various regions of the world, take this book and have it read to you. . .[99]

Polo and Rustichello were addressing a general audience, aristocratic and popular, in the vulgar tongue. Their appeal was to curiosity and the desire for knowledge alone. Certainly the European protagonists of the journey, Marco Polo and his father and uncle, were made to appear as collaborators with the pope and his missionary purposes, carrying letters back and forth between Latin Christendom and the court of Kubilai Khan. But their mission was on the whole a private enterprise which began as a business venture and ended with the peculiar job of serving the Great Khan as part of his extensive foreign contingent in China. The book, as such, was a combination of pure ethnography and historical or legendary material based on hearsay, organized geographically and framed by an account of Marco Polo's travels which did not tell much about himself but rather served to guarantee the truthfulness of the book. The traveller therefore appeared mainly as a guarantor of either empirical observation or hearsay (much of the 'miraculous' and 'marvellous' material is not, as has often been suggested, a deformation of empirical reality caused by Marco Polo's Latin Christian prejudices, but rather a tribute to his willingness to tell a European audience what some Oriental peoples had told him about other Oriental peoples and places).

What makes the work original is that the focus of the book is neither the traveller as adventurer, nor his political or religious mission, but rather the depiction of human empirical diversity, as the preface quoted above makes clear. It has been noted that Rustichello relied on his own Arthurian compilation for this preface, but this in reality only illuminates the way an audience for a new kind of book could be reached: Polo and Rustichello used the well-tried rhetoric of a literature of entertainment in order to create a niche for an empirical geography of human diversity. Occasionally the narrative of wars in distant kingdoms also relied on the late medieval rhetoric of chivalric warfare. But the crucial innovation of the book, and what explains its influence in cartography and its ability to inspire future explorers, was the way in which the figure of the traveller became a rhetorical justification for the use of popular vernacular descriptive language in a 'realist' (if rhetorically stereotyped) manner. Nothing could be further from the abstract landscape of enchanted forests and castles of Arthurian literature than the long lists of specific places and their conditions and customs in Marco Polo's *Description of the World*.

When the traveller leaves Ceylon and sails westwards for about sixty miles he arrives at the great province of Maabar [the Coromandel coast], which is called Greater India [. . .] it is ruled by five kings, who are all brothers [. . .] You must understand that in this sea is a gulf between the island and the mainland [. . .] it is in this gulf that the pearls are gathered [. . .] can assure you that the king of this province derives an immense duty from the revenue paid on this fishery [. . .] must tell you that in all this province of Maabar there is no master tailor or dressmaker to cut or stitch cloth, because the people go stark naked all the year round [. . .] except that they cover their private parts with a piece of cloth. . .[100]

And on and on. We find here not an irrational predilection for marvels and monstrosities but rather someone on the lookout for that which is novel and different – the 'true marvels' announced by Rustichello – and which encompasses in a fairly orderly fashion geography, climate, politics, economy and social customs. The limitations of the book are therefore those of Marco Polo's relative superficiality as observer, of his (and Rustichello's) difficulty in organizing a combination of notes and memories in order to create a book, of the differing quality of Polo's observations made over the course of many years, and above all of the need to adapt many observations originally made for an Oriental employer and possibly in an Oriental language to the religious and civil assumptions of Europeans who had no means to test the veracity of what was being said.[101]

A book like this of course created numerous difficulties. It did not deny the superiority of Christianity: the analysis of manuscript variants shows that Marco Polo, Rustichello and many later interpolators often felt obliged to cut or to add in order to emphasize the point that idolaters were devilish and so on. But the focus on the diversity of customs and, occasionally, on the 'local rationality' of alternative beliefs, including the image of admirable non-Christian urban civilizations, certainly tested the common assumption (implicit, for instance, in Dante's vision) that the Christian way of salvation and European civility formed a harmonious and comprehensive whole. A book that satisfied curiosity for diversity, here referred to a lay rather than to a clerical audience which might have subjected the analysis of idolatry and strange customs to missionary or theological purposes, also encouraged the kind of worldliness which Dante had condemned when he made Ulysses sink. But Marco Polo also created a problem for the lay readership: if the traveller stood individually for the truthfulness of his observation, how could he be trusted?

Only the spectacular increase in travel narratives and the establishment of regular contacts with many different parts of the world after the sixteenth century transformed Marco Polo, who was an exceptional character in his period, into the celebrated pioneer for a new authoritative discourse on human geography. But obviously, even when mistrusted, the empirical traveller represented an important novelty: the issue about him was no longer salvation, not even moral wisdom, but rather the reliability of knowledge, a kind of science of nature and mankind. After Marco Polo the authority of the traveller replaced that of the book; the book was only authoritative if the traveller whose report it contained was authoritative too.

It is perhaps for this reason that the most successful medieval travel text after Marco Polo, that of Sir John Mandeville, represented a purely fictional traveller, an invention devised to render a compilation of pre-existing travel accounts more coherent and convincing. The *Book of Sir John Mandeville* of *c.* 1356 can now be read as a clever fiction because modern critics have been able to trace the vast majority of its statements to its written sources, but for the late fourteenth-century reader – in a period when actual contacts with the East had again been interrupted by the collapse of the ephemeral Pax Mongolica – the familiarity of its statements was only proof of its veracity.[102]

However, the point about Mandeville is not simply how successfully the first-person fictional *persona* of the traveller allowed an anonymous writer to weave together his sources, thus creating a 'false' Marco Polo who fooled generations of readers, but that the intention of the book was clearly contrary to the spirit of Marco Polo's lay empiricism. John Mandeville is a pilgrim, and his book is a conventional fourteenth-century pilgrimage to the Holy Land, although with the unprecedented addition of an extended journey to the East, India, Cathay, the land of Prester John, and the walls of Paradise (Paradise itelf is unreachable). As the traveller explains when he introduces himself:

Since it is so that the land beyond the sea, that is to say the Holy Land, the land of promission [Mandeville's own word, meaning where the ultimate promise may be fulfilled], is among all other lands the most excellent and noble, and lady sovereign of them all; and was blessed, sanctified and consecrated by the precious body and blood of Our Lord Jesus Christ, in which land it pleased him to become human in the Virgin Mary [. . .] and that land he raised among all others as the best and most virtuous and noble land in the world, for it is the heart and the middle point of all the land of the world [. . .] And for as much as it has been a long time since there has not been any general passage to the land beyond the sea, and many people take pleasure in hearing about the Holy Land, and find recreation therein, I, John Mandeville, knight, though unworthy, born and brought up in the town of Saint Albans in England, who have travelled over there . . . [103]

This vicarious pilgrimage, written for a generation who lived without hope of a successful crusade, is much more than an excuse to begin an imaginary journey to India. The coherence of the text relies on the sophisticated intentionality of its author and is brought forth by a comparison of the text with its well-known sources, and also with its many later variant transformations (the manuscripts are as abundant as they are diverse).[104] In effect the extended pilgrimage serves two purposes for the writer: first, to re-create the theology of a sacred geography by combining a journey to the centre of the world with an account of as complete as possible a journey to its edges; and, second, to express his concerns for religious reform within Latin Christianity by using the 'exotic other' – the Oriental Christian, the Muslim, the virtuous gentile – to question ironically the shortcomings of a Roman Christendom caught in a crisis of inner strife and ecclesiastical abuse, the best expression of which was perhaps the repeated failure of the crusades.

We do not know who the author was, other than that he wrote in French (even if Mandeville was presented as an English knight). The sources he used have been successfully identified for the most part, and the vast majority belonged to a compilation of travel acccounts translated into French by Jean le Long, a Benedictine monk of Saint Omer, around 1351. The key texts around which the two main parts of Mandeville's travels were constructed were the pilgrimage narrative of William of

Boldensele (1336) and the narrative of the Franciscan missionary to India and Cathay Odoric of Pordenone (1330) – although not, interestingly enough, the earlier book of Marco Polo. Jean le Long may or may not have been the author, but what is clear is that the writer of the *Book of Sir John Mandeville* had a religious aim in mind, one which amounted very much to erecting a Polo type of narrative *persona* as authority for a theologically compelling 'description of the world'. Salvation was, now again, the issue, and the different descriptions of cultural diversity, the encyclopaedic ambition, even the geographical speculations describing a world that was round and could be travelled in circles, were all geared towards moral self-reflection and cosmographical re-centring. Mandeville's world was one where different customs eventually pointed towards a universal natural reason and where distant lands were opposite mirrors to a Christian sacred geography.

Mandeville in this way represents both a conservative attempt to reinstate a past vision in a period of doubt and a concession to the new authority of the traveller as direct observer. The book persistently points back towards Marco Polo and beyond him, in a way which is extremely significant for the history of travel literature in late medieval Europe. It seems clear that the narratives of the travels by Marco Polo and Mandeville were the most influential in this period – something that is borne out by the number of surviving manuscripts, the variety of uses to which they were put, and the number of languages into which they were translated. Their opposition also exemplifies the key issue of how an empirical travel literature centred upon the description of anthropological and natural diversity rose against a dominant religious background. Although pious pilgrimage was still a lively genre in the seventeenth century (as an example we may refer to the many editions, translations and plagiarisms of Jean Zuallart's *Il devotissimo viaggio di Gerusalemme*, originally published in Rome in 1587),[105] in the long term the victory was Marco Polo's rather than Mandeville's. Marco Polo triumphed as the medieval traveller who best represented the new myth of the modern traveller as a curious observer able to explore human cultural diversity through geography. In the following centuries, as the religious vision went through successive crises (of which the more spectacular would be the Reformation) and slowly faded, the truth of empirical observation became more established as a desirable aim for travellers.[106] Even pilgrimage literature, after the fourteenth century more abundant than ever, became increasingly a vehicle for empirical research. It is interesting to note that many of the pilgrim narratives of this period are full of chapters describing the customs of Egyptians or the landscape, rather than simply the meaning of a Christian experience, in Mount Sinai or the Holy Land. One example is the Tuscan narratives by the Florentines Lionardo Frescobaldi, Simone Sigoli and Giorgio Gucci, who travelled together (as was usually the case, from Venice) with a few other pilgrims in 1384. There is no lack of piety and interest in miraculous stories in each of their accounts, but like Marco Polo they all combine this traditional belief in religious magic with a great deal of empirical curiosity. One of the best examples is Sigoli's description of Cairo, which ranges over many subjects, from mosques to local customs to elephants:

I shall now describe the nobility of the Sultan and of the city of Cairo, and in addition will record many customs which have not been previously noted [. . .] it would be a long thing to describe the churches of the Saracens, which are called mosques and have tall towers [. . .] the men have beautiful bodies, much more than us, and all have very large beards, and there are many old men over 80, and it is a great pleasure to see how they carry themselves, because they appear majestic to the eye . . .[107]

For Sigoli the Saracens were no less important than the religious indulgences he had gained in his journey (of which he provided a detailed list). Empirical descriptions were not however a phenomenon exclusive to a sophisticated urban milieu such as the city of Florence, arguably under the influence of early Humanism. As early as 1323–4 an Irish Franciscan, Symon Semeonis, could spend long chapters of his pilgrimage narrative decribing Crete and, in much greater detail, Alexandria and Cairo.[108] Similar attention to geographical detail can be found in the Latin narrative by William of Boldensele, in reality Otto of Nyenhusen, a Dominican who travelled in 1334 (as an imposed penitence) and was the key source for Mandeville's own 'pilgrimage', or in Ludolph of Sudheim's account of his travels through the Orient in 1336–41 as chaplain of a nobleman in the service of the king of Armenia, which was as full as it was confused and grew, Mandeville-like, almost to became a geographical encyclopedia.[109] These trends persisted in the fifteenth century. In 1496–9 the German pilgrim Arnold von Harff, a knight from Cologne, did not content himself with visiting the Holy Places and describing at length his adventures in Cairo, but he also had to add his further travels in Rome, Compostela, India and to the sources of the Nile – journeys which, since he had not really been to any of these places, he had to make up by copying other sources (including one of the early printed versions of the book of John Mandeville). Even in a case like this, in which the intention was obviously pious (all the places which von Harff added to Jerusalem were meant to make his sacred geography complete), the prestige of the exotic traveller was perhaps more important than that of the simple pilgrim.[110] By the time we reach Ludovico de Varthema, who travelled East in 1502–8, openly out of intellectual curiosity, as we have seen, he could skip Jerusalem altogether in order simply to pursue Mecca, the Indian Ocean and the Spice Islands.

A similar tension between piety and the worldliness of attention to human life is implicit in Geoffrey Chaucer's *Canterbury Tales* (1386–1400). The pilgrimage to the saint's tomb is almost completely subsumed within a game of story-telling which, seeking to integrate humanity within the Christian vision in the name of literal truth, is in danger of burying the religious dimension altogether. As the Host who proposed the story-telling contest reveals:

> And I don't doubt, before the journey's done
> You mean to while the time in tales and fun.
> Indeed there is little pleasure for your bones
> Riding alone and all as dumb as stones.[111]

It is not therefore surprising that a little more than a century later the Christian Humanist's response, famously that of Erasmus, was to condemn pilgrimage as a waste of time altogether in a move which, however pure in pious intention, effectively destroyed what was left of the medieval paradigm of the religious journey.[112] But this same sort of tension between religious and secular concerns deeply affected the other major genre of the period in which travel played a key role, namely chivalry. We do still find, of course, images of the Christian knight. For instance the anonymous Middle English poem *Sir Gawain and the Green Knight*, written in alliterative verse, has as its main theme (like Chrétien's *Perceval*) an enigmatic quest which involves a process of self-knowledge. The knight, armed with an impressive array of Christian virtues, travels to his confrontation with an ambiguous figure. These alas, despite a rather impressive performance, do not entirely suffice, but Sir Gawain's weakness (a sin of fear for self-preservation rather than one of licentiousness) is seen by all but himself as minor and understandable from a human perspective – which allows the writer both to re-state the highest ideal and to humanize it a little with humour.[113] But besides this and other examples of traditional chivalric idealism we also find in the fifteenth century a number of chivalric novels which clearly take a more decisively realistic turn, taking both the setting and the humanizing tendencies to extremes, which often affects profoundly the meaning of travel as a narrative theme.

Two of the most interesting novels of the fifteenth century, Antoine de la Sale's *Jehan de Saintré* (1456) and the anonymous Catalan *Curial e Güelfa* (probably also written in the middle of the century), share the premise that the knight will be initiated not by a hermit but rather by a woman, a widow of position who trains a young page at court to become not just a good knight but, especially, a good lover. We are here not only confronted with a world of moral ambiguity in which the psychological interaction between non-conventional lovers takes centre stage at the expense of the quest, but also with a world which is clearly rooted on a recognizable geography and history. Antoine de la Sale (1386–1460), a nobleman in the service of the Counts of Anjou, was himself active in Sicily, North Africa and Naples, and his novel is set in a recognizable Europe where his hero, Jehan, is victorious in Paris, Barcelona, Calais and on the Prussian frontier, against Christian rivals and Muslim enemies alike. For the author of the *Curial*, similarly, the setting is precise – the court of Montferrat in Italy – and the adventures take place in a defined

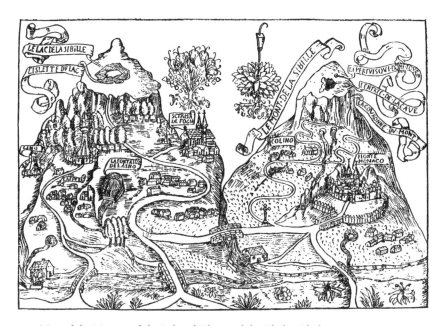

Map of the Mounts of the Lake of Pilate and the Sibyl, with the entrance to the legendary cave, from Antoine de la Sale, *La Salade* (Paris, 1521).

historical period, with precise figures (such as Peter the Great of Aragon) as protagonists, and a war against the Turks as the climax of a chivalric career. The novels present, of course, important differences. Jehan de Saintré succeeds, through his chivalric virtue, in overcoming his devotion to a woman who had captured him for her own pleasure and rejects her when her unfaithfulness becomes apparent, while in a far less misogynistic scenario Curial uses his military success at home and abroad to strengthen his own moral virtue in the face of changing fortune and thus regains the favour of his perhaps justifiably jealous lady. In both cases, however, what is striking is how the traditional roles of chivalry, even those of pilgrimage and crusade, act as proofs of virtue for a purely human scenario. What is at stake in these late medieval novels is not the Christian and chivalric codes of virtue and love, but their revision in the light of a more empirical understanding of human psychology and circumstances.[114]

We have Antoine de la Sale's account of his actual journey in 1420 to the two peaks of Mount Pilatos and Mount Sibyl in the Apennines – where, according to a local legend with great diffusion, the Sibyl was supposed to live – as illustration that this new attitude involved an element of scepticism and experimentation. The *Paradis de la Reine Sibylle* (1437), dedicated to the Duchess of Bourbon, took as its starting point a tapestry of the mountain owned by the Duchess, and various stories which were told about the supernatural goings-on inside.[115] La Sale offered both a narration of his actual journey and a picture – a kind of map – in which he noted how different reality was from legend (see opposite: this 'realist' picture was faithfully reproduced in an engraving included in the Paris edition of 1521). This, in effect, was the key theme of this fascinating narrative. To begin with, the local legends about Pontius Pilate having been buried on the mountain are scrutinized and refuted on the basis of written authorities (e.g. Orosius) according to an idea of historical coherence. The narration of la Sale's own visit is extremely precise in its geographical descriptions, leaving nothing to chance. Throughout his ascent and after reaching the cave on Mt Sibyl, la Sale systematically opposes his empirical observations to the supernatural stories he is told:

I cannot tell you about the other things and marvels which the cave hides, because I never went further in. This was not in any case my business there, but even if I had tried I would have had to put my life at serious risk [because the hole was so dark, narrow and steep]. Therefore, in honour of truth I should say no more, other than I was there in the company of a learned doctor from that country

[. . .]Whilst we were there we heard a long cry which seemed to come from a long
distance and was like the sound made by a peacock. Then the people said that the
voice came from the paradise of the Sibyl, but as far as I am concerned I do not
believe this at all. Rather, I think that we heard my horses whinnying from the
bottom of the mountain . . .[116]

This is followed by three successive accounts, each more fantastic than
the former. A few men penetrated the cave, only to reach a windy gallery
which they dared not cross. This la Sale, who spoke to them, is prepared
to believe. A priest claimed to have been further inside the cave, and
described a magical landscape of bridges over dark rivers and statues of
dragons guarding the road, but he did not cross the tantalizing metal
doors at the end of the path. However, he is dismissed by la Sale (who also
met him) as a lunatic. There finally follows the more significant story of a
German knight who actually reached the magnificent court of Queen
Sibyl – at which 'some laugh, whilst others believe very much in the stories
that the common people have been telling from old times'. In the paradise
of Queen Sibyl the German traveller fell into a life of unbounded carnal
pleasures for many days until, remembering God, he decided to return.
He also realized that the Sibyl and the ladies of her court, every Friday
night, became snakes, only to return to their lovers more beautiful than
ever in the morning. Obviously this is the legend of a Melusine-type figure
of a female magician, a well-known topos in this period and here clearly
associated with the devil. This is not therefore a real paradise, but instead
a typical allegory of sin and perdition in the chivalric mould. The knight,
who managed to escape, the story goes on to explain, confessed in full to
the pope in Rome, but the pope wilfully delayed absolution in order to
make an example of the German to the world. In desperation, the sinner
returned to the false paradise.

There is perhaps some ambiguity in la Sale's attitude towards this story.
He has told these various tales to disprove them, and he also refuses to
believe that the devil might have any magical power over men after the
death and resurrection of Christ. On the other hand he seems attracted to
the empirical feasibility of many of the historical details of the German
knight's story (such as the visit to the pope, whom la Sale tries to identify
historically), and he is impressed by the names he finds inscribed on the
chamber at the entrance of the cave. He inscribes his own name too, but is
careful to stress that he did not penetrate further inside, something which
(as the German's tale confirms) has been expressly forbidden by the pope.
We do not therefore find here a denial of the Christian theme of the
German's story (including the suggestion that travelling knights moved by

curiosity and the desire for adventures, instead of a sane crusading spirit, may fall into perdition), but rather a prudent scepticism towards allegory, which finds its guiding principles in attachment to observed experience, historical feasibility and theological coherence.

The final questioning of the chivalric ideal came with Cervantes's *Don Quixote* (1605–14) as an end product of the Hispanic Renaissance. The values and myths of medieval chivalry had been inscribed in the imperial ideologies of the sixteenth century, in Portuguese Asia as well as in Spanish America.[117] It is for this reason that the criticism, when it finally came, was so poignant – because this was a society which cultivated the imaginary world of the fantastic quest at the same time as it organized the systematic exploitation of fabulous silver mines with forced labour in a newly-found and distant continent. When Cervantes transformed a poor rural gentleman into a parody of the knight-errant, he was not therefore targeting the more historically plausible knights such as Jehan de Saintré and Curial, but rather the more fantastic and popular figures such as Amadís of Gaul, the hero of a late medieval chivalric romance written in Spain and popular throughout Europe. The point of *Don Quixote* was that the magic quest was over. Instead a different journey was offered, one which would lead to a realistic, self-critical assessment of the true nature of Spanish society and its values under the most Catholic monarchy. Beyond the mere practice of empirical observation, modernity began as disenchantment:

Don Quixote replied – 'I find that you are the one without judgement and under some sort of enchantment, since you have declared so many blasphemies concerning something so well received in the world [. . .] because to pretend that the knight Amadís did not exist in this world, nor any of all those adventurous knights of which the histories are full, would be like trying to argue that the sun gives no light, ice does not make things any cooler, or the earth does not hold us. Who in the world will be able to argue that that thing about Guy of Burgundy and princess Floripes was not true, or the story about Fierabreás and the bridge of Mantible? This happened at the time of Charlemagne [. . .] If this is a lie, surely there were no Hector and Achilles either, nor a war in Troy, nor the twelve Peers of France, nor king Arthur [. . .] and the quest for the Holy Grail was a lie too. . .'[118]

Don Quixote's refusal to disbelieve even after long and often painful experience was more than a satire on the power of fantastic literature to blur the edges of perception: it also raised the issue of what there was to believe in.[119]

Despite the continuing importance of the traditional genres of pilgrimage and chivalry in the fifteenth and sixteenth centuries, the transition from occasional to systematic empiricism in travel literature first took place in the more practical field of political reportage. The reason is that ambassadors and spies were always responsible for accurate observation. This, for example, explains the extreme (if rather pedestrian) realism of the report of Ruy González de Clavijo's journey to Timur's Samarqand in the name of Henry III of Castile in 1403–6, or the more penetrating report by Bertrandon de la Broquière, sent to the Near East in 1432 by the Duke of Burgundy, Philip le Bon, in order to assess the opportunities of a crusade against the Turks which would prevent the Muslim conquest of Constantinople. Bertrandon learnt to travel in disguise and to rely on local contacts in order to obtain systematic information.[120] Within this emerging genre of political reportage the merchants and ambassadors of the Venetian Republic often led the way, both in descriptions of European and non-European kingdoms, so that it was in Venice where many of the accounts of the history and customs of the Turks were published in the fifteenth and sixteenth centuries.

In this context of an emerging systematic empiricism led by a combination of curiosity and practical needs, and, fuelled by the persistent crisis of the medieval religious vision, the impact of Humanism was double. On the one hand, it offered philological tools and classical literary models which made the empirical enterprise more precise and systematic; we see this influence in exotic travel literature from Poggio Bracciolini's account of the travels of the Venetian merchant Nicolò Conti in his *De varietate fortunae* (c. 1447) to the travel collections of the following century, of which the most important was undoubtedly the *Navigationi et Viaggi* edited by the Venetian Humanist and civil servant Giovanni Battista Ramusio (1550–59).[121] The second contribution of Humanism was to offer a positive ideology of travel as education within a system of lay, secular learning, that made the empirical traveller who had been emerging since the late middle ages not only as authoritative but also an admirable figure. Marco Polo and Columbus were recognized by their Humanist-educated biographers as men with mythical significance. Ulysses was similarly rescued from the bottom of the sea and enthroned as a model for a worldly wisdom which the most sophisticated European elites came to embrace through the sixteenth and seventeenth centuries. We find here, therefore, the ideological origins of the Grand Tour, as well as of the extended pilgrimages of curiosity of the turn of the seventeenth century (like those performed by the English Anglican George Sandys or the Roman Catholic Pietro della Valle) in which even the religiously orthodox pilgrim became an ethnologist and antiquarian – indeed, an Orientalist.[122]

TRAVEL AND MODERNITY: A HISTORY OF FRAGMENTATIONS

The importance of the modern theme of travel as a quest – often a negative, pointless one – and of travel literature as a fundamental part of a system of empirical narrative practices is best understood historically, in the light of the traditions that have defined Western culture through Antiquity and the Middle Ages. The ten articles in this book explore in some detail a number of aspects of this history, from the Renaissance to the present day. They do not attempt to cover all the ground, which would be impossible, but they provide the basis for a continuous historical perspective. We will therefore end this introduction by suggesting the way in which these different articles, read together in the light of the preceding analysis, contribute to the creation of this general perspective.

One first important observation is the obvious existence of a succession of European imperial cultures which, through the last five centuries, have substantially conditioned the production, reception and ideological leanings of a great deal of travel writing. As one would expect, these imperial influences are especially evident in those travel narratives that are themselves generated by colonial experience. What is perhaps more interesting is to observe how these imperial paradigms variously combined universalist claims with a national focus. Although there were many moments when rival imperial projects co-existed, as well as a number of minor powers which generated their own imperial traditions, the main line of succession is clear. It runs from the Hispanic Renaissance, in this book discussed with reference to the New World, through the French cultural models which were crucial in the period from the late Renaissance to the end of the Enlightenment (evident in the essays on Montaigne, Bernier and the Grand Tour – here seen, as in a mirror, from the Neapolitan end), to the Anglo-Saxon dominance of the nineteenth and twentieth centuries. Nigel Leask's essay is particularly illuminating of the clash between two imperial appropriations – Hispanic and Anglo-Saxon – of the Mexican landscape in early nineteenth-century Mexico, against the background of an earlier native imperial tradition which was, however, by then little more than an object of literary re-creation. Within this latter Anglo-Saxon paradigm we may still distinguish the British tradition, here discussed with reference to scientific travel and to mountaineering in the nineteenth century, from the American one, mainly analysed with reference to post-War fiction.

If any pattern can be suggested at this stage, it is that there is no one single history of European imperialism in travel writing, but rather a succession of nationally tinged paradigms, with some interesting differences of emphasis, within a common European tradition. From the time of the discovery of new maritime routes by Columbus and Vasco da Gama, which made possible the growth overseas of two Hispanic imperial traditions (Spanish and Portuguese), to the popularity of American images of the exploration of outer space throughout the world today, there is a marked tendency in the history of European colonial empires towards an ever wider reach of imperial dominion (direct or indirect, the latter often more insidious). Travel writing has been a key instrument in the cultural aspects of this process. On the other hand, against the background of a modern world which is more interconnected than ever before, we should also consider that universalist assumptions were already explicit in Classical Rome (as self-centred as all pre-modern imperial cultures), and also in the paradigm of pilgrimage and crusade of the Middle Ages – however limited the actual European dominion of the world. The first essays in this book make it clear that early modern Europeans adopted and transformed their dual universalist inheritance, Roman and Christian, on a larger scale than had ever been possible.[123]

If imperialism provides a common thread in the history of European travel, empiricism offers another. The article by Jesús Carrillo usefully combines both, relating the subjective gaze, as developed by the first great European Humanist Petrarch, to Gonzalo Fernández de Oviedo's formulation of a scientific imperialism in the early stages of Spanish appropriation of the New World. This clarifies the role of Humanist sensibility in the transition from allegory to science, defining a paradigm of subjectivity for the early modern period which goes beyond the sensual, narrative empiricism of Marco Polo or even Antoine de la Sale. In this respect the theme of ascent to mountains, with its rich symbolic significance, provides a basis for comparison. Antoine de la Sale, as we have seen, in his account of a journey to Mount Sibyl is struggling between the supernatural in traditional legends – interpreted morally as a struggle between sin and virtue – and empiricism as a principle for sceptical prudence. Petrarch, more decisively, abandons any allegory of conversion altogether in order simply to turn the gaze upon himself. Oviedo, an imperial builder, turns this new subjective gaze outwards for a new project – measuring dominions. Thus in his ascent to the volcano in Nicaragua he establishes the principle of personal observation as a basis for objective description in order to fulfil the universalist claims of the Monarchy he serves. What separates him from Marco Polo is not simply the European political system that he serves, but also the subjectivism and ideological naturalism upon which his capacity to oppose his observations to those of others rests.

Oviedo's positive affirmation of imperialist values, however, only reveals the outer crust of the Renaissance paradigm of travel. New opportunities for economic profit, unprecedented success in overseas conquests and a staggering expansion of the horizons for missionary work: all of these characterize the Hispanic Renaissance and yet, as the article by Joan-Pau Rubiés shows, travel literature not only stated the objectives but also revealed their futility. This discovery of futility, which recalls the disenchantment with the chivalric ideal expressed by Cervantes, suggests that sixteenth-century travel literature represented the effective end of the medieval paradigms which it had sought belatedly to fulfil. The article on Montaigne's pilgrimage by Wes Williams reveals the same process in European travel. Here the traveller to Rome talks about miracles but does not expect any. Instead, in an exercise of self-reflection, he sceptically explores changes in cultural and personal identity, the limits of belief, and the very value of the journey itself.

Montaigne's scepticism towards pilgrimage and, more pointedly, towards the educational value of travel can be read not simply in the light of the waning paradigm of religious travel (already criticized by Erasmus and effectively abandoned by the Reformation), but also in the light of the emerging paradigm of the Grand Tour. In some ways Montaigne manages to challenge both the past and the future history of travel. The aristocratic ritual of the Grand Tour, based on the Humanist idea of travel for education – in languages, academic learning, courtly refinement and political experience – was in effect the fundamental contribution of the late Renaissance to the history of travel in the West and defined a paradigm that would dominate until the nineteenth century. It functioned, alongside travel for empire, as a replacement for pilgrimage and crusade, and it implied an interest in cultural diversity and comparison that was only possible because the empirical travel literature of the period also made the issue of human diversity central.[124]

There were, certainly, debates concerning whether travel abroad was really good: would not the young nobleman lose his moral balance, rather than strengthen it, under foreign influence? Whilst strictly Catholic rulers such as Philip II in Spain issued prohibitions in order to isolate the nation under his care from heretical influences, other countries, mainly Protestant ones, eventually embraced the new ideal, in a clearly secular fashion given that they often went to Catholic Italy. The English writer

Henry Peacham explained it succinctly in his chapter 'Of travel' for his educational treatise *The Compleat Gentleman* of 1622:

nothing rectifies and confirms more the judgement of a gentleman in foreign affairs, teaches him knowledge of himself, and settles his affection more sure to his own country, than travel does [. . .] where may wisdom be had, but from many men, and in many places?[125]

François Bernier represents the ideal of the educated traveller in an exotic setting in an age when the Hispanic imperial systems had largely collapsed under the pressure of northern European military and commercial enterprise. What characterizes his contribution, related – as Peter Burke shows – to the political and religious debates of the court of Louis XIV, is the emphasis on self-reflection. He was able fiercely to criticize Indian beliefs and practices, but not because they were foreign: rather, he invited his readers to extend much of the criticism to their own society. Bernier's use of sceptical arguments separates him from earlier, more conservative, educated travellers such as the Englishman George Sandys and the Italian Pietro della Valle, even though they all shared the seventeenth-century ideal of independent observation and learned curiosity. His scepticism, on the contrary, points towards the Enlightenment, and specifically towards the systematic use of comparison between European and non-European cultures in order to elucidate a new system of European cosmopolitan values – a civil progress founded upon criticism, tolerance and rationality against images of barbarism and despotism. However, these new values were also defined against Europe's own religious past, marked from this perspective by ritual superstition and violent fanaticism. In this way the educated traveller contributed to the break between the Enlightenment and the medieval inheritance of pilgrimage and crusade.[126]

Alas, the cosmopolitan ideals of the Grand Tour were not without contradictions, and belief in rational civilization would often prove a poor substitute for the discarded paradigm of other-worldly salvation. Melissa Calaresu's essay on Neapolitan responses to travellers' stereotypes of their own society illuminates the existence of a centre and a periphery within the enlightened discourse of civilization, one which did not simply separate the European from the non-European, but also some Europeans from others. The importance of the example of Naples partly lies in the fact that, as an ancient site which occupied a prominent place in the early modern aesthetic and moral ideal of a return to Classicism, it was impossible not to reflect upon the discrepancies between that ideal and the

reality. The efforts of the Neapolitan elite to adopt the Enlightenment only made this awareness all the more inevitable and painful.
Montesquieu's influential (although not entirely novel) appeal to climatic
explanations, or the insistence of some Neapolitans on the existence of
political and institutional causes for their problems, together pointed
towards a future vision of national hierarchies and historical particu-
larism which, in effect, modified quite substantially the effects of the
cosmopolitan ideal. The combination of a model of civilization set
by the most successful European nations, with attempts to explain the
deficiencies of those who lagged behind, would often characterize the
new imperialism of the nineteenth century.

At the turn of the nineteenth century the Grand Tour was perhaps over,
but the process of European expansion, led by Great Britain and largely
prompted by the need to fight Napoleonic France, entered a more ambitious phase.[127] Michael Bravo's discussion of the scientific ideal of
precision in this period helps us to understand the transition from the
aristocratic natural histories of the enlightened generation of Cook and
Banks to the more systematic geography of Rennell – the one that set the
ambitious scientific standards of Ali Bey and Richard Burton. To some
extent this seems to have been a transition from the systematic use of
qualitative categories to a new emphasis on quantitative precision, and
it led to an ideal of comprehensive mapping – of which Rennell became
a master – which implied a subjection of the traveller's observations to
very strict requirements, the aim of which was to create objectivity. The
classical conventions which had inspired the Grand Tour for centuries were
sacrificed to precision in this shift towards a more open-ended vision, one
which allowed William Hodges (the painter on Cook's second voyage) to
suggest, in the light of his exotic travels, that Greek standards of architecture were not universal, but simply the result of European education.[128]

Following this development, it is not surprising that – at a time when
belief in the superiority of Western civilization as the apex of a universal
system of historical evolution became ever more rigid, and whilst the
emphasis on scientific precision created a virtual religion of empiricism –
the sense of the other as unattainable, a romantic desire for difference,
also grew. The period is rich in travel accounts which reflect this yearning.
Alexander von Humboldt, by subjecting the travel journal (e.g. the *Personal
Narrative of Travels to Equinoctial Regions of America*, first published
in French in 1814–19) to his desire for a global, meaningful scientific
vision, decisively married empirical observation with imaginative speculation, a method which also influenced Charles Darwin during his voyage

on the *Beagle* (1831–6). As we saw, in Richard Burton the romantic fascination with cultural difference also expressed an awareness of what Europeans, by becoming civilized, had denied within themselves and left behind.

Nigel Leask offers further insights into this romantic imagination, located in the 'orientalist' setting (if we may abuse the expression) of the Mexican civilization destroyed by the West. If in the European imagination the Orient represented the challenge of an alternative civilization which can never be domesticated, the Americas were the most obvious location for Western agency and transformation. As Anthony Padgen has noted, in Humboldt's influential vision their discovery was a historical landmark of universal significance, representing the beginning of modernity as an open-ended intellectual conquest.[129] Leask's analysis of Fanny Calderón's *Life in Mexico* – contemporary to Humboldt's *Cosmos* – has the special interest of focusing on a female writer, when so much of the European traveller's identity seems to have been specifically male. This female writer was supposed to write 'subjectively' about Mexico's inner social life, rather than 'objectively' about its natural constitution (like Alexander von Humboldt) or its vulnerability to European conquest (like Fanny's mentor, the historian William Prescott). As Leask reveals, on the whole Fanny Calderón managed to be almost as full of Western prejudice towards the native as the average male writer. One finds differences, however, when the analysis is taken to subtler points, so that Leask opposes Fanny's identification with Doña Marina – Ferdinand Cortés's Indian mistress and interpreter – to Prescott's identification with the heroic virtues of the conqueror. Similarly, Fanny evokes Aztec civilization as beautiful in a way which subverts Prescott's historicism.

The romantic female traveller's voice is not, one may conclude, totally opposed to the imperial paradigm but offers variations, sometimes specifically related to gender identities, which more often than not imply a dialogue with a dominant male voice. (This is still true of a great deal of post-colonial, late twentieth-century female Anglo-Saxon travel writing: as Dea Birkett and Sara Wheeler explain in their introduction to a recent anthology of women's new travel writing, since 'the writer's inner journey is the most important part' and 'the story of transformation is often the central theme', their real point of reference is not the Victorian female traveller but rather the creative imagination of contemporary travel writers, the majority of them male, of which this century has produced a 'golden age' between the wars and a couple of influential generations afterwards.)[130]

Gender is not of course the only distinction that needs to be considered. There were also differences in the way the romantic imagination affected different nations and different individuals. One of the contributions of Edward Said's *Orientalism* is the distinction between a British attitude of imperial surveying – the one represented by Rennell and Burton – and the French sense of imperial loss after Napoleon's defeat, echoing the earlier defeat of the French-led crusades. This sense of loss helps to explain, for example, why Chateaubriand's Orient became a locale for his 'private myths, obsessions and requirements'.[131] Burton occupied 'a median position' between the fantastic subjectivism of French writers and the authoritative, 'detached' observer of the British imperial system – one well represented in the Orient by the extreme empiricist rhetoric of Edward Lane's *Manners and Customs of Modern Egyptians* (1836). One needs to remain sceptical, however, of Said's suggestion that European discourse had nothing to do with the reality of the Orient. Even in this age of exaggerated imperialism, much of the evidence from travel literature points towards the existence of a cultural exchange, however unequal, between the European and the non-European.

Peter Hansen's essay on British mountaineering explores this point. According to his analysis of mountaineering as a substantial part of British imperial culture between 1850 and 1950 (paradoxically, a period marked by the effective loss of British imperial hegemony), what was at stake in climbing the Alps or the Himalayas was not demystification as in Antoine de la Sale, nor self-knowledge as in Petrarch, nor even imperial measurements as in Oviedo, but rather a pure, gratuitous symbol of conquest and masculinity that separated those who had done it from those who had not. This desire responded to some extent to the crisis of the romantic ideal that nature, or the exotic, could offer a vision which transcended the familiar; in effect the mass tourist industry destroyed this illusion by eroding the traditional elitism of aristocratic travel.[132] For mountaineers, climbing offered a challenge that created a new elite. The trouble was that this elite was not simply British, because a great deal of local knowledge – offered by Swiss guides or by Sherpas – was essential to a successful climb. In effect a complex negotiation took place, one which combined hierarchies with the principle of equality and which meant that the significance of the climb could not remain static. Contrary to the assumption that Europeans did all the doing (and the undoing) in the definition of this relationship, Hansen emphasizes the importance of the Sherpas' identities and strategies in the final outcome.[133]

The history of mountaineering between 1850 and 1950 can help us understand the cultural significance of the evolution of European imperialism in the period of its maximum and most decisive impact, from the intense national rivalries and aggressive appeals to the progress of civilization at the turn of the century to the process of decolonization after the Second World War, with its concomitant ideas of commonwealth and partnership. Possibly the most significant contribution of travel literature at the turn of the twentieth century was the discovery of futility in the idea of progress; and perhaps no scenario was as revealing, because of its intractability, as the 'dark Africa' of Livingstone and Stanley. As the sailor and novelist Joseph Conrad wrote of those famous African explorers who stirred the popular imagination in this period, they were 'conquerors of truth', not because they filled in blank spaces in the map (like, as we saw, Richard Burton claimed), but rather because they explored ways of reading the unknown.[134] Henry Stanley, with his controversially violent and expansionist attitudes, contrasting with the gentlemanly religious idealism of Livingstone, is the background figure who helps us to understand Joseph Conrad's literary judgement on this 'conquest of truth'.[135] Conrad's *Heart of Darkness* (1899) is a fictional re-creation of an autobiographical experience of a journey up the Congo in 1890. This experience shattered the writer's romantic ideals and left him with a feeling of profound failure – one which echoes some of the themes discussed in Rubiés's essay on narratives of travel in sixteenth-century America.[136] More important than the experiences themselves is the symbolic reading to which they are subjected. Hence a return to allegory, as opposed to empiricism, allows Conrad to penetrate the meaning of Europe's belief in progress and civilization, ideals which shatter as the African journey in search of the mythical traveller Kurtz progresses. Allegory allows Conrad to transform the geographical heart of darkness into the darkness of the human heart. In this way he inaugurates the twentieth century – which is also a century of pervasive cultural Westernization – with a very harsh judgement on the depth of the values that sustain Western belief in reason and civilization. The traveller concludes, when explaining his survival and return:

Droll thing life is – that mysterious arrangement of merciless logic for a futile purpose. The most you can hope for is some knowledge of yourself – that comes too late – a crop of unextinguishable regrets. I have wrestled with death. It is the most unexciting conquest you can imagine. It takes place in an impalpable greyness, with nothing underfoot, with nothing around, without spectators...[137]

Paradoxically, Conrad is only able to explain the journey because he did not fully confront the darkness – the 'horror' seen by Kurtz, the successful traveller.

Marlow's story, told on a boat on the River Thames, begins with the recognition that 'this also has been one of the dark places of the earth' – a historical observation that suggests not only reversibility but also the progress of the boundaries of civilization (however dark its insides). What characterizes the twentieth century is almost the completion of this process, with the subsequent decline of exoticism as a genuine commodity: the collective fall into the condition of tourists. This new situation is explored in Kasia Boddy's essay on the American journey to Europe after the Second World War. Not only does the Old World now become the object of attention – of a 'cultural pilgrimage' – by the new dominators, but the emphasis also shifts to literature and film. Who needs bare empiricism in an age overloaded with information? Now we know that naked empiricism does not even exist. The authenticity of this postmodern condition is of interpretation rather than of experience, and one of the issues explored in Boddy's essay is whether Europe, a collapsed civilization rescued by Americans after the wars, has anything to offer a traveller who can only repeat or parody a previous traveller's experience. Is there anywhere 'different' to go? It is remarkable how closely this postmodern anxiety resembles Montaigne's sixteenth-century reflections.

We may conclude here with this sense of ultimate futility about the cultural significance of travel, after the imperial, the scientific and the romantic illusions of modernity have all been dealt such apparently deadly blows. However, Boddy is reluctant to announce an end, and Edward James, in his essay on space travel in science fiction, offers an illustration of why this is the case. Undeniably, the landing on the Moon in 1969 can be presented as the symbol of humankind's success in creating new frontiers and of the hope for future conquests under the impulse of scientific and technological dicoveries. The space frontier functions, in particular, as an extension of the American dream: it is the other side of the educational excursion to Europe (much as the acquisition of overseas colonies once was the other side of the Grand Tour). And yet there are also troubling questions here, expressed by the fact that the image of the expeditions to the Moon today elicits more *nostalgia* than *hope*. As in Jerry Oltion's 1996 story 'Abandon in Place', discussed by James, the solution can only be magical. James's analysis makes it quite clear that behind the dream of galactic space travel there is a great deal of bogus science – that the mythical is in essence more important than the practical. Can we really believe in space travel? Or, more to the point, why do people still believe in space travel?

The example of A. E. Van Vogt (born in 1912), a Canadian science-fiction writer of the generation which defined the genre in the 1940s, offers an important insight. In his novel *The Voyage of the Space Beagle* (1950) an all-male crew of scientists meets a number of incredible challenges and defeats them all, much like Arthur's knights defeated all the monsters they encountered in largely imaginary landscapes (one of these encounters became the inspiration for the major 1979 SF film *Alien*).[138] The human virtue that allows them to accomplish all this is the use of science. Not simply atomic power and anti-acceleration drives, described in ways which modern physicists will frown at, but also a new scientific synthesis called 'Nexiology' – the hero's contribution – which integrates all existing disciplines into a single system. This supra-scientific vision, which will lead mankind to a new stage of evolution, may remind us of Ramon Llull's thirteenth-century vision of an *Ars* which would make Christian faith, with the Trinity and the Incarnation, fully rational. Indeed, soon after writing this book, Van Vogt became a follower of Scientology (first called Dianetics), a religion of 'scientific' self-improvement created by L. Ron Hubbard (another SF pulp writer) and which prospered from the 1950s to become a multi-million-dollar religious operation.[139]

James suggests, like Boddy, that the romantic dream is here to stay. It has been our argument that the succession of cultural paradigms which have sustained travellers' quests – wisdom and salvation, education and science, progress and civilization – have all eventually collapsed. Travellers' tales, real or fictional, have repeatedly served to build, re-inforce, question, alter and destroy these paradigms. Rather than the persistence of a vision, then, what perhaps we find within this legacy of fragments is the persistence of desire.

From Mt Ventoux to Mt Masaya: The Rise and Fall of Subjectivity in Early Modern Travel Narrative

JESÚS CARRILLO

In a letter dated 26 April 1336, Petrarch wrote to an old friend from the time of his studies in Paris, the Augustinian Fra Dionigi da Borgo San Sepolcro, telling the story of his climb of Mont Ventoux.[1] Fictional as it may be, the letter describes the preparations for the journey, the arduous ascent to the top, the contemplation of the views, and the trip back to Malaucène, where Petrarch felt impelled to recount his experience to Fra Dionigi. This brief and apparently simple autobiographical account has often been taken as the manifesto of Renaissance subjectivity, as well as an announcement of the narrative patterns of modern discourse.[2]

Recent studies have explored the close relationship of Petrarch's letter with a book which Fra Dionigi gave him as a reminder of their friendship and which Petrarch took with him on his ascent of the mountain: St Augustine's *Confessions*.[3] Like the famous episode of Augustine's psychological agony and Christian conversion in the garden of his lodgings in Milan (*Confessions*, VIII, 19–29), the journey to Mt Ventoux provided Petrarch with the occasion for an exercise in self-examination.[4] But, unlike his illustrious model, Petrarch's peripatetic thoughts did not lead him straight to conversion. They drew him instead into a meandering reflection on the difficult task of making sense of life in terms of the love of God:

I will not speak of what is still left undone, for I am not yet in port that I might think in security of the storms I have had to endure. The time will perhaps come when I can review all this in the order in which it happened, using as a prologue that passage of your favourite Augustine: 'Let me remember my past mean acts and the carnal corruption of my soul, not that I love them, but I may love Thee, my God'.[5]

In his essay 'The Ascent of Mt Ventoux and the Crisis of Allegory', Robert M. Durling interprets Petrarch's letter as an implicit but systematic critique of the allegorical world-view associated with Augustinian theology.[6] Petrarch's description of his physical climb to Mt Ventoux is not a typical medieval illustration of the spiritual ascent of the soul as pre-established by Catholic tradition and best exemplified by Dante's mountain of Purgatory. Rather, Petrarch's fluctuating point of view – and the subtle irony which he deploys throughout the letter – bear witness to the rise of a new and restless sense of subjectivity, striving to occupy the centre of discourse.[7]

One significant aspect in Petrarch's account is his initial reference to a classical precedent for his journey: Philip of Macedon's climb of Mt Haemus, as related by Livy, from the top of which he had a simultaneous vision of both the Adriatic and the Euxine seas.[8] Like a modern Philip, Petrarch sought to expand his visual field beyond the narrow limits of everyday-life perception. The broad and continuous panorama which he discerned from the top of Mt Ventoux was the scope of a new individual who was willing to take control both of his own destiny and of the world as it extended beneath his vision. This subject appears again in the first four books of Petrarch's epic poem *Africa*, where he develops the theme of the *Somnium Scipionis*. The *Somnium*, as found in book VI of Cicero's *De republica* and in a famous commentary by Macrobius, relates the dream-flight of the Roman general Scipio Aemilianus during which he enjoyed a bird's-eye view of the world and realized the actual domain of human ambitions. Petrarch's aspiration to comprehend the world from a single and focal viewpoint lies at the origins of a fundamental development within European subjectivity that would culminate in the radical subjectivism of Descartes.[9]

Petrarch's continuous view, as symbolized at Mt Ventoux, was ultimately incompatible with the radical discontinuity of human experience implied in Augustine's allegorical interpretation of earthly matters.[10] Petrarch's ideal was not exclusively that of conversion as described in the *Confessions*, but also included the heroic figure of Scipio 'the African', grandfather and guide of Aemilianus in his dream.[11] Scipio, the Roman general who saved the *respublica* from the threat of Hannibal's troops, deserved the longest section of Petrarch's *De viris illustribus* and played the part of the hero in *Africa*. Scipio incarnated the possibility of salvation through the accomplishment of actions and deeds worthy of immortal fame and glory.[12] However, the model of active life and civic virtues that Petrarch saw in Scipio lay more in a nostalgic evocation of a glorious

Roman past than in the present circumstances in which Petrarch himself was living. Petrarch's anachronistic attitude is most clearly realized in the letters which he addressed personally to Livy, Cicero, Seneca and Varro as if they were his actual contemporaries. In part as a result of his enduring dissatisfaction with the present and in part because of his craving for new experiences, Petrarch became a vocational traveller who spent most of his life moving from one place to another.[13] In a letter to the Venetian doge Andrea Dandolo, written ten years after his expedition to Mt Ventoux, Petrarch described his period of training as the voyagings of a Homeric hero, always seeking to see new places and to accumulate new experiences: 'I must confess that during my early years of study, I followed the path of Homer eager to learn about the customs of many peoples, to visit cities and to contemplate new landscapes with curiosity – the highest peaks, praised lakes, famous fountains and rivers and distinct locales'.[14]

Two hundred years after Petrarch's letter to Fra Dionigi, around 1539, Gonzalo Fernández de Oviedo (1478–1557), the official chronicler of the Spanish empire in the Indies, recorded a journey to a very different kind of mountain: in his *Historia General y Natural de las Indias*, Oviedo describes the volcano Masaya in the province of Nicaragua, which he had visited ten years earlier.[15] Oviedo's description prefigures in many respects the scientific expeditions organized by colonial powers in the following centuries, as well as modern methods of observation.

Oviedo's life is paradigmatic of the way in which the discovery and conquest of America affected the life and views of the first generation of colonists: in this case an individual who presented himself as the perfect incarnation of the values of the society to which he belonged. A courtier since his youth, Oviedo was brought up in the manners, ideology and world-view of the European elite of the early sixteenth century: the courts of Isabella and Ferdinand in Spain, the Sforza, the Gonzaga, the Borgia and the Neapolitan Aragonese in Italy, and the imperial Habsburgs back in Spain.[16] From his arrival in the 'New World' in 1514, Oviedo became the most enthusiastic propagandist of the Spanish Universal Monarchy, at the same time as being one of the first champions of 'Americanness'. The ambitious scope of his major work, *Historia General y Natural de las Indias* (*c.* 1535–49), was the physical description of the whole territory of America on behalf of the Spanish empire – or, more precisely, the Castilian monarchy – whose possession it was claimed to be, by right of discovery and conquest. At the time of his journey to the volcano Masaya, Oviedo was official supervisor of mining and the fusion of precious metals in Nicaragua. When he included the account of his expedition in the third part of his *Historia General y Natural* ten years later, Oviedo was the royal chronicler and the *alcaide* – warden – of the castle of Santo Domingo in Hispaniola.

Petrarch's letter deals with a journey to a familiar point in his personal landscape: 'For many years I have been intending to make this expedition. You know that since my early childhood, as fate revolved the affairs of men, so I have revolved around these parts, and this mountain, visible far and wide from everywhere, is always in your view'.[17] The peak of Mt Ventoux was strategically located at the core of Europe, between Italy and France, and from it Petrarch could contemplate a significant portion of the world he knew, which was, at the same time, the world once inhabited by the Roman authors referred to in the text: Virgil, Livy and Ovid. The person he chose to accompany him on this personally significant journey was a close relative, his beloved brother Gherardo; and the recipient of his intimate confession of the trip, Fra Dionigi, was an old friend and confidant. The explicit motivation of Petrarch's journey was the desire to enjoy the views from the top ('Nothing but the desire to its conspicuous height was the reason for this undertaking'),[18] an aesthetic impulse which, as the warnings of a local shepherd inform us, was not shared by the majority of his contemporaries. By climbing to the top of Mt Ventoux, Petrarch was consciously marking a difference with regard to normal standards of perception.

By contrast, the value of Fernández de Oviedo's description of Mt Masaya rests upon the official character of the expedition and the exotic nature of its object: a volcano located in a newly discovered land of which the classical authors knew nothing. His travel companion was an anonymous African assistant (of whom Oviedo only reveals that he was 'rescio e mancebo' – strong and young) and his formal addressee was the Council of the Indies, which in fact examined an original version of the account. Oviedo frequently remarks that he did not plan the journey in search of wealth or personal glory but with the aim of investigating the truth in fulfilment of his official duties. The format of Oviedo's historical description remains the *relación*, an official report such as the one he actually submitted to the Council.[19] Unlike Petrarch, Oviedo saw nothing worthy of note as he climbed Mt Masaya, either in relation to his personal destiny or to the surrounding panorama. He focused all his attention instead on careful observation of the volcano itself, which he described from three positions – as he approached the site, from the edge of the crater and, finally, from twelve leagues away.

My aim in comparing these two descriptions of the ascents of mountains is not to establish a precise relationship between two isolated texts, but rather to trace one of the possible paths connecting two chronologically and geographically distant landmarks of modern discourse. Nevertheless, the relationship between these two travel accounts and, consequently, between their implicit narratives of modern subjectivity and empire looks rather less arbitrary when we analyse the Petrarchan foundations of Oviedo's writing on American natural history. There are numerous traces of Petrarch and Petrarchan literature in early colonial discourse, especially in Columbus's letters and in Oviedo's *Historia General y Natural*.[20] This presence was not merely anecdotal: in Roland Greene's words: 'Petrarchism shapes colonial experience as we know it, and as the sixteenth century knew it, in certain canonical texts'.[21] I have explored elsewhere the extent to which Oviedo's representation of American nature derives from his own practice of ekphrasis (or literary description) and the paraphrasing of poetic texts, most frequently borrowing from Petrarch.[22] Indeed, the highly sensuous and vivid character of many of Oviedo's descriptions reveals his application of the techniques of Renaissance lyric poetry. In this essay, however, I wish to focus attention on the gradual transformation and crisis of the Petrarchan model in Oviedo's economy of representation. I intend to sustain the same degree of ambivalence which Durling pointed out twenty years ago when he commented on the title of his own article: 'to which crisis (of allegory) does it refer, to Petrarch's or to our own?'[23] The choice of Oviedo's account of Mt Masaya implies on my part, however, a very different approach to the genealogy of modernity.

In one of the most elaborate descriptions of a new species found in the *Historia General y Natural*, an account of the exotic bird brought to him by a certain captain Urdaneta, Oviedo rhetorically dismissed the attempt to provide a complete depiction of this American wonder. No human artifice, Oviedo maintained, could replace the direct experience of something that was itself an unmatchable work of art. He pointed out the gap between the surrogate or second-hand experience that he was currently offering his readers and the unique aesthetic confrontation that he had once enjoyed:

For what I said above, I must conclude that there will never be a painter able to portray this bird. However, as I read my description above with the bird beside me, I get the impression that there is something valuable in what I have just said. And I wrote it while looking at the bird and giving thanks to God for having created such things. And this is, in my opinion, the gentlest bird and the one with the most extraordinary plumage that I have ever seen, and the one which has provoked the most admiration in me. But it was created by such an artist and by such hands that nobody could or should think that He employed all His art in this. And no painter, sculptor or orator will ever be able either to express or to communicate His works to human understanding in a manner as natural and perfect as they are in reality.[24]

The notion of the irreproducibility of life and the radical superiority of the natural over any artificial substitute had already appeared in Augustine as a combination of Platonic themes, probably filtered through Cicero and Seneca.[25] However, Oviedo's literary, rather than philosophical or theological, background suggests an alternative path for his discovery of this theme: the representation of the female beloved as developed in Petrarch's *Rime sparse* (the so-called *Canzionere*), which provided the main model for a language of desire in the Renaissance. In fact, it was during a discussion of the possibility of portraying female beauty that Oviedo formulated the irreproducibility topos most perfectly. When in 1500 he met Don Hugo de Cardona, a Sicilian nobleman of Catalan origin in the service of Frederick of Naples, Oviedo particularly noted his *invención*, or personal device. This chivalric emblem consisted of an image showing a painter drawing a lady followed by a motto which set the real woman above any representation. Oviedo comments: 'It is just as don Hugo puts it, because nature is, without comparison, far better than any artifice; the difference between the two of them is that between the living and the dead, between truth and the tricks of deception'.[26]

The object of Oviedo's statement about the essential inadequacy of representation was the natural beauty of the lady with whom the painter – or the patron of her portraits, in the case of Hugo de Cardona – was in love. This specific amatory turn, which ultimately derives from one of Lucian's dialogues, was to affect the whole debate on the nature and limits of representation in the Renaissance.[27] As both Robert M. Durling and John Frecero have argued, Petrarch introduced a radical shift in Western semiotics when he made the longing for the historical and physical presence of Laura the subject of his poetry.[28] In his sonnets Petrarch placed subjective experience and individual psychology at the centre of the representational process. The evocation of the sensual qualities of his beloved and the emotions inspired by her absence were the coordinates for a new personal universe free from the constraints, but also the certainties, of the eternal structures which had ruled Dante's love for Beatrice. According to this new topos, the lover was condemned to an endless pursuit of the absent beloved, being forced to recall her image only in a fragmentary way by evoking a texture, a perfume, the shape of a particular part of her body and, above all, by using comparisons, metaphors and indirect allusions. The desire inspired by the beauty of the absent beloved – the very quality which challenged any attempt at reproduction – triggered the representational process, provoking a compulsive display of fragments and surrogate images.[29] The impossibility of reconstructing the experience of the desired object – in Oviedo's case, the mysterious bird brought by Captain Urdaneta – was the rhetorical justification for the meticulous dissection and the detailed description of all its components.

Although never perfectly visible to his readers, the referents of Oviedo's descriptions were always specific physical realities which the author had actually seen and touched. The truth obtained from a reading of his account of Urdaneta's bird was not the result of the revelation of an allegorical meaning lurking behind sensual appearances, as in the Pauline and Augustinian epistemology favoured by the Middle Ages.[30] It consisted, rather, in the partial and imperfect realization of an absent – though historical and tangible – reality, through the subjective mediation of the chronicler. As Hugo de Cardona confessed to Oviedo, imperfect as they were, the female portraits that he collected obsessively were not completely spurious, since they somehow reflected the true love that lay buried in his soul:

Laughing together one day about these portraits and making comments on their different degrees of resemblance while looking at them, I asked him about his plans for all these persons or artificial women. After a loud sigh, don Hugo answered saying: 'God knows how much more I love the living one than the pictures, but it would be a crime nonetheless to touch them or to stop loving them, because they reflect what I keep deep in my soul'.[31]

The trope which turned the American bird into an object of desire and, therefore, into an object of description necessarily implicated the narration of the chronicler's subjective experience, with the evocation of feelings provoked by his encounter with a new reality. This provided Oviedo with a very effective means to communicate one event in the ongoing assimilation of a distant and different world, but, by the same token, it also allowed him to restrict full access to that reality to those who – like Oviedo himself – were actually living in America. The 'Petrarchan style' thus worked as a perfect instrument of territorialization.

Oviedo's use of images in the first edition of part I of the *Historia General y Natural* (Seville, 1535) corresponds to this logic. The introduction

of each illustration is explicitly justified in the text as a way of making the
eyes of the reader *participar* – participate in or, rather, partake of – a
reality which existed beyond their reach. Frequently, Oviedo's images are
said to reproduce the *forma* or *figura* – the more or less abstract shape –
of what is described, in order to make intelligible – *dar a entender* – what
would otherwise remain obscure owing to the lack of suitable terms for
comparison. In fact, most of the botanical illustrations to the 1535 edition
only render a leaf or, more precisely, the shape of a leaf, instead of the
whole plant or tree. The figurative features of these images correspond
strictly to the function of conveying the meaning – size, shape, texture,
tonality – predetermined by the text, while avoiding any superfluous element that may disturb that function. Any further visual stimulus would
be an excess, even – using the terms articulated in the Middle Ages by
Bernard of Clairvaux – an invitation to curiosity and intellectual wandering.[32] A good example of the subordination of the image to the word of
the chronicler is the illustration of the leaf of the perebenuc, whose shape
and shades only conveyed information through the explicit references
made in the text: 'You should interpret the shade at the end of the leaves in
the picture as that purple bit that (I said) they have.'[33] While the illustration helped the chronicler communicate his visual experience, it also
served to remind the reader that the full vision – and, with it, the full

Leaf of perebenuc, from Gonzalo Fernández de Oviedo,
Historia General y Natural de las Indias (Seville, 1535).

understanding – was essentially attached to that experience, a fact that neither the text nor the image could ever replace. What the reader received, when contemplating the image and reading the text, was not a vertiginous glimpse of an unknown and distant phenomenon but participation in a parallel reality as perceived and lived by the chronicler.

The 'Petrarchan' representation of American experience overlaps in Oviedo's text with another mode of description – concerned with specific acts of measurement and reckoning, and with the display of an unpassionate objectivity – which is particularly manifested in the narration of the expedition to Mt Masaya. Although both 'styles' co-exist throughout the *Historia General y Natural*, the more 'objective' style is particularly frequent in the description of controversial phenomena, such as the mermen of book XXIII and the Masaya volcano in book XLII.[34] One may also note the development of this type of description in the latest stages of Oviedo's long process of production of the *Historia General y Natural*.[35]

The distinctive feature of this second 'style' is its emphasis on measurement and reckoning, and its restrained objectivity – utterly different from the highly subjective tone of his other descriptions – which Oviedo ascribes to the performance of his duties as an officer of the Crown. The description of the enormous *ceiba* tree of book IX provides a good example of the evolution of Oviedo's position in this respect. In the Seville edition of 1535, Oviedo started his account of the *ceiba* with the news of a large specimen brought back by Admiral Diego Columbus and his companions. According to their testimonies, the circumference of the trunk of the *ceiba* was as great as fourteen men with outstretched arms.[36] In the new version of the chapter, drafted sometime before 1542, this second-hand account was replaced by the consecutive narratives of three separate occasions on which Oviedo himself had the chance to see and size a specimen of the tree. The exact measurements of the first of these *ceibas* were recorded after Oviedo, exercising his duty as judge and captain – *justicia y capitán* – of the town of Santa María del Darién, ordered the tree to be cut down so that he might make a bridge with its trunk: 'This tree was sixteen spans wide in the thickest part and made a very good bridge which stood more than two cubits over the surface of the water'.[37] In the second episode, Oviedo described how he had climbed half of the height of a *ceiba* in the province of Guataro when, in his official capacities, he was pursuing a rebel *cacique* (native leader). The exclamation: 'It was wonderful to see the great extent of land on the side of the Abraime province which could be surveyed from there',[38] fits perfectly both with his description of a tree that he compared with the tower of San Román of Toledo (a belfry that was the place of long-distance views *par excellence* in Hispanic tradition) and with the policeman's task of surveillance that Oviedo was then undertaking. In the third case, the first-person account of his encounter with a *ceiba* in Nicaragua relates a premeditated act of measurement:

I measured that tree with my own hands using a thread of *cabuya*. The diameter of the base was thirty three *varas* long,[39] which makes one hundred and thirty-two spans. As the tree was by the riverside, it was impossible to take the measure from the lowest part, near the roots, which might well have been more than three *varas* longer. I think that, correctly measured, the diameter of the tree was thirty-six *varas*, which makes one hundred and forty-four spans.[40]

The precise quantification of the phenomenon appears here as the consequence of the correct performance of a specific ritual. The account reflects upon its author as the royal chronicler/supervisor/notary represented in the accomplishment of his official duties – in this case, recording the existence of a natural phenomenon in the territory under his jurisdiction. The high degree of accuracy and precision which characterizes the description in these cases is the distinctive sign of a very specific way of apprehending reality, one performed on behalf of the monarchy in the interests of empire.

Oviedo's description of his ascent to the top of Masaya in 1529 starts with the planning of an expedition to Nicaragua made four years before the actual journey with the aim of discrediting some dubious news about a wondrous city of 'tres leguas en luengo', propagated by certain clerics from the pulpits of Toledo.[41] The detailed account of Oviedo's official journey from Leon to Managua, from Managua to Lenderi and from Lenderi to Masaya is rhetorically opposed to the relation of wonders he intended to refute. Oviedo noted carefully the dates and the precise distances between the different points of his itinerary, as well as the name and duty of each of the Spanish officials who guided his steps in every administrative demarcation he had to cross.

The unfolding of Oviedo's description of the volcano follows the strict chronological pace of a *relación*, or official report. As mentioned above, the description of the expedition to Masaya was part of a *relación* that Oviedo submitted to the Council in 1539, probably around the same date that the chapter of the *Historia General y Natural* was originally written. The institutional tone which Oviedo gave his account is not simply an unconscious repetition of the official pattern but, rather, it represents a premeditated appropriation of authoritative language in order to participate in, and influence, an ongoing debate. Indeed, the content of the *relación* to the Council, as summarized by the royal cosmographer Juan Bautista Muñoz in the eighteenth century, reveals Oviedo's intentions to discredit the accounts of other expeditionaries who the previous year had visited Masaya in search of gold, silver and other precious metals.[42] In the same way, Oviedo reinforced the authority of his description in the *Historia General y Natural* by including, in the subsequent chapters of book XLII, a report by one Fray Blas del Castillo on a similar expedition to Masaya which occurred five years after his.[43] In order to compare the two accounts, Oviedo doubled his voice in two different personae – the impartial chronicler and the eye-witness informant – the latter being referred to in the third person as if in judicial proceedings. Unsurprisingly, Oviedo's final verdict sanctioned the higher reliability and accuracy of his version over Fray Blas del Castillo's testimony.

As a member of a family of civil servants,[44] Oviedo was perfectly aware that the full completion of the bureaucratic procedure determined a degree of exhaustiveness, comprehensibility and authority unthinkable in the more selective and always dubious account of a private individual, especially when dealing with the description of such a natural portent as a volcano. The institutional and ideological framework of his official mission justified the detailed and systematic recording of empirical data as part of a general process of taking possession of the newly discovered territory; at the same time it provided the formal procedure to undertake such a task.

As he approached the mountain and ascended towards the crater, Oviedo transformed his body into an instrument of observation ready both to record the effects of the changing physical conditions – fatigue, heat, odours, noises and visual impressions – and to translate those sensorial stimuli into quantitative data. His eyes progressively turned into optical instruments to be corrected by the estimation of his relative position with regard to the object to be observed, and his nose into a detector of the chemical composition of the magma boiling inside the volcano. The description of the interior of the crater reproduces with extreme detail the physical processes happening in an active volcano. The agent of the experience disappears from the account after an initial '*digo*' – 'I say' – which repeats the formula that Oviedo had often used when writing official reports for the Council:[45]

I say that at the bottom of the hole – or as deep as I was able to see – there was a fiery liquid like water or whatever substance it was. Its colour was brighter than burning coal and I would dare say that it was more fiery than any other fire could possibly be. The boiling liquid which covered all the surface of the crater did not boil all at the same time, but only in certain areas. The bubbles changed place from time to time, moving from one extreme to the other without interruption. The parts in which there were no bubbles – or where the boiling had ceased – were immediately covered with a crackled layer of nap whose cracks allowed me to perceive the fiery liquid like water which underlay the whole surface of the plateau. Every now and then all the matter rose up impetuously, throwing to the air thousands of drops which would fall again into the same fiery stuff. I reckon that the drops ascended more than one stadium.[46]

Here, the chronicler sacrifices the subjective voice which had once praised the extraordinary beauty of the bird brought by Urdaneta in order to become a *tabula rasa* on which physical reality could leave its imprint. However, the accomplishment of the official procedure also involved the performance of specific actions, such as the collection of samples, typical of modern scientific inquiry. After his long recording of volcanic activity, Oviedo attempted to measure the depth of the crater by calculating the trajectory and the time that it would take a stone to arrive at the bottom:

Further, I say that I threw some stones into the hole, and I made the negro do it as well because he was quite young and strong. However, I never managed to see the place where the stones either stopped or struck, and it seemed as if once we threw the stones they followed an arched trajectory which led them beneath the scope of our sight. The fact that none was seen to stop is a notable indication of the great depth of the hole.[47]

This experimental attitude connects with the operations which Oviedo undertook when performing his duties as royal supervisor of the fusion of precious metals. This relationship is very clear in the report about the nature of the minerals boiling in the crater, which an anonymous informant submitted to the governor of Nicaragua, Rodrigo Contreras, a few years after Oviedo's expedition. On this occasion the experiment was performed by professional goldsmiths searching for precious metals under the supervision of an officer of the Crown:

Ore and stone were extracted from the depths of the volcano and they were melted in a crucible in the city of Léon on May the 15th, in the Governor's presence. The silversmiths said that there was no metal, but stones burning like live coal because of their high content of saltpeter. The treasurer Pedro de los Ríos attended the experiment.[48]

The most patent illustration of this evolution is probably in one of the drawings which Oviedo produced for his account of the expedition to

Masaya. Although the original manuscript version of book XLII has been lost, the copy ordered by Andrés Gascó around 1565 contains two drawings authenticated by his initials – AG.[49] Of the two, the most interesting is the simple diagram consisting of three eccentric circles, one within the other, which Oviedo drew as a representation of the crater. The inner circle, schematically shadowed in order to suggest depth, bears the label 'pozo' – well – to indicate the hole of the crater. The second is identified as 'la plaza de abajo' (the lower plateau) and the external one as 'este es el círculo alto de la abertura del monte para abajo' (this is the upper rim of the mountain). Four labels with the cardinal points orientate the picture.

The illustration is introduced as part of a formal process of collecting information which entailed, as Oviedo describes, the trip to the site, the careful observation of the phenomenon ('I stayed looking at what I have just described for more than two hours, until it was about ten o'clock on the day of the glorious St Anne')[50] and, finally, the production of a drawing which would convey the information to the Council: 'and I draw the shape of this mountain on paper as I put it here'.[51] This simple picture

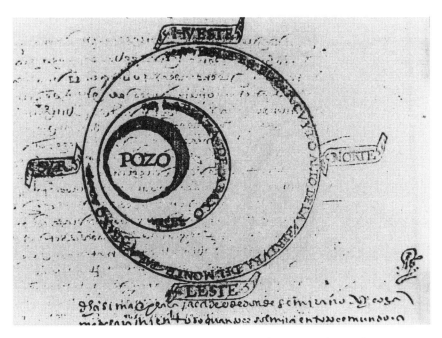

Crater of Mt Masaya, from a manuscript copy of Fernández de Oviedo, *Historia General . . . (c.* 1565). Library of the Palacio Real, Madrid.

is not the trace of an experience, nor the visual proof of a testimony, nor does it offer the reader a vicarious participation in the vision of the chronicler, as do most of the illustrations in the 1535 edition. It is a diagram, a conveyor of information.[52] In the case of Masaya, the account of Oviedo's experience – more than two hours of attentive observation – was offered as a proof of the truthfulness and accuracy of the drawing, and not the other way round. In what can be considered a Copernican turn, biographical time has been transformed into time of observation and subjective experience has stopped being the central object of representation in order to become a specialized instrument to obtain a certain knowledge of the world. This knowledge would be consequently encapsulated in a diagram, a primitive 'combinable mobile', using the term employed by Bruno Latour, which, like a navigational chart, was capable of carrying back home the information it contained.[53]

The many new botanical drawings which Oviedo produced for the projected, augmented, version of part I of the *Historia General y Natural* are the most obvious consequence of this transformation. A good example is the picture of the *perorica* included in chapter VIII of book XI.[54] In this case the image does not represent a fragment of the plant or a leaf, as had been the case in the 1535 edition, but a complete specimen – roots included – as in contemporary printed herbals. Unlike the illustrations of the 1535 edition, this image now occupies the centre of the page without the need of any reference from the text.[55] No verbal explanation seems necessary since the lifelikeness of the drawing justifies its appearance sufficiently. Whereas the image of the perebenuc of 1535 was adapted to the didactic purposes of the written description, in the case of the *perorica* the text comments *a posteriori* on the different parts of the picture. In this 'second style' of Oviedo's writing, the subjective mediation of the chronicler is completely unnecessary and anecdotal since the illustration stands by itself as an autonomous representation of a phenomenon from America.

Despite the dominance of procedural correctness, Oviedo's description of his expedition to Mt Masaya is cut across by a series of biographical episodes and literary references which reveal a link between the objective institutional recording of data and the aesthetics of Petrarch's account of subjective experience. Although Oviedo did not omit the connection between his expedition and the accomplishment of his official duties in the province of Nicaragua, he also wanted to present the episode as the result of a personal quest for truth. This quest had been initiated several years earlier at the symbolic centre of his own world – like Petrarch – when

Oviedo attended the general meeting of the Castilian Cortes in Toledo in 1525, where he presented the beginnings of his natural history of the Indies to the emperor, Charles V. In addition, as Oviedo informs his readers, the observation and recording of an extraordinary phenomenon (such as an active volcano) was not new for him, since he had belonged for many years to the elite milieu in which such observations were a normal activity. According to his own testimony, he accompanied the royal court of Naples several times to both Vesuvius and Etna in expeditions filled with classical echoes of episodes in ancient history related by Pliny and Ovid. The classicist flavour in the elite ritual of visiting volcanoes and other natural portents acquired special connotations when performed by the official chronicler of the empire. If Petrarch emulated King Philip of Macedon in his ascent of Mt Ventoux, Oviedo was explicitly enacting an equivalent trip performed by Pliny, the natural historian at the service of the Roman empire, who – according to the account given by his nephew, Pliny the Younger – died in the eruption of Vesuvius as the result of an excess of zeal in observing and recording the natural phenomenon. Oviedo's emulation of Pliny imbued the simple act of gathering empirical data in a peripheral corner of the world with the historical significance of an imperial activity sanctioned by classical literature – an activity which, disregarding the tragic outcome of Pliny's adventure and the impractical character of Oviedo's expedition, expressed the intervention in the natural world of a historical agency claiming universal power.

Paradoxical as it may seem, Oviedo's ability to shift the scope of his gaze from subjective impression to objective observation depended upon Petrarch's move two hundred years earlier. The ascent of Mt Ventoux illustrated Petrarch's desire to attain a more global view of the world. Only from that global vantage point could Oviedo gain sufficient perspective both to imagine the historical role of the new Spanish empire and to cast himself 'as a participant in an imperialist interprise'.[56] But, if the conditions for the description of Mt Masaya were already implicit in Mt Ventoux and in Scipio's dream, the actual participation in the imperial enterprise required from Oviedo a further act of imagination – an act which would ultimately bring about the crisis of the subjective model. Neither Petrarch's emphatic self-consciousness nor his retrospective view of a glorious past were suitable positions from which to distinguish the boundaries of an empire of unprecedented dimensions. The new imperial gaze had to be released from the physical limitations

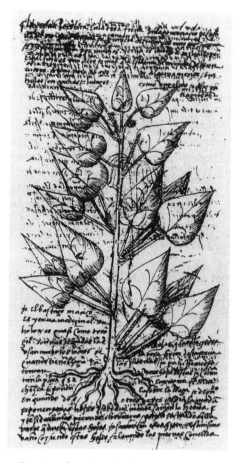

Perorica plant, drawing in a manuscript of
Fernández de Oviedo, *Historia General . . . (c.* 1548).
The Huntington Library, San Marino.

of subjective perception to reach a super-human status. On one occasion, Oviedo expressed the need for a general reappraisal of human intellectual capacities with regard to the new circumstances:

Thales of Miletus also said that human intellect is the fastest, lightest and promptest thing in the world. But, in my opinion, he should rather say the mind and thought. Because whereas there are many things that human understanding can hardly grasp and comprehends either very slowly, very late or never, our memory or thought, on the contrary, moves so rapidly through everything that, in my opinion, there is nothing so fast and prompt. Because, in one moment, it is in these [Western] Indies where I am now and, all of a sudden, it is in the land of the Prester John in the Indies,[57] or it goes to the Colupios Mountains.[58] Then it comes back to New Spain and Mexico and travels from there to the Lake Meotides,[59] to return finally to the Lakes Enderi and Ara in the province and government of Nicaragua.[60]

This kind of super-human flight of fancy appealed to many of Oviedo's contemporaries concerned with the creation of a new global consciousness. The Europeans of the sixteenth century did not find any psychological or geographical barrier to their gaze, but the access to this expanded view implied an act of disembodiment and a renunciation of subjectivity which both culminated in and cancelled out the process initiated by Petrarch two hundred years earlier. In the cases of such Humanists as Juan Luis Vives and Juan Maldonado, this was fashioned as an adaptation of Scipio's *Somnium*, albeit applied to the present: a releasing dream in which the individual suspended his natural tendency to take himself as the measure of the world and turned into a disincarnated eye capable of sizing things as they actually were.[61] This was the eye of cartography and precise reckoning. Of the same nature was the somnambulistic state that I described when analysing Oviedo's shift from his usual subjective rhetoric to the objective logic of the official procedure. Technology and imperial bureaucracy, intimately related, seem to have taken the place of individuals as agents of the new colonial situation. A clear symptom of this evolution may be the return of allegory in the late Renaissance and the Baroque period, a discourse in which the individual was again 'possessed' by the transcendental significance of his actions in an infinite, changing and incommensurable world.[62]

2

Futility in the New World: Narratives of Travel in Sixteenth-Century America

JOAN-PAU RUBIÉS

'What is the history of America, other than a chronicle of the real-marvellous?' With these words the Cuban novelist Alejo Carpentier concluded the prologue to *El reino de este mundo*, one of his vaguely historical novels, thus defining magic realism as something more serious than just a mode of writing fiction in this century. As he explained, 'because of the virginity of the landscape, because of the formation, ontology and faustic presence of the Indian and the Black, because of the revelation of its recent discovery and the fecund racial mixtures to which it gave way, America is far from having exhausted its flow of mythologies'.[1] The fundamental aspect of this vision of American cultural identity (which here is, of course, Latin American) is that historical reality and myth do not cancel each other out entirely. We could analyse this co-existence by saying, more generally, that in order to be meaningful, historical discourses either sustain or refute myths – and that, in order to be credible, myths draw their inspiration from a perception of historical realities.

This theme goes back to the literature of discovery and conquest and finds there a fundamental source of inspiration, with the combination of real Caribbean islands and mythical Cipangus, real gold and mythical *el Dorados*, real empires of the sun and mythical Amazons. Columbus defined this tension (which is at least in part an intellectual tension) within his very first journal of discovery, in his attempt to prove to himself and to his masters that he had found what he sought, or in any case found something worth finding.[2]

In this tendency towards constructive self-delusion, as in many other things, Columbus set the tone for what was to follow. The literary fusion of desire and experience pervaded the accounts of discovery of the following century as, within an improvised and unstable colonial system of authority, there were always new frontiers to be explored, new landscapes upon which the greed of the conquerors projected dreams of wealth and providential success, although often in a context of ruthless cruelty and deprivation. It is therefore not surprising that much of the interpretation of early European encounters with non-Europeans, and in particular the peculiar and remarkable Hispanic colonial construction in the New World, has focused upon this clash between ideals and realities, variously defined as contrasting principles of dominion and miscegenation, alterity and appropriation.[3] If any general conclusion can be drawn from the recent interest in this otherwise classic theme, it is that any interpretation of the literature of travel and discovery must be an exercise in cultural history which acknowledges the apparent contradictions between the rhetoric of triumphant imperialism, too often portrayed as a one-sided force both by critics and apologists, and the ambivalence of the actual encounter with an indigenous world, human and natural, which was neither passive nor homogeneous.

This contradiction, apparent at a very early stage, was only multiplied by the speed and scale of the early phases of conquest. In the mad frenzy of a few decades, a few thousand men squandered the traditional order of indigenous America in the pursuit of myths. But the tangible gains – gold and silver, sex, labour, land, geographical knowledge too – very often fell short of the desires expressed by the myths. In a perverse twist, the myths themselves grew out of the historical frustration of a majority of European invaders who could not settle to benefit from their adventures, as their ability to convert the enormous resources encountered in America into a system of shared prosperity was severely limited. As the Florentine merchant Galeotto Cei sceptically observed on the arrival of Francisco de Orellana's expedition in Santo Domingo in 1544, ignorant men, who could not give an account of what they were talking about, sustained the belief that there were actual Amazons – the society of women warriors of antiquity – in the huge river that, as Orellana had accidentally found out, flowed from Peru to the Atlantic (indeed the river that today we know as the Amazon).[4] Cei was convinced, from talking to one of the members of the expedition, that they had only seen Indian women who fought alongside their men, like Swiss women did in Europe, and that the Spanish had simply exaggerated their discoveries in order to attract more people to new expeditions. But the fact is that, as would often happen in the conquest of America, the myth of hopeful conquerors proved more powerful than the common sense of a merchant, and similar expeditions would be launched again to the Brazilian rivers searching for wealthy kingdoms like *el Dorado* in the following years.

Against the image of the real-marvellous as a pure creative force, I wish to insist here on the profoundly tragic quality of this construct. This is not only the tragedy of wanton cruelty and unintended genocide which we encounter if we focus our gaze on the American Indians but also the tragedy of the European identities – religious, political and social – projected upon the new continent.

Few sources reveal with the clarity of travel accounts the subtle tension between the projection of ideals and the discovery of futility, because these numerous writings incarnated simultaneously the rhetoric of empire and evangelization, the projection of personal aims, desires and disappointments, and the formation of empirical discourses, historical, anthropological and geographical. That is to say, the traveller and his chronicler (who was not necessarily the same person) were working creatively at three simultaneous levels: a definition of the global ideology of imperial legitimation and imperial strategy according to a special bias, the expression of personal experiences geared towards a profitable social recognition, and the collective construction of an empirical body of information concerning the lands and peoples of the New World.[5]

In this article I shall seek to distinguish the development of a sense of futility within narratives of travel which purportedly shared in the general rhetoric of imperial success. I will do so by focusing on a number of examples, some very well known and others much less so, in order to explore the three fundamental social forms of discourse of the Renaissance: the gentleman *hidalgo* as conqueror, the merchant as adventurous traveller, and the missionary as religious pilgrim. I shall thus illustrate the transformation of a medieval sense of the marvellous into the discovery of the futile in the secret codes of the Hispanic Renaissance, emphasizing the special role of the literature of discovery in this process and seeking to define the cultural mechanisms which allowed this literature to enshrine such powerful contradictions.[6]

The search for marvels which characterized the medieval figure of the traveller would appear to have been transferred to the New World as a result of the profound cultural continuity between the development of medieval Christian Spain and its overseas expansion. As a pilgrim, the medieval traveller sought the marvellous signs of divine creation and historical order. As a lay traveller he could issue a new voice beyond the strict utilitarian aims of his practice only in order to depict the marvellous world of human diversity – and this is how Marco Polo's extraordinary narrative as merchant–adventurer could be justified and assimilated. As a chronicler, the medieval writer would depict the marvellous victories of kings and chivalric heroes, all providentially assisted when fighting infidels and enemy Christians alike. The main paradigm for the appropriation of the New World was, not surprisingly, a language of marvels which would inscribe territorial expansion and profit-seeking within a providential plan and widen the horizon of natural and human diversity in a vaguely humanistic project.

This paradigm is perfectly expressed through the ambitious conception of the *Natural History of the Indies*, written by the chronicler–settler Gonzalo Fernández de Oviedo (1478–1557) on the basis of the experience of the four central decades of the unfolding of the process of discovery in the American mainland – roughly speaking, between 1515 and 1555.[7] Oviedo's appeal to classical models in his encyclopaedic account of the conquest and its setting, and his evident sense of historical perspective, do not detract from a system of values which was essentially medieval in its emphasis on divine intervention, moralistic explanation, aristocratic military ethos and nationalist mythology. These medieval principles, however, could not be transferred simply to the New World, however analogous this experience was to earlier forms of conquest and colonization in the Mediterranean and the Atlantic. On the one hand, the American setting, with its sheer vastness and novelty, multiplied the possibilities for mythical construction. On the other hand, the European context was also rapidly changing, and, as the key power in the Habsburg Monarchy, the kingdom of Castile (within whose jurisdiction the American conquests came to be incorporated) could not fail to adapt and develop the new cultural forms coming from Italy.[8] Essentially, the expansion of historical discourse throughout the Renaissance put a severe strain on the theological system by shifting the emphasis towards the criticism of human passions and the analysis of political and economic forms. In support of a system of secular politics the traveller became a spy, the geographer an ideologue and the educator a moral critic. Although the Hispanic Renaissance was essentially a traditionalist one, which sought to perpetuate religious definitions and political forms against new alternatives, these traditional values suffered a transformation in the New World. The New World not only amplified millenarian hopes, imperial ambitions and economic prospects, it also created a privileged ground for de-sacralization and disillusionment.

Thus the fragility of the language of conquest as a language of Christian civilization and its contradictions were precisely recorded by

Oviedo in his attempt to explain the barbarism and greed of the Spanish, the vacuity of the rhetoric of indigenous conversion, the foolishness and failure of many conquering expeditions, and the civil wars that stained the spectacular conquests in Peru. Having enlisted historical experience as a witness to providential history, he now needed to explain the often disturbing evidence which, as official chronicler appointed by the emperor, he received from all quarters from his base at Santo Domingo in *Española* [Hispaniola]. This very island where he lived was in itself a reminder that something was going terribly wrong, since the peaceful and ready-to-be-converted Indians among whom Columbus had settled were now completely decimated by violence, illnesses and lack of adaptation. However emphatically Oviedo had insisted to Emperor Charles in 1526 that Santo Domingo was as good as any Spanish city, with houses made of stone and well-laid streets that not even a beautiful European city like Barcelona could surpass, things were changing rapidly and would continue to do so.[9] As interest shifted to the mainland after the success of Cortés in Mexico, Cuba and *Española* had quickly become a colonial backwater, altering the significance of the proud capital city from a precocious symbol of the spread and perfection of Christian civilization to one of premature decline.

One of the passages in Oviedo's chronicle which expresses this need of making sense of the evidence of failure is his account of the expedition led by Pánfilo de Narváez into Florida in 1528, for which he relied on the evidence supplied by four survivors. Narváez was one of the prominent conquerors of Cuba. In 1520 he had been sent by the Governor, Diego Velázquez, to imprison Cortés so that he would not conquer Mexico on his own, sidestepping the authority of the Governor. Outmanoeuvred on this famous occasion, Narváez was however sufficiently impressed by the achievement of Cortés to attempt an ambitious expedition into Florida. It is important here to remember that, in the context of the Spanish exploration of America, the civilizations of Mexico and Peru were truly marvellous, extraordinary discoveries rather than the rule. However, they confirmed the myth-making tendencies of a young colonial society always on the brink of economic decline. The expedition led by Narváez ended up in unprecedented disaster, as the men lost sight of the ships and attempted to penetrate difficult terrain where, instead of another civilization of cities and gold ripe for the taking, they met with deprivation and tenacious opposition from the local Indians. Retreating with huge losses, they improvised rafts and navigated along the coast until the sea threw them onto the shore of modern Texas. There, in the following winter months, the majority died of cold and hunger under the ambivalent gaze of the local Karankawa Indians, themselves living in a fragile subsistence economy. Oviedo could not fail to comment on this fate:

Oh God, what excessive labours for a life as short as man's! [. . .] How did the captains and ministers pay for these travels, which led so many sad men, and so thoroughly deluded and deceived, to die such deaths? It can be answered that they paid with their greed, which guaranteed their words. We now know that Pánfilo de Narváez never was in that land where he thought he was leading this people. He thought he would be Governor and lord, but he was not able to govern himself. Can there be more frivolity than listening to these leaders?[10]

Oviedo went on addressing the unfortunate men – gentlemen, squires, artisans and peasants – who had left their modest but safer and well-ordered background to undertake the adventure of conquest. That, he said, was a moral mistake. What horrified him, what made him deny any heroic element in the Spanish enterprise, was the reversion to barbarism entailed by failure: the Spanish became naked, hungry, cannibalistic, isolated beings, barbarians among barbarians after their defeat. And Oviedo's concern was not limited to the members of this particular expedition: it extended to many other stories of unbridled ambition, unrealistic hopes and miserable death. The whole enterprise became the subject of critical scrutiny: the Indies, which some called the New World (Oviedo, eager to leave his mark, preferred to call it 'here', or 'the other half of the world'), was vast beyond any measure that Europeans had conceived. People 'over there' did not quite understand what they were up to. The rulers of Spain, Oviedo suggested, played a perverse role in this enterprise. They did not take responsibility for the organization and financing of the expeditions: they let privateers invest their own resources and risk their own lives, giving them authority on paper and a few good words (in this way, we can complete the argument, they could collect the fruits of success where there was success but remain immune to the many failures). Friars in Seville further excited people's imagination with their preaching about conversions and untold wealth, thus contributing to the delusion that sent many across the Atlantic, often after having sold everything and gone into debt in order to finance their expeditions. In this way the pressure to succeed, albeit tragically on false assumptions, was at the very origin of the journey. Feeding on men's cupidity, poverty and foolishness, travel to the New World was for the majority a journey of no return.[11]

The power and lucidity of this passage is most remarkable if we consider that Oviedo was himself a successful traveller and settler, well connected at court and acting as official chronicler of the Indies. Essentially Oviedo is here undermining his own imperial, providential vision. What separates Pánfilo de Narváez from Cortés or Columbus, Oviedo's heroes, is that the latter succeeded, not that they knew any better what they were doing when they set out. Oviedo tries, of course, to distinguish between just cause and greed: the man who travels and discovers according to a high divine purpose, which is to say according to a coherent plan and authority, is a great man, who deserves fame for bringing an entire new continent under the jurisdiction of Catholic rulers or for subjecting a mighty empire of barbarians to legal Spanish rule. The futile death is the death of the greedy and irrational conqueror who pursues dreams in unknown lands. The problem is that Columbus and Cortés were no less greedy than Narváez and, as experience was later to show in Peru, the subjection of a mighty empire could be accompanied by the most cruel and illegal behaviour, by civil war and by rebellion. Could this be a heroic fulfilment of a divine plan? From a logical standpoint Oviedo's argument was contradictory because, however foolish Narváez had been (and Oviedo had personally tried to dissuade him before he set out), the fact remains that the whole enterprise of discovery and conquest depended upon men like Narváez. Since the success of Columbus, Cortés and Pizarro (relative as it turned out to be) could not be reached independently from the failure of many others, what condemns Oviedo to his discovery of futility is simply his task as historian.[12]

One of the few survivors of Narváez's expedition was Álvar Núñez Cabeza de Vaca. His account of his survival among Indians, for a period of ten years, and his long journey with three other companions across northern Mexico all the way to the Gulf of California is perhaps the most beautiful and illuminating account of travels in sixteenth-century America.[13] The narrative of this journey completed by three Spanish men and a Black slave of Moroccan origin was used by Oviedo and was published separately by Cabeza de Vaca in a more personal, detailed version (in 1542 and 1555).[14] It is a unique document of the psychological progression of a leading conqueror, an *hidalgo* of some means and education, from a position of power to one of thorough dependance upon the Indians and then, interestingly, back to a position of power on a later expedition of discovery and conquest, this time to Paraguay (the implications of this second phase is certainly the aspect that has been less studied).

One of the most striking features of Cabeza de Vaca's account is that his itinerary amounts to a progressive reversal of roles. The Spanish enter the land as conquerors, but they have to retreat and end up at the mercy of

the Indians. In that situation, they are afraid of being eaten by cannibals
(those who knew Mexico, in particular, could see themselves being sacrificed to Indian idols). Instead, they are promptly fed and given emotional
support: contemplating their misery, the Indians even cry with them.[15]
Soon we learn that it is the Spanish who, hungry and desperate, are eating
each other, which creates a great scandal among their hosts.[16] The few
Spaniards who manage to survive learn to live like Indians; if they are
permanently hungry, it is not because they are mistreated but rather
because they share a life of hunger.[17] The account of native customs that
accompanies this tale of reversal to barbarism is remarkably sympathetic
to the Indians, who are portrayed as child-loving and very generous
(although eventually they made Cabeza de Vaca work hard, collecting
roots or participating in their rituals of medicine). They may be superstitious and brutish, and they have many strange customs, but when reduced
to nakedness and lack of civilization the Spanish become part of that
same world (and one suspects here that not all the story could be told,
because the narrative in part had to function as a ritual of return to

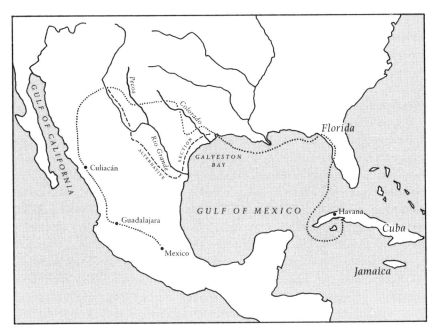

Approximate route of Cabeza de Vaca, showing the route proposed by
Cleve Hallenbeck with the alternative section proposed by Alex D. Krieger
(see p. 290, n. 13).

Christian civilization). To that extent, there can be little doubt about the fundamental equality of the human condition shared between Indians and Christians.[18] They were all animals with souls, with a common spiritual calling as children of God and even a common political horizon as vassals, or future vassals, of the kings of Castile. The condition that they actually shared as naked humans and the condition that they should ideally share as European-like Christians stood as markers of absolute equality at two ends of an unequal hierarchy of religion and civilization. Cabeza de Vaca does not invent, but rather experience and retrieve, the minimalist equality carefully defined by the Spanish theologians and lawgivers, but hardly ever reflected by the practice of colonial dominion.

In the face of this dramatic role reversal one seriously wonders how much of the account is fictional. This is not easy to settle: while the basic facts must have been accurate enough to provide an official explanation of an extraordinary survival among Indians over many years, and an account in any case corroborated by the four survivors, there can be little doubt that an element of rhetorical fictionalization also exists.[19] The surviving Spanish were not likely to present themselves in a negative light, and Cabeza de Vaca, in particular, was eager to develop those roles in which he saw himself as protagonist (a tendency revealed by his occasional departure from the joint report by the three white survivors used by Oviedo). Beyond the contextual coherence of the narrative account, which is pretty solid, what makes it compelling is precisely the obvious existence of an effort of moral interpretation within an otherwise bewildering empirical narrative.

It would in fact be misleading to define Cabeza de Vaca's discussion of American Indians as essentially idealistic. Having completed the first stage of a reversal of roles between conquerors and conquered, Cabeza de Vaca was not so nicely treated. He thus ran away from slavery among the islanders and lived for some six years as a trader in the mainland (across from Galveston Island), selling sea-shells in the interior, buying hides, dyes and other products fom mutually hostile tribes and thus obtaining food and freedom, but isolated from the remaining Spanish, who had travelled ahead.[20] It was thus a long time before the few survivors managed to connect up again and decide to set out on a return journey westward. But they encountered special difficulties among the 'Mareames' (a Coahuiltecan tribe), who are portrayed as cruel and lazy and far less sympathetically than the 'Han' and 'Capoques' (Karankawa tribes) before.[21] The Spanish were treated harshly and felt vulnerable all the time. After they managed to escape, however, things improved steadily. Above all they adopted the role of magic healers, and this allowed them to travel from tribe to tribe towards the north and the west, in an increasingly triumphal progress that took them from the frail seasonal diet of the Gulf of Mexico to the relative luxury of meat and corn in the interior, and from virtual slavery to a position of leadership as travelling 'sons of the sun'.[22] Eventually, this extraordinary journey took them from their isolation among Indians in an unknown land to a famous return to their own society.

When discussing this progress, it was easy for Oviedo to insist that God chose to deliver the Spanish from their captors by performing miracles through them. For contemporaries this unprecedented account of misfortune and survival needed to be cast as a moral story in order to be historically true (indeed this need to interpret the experience, which is also apparent in Cabeza de Vaca's published version, is a mark of its genuine character). But this would seem to bring the narrative back to the official rhetoric of providential marvels, neutralizing its otherwise relativistic denial of conventional roles. Is the ultimate superiority of the Spanish the key to the text? Were they skilful readers of signs and manipulators of beliefs, as Cortés is often depicted in his confrontation with Moctezuma?[23]

In fact, only a very superficial reading of Cabeza de Vaca's personal account could lead us to believe that the Spanish managed to travel because they *knew* how to manipulate Indian superstitions. Instead, if we read carefully, what we are confronted with is the evidence of a complex process of exchange by which the Spanish are *adopted* by the Indians to perform a magical role, and at the same time they manage to secure their passage in exchange for playing along. But there is more to it. As they insist on pursuing their journey beyond any single Indian community, the foreigners do not (indeed, could not) obtain a traditional role as, let us say, tribal healers or regional traders. The Indians and the Europeans, confronting their mutual needs, invent a new ritual which neither could have made up on their own: the Spanish are accompanied by each tribe to their following destination, but then the Indians plunder their neighbours as they deliver the special men, three white and one black, with a commendation. Cabeza de Vaca is clear about this point: they did not control the ritual, they had to adapt to the role placed upon them as 'new customs' were introduced by different groups.[24] They could argue for their own needs: in particular they insisted that they wanted to travel in certain directions which did not always agree with the preferences of a given tribe. They could manipulate their role as special men in order to achieve

this, but it was always a risk and it often involved magical threats. Thus
at some point, the Indians attribute a mysterious illness that has suddenly fallen upon the tribe to the anger (rather than the presence) of the
foreigners. This gave the Spanish the chance to impose their own agenda,
even though they were themselves frightened of the possibility of being
abandoned as a result of the same illness.[25] As the Indians held their own
mythologies of miraculous illnesses and cures, they sustained their
own side of the ritual construct, the full meaning of which was unknown
to the Spaniards. What is most extraordinary is that this mechanism of
'interactive mythologies' held up for as long as the Europeans needed
to travel.[26]

The element of futility insinuated itself precisely when the Spanish
reached their destination: Christians, or more precisely Spanish Christians.
They found them hunting slaves among the Pima Indians, who had
deserted the land in terror.[27] In order to finish their journey the Spanish
needed now to adopt a final role, the role of peace mediators. They had to
promise the Indians that if they accepted Spanish dominion they would
no longer be enslaved. At the same time, they had to promise the Spanish
that if they ceased their persecutions, the Indians would return. At that
crucial moment Cabeza de Vaca's heart was, definitely, on the side of
the Indians who had facilitated their passage, and even Oviedo, so often
negative when describing Indians, felt obliged to draw a moral from
the scene: 'Is it not worth considering, my Christian reader, the contrast
between those Spanish in the land, and the four travellers? while the
former were slave-hunting and stealing, the others came healing the sick
and making miracles...'

Naked like the Indians, Cabeza de Vaca and his companions contemplated with horror the evil intentions of the civilized. Momentarily the
travellers prevailed in their improvised role as pacifiers, because their
credibility among the Indians as sons of the sun, explains Cabeza de Vaca,
was superior to the credibility of the slave-hunters who called themselves
Christians. But this humanitarian stance cannot hide the fact that the
terms of analysis had quickly settled on the side of the language of the
Christian conquerors. What Cabeza de Vaca was to propose to the Crown,
here and on other occasions, was the feasibility of peaceful conquest
and peaceful conversion. Among the Indians he had known, no obvious
idolatry had been found, he claimed, while their willingness to take the
Europeans as sons of the sun surely suggested a willingness to accept
Christianity too. Thus these Indians might not be evil, but they were
certainly spiritually and politically incomplete.

This sudden restoration of the imperialist project (a 'soft', paternalistic kind of imperialism, indeed an ideological alternative well attested from the times of Columbus) allowed Cabeza de Vaca to end his narrative on a note of hope: it brought back the humanitarian ideals to the official system, and it vindicated his whole, painful experience as a meaningful process. The survivors from Narváez's expedition had gained a new insight into the methodology of conquest. Unfortunately, as events were to prove, this model was fatally flawed. The Pima and Opata Indians had not understood or accepted Christianity, nor had the conquerors of the northern frontier of New Galicia (the modern Mexican state of Sonora) abandoned their essential aim of profiting from whatever was most convenient: if gold did not appear, if the Amazons (also reported in this area) were not, as Oviedo suspected, real Amazons, taking slaves was often the main alternative option.[28] Certainly the laws were against it, but all laws, if they were to accommodate the needs of empire, could be twisted, and the Spanish laws in the Indies, for all their humanitarian concern, repeatedly were.

One cannot blame Cabeza de Vaca for failing in a context in which he was ultimately powerless. The full measure of his idealism and its flaws comes across, however, in his next expedition in Río de la Plata – and more precisely, his governorship of this area of conquest begun in 1540 (that is, only three years after his return to Spain with his tale from Florida). He had apparently bought the position of *adelantado* (a title that gave wide authority in unexplored areas) from the Crown by promising to invest the handsome sum of 8,000 escudos, following the then current practice. This implied that he would need to obtain *at least* that sum through his office as governor and conqueror among the Indians of Paraguay. It seems likely that he also promised to deal peacefully with the Indians according to the unique insights gained in the north, thus allowing the Crown to experiment, through Cabeza de Vaca, with less callous methods of conquest. Unfortunately for him, but perhaps not surprisingly, this radical transfer from one open frontier to another proved remarkably unsuccessful. His expedition north from the settlement of Asunción led nowhere but to the unhealthy climate of the rainy season. Worse than that, he alienated his men, and while he lay ill in bed he was deposed, imprisoned and, eventually, sent back to Spain as a criminal.[29]

Reading the *Commentaries* that he dictated to his scribe Pero Hernández on his return – a document that must be interpreted as a veiled apology – one can believe that Cabeza de Vaca had indeed suffered from

the impossibility of his legalistic policy: either he fed the ambitions of
his men, or he lost all authority. In particular, his attempt to protect
the Indians from excessive abuse took away from his men one of the
few things that they could enjoy in their grim environment: the power of
command over someone else and, in particular, access to a great deal
of unrestricted sex and free labour. These expectations, and the incon-
fessable realities to which they led, are perfectly revealed by the description
of Indian women of the Maipai tribe by Ulrich Schmidel, a Bavarian
common soldier under Cabeza de Vaca's authority who spent twenty
years in the Indies: 'they do nothing but spinning and weaving cotton,
cook meals, and what the husband wants, or other men if they are asked
to, but I do not want to speak further of this. If anyone does not believe
this, go there and see, and you will find nothing else'.[30] Although Cabeza
de Vaca depicted the events of his governorship with an obvious bias (the
adoption of the third person was of course a rhetorical trick inspired
by Caesar's own *Commentaries*), we can reconstruct the mechanisms
through which his men lost respect for him because we also have Ulrich
Schmidel's autobiographical account, which was published in German in
1567. In it he presents Cabeza de Vaca in a negative light as a man who
failed to connect with his men.[31] Schmidel was, obviously, one of the
adventurers who followed Cabeza de Vaca's leading opponent, Domingo
Martínez de Irala. But his account also reveals the extent to which the
Spanish in Paraguay were an isolated and disorderly lot, prone to rebellion
and civil strife.

Despite all his idealism, Cabeza de Vaca was a vulgar conqueror when
it came to the actual mechanisms of conquest: he had invested a fortune
for the sake of a speculative discovery, and his eagerness to move ahead
was part of the rush for the spoils of the Peruvian empire discovered only
a few years earlier by Pizarro. The idea was not entirely absurd, since the
men from Paraguay sought to reach from the east what is now Potosí, but
it was inevitable that a significant gap would grow between the reality of
life in the jungle and the distant aims of plentiful gold and silver.[32]
European hopes were fed by mythical stories extracted from the Indians
through the biased method of repeatedly asking for signs of wealth –
signs that many Indians soon learnt to administer according to what they
believed was more advantageous to them.

In the 1540s there was still hope for another Peru, and to a great extent
Cabeza de Vaca only discovered the full measure of his failure when he
was unable to convince the officials of the court in Spain that he was
innocent of the crimes for which his men had imprisoned him. It is

Francisco de Ribera entertained by the Xarayes (1543–4), from Levinus Hulsius, ed.,
Vera historia admirandae cuiusdam navigationis quam Huldericus Schmidel,
Straubingensis, ab anno 1534 usque ad annum 1554, in Americam vel Novum Mundum
iuxta Brasiliam & Rio della Plata confecit (Nüremberg, 1599).

possible that his final, sad poverty in Spain after so many years of suffering in the Indies was the result of the political realism of the men at the
court: he was a spent force now, unable to assist the extension of royal
authority in a continent that was erupting into civil wars, as the spoils
of conquest were quickly distributed among a small oligarchy in an
attempt to construct a new social order, and thousands of soldiers were
left with nothing but a sense of betrayal.

The culmination of this process, the extreme sense of emptiness to
which it led, is apparent in a slightly later expedition of discovery and
conquest: the one led by Pedro de Ursúa from Peru down the Marañón
and Amazon rivers in 1561, which ended in the famous episode of his
murder and the rise of an obscure Basque soldier, Lope de Aguirre, as a
rebel against the king. In the context of a colonial society in which, even
in Peru, less than 20 per cent of the Spanish adventurers had obtained
repartimientos of Indians or other royal offices to satisfy their ambition,
this violent rebellion in the face of diminishing prospects was not an
exceptional event, and perhaps Cabeza de Vaca should count himself
lucky for not having suffered a fate similar to Pedro de Ursúa's.[33] Among
the many fascinating documents generated by this expedition, perhaps

the most surprising, albeit horrid in the same proportion, is the letter that Lope de Aguirre wrote to Philip II when he reached the island of Margarita (off the coast of modern Venezuela) after leaving the mouth of the Marañón river. Here the notoriously cruel 'tyrant' (as his companions would call him) addressed the king in a characteristically direct fashion, almost like a son speaking to his father, in order to present himself as a humble but honourable vassal, victim of gross injustice:

In my youth I crossed the Ocean sea towards Peru to improve my condition with the lance in hand, and to fulfil my obligation as a good man. Thus in 24 years I have done many services to you in Peru, conquering Indians, populating towns for your service, and especially in many battles and encounters which have been fought in your name, always to the best of my forces and without disturbing your officers for my pay, as will be seen in your royal books. I firmly believe, most excellent King and Lord, that to me and my companions you have not behaved as such, but have been cruel and ungrateful. . .[34]

This 'good man' was prepared to accept that King Philip had been deceived by his agents in the Indies 'because of the great distance', but that did not prevent him from declaring his personal rebellion against 'the great oppression and punishments that your ministers give us, who in order to favour their sons and followers have stolen our fame, life and honour'. What is most interesting is that while declaring this rejection of Philip's authority, Aguirre maintains his commitment to the collective pursuit of empire and the underlying values of the Catholic monarchy. Not only does he provide a criticism of colonial government (including clerical corruption), he also claims that when he heard about the Lutheran schism he had a German member of the expedition cut to pieces. This rather crude, symbolic statement of orthodoxy (which, need-less to say, is rendered sterile by a large number of obviously unchristian actions) is however accompanied by some rather more constructive attitudes. Thus after explaining his seizure of power, which was followed by a number of further killings, Aguirre's letter offers information about what the Spanish had found – and not found – down the river:

We went along our route, suffering all these deaths and unhappy events in this river Marañón, and we spent more than ten and a half months until we reached its mouth [. . .] our journey was 1,500 leagues long, it is a large and fearsome river [. . .] it has 800 leagues without any inhabitants [. . .] God only knows how we escaped this fearsome lake! I warn you, King and Lord, not to organise nor allow any fleet to be sent to this river of such ill fortune, because for my Christian faith I swear, King and Lord, that if 100,000 men were to come none would escape, for the false reports. In this river there is nothing but despair, especially for those who have recently arrived from Spain.[35]

Beyond any intended rhetorical effect, what dominates Aguirre's letter is therefore his attachment to the unfulfilled idea of conquest, which requires a commitment to 'true relations' as opposed to fanciful tales. Aguirre the rebel affirms in the end the Hispanic values, political and religious, that made him a conqueror, despite his denunciation of the existing structure of authority as unjust. This is why the final statement by Aguirre and his men is a prayer for the restoration of their success as conquerors:

We pray to God our Lord that your fortune be ever increased, and your success be assured against the Turk, the French and all those who in those parts have wars against you. In these parts, God grant us His grace so that by our force of arms we may achieve the rewards owed to us, because they have denied to us what belonged to us by right.[36]

Aguirre, declaring himself a 'rebel until death for your ingratitude', resolved his sense of futility by doubly affirming his *persona* as a traveller. He was a traveller as wanderer, that is, as a dispossessed person and thus a rebel (he actually signed his letter *el peregrino*).[37] But he was also a traveller as explorer and observer, as direct discoverer of the truth of futility in the midst of the river and the jungle, rather than *el Dorado* which had been promised to him. His letter is so revealing because in it rebellion appears as a genuine expression of the moral economy of the conqueror, a logical consequence of his pursuit of dreams and experience of failure. It is of course also true that in the ideological and logistical context of the Spanish American empire rebellion was invariably self-defeating, whether in civilized Peru or in the inhospitable jungle. Rebellion was an act of desperation and therefore tragic. And yet, through this act, Aguirre articulated a criticism of the injustice of the empire from the perspective of the soldier who made the empire possible in the first place, rather than from the perspective of a foreigner excluded from the Castilian monopoly, or the missionary as protector of Indians. Obviously, Aguirre's idea of justice was incompatible with the idea of justice of those among his Spanish companions who had protested because, in the face of scarcity, he had decided to abandon to certain death a hundred Christianized and Hispanicized Indian women (in fact virtual slaves) which they had brought with them, all the way from Peru to the mouth of the river.[38] We must here conclude that the rhetoric of justice only attempted to explain the evidence of failure.[39]

So far I have focused on the discovery of futility by the conqueror as traveller, and we may wonder whether other social groups had a different perspective and experience. Merchants, for instance, may have been far less dominant in the official rhetoric of Hispanic imperialism in the New World and yet they perhaps adopted a more realistic stance, based on a discourse of profit rather than conquest. We do have evidence of a specifically mercantile perspective in the same period. However, a brief analysis of the account of the travels of Galeotto Cei (1513–1579), a Florentine trying to reach Peru from the Caribbean (although he ended up in modern Venezuela and Colombia), reveals that in essence this is, I would argue, another version of the discovery of the futile.[40]

Cei's narrative is extremely informative, but we have seen in the examples of Oviedo, Cabeza de Vaca and Vázquez–Aguirre that this alone does not constitute an affirmation of the marvellous according to traditional European ideals. Rather, we might say that precise description often sustained a kind of demystification. In order to interpret Galeotto Cei's narrative it is therefore necessary to consider both the progress of his travels as part of a general autobiographical itinerary and the particular comments which accompany the empirical description of events, places and peoples. At both levels a distinctive structure of success and failure is proposed, based on the values of the Renaissance merchant–patrician rather than those of a conqueror with chivalric and crusading ideals. As a merchant–patrician, Galeotto Cei appears in the first place as the culti-vator of a genre of travel memoirs which is addressed to his fellow citizens, friends (often merchants) who have requested an account of his experi-ences in the New World.[41] Like a modern Marco Polo, Cei needs to defeat their scepticism and, simultaneously, satisfy their sense of wonder. In this sense his account is, inevitably, a book of marvels, 'true' marvels as opposed to traditional ones (true marvels, as novel and extraordinary observations, are meant to be both useful and entertaining). Galeotto Cei is therefore offering two things at the same time: a picture of the prospects of the merchant in the New World, incarnated by himself, and a picture of the New World as such.

On both accounts, however, the merchant turns out to be a demystifier. His apparent success as a civilized and wealthy patrician, who has married a younger woman who bears him many children, has, it turns out, little to do with his years in the Indies (as he calls them) and more to do with a change of his relationship with the Medici regime which now controlled the Florentine Republic. Galeotto's father had been executed for his anti-Medici activities in 1530 and his fortune was confiscated, leaving his sons in a vulnerable position. Still an exile from the city when he sailed from Seville in 1539, Galeotto only managed to return to Spain in 1553 and was then pardoned by Duke Cosimo of the Medici, who restored his fortune. His actual experience of fourteen years in the Indies was instead a succession of commercial experiments which were often risky, sometimes unprofitable, always unsavoury, and never took him exactly where he wanted to go – to the mythical wealth of Peru. Throughout the 1540s Cei carried slaves from Africa to Santo Domingo, attempted to exploit pearl fisheries, carried slaves between the islands and the mainland, was obliged to join expeditions of conquest and colonization in Venezuela, waited for years for a licence to trade, carried cattle across the mountains towards New Granada (modern Colombia), and dreamt, but never achieved, the project of a gold mine (when he finally saw one he realized that inflationary pressures and the need for a substantial investment often rendered such findings useless). He suffered a great deal of physical hardship and was often forced to sell at a loss. He also became aware of a world which was brutal and dishonest but unable to fulfil his economic dreams. There is, therefore, a global message, an autobiographical confession which Cei summarized early on when he justified, in the first page of his account, why he had returned poor from his long travels in 'India':

There is never a lack of people who want to learn about India [. . .] the majority because I have returned poor, as if it were shameful to return without a big treasury, and as if all the parts and provinces of India, which is such a large country, were very rich, while in fact they are not. Many are extremely poor, and whoever knows this is marvelled how the poor Christians live over there [. . .] the majority go there foolishly (following this false opinion) and stay because they are ashamed (not wanting to return poor), and from these people most of India is populated, although the majority are commoners and people of low condition, who in Spain in order to live needed to labor the earth, look after pigs, go after a mule all day, or do other jobs and mechanical professions. Finding themselves in India with one or two Indian women to serve them, they are happy with that miserable condition.[42]

In this way the account of personal misfortune becomes a negative comment about the nature of the colonial society of the New World. The double demystification is in fact a single process, because the nature of the marvellous is transferred from the particular observations of strange peoples and exotic products to the unexpected realization of overall material poverty and moral corruption. The merchant does not become wealthy because the Indies are not what they are supposed to be – and this distorted response to European desires becomes the key marvel, the marvel of unexpected truth. Galeotto Cei 'marvels' at the poverty of the Christians in the New World. He also marvels at how fast the Indies are becoming depopulated and, above all, at how easily people in Europe believe wonderful reports about untold wealth and are even able to print them.[43]

The whole catalogue of negative experiences described by Galeotto Cei is certainly too vast to discuss here. It is important however to empha- size that it encompasses a wide range of considerations, from practical to moral ones. The merchant was not therefore only discussing economic profit, but rather how profit related to justice, religion and civilization. In the New World economic and moral failure were a reflection of each other. Thus, to begin with, he complained that European women in the Indies were lazy and dishonest and had acquired an enormous amount of sexual power (Galeotto Cei was obviously fascinated by sexual activities and sexual organs, a fascination that often verges on the voyeuristic). Sex was a compensation when wealth was elusive, but the alternative of a lascivious life frightened the Florentine merchant–patrician, as he associ- ated it with loss of power, ill-health and the many insects of a hot climate.[44]

This alluring inner weakness found correspondance in the political and economic spheres. The business of discovery was a tale of rivalries and betrayals between Europeans, often accompanied by cruelty and exploitation towards Indians. The exploitation of Indians was done with little economic benefit or discrimination and was in fact a reflection of economic incompetence in the first place. Thus, settling a new town in a new area of the mainland of the southern continent was extremely diffi- cult: 'we made our village, each of us a house made of reeds, hay and wood, all of which were abundant there, and then began our struggle against hunger . . .'[45] Life in coastal towns, like Nombre de Dios, was like hell – both expensive (since everything was scarce) and dangerous (since there were so many illnesses). 'Discovering' a new area in what is modern Venezuela was about robbing Indians of their food and then enslaving them, causing their destruction without bringing any permanent wealth to the Europeans (Galeotto Cei criticized this cruelty, but often we find him joining in).[46] In the Caribbean, pearls were fished out of the sea at the expense of condemning Indian slaves to a dog's life, forced to dive and otherwise kept in prison, 'and of six Indians that they put there, four die'.[47] This exploitation was the result of abuse of the laws, because 'here in the Indies people do not fear God, but only the king's justice'.[48] Fear of punishment was of course not sufficient to make men virtuous.

On the other hand Galeotto Cei shared the anti-clericalism of many

Spanish settlers and in particular complained about the priests' insistence that Christians should teach religion to their Indians (he provides an example of his dialogue with the Indians about God in Heaven, to which they reply 'how does he know' and 'if he has been there', in order to suggest that Christianization is a futile exercise). His fundamental belief here was that without civilization there could be no Christianization (this the Indians understood by claiming that in order to go to mass they should be able to dress like Spaniards – not the trivial point that it may seem from an abstract theological perspective). However, the bad example set by the Spanish made civilization impossible: 'there are more Christians who become Indians than Indians who become Christians [...] We are like our friars, we want them to do what we tell them to do, but instead they do what they see us doing'.[49]

As for the Indians themselves, with all their different habits and customs, they are portrayed as simple and irrational, some (not all, he carefully distinguished them) were cannibals and sodomites, and in general 'they have no religion, nor anything good, nor law, nor civility'. Young women abort regularly so as not to have sagging breasts, 'and often, in order to kill the child, they also die, like beasts'. They live a life of sexual disorder, fathers copulating with daughters and brothers with sisters, and with a complete lack of criminal justice, 'because they know neither vice nor virtue, nor do they have charity, shame or piety'.[50]

The moral vacuum of the Indians was in fact the reason for the moral corruption of the Christians, who 'marry whores' and, 'having lost their shame here, lose it in everything else, so that here one does not find truth, honesty, charity nor any other virtue'. Thus, in an ironic reversal of the meaning of Cabeza de Vaca's *reductio ad naturam*, 'the Christians can be said to have become Indians'. This negative transfer ('here one can see that men always pick up the worst') corresponded however to the cruel treatment which the Europeans gave to the Indians, which, as we have seen, is clearly portrayed. The travels of Galeotto Cei do not lead him to the simple discovery of Christian European corruption (his discourse is not therefore the discourse of the defender of the Indians) but rather to the discovery of a natural world devastated by the interaction of human imperfections and in which the new setting is in itself, and against all dominant expectations, an invitation to failure.

Galeotto Cei logically rejected life in a colonial society (he clearly states that he could have married and stayed in Santo Domingo, maintaining a stable if mediocre life as a trader with other Florentines, but that he ran away from the idea). The discourse of personal profit, the expectation of marvellous possessions we may say (to echo Stephen Greenblatt's title – see note 3) had led to the revelation of collective deceit, and a retreat to the security of Florentine conventions: economic (with his fortune restored by his father's enemy), sexual (with a young, European, submissive wife) and civil (with a number of pseudo-republican public responsibilities in the Duchy of Tuscany to culminate his career).

The discourse of travel as profit was not more able to deliver medieval marvels than the discourse of travel as conquest, but surely the discourse of religion was even more fundamental. After all, the activities of men of religion both legitimized conquest and gave a structural identity to the new colonial society. Travel as mission immediately became a moral obligation within the official system, but travel as pilgrimage only became a possibility more slowly, as the Europeans did their best to destroy the indigenous mythical landscape and instal their own religious system, with St Thomas the Apostle, the Devil, the Virgin and other apparitions. The location of these mythical events within the new geography was an essential complement to the establishment of Christian doctrine, ritual and authority. It is in the context of this need to fill a spiritual vacuum that the last document which I wish to analyse becomes significant.

In 1587 the remarkable Jesuit missionary and historian José de Acosta sent a peculiar biography of one of the brothers in Peru, called Bartolomé Lorenzo, to the General of the Society of Jesus in Rome. It was an account of his travels in the Indies until he joined the Society. He began as a poor man, wandering from place to place in a kind of unconscious pilgrimage, until he was led by a tortuous path to his final destination in Peru. It was possible to see his numerous adventures as a number of false alternatives, which Bartolomé Lorenzo never embraced with enthusiasm. He thus rejected the lure of the flesh and the lure of conquest, even the lure of the friars (rivals of the Jesuits). However, while it is obvious that Acosta told this story as an exemplary tale, an allegory of a spiritual quest which could only culminate in the Society of Jesus (and as such was published in 1666 by the Jesuit Alonso de Andrade), a careful reading reveals something else, perhaps a final glimpse of a journey which was not really a conventional discovery of Christian truth and salvation.[51] Thus this narrative merits close scrutiny, not only because José de Acosta was an extremely important figure in the development of a religious strategy for the New World, but also because here futility insinuates itself even in the sacred core of the European system of meaning.

One must however read between the lines in order to interpret this document, which is neither fully realistic nor entirely fictional. Acosta

could not 'invent a novel' and at the same time maintain his commitment
to 'a true relation' (he was after all writing to the General in Rome). Like
conquerors and traders, Jesuit missionaries interpreted their experiences
in the New World with a bias that did not exclude an idea of historical
truth. On the contrary, the idea of empirical truth was essential to the
belief of the Spanish in a meaningful imperial experience (and this
obviously distinguishes the enormous body of writings generated by the
sixteenth-century colonial expansion from much of medieval literature).
Of all people, Acosta was a key example of rationalistic historical writing
about the Indies. His manipulation of Bartolomé Lorenzo's account can
therefore be seen as a subtle attempt to insinuate meaning, rather than an
outright fictionalization. One possible rhetorical model seems obvious:
the Jesuit practice of recounting their lives to each other in a spiritual key
as a process of agonizing search, which, invariably, could only find conso-
lation (through the acceptance of God's will) within the new religious
order. This self-fashioning practice developed quickly in the 1550s and
1560s and found its supreme example in Ignatius' own autobiography,
which was cast as a pilgrimage.[52] It can thus help us make sense of
Bartolomé Lorenzo's narrative. However, the question is, can we retrieve
another, less ideological voice behind Acosta's interpretation?[53]

The first important observation is that Bartolomé Lorenzo was a poor
Portuguese who had embarked for America because he had to flee his
country, accused of a mysterious offence, 'an unfortunate incident in
which a man's honour was stained'.[54] It is implicit that this was a sexual
scandal, and Acosta adds that, despite some evidence to the contrary, 'he
was innocent'. Lorenzo was therefore a fugitive from justice, whose
original flight was constructed by Acosta as a first step towards the
rejection of temptation and thus on the path of spiritual discovery.

Once in the Spanish Caribbean, Lorenzo joined the ranks of the many
Europeans who did not have enough influence and wealth to find a stable
position in a harsh colonial society and was driven, through a remarkable
series of misfortunes, to the edge of human society. The narrative conveys
continuous dangers. As early as the Cape Verde islands his survival,
Acosta insinuates, was due to a miraculous intervention by 'a woman'
who gave him water. Afterwards he also survived an attack by French
pirates, and a number of illnesses. But perhaps what is most interesting is
Lorenzo's growing rejection of human society, his 'desire of solitude'
which led him to seek the countryside. This attitude is the key to interpreting his travels. Despite Acosta's attempt to put a gloss on these events,
we learn that Lorenzo was still running away from the authorities (the

Portuguese, as foreigners, needed a licence to be in *Española* or anywhere else in the Indies). This is what led him to Jamaica, and then he fled Jamaica in order to avoid having to work in the militia or being caught up in another sexual scandal. Behind the story of a man who rejected the world as sinful or vain, the picture emerges of someone running away from the cruelty and punishments of a world in which he occupied a low position. Bartolomé Lorenzo's choice of solitude and the wilderness was an entirely negative choice, the directionless escape of a vulnerable man who seemed unable to seize his fortune. He was unhappy and often scared, and had a special ability to get lost in the wilderness. Typical of his incompetence is that he would burn some weeds in order to clear his path only to provoke a huge fire that destroyed mountains and fields and almost killed him.[55]

The narrative obviously suggests that Lorenzo found more peace surviving alone in the wilderness, or living among runaway slaves, than in a colonial society which relied on enslaving innocent Indians and which was prey to the passion for worldly honour and worldly flesh. These dangers are all repeatedly illustrated. In Jamaica he was welcomed by a gentleman, only to be later accused of adultery with his wife (Acosta, of course, insists on his innocence). Attempting to escape that island for a second time, the providential hand of God, Acosta suggests, protected him from deadly shipwrecks, which he accidentally missed. What is perhaps more significant is that the dangers and shortcomings of the civilized order changed Lorenzo's attitude towards the dangers of the wilderness. Thus, after reaching Nombre de Dios on his way to Peru, he decided to cross towards Panama with a companion, 'without any fear of the *cimarrones* (runaway black slaves) which all warned them against, and he said that if they found him, they would probably feed him and his companion rather than rob them'.[56] And indeed, the Black men encountered the two travellers in the jungle of the Isthmus, marvelled at their simplicity and helped them find their way, so that 'those who usually attack and take the life of other people, gave Lorenzo his life back, for his good faith'.[57]

It is quite clear that Acosta decided to turn Lorenzo's rejection of social life into a paradoxical introduction to God's calling. Lorenzo's incompetence becomes a sign of his sainthood, and his rejection of colonial society a religious choice. It is however difficult to define Lorenzo's actual position beyond the observation that it is essentially negative. 'Lorenzo was unhappy in Panama, and because he could not go to Peru, he decided to go to an island nearby, to live in the countryside, a life which he desired, even though in Panama he lacked nothing. . .'[58] After a shipwreck, which got him stuck in a jungle (on the western Pacific coast of the Isthmus) infested with mosquitoes and tigers, the unfortunate traveller was received by a priest, another remarkable man who had decided to live there in order to look after the souls of a number of Black runaways. Lorenzo however continued his elusive search: 'after living a few days with the priest in the loneliness of those mountains he felt that to be a life of idleness, said goodbye to him, and went further inland, where he cultivated the land and led a solitary life. . .'[59] This accidental life as a naked hermit for a number of months is the logical conclusion of the failure of every other alternative. Although we have a clear sense of the vague uneasiness which led Lorenzo to this point, Acosta can present little evidence of an actual religious enthusiasm (he is even obliged to explain that, although Lorenzo sometimes went to hear mass with the priest, he rarely partook in the Eucharist). The Jesuit writer is therefore obliged to fill in the picture by referring to continuous orations and inner experiences that Lorenzo 'was unable to explain well, but felt deeply'.[60]

The fact is that as soon as he had a chance Bartolomé Lorenzo accepted to be rescued and continued his journey towards Peru. It was not a passage devoid of further incident (he was injured in a violent fight, although, of course, he was only the victim). However, unlike Galeotto Cei, Lorenzo did after all reach the mythical kingdom of Peru, only to experience there his most radical rejection of the practices that sustained the colonial system, in particular the cruel enslavement of Indians. Having been forced to participate in an expedition against some villages, after seeing what it was all about, he decided that he would never do it again, 'because he did not see the reason for taking away from others their homes and freedom, not having received any ill from them'.[61] He thus had to run away yet another time, escaping a role that had been forced upon him.

After yet another phase of wilderness, illness and rescue, a religious life would be Lorenzo's final refuge. The narrative presents his incorporation into the Society of Jesus as the culmination of a process of rejection of the sin of the world and at the same time a response to a providential calling, a natural sainthood. Peru is the traveller's destination because in Peru he joins this religious order. We have however seen that Lorenzo had always been looking for a way of escaping his marginal position within society, his poverty and vulnerability, and all the accusations of illegal behaviour (sexual and other) that a poor foreigner was likely to attract. His flight into the wilderness was not a discovery of real peace but rather a way of getting lost and surviving nevertheless. His journey towards Peru was perhaps the last remnant of a conventional hope for someone who had always travelled in the New World against his wishes and without a proper legal right. All the signs (if we put Acosta's insinuations between brackets) suggest that this was a man ill adapted to colonial society, fleeing any kind of conventional role in that society. His religiosity was made up of aimless contemplation and compassion for Indians and Black slaves, not of any attachment to the ritual observations and official doctrines of the Church. The Jesuit order, where Lorenzo would eventually lead a quiet, modest, passive life, appears then as the final place for escape, preferable to both the mosquitoes of the jungle and the injustice of the social world. One may suspect that this is the subtlest, but also the most profound, discovery of futility. Lorenzo had reached Peru, his destination, to know that there was nothing there to be found and nowhere else to go. There is here a renunciation rather than an act of faith.

The marvellous in the Middle Ages was that which was extraordinary and noteworthy, and it remained so during the Renaissance. But the connotations of the concept changed significantly from the times of the *Mirabilia urbis romae* (a twelfth-century Latin guide to Roman churches and ancient buildings), the *Llibre de meravelles* (Ramon Llull's thirteenth-century spiritual novel) and the *Livre des merveilles dou monde* (which is how Marco Polo's book was sometimes known in the late Middle Ages) to those of Oviedo, Cabeza de Vaca, Cei, Aguirre and Lorenzo. The marvellous in the Middle Ages evoked magic and exoticism, and both were understood in relationship to a divine order that was either seen or sought. The Renaissance sought to conquer, intellectually and physically, and for this reason the New World was not incorporated as just another marvel: it was systematically mapped and rapidly traversed, furiously described and violently subjected to dominion. Gonzalo Fernández de Oviedo sought to have it all in his history, adding one book after the other as new lands were uncovered, new peoples encountered and as new reports arrived. He and many others were emphatic that this was providential history, that God's hand was behind the success of the Catholic kings and of Emperor Charles V, in America as in Europe. Above all, the conversion and civilization of so many infidels was a task of a huge magnitude that alone seemed to justify many efforts and losses.

And yet the connection between the marvellous as extraordinary and the marvellous as divinely ordained had been broken. It might persist in the official rhetoric, but it had been left behind in the minute accounts of travels by conquerors, merchants and missionaries, and this loss even inundated the official chronicle. Scepticism about conversion was clearly expressed – Oviedo even had a whole dialogue between an Indian and a friar to prove that mere baptism did not make the Indians of Nicaragua any more Christian than they had been before.[62] Galeotto Cei, questioning common assumptions among the citizens of Florence, marvelled often: he marvelled that everybody in Europe thought that the Indies were wealthy, while in fact they were often extremely poor; he marvelled at sexual customs which gave more pleasure to women than to men, and which did not sustain a rigid social order; and he marvelled at how quickly millions of Indians had been decimated after meeting the Spanish, enslaved and overworked until they desired to die rather than to breed children. Oviedo had explained this obvious catastrophe by suggesting that God must have decided their extermination, for their sins. Were these the peoples whom the Spanish were supposed to make Christians? If they were vicious by nature, how could the Spanish seek to make them fully civil? No matter what a few idealist friars like the notorious trouble-maker Bartolomé de Las Casas may have written, it was better to forget about a legitimacy based upon hopes of conversion. Oviedo simply claimed that the Crown of Castile owned America because the Spanish had conquered it before anyone else – and, if necessary, the Indians themselves were made out to be the descendants of the mythical medieval Hispanic king Hesperus in order to support this claim.

It was true that the hand of God was still to be seen in the life of such exemplary saints as Bartolomé Lorenzo or in the miracles that he performed for the salvation of Álvar Núñez and his companions. However, the travellers' accounts, on close scrutiny, say otherwise. Bartolomé Lorenzo was driven to religion through a simple, unideological rejection of a society that tortured him, and he had no positive marvels to show for his incorporation into the Society of Jesus, nor any missionary project either, unlike his hagiographer Acosta, whose formidable aim was instead to reconstruct the missionary project as intellectually valid.[63] Cabeza de Vaca, on the other hand, beyond the language of miraculous cures, describes an experience of exchange with Indians, a negotiation of fear (as it has aptly been described by Rolena Adorno) in which he was simultaneously the manipulator and the manipulated. His hurried conclusion upon his deliverance was that there was an alternative conquest: not one based on violence, but one based on peaceful conversion. With those ideas he tried a second time and failed, because his men would not follow, nor possibly the Indians either. As he was finally imprisoned and impoverished in Madrid by the men who had sent him as conqueror, his last hopes for marvellous vindication were directed towards those Amazons whom he had been so close to finding in Paraguay, and who stood as the unequivocal sign that the Kingdom of Gold was near. And as year after year men like Lope de Aguirre sailed down the rivers of South America in search of Amazons, to find nothing but brutality, especially their own brutality, the shreds of New World marvels sank deeper into the equatorial forest.

Beyond the conquest, the real-marvellous is still part of Latin American life; this will be claimed by such cultivators of the magic–realist novel as Alejo Carpentier. But the roots are clearly contradictory, as the sixteenth-century travellers who discovered futility fully testify, because the ideal claims are so distant from the actual practice, and yet they permeate so fully the rhetoric of being. What is marvellous in America since the conquest is the spectacular clarity with which history and myth, tragically, co-exist.

3

'Rubbing up against others':
Montaigne on Pilgrimage

WES WILLIAMS

I

But at such an age, you will never return from so long a journey.
What do I care? I'm not going on this journey either so as
to return from it, or to complete it. I'm only going so as to
move about while I still enjoy movement.[1]

On Sunday, 10 September 1581, Michel de Montaigne, out riding alone after lunch in the hills above Lucca, pauses for a moment to admire the view. These are, he writes in his journal, 'the most beautiful, fertile, and pleasant inhabited slopes that could possibly be seen' (p. 1020). That 'inhabited' is important, for Montaigne is not really admiring a view here so much as describing a place where people live. The quality which causes him to pause, and to remark on the 'piaggie abitate', is not the picturesque. He is not experiencing the Romantic sublime, nor is his Italian journey undertaken in search of his sentimental self, in flight from the crowd. Nor, finally, is the reference to cultivated, peopled slopes mere commonplace, one of those remarks that signal the stages of a gentleman's journey. Rather, Montaigne's desire for contact breathes life into the topoi of Renaissance civility; his attention is aroused by the possibility of an encounter, and by the imagination of himself as other. This is a place where he might have lived, had he not become what his house and family at Montaigne have made him. As the essay 'On the education of children' makes clear, for Montaigne, 'rubbing up . . . against others', learning from them, imagining oneself as one of them, is the purpose of travel (p. 112); he left home partly in search of just such an inhabited place.

The descriptive hiatus surveys the ground. The stage is set, and there follows an exemplary 'scene', the desired encounter between inhabitant and traveller. The speaking parts are taken by an unnamed 'very elderly man' and Montaigne, himself at once pilgrim and patient in search of a cure at the local baths for the pain of gallstones from which, like his father Pierre before him, he is dying. The scene begins as follows:

Talking with the natives, I asked one very elderly man whether they used our [sic] baths, and he replied that it worked out with them as it did with the people who live near Our Lady of Loreto: that those people rarely go there on a pilgrimage, and that there is little use of the baths, except for the benefit of foreigners and those who live far away. (p. 1021)

It comes as some surprise, in the context of Montaigne's energetic publicizing of the worth of travel in the *Essays* and elsewhere in the *Travel Journal*, to find him giving so much textual room to the sceptical sage. Montaigne's 'our baths' – imagining perhaps a community of travellers and locals mixing in the waters – clearly does not include the old man, who argues the futility of travels to this place by way of an analogy between pilgrimage and cure that works to the detriment of both. The lessons of local experience, given Montaigne's own declared status as pilgrim and patient, are unsettling.

In the context of other Renaissance pilgrim dialogues and narratives, however, this encounter reads as rather less strange. Reformers both within and without the Church had been working for some time to cast doubt on the value of pilgrimage. Erasmus, giving new voice to ancient anxieties in the dialogue *Peregrinatio religionis ergo*, has Menedemus (Mr Stay-at-Home) mock his pilgrim neighbour Ogygius (Mr Gullible) for his faith in such things as phials of the Virgin's milk and letters dictated by angels. But Ogygius is unmoved by his neighbour's argument, and Erasmus' playfully ambiguous use of the dialogue form obliges even the sceptical reader to admire the pilgrim's stubborn faith.[2] The *Enchiridion militis christiani*, less a playful dialogue than a militant treatise, sharpens, however, the focus of Erasmus's attack on those (few) who, although able to read, nonetheless prefer the reading of bones to that of scripture: 'You make much of a piece of his body visible through a glass covering, yet you do not marvel at the whole mind of Paul shining through his writings?'[3] Rabelais, taking the argument into the vernacular, has his philosopher–king Grandgousier adopt a similar tone as he quotes Paul to scold Lasdaller (Mr Tired-of-Walking) and his fellow pilgrims for leaving their homes unprotected to undertake such 'lazy and useless travels as these'.[4] And for his part Calvin moves away from the gentle sarcasm with which the home-owners and rulers, Menedemus and Grandgousier, speak to the 'simple' pilgrims. His treatise on relics is less concerned to establish different orders of believer and different kinds of reading, than to declare, insistently and directly, that it is the duty of all to recognize that pilgrimage is, and is only, an invention of the corrupt Church, an idolatrous trade, a means to the commodification of both the body and the word.[5]

Nor is the critique of the journey itself purely a Reformist theme. The Counter-Reformation Church, when it is not confirming the re-invention of pilgrimage as the Stations of the Cross (and thus denying the need for actual travel beyond the parish bounds, let alone those of Europe), subjects the journey proper to careful scrutiny. Post-tridentine legislators are keen to establish a new model pilgrim. They do so by warning against rubbing indiscriminately against others and by producing a rhetorical technology of distinction between good and bad curiosity, between right and wrong motives for travel, and between legitimate and unreasonable forms of encounter.[6]

In what follows I want first to present the broad outlines of the arguments for and against pilgrimage in the Renaissance, and then to explore one man's particular response to the challenges and pleasures of early modern travel and travel writing. I shall do this by way of a close reading of a number of encounters in Montaigne's *Journal*, the record of his journey to Italy and back in 1580–81. Montaigne is many things besides pilgrim and patient, and he has a host of political, scholarly, linguistic and sexual aims in mind as he travels. His text is correspondingly plural: it is written in both his own and his secretary's voice, and in both Italian and French. Few of us – Montaigne included – are ever on just one journey at a time, and it is Montaigne's avowed confusion of intentions, languages and narrative forms that interests me here. For it is this which provides a means to understanding the relations between pilgrimage and other forms of travel discourse in the Renaissance.

Montaigne is not simply pious or in pain; he heads for the new holy land – Italy – to read the Seneca manuscript in the Vatican Library and make contact with other notable nobles as much as he does to see relics and meet God.[7] But the memory of how pilgrims travel, and the fantasy of what it might be to read the land and the body as a pilgrim, nonetheless accompanies him all the way to Italy and back. It informs what we might hastily think of his learned, self-conscious modernity on more than one occasion. Travelling as a pilgrim for Montaigne does not mean adopting an attitude of holy separation, or denying the effects of elsewhere and others either on his body or his text. Rather, as we shall see, what he terms an 'honest curiosity to inquire into all things' (p. 115) brings him into conversation and contact with many people in the course of the journey.

On occasion it will cause him, and them, to reflect on the worth of the project on which he is embarked and even to doubt the value of the journey which brought them together.

The questions Montaigne's journey raises might run as follows. How can we ever encounter absolute otherness; for if we did, how would we recognize that we were doing so? Are the differences in ideas, customs and faiths we hold really in large measure a function of place, and are we really, as the aphorism has it, 'Christians by the same title that we are Perigordians or Germans' (p. 325)? If so, then by changing place, surely we can – we cannot but – go some way towards changing faiths. Or do we stop changing at a certain point in our journey; if so, where?[8] The *Journal* itself turns aphorisms into questions, into a lived argument concerning the relation between, on the one hand, the discourses of officially sanctioned travel and, on the other, the contingencies of the road. In doing so, it also sharpens and personalizes the focus on the body still further: can I ever, Montaigne wonders, properly leave home when my father, Pierre, in name and disease, is embedded deep within what I took to be my own body?

The terms of all of these questions are generated by the context of pilgrimage discourse; by reiterating them and by reinscribing his own travels within this field Montaigne is able both to perpetuate the life of pilgrimage – as both rhetoric and practice – and to extend its scope and value. In the latter part of this essay I want to point, very briefly, to three moments of encounter in the *Journal*. They represent three different questions concerning the value of travel and the way we organize knowledge about ourselves and others that Montaigne puts to his – unintended – readers.[9] Each question arises in a different place, language and modality of narrative exchange. The first, narrated by his secretary, takes place in Germany and concerns Latin polemic regarding the location of the sacred. The second, narrated by Montaigne himself, in Italian, is the dialogue with the old man in the hills above Lucca and addresses the futility both of pilgrimage and of journeys to baths in search of a cure. The last takes us to a site of pilgrimage proper and returns us to Montaigne's native French, as he retells the story of a miracle cure which resulted from a fellow French nobleman's dream at Loreto. I shall focus on the first two and gesture towards the last, rather than analyse it in detail. This is not pure tease. There is, crucially, something irrecuperable to analysis about Montaigne's experience at Loreto, and it is this aporia that best represents his own relationship – and perhaps that of other readers and travellers – to the rhetoric and practice of pilgrimage.

II

Death is the same to me anywhere. However, if I had the
choice, it would take me, I think, rather on horseback than in
a bed, it would be out of my house, away from my people. . .
Let us live and laugh among our friends, and let us go die and
look sour among strangers. (pp. 747–8)

If Montaigne is waiting to be surprised by death in the course of his journey, he is disappointed. While in Lucca – a few days before we met him in
dialogue with the old man – he had received a letter calling him back to
take up the position of Mayor of Bordeaux to which he had been elected
in his absence (p. 1020). He could not refuse and returned home, never
undertaking such a journey again, to live for a good many years yet.
Rather than tell of sudden death, then, the *Journal* details the slow
progress of a medical self-examination in often excruciating detail. It
traces the fitful and scraping movement of stones, dislodged either by
water or by wind, from Montaigne's kidneys or bladder through his penis
to the pot in which he measures the amount of blood and urine passed in
relation to the amount of water swallowed, and the size of the stones,
their colour, their shape and their weight, hoping in the recording of such
detail to calibrate some sense of progress in the illness at least, if not quite
of cure.

The movement of Montaigne's body represents, furthermore, a reiter-
ation, a repetition of a number of other, earlier journeys. Particularly
important are those relating to his father, who had, Montaigne tells us,
'taken a very long part in the Italian wars, of which he left a diary in his
own hand, following what happened, point by point, in both public and
his own private matters' (p. 248). The Italian journey and the writing of
the journal, like the stones passed from father to son, suggest a continuity
of experience from one generation to the next. What has changed is the
locus of battle, and with it the motivations for travel. The war has moved
from Italy to France itself, and the son moves to Italy in part to escape the
'guerres intestines' which are tearing France apart. By way of a cruel pun,
the intestinal wars have also moved from the father's body to that of the
son: the name of the father – *père*/Pierre – has been literalized in the
stones – *pierres* – lodged in Montaigne the son's body. In order to free
himself from his lethal inheritance, Montaigne knows he must repeatedly
pass 'pierres' through his penis. Yet doing this also reinforces his failure as
a son, as a husband, and as a member of his caste. For his journey, marked

by the deposition across Europe of the stones his father left him, reads as proof of his own bad husbandry of the other stones he has inherited and squandered – those which make up the walls of the house at Montaigne which, like France, is falling apart.[10]

The difference between the experience of one generation and the next is further underlined by way of a further, bitter play on words, more directly concerning the issue of travel. When noting his father's presence in Italy before him, Montaigne tells a miracle story about a virgin. The virgin in question was his father and the 'miracle' (Montaigne's term) was that he remained so throughout his long service in Italy, before returning home to marry (p. 248). As Montaigne will learn, and as we shall see below, no miracle will be granted to the son, even though he comes as a pilgrim, not a soldier, and even though he travels to the Virgin's house at Loreto.

Travel reads here, much as in 'On vanity', as at once a sign of increasingly errant times and a figure for the uselessness of writing:

The Law ought to impose restraints on foolish and useless writers, as it does on vagabonds and loiterers. Then both myself and a hundred others would be banished from the hands of our people. I'm not joking: scribbling does seem to be symptomatic of an age of excess (p. 721; altered).

This is, in one of the oldest and most persistent of moral tropes, to equate writing with error, the writer with the vagabond. Such figurations of writing are reinforced in relation to travel narrative, particularly in the Renaissance, when few nobles wrote their own accounts. If the details of travel (rather than those of battle or military machinery, say) were worth recording at all, then secretaries were employed to take notes under dictation. The *Journal* has Montaigne at times sorely doubtful of the worth of such records, particularly when they concern the details of his own body. Whereas the *Essays* celebrate details of bodily movements and accommodate them to the rhetoric of self-expression, in the *Journal*, where the immediate physical stakes seem to be those of cure, not merely expression, the project of measured self-discovery seems more subject to frustration and doubt: 'Such a stupid habit, this, keeping an account of [*compter*] what you piss' (p. 988).[11]

But in truth the opposition between physical cure and 'mere' self-expression is never less tenable than here, where the literal expression of stones from within his body and the business of '*compter/conter*' – keeping an account, in both a numerical and a narrative sense – carry equal importance. For, along with the frustration and doubt as to the worth of his project, the travelling Montaigne also expresses an exemplary resistance to the 'rules' of travel narrative as they are developed in the Renaissance. In both the *Essays* and the *Journal* he argues that the boundaries legislators seek to build between categories of experience – sacred and secular, literal and metaphorical, homely and foreign – are porous. His argument translates itself textually into the juxtaposition of personal physical details, lengthy philosophical digressions, and narratives of others' experiences. It is a textual performance which enacts resistance to the at once medical, rhetorical and spiritual prescriptions of Counter-Reformation legislators on how to write and travel.

It will not do, for instance, to argue for hard and fast distinctions between literal and metaphorical movement, between the identity of the writer and that of the traveller. For, as Montaigne makes clear, the body in the library is always in literal motion, both externally when writing, dictating, turning pages or pacing up and down, and internally, when subject to arousal or tears, or the movement of grief or of stones. Equally, the body is no less subject to metaphorical displacement for being away from home and on the road. If he sets out from home to 'move about while [he] still enjoy[s] movement', Montaigne also knows that he cannot escape self-observation or interpretation simply by getting on his horse. Physical movement is always already metaphorical, and no motion, nor any emotion, is entirely free from expressive or interpreted value. But this value is not fixed, and the rhetorics of presence elaborated both in the *Essays* and in the *Journal* – by way of stubborn recording of dates, times, places and measured detail – project the hope that it might be possible to experience pleasure and pain in terms other than those set by the Law, any Law. The force of the *Journal*'s resistance to narrative prescription is especially clear when we consider Montaigne's relation to the specific laws of conduct elaborated during the Renaissance by those who sought to define and police the subjectivity of the pilgrim.

The most adamant of these is one Henri de Castela, from Toulouse, whose guidebook on how to be a pilgrim, first published in 1604, marks a defining moment in the history of Renaissance pilgrimage writing. Castela presents both a vernacular French compendium of pilgrim advice – gleaned from those of earlier writers in Latin and French – and the most considered Counter-Reformation response to the development of the secular arts of travel which had been developed by the Humanists of the Protestant north. The essence of being a pilgrim, as Castela sees it, is *not* rubbing up against others: the pilgrim should always travel in the protection of guides, should never leave pilgrim company, never address locals, never be caught writing *in situ*, for fear of 'being caressed as spies are caressed'.[12] He (for it is always he) must be careful not to travel in order to 'be able to boast afterwards of having seen this or that rare or singular thing' (*ibid.*). Castela's advice to the pilgrim is summarized by way of brutal analogy: 'you must counterfeit, when amongst others, the deaf, dumb and blind man' (Castela, fol. 60v). His ideal pilgrim would be a traveller without a body.

This image is the culmination of a polemic which attempted to reassert the value of pilgrimage as against the new forms of travel which were becoming practically possible and, crucially, were developing theoretical validity within Europe. Zwinger, Turler, Pyrckmaier and Lipsius were all training the young noblemen of the Protestant north in ways of seeing and being on the road which bore no stated relationship to pilgrimage. In this context, Castela's guidebook seems like a last-gasp effort of pilgrimage to lay exclusive rights to the territory of travel.[13] Yet it is also part of a far longer, and more enduring, argument within pilgrimage discourse itself about the effects of curiosity on what Castela terms 'la personne Chrestienne'. These effects are characterized, often, in terms of contagion and an anxiety regarding the health, both physical and spiritual, of the pilgrim when he exposes himself to the dangers either of the road or of writing. It is in the context of this particular anxiety, and the larger debate concerning the effects of others and elsewhere on the travelling Christian, that Montaigne undertakes his pilgrimage and seeks a cure for his stones. We return to Montaigne in a moment; first, a sketched, and very brief history of curiosity and change within pilgrimage discourse.

Change can carry either a negative or a positive charge in pilgrimage writing. When positive, it is recognized as part of the rhetoric and practice of *imitatio*. To touch the hand of a (dead) saint is to participate in his or her (still present) holiness; to stand in the 'place where Christ stood' is to become fully identified with him – it is, in a sense, to become Christ. In the narrative of such imitative transformation, the act of pilgrimage is often represented as leading to a central point, a peripeteia which is geographically and historically expressed in Jerusalem: a place which is at once the centre of the physical world and the turning point in salvation history. So Nicole Huen, one of the earliest printed French pilgrims, writes of having been motivated by 'holy curiosity (in a manner of speaking)' and stresses that the pilgrim on arrival in the Holy Land, 'even if he were the worst possible kind of person, could not but be changed [. . .] *pour veoir*'.[14] The last words here, 'pour veoir', amount to a pun: on seeing, and in truth. The pilgrim is figured as a witness, and the truth of an event is understood in terms of its connectedness to a place which the pilgrim can now, still, see. Within such a powerfully recuperative narrative, curiosity and change, if mediated through the channels of scripture to the pilgrim's physical experience, can only work for the good.

But there is also a different reading of the effects of curiosity and change on the pilgrim within the Christian tradition, one which is negative in charge precisely because of the physicality of the pilgrim experience. The pilgrim not only travels in search of dialogue, he also leaves home, like Montaigne, anticipating death. This is not mere metaphor, since it was required of early modern heads of household, if they undertook pilgrimage, to draw up a will and make arrangements for the eventuality of not returning. The pilgrim can thus be thought of as a kind of liminal figure, suspended mid-way between life and death, freed from adherence to the social structures which normally regulate the Christian person.[15] But in being so suspended, the liminal pilgrim runs – as Castela warns – the risk of being consumed by the fires of desires he never even knew he had. Most insistent of those who express such anxieties regarding the pilgrim's liminal status, and the first of many to define the problem in terms of contagion, is Gregory of Nyssa. His letter on pilgrimage, first composed in the fourth century, was edited and translated in both Latin and French throughout the Renaissance, giving rise to heated and occasionally furious debate both within and without the Church.[16]

The problem with pilgrimage, as Gregory defines it, is one of limits. Focusing on the 'inns and hostelries of the East' where pilgrims are obliged to bed down for the night, he asks: 'How is it possible to thread your way through such seats of contagion without becoming infected by the smoke found therein? Where the ear and the eye are defiled, so too is the heart.'[17] It is in response to this fear of contagion – at once physical and spiritual – that Castela advises keeping mouth, ear and eye closed to the claims of others on the road. This is the only way to resist the negative changes brought about by encounters which the travelling pilgrim cannot help but experience on the journey.

In this last context, Montaigne's valorization of the body's claims seems all the more striking; it is less so when read as part of the earlier tradition of positive change within pilgrimage writing. Whether change is figured as positive or negative, however, it is clear that pilgrimage is understood to be a discourse grounded in the body. Which is to say that it is a practice in which the relation between bodies and rhetoric is paramount. In its attachment to the materiality of the physical signs and relics which are its focus, the pilgrim's journey is performed in defiance of the potential for harmful contagion amongst the faithful: no pilgrim writers suggest that relics themselves might be carriers of disease. The danger of contagion comes either from non-pilgrim others or from desires which the conditions of travel release within the Christian person and which cannot be recuperated to the rhetoric of pilgrimage. This fear has to do with return and with recollection; it bears on the question of pilgrim identity and the changing effects of encounters with others. The concern is not only that expressed in Montaigne's essay 'On vanity' cited above: 'how can you be sure you will return from so long and arduous a journey?'. Nor is it even: 'will you stay there, become a renegade, and abandon your Christian self?' The fear is rather that on return, the pilgrim will be so changed by his experience as to be unrecognizable either to those at home or to himself.

The danger of the traveller losing himself on the journey was not, of course, recognized only by pilgrim writers. Indeed it was a commonplace theme in writing of the period: all the conduct manuals for secular travel noted above, and those of Turler and Lipsius in particular, give voice to an identical anxiety, often in near identical terms. Not least since they, like pilgrim writers, understand that, when expressed in this way, anxiety can be – to some degree – overcome and the value of travel re-established. For it can be figured as less to do with the place itself than with the person of the traveller; less a question of where you travel than how. Pilgrim legislators in particular see in this focus on what Castela terms 'la personne Chrestienne' a means of rescuing the journey proper from its detractors. Christians can be encouraged to travel on condition that rules of conduct be carefully elaborated and limits set to liminality. Before leaving home and running the risks of the road, the pilgrim must be able to demonstrate his ability to distinguish his intentions from those of other travellers, insufficiently schooled in the art of travelling well, and the journey itself becomes a spritual exercise in the avoidance of harmful curiosity and negative change. Castela's guidebook thus measures the success of a pilgrimage in terms of its resistance to the effects of others. For him pilgrims search out alterity only in order to deny its attractions. The saintliness of the pilgrim now resides not so much in his contact with sacred sites as in his travelling to places of seduction and there resisting what he sees, smells and hears. The pilgrim's heroism is a function of his having gone away to visit Gregory's 'seats of contagion' and having returned fundamentally unchanged. This is, as we have seen, not how Montaigne travels; nor, as the second of our two encounters will show, is this his reading of pilgrimage.

III

> ISNY, two leagues, a little Imperial town, very pleasantly laid
> out. Monsieur de Montaigne, as was his custom, promptly
> went and found a doctor of theology of this town, to pick up
> information [*prendre langue*], and this doctor dined with our
> party. (p. 893)

Against the advice of the pilgrim manuals Montaigne often, and insistently, engages in dialogue with people he meets on his journey. He goes
out of his way to speak with those whom pilgrim legislators (and some
pilgrims) run in fear of: heretics, Jews, even renegades.[18] In the process, he
'picks up information' as traders do goods or pilgrims indulgences; the
French for this phrase has less to do with knowledge and more, perhaps,
with pleasure. *Prendre langue*: there is a physicality to this process of
encounter which correlates not only with the invitation to dinner
(Montaigne on the road is a Symposium in movement) but also with his
desire to 'go native' in other respects. 'On vanity' anticipates the terms of
Castela's fantasy pilgrim identity, castigating those who 'travel covered
and wrapped in a taciturn and incommunicative prudence, defending
themselves from the contagion of an unknown atmosphere' (p. 754).
When on the road himself, Montaigne is intent on subjecting himself to
just such contagion. He insists on 'seeking out the tables thickest with
foreigners' and on being served local food, the better to taste the locality;
he is careful to take his wine the way the locals do – diluted exactly as
regional taste, rather than his own, demands. So too he writes in the local
language where he can, dismisses his secretary, the better, perhaps, to
'taste' the business of writing the *Journal* himself (p. 947). He shifts after
a time into Tuscan, since '[he] was in this region' (p. 990), before reverting
to French on crossing the Alps (p. 1036).

This ingestion of otherness, though counter to the advice of pilgrim
legislators, is consonant with the theoretical and pedagogical thrust of
the *Essays*. Like a language tutor advising second-year students on where
to spend their year abroad, Montaigne warns against large towns: 'you'll
find only French people there . . . rallying round and condemning all
the barbarous customs that they see' (p. 754). What is at stake here is a
rhetoric of distinction: Montaigne defines himself as a *real* traveller by
searching for authentic otherness. He does not 'seek out Gascons in Sicily
– I have enough of them at home' (*ibid.*). This is advice contrary in direction to the Counter-Reformation pilgrim guidebooks; but the structure of

exclusion within the ranks of travellers – we are the real pilgrims/
travellers, *they* are not – is repeated. Much as pilgrim legislators do,
Montaigne argues against the way others travel, and this rhetoric of
distinction can be seen to be historically circumscribed in that it has to
do with a particular moment at which the hegemony of pilgrims and
merchants on legitimate travel was being challenged by the educational
traveller, the antiquarian, the botanist: professional tourists. But this
rhetoric and its effects also have a long life. The terms of Montaigne's
complaint in Rome anticipate those of many a recent traveller to, for
instance, Calcutta: 'you hardly see a beggar here who does not ask alms of
us in our own language' (p. 962).[19]

The complaint stresses how, for Montaigne, to travel properly is to
speak with others in their own terms, to rub words as well as bodies
against each other. If in Germany Montaigne is pained by the fact that he
can speak to none but the Latin-learned, he makes up for this by addressing the terms of their local faiths, often questioning them in detail. So, for
instance, he discovers from the Isny doctor of theology that the Lutheran
church had been 'usurped, like others in Imperial towns, from the
Catholics'. He notes that the style of worship changes, but the place
remains the same. This note is then immediately followed by a discussion
about another process of 'usurpation' in connection with place: that of
transubstantiation and the doctrine of ubiquitism.

Ubiquitism, as Montaigne learns on his journey, is a doctrine which
early modern theologians take primarily to concern the host. The account
of the heresy as given in the *Journal*, explained to Montaigne by 'several
Calvinists' who say it is held to by 'many Lutherans', and which he in turn
outlines to the Isny theologian, is admirably clear and is worth quoting at
length:

[T]hey maintained that the divinity is inseparable from the body, wherefore, the
divinity being everywhere, the body was everywhere also; and second, that since
Jesus Christ had always to be at the right hand of the Father, he was everywhere,
inasmuch as the right hand of the Father, which is the power, is everywhere . . .
and that the body of Jesus Christ is thus everywhere, as in the host. Whereby they
fall into the same difficulty as Zwingli, though by a different path, the one by
being too sparing of the presence of the body, the other by being too prodigal of
it (for by this reckoning the sacrament had no privilege over the body of the
Church or the assembly of three good men). (p. 893)

Often characterized, as here, as a particularly Lutheran heresy, ubiquitism
in fact has a long history, stretching back (at least) as far as Gregory of
Nyssa, whose letter on pilgrimage already cited argues its relevance to

the institution of pilgrimage. Gregory uses the notion of the omni-presence, or ubiquity, of the divinity to argue the strict worthlessness of the journey proper. Christ is as close to believers in churches in Cappadocia as in Jerusalem: outward movement cannot bring us closer to God. What is of interest in the *Journal* is that this application of the doctrine is never evoked. Nowhere are Gregory's arguments about ubiquity used to decry the practice of pilgrimage; they are diverted into arguments about the nature of the host. Though ubiquitism is encountered, and explained, its lesson is ignored, perhaps because it runs counter to the anecdotal, experiential evidence of the traveller himself. Indeed Montaigne celebrates the fact that his understanding of the doctrine about the worthlessness of travel has been acquired 'en chemin'.

Though they are of different faiths – let alone nationalities – these two good men speak the same language of theological argument. The rigorous structure and the consequential, Latinate phraseology of this language is represented in the sentences which summarize their debate. As a consequence, the *Journal* moves from being a list of place names and distances into echoing the voices of the encounter *in situ*. In the process, doctrine modulates into discussion and verbs of travel become metaphors for thought and for belief: people are 'in error', they 'fall into difficulty ... albeit by different paths', and so on. The problem, and the pleasure, of such discussion is that of religious language and the adequation of faith to understanding. For Montaigne, this is less a reason for conflict than a means to study, distinguishing between kinds and degrees of otherness both abroad and within Christendom. And, rather than offer the occa-sion for a critique of pilgrimage, the discussion of ubiquitism serves him as proof of the worth of travel, since it is the journey which has allowed him to suspend his judgement for a time and thereby broaden his under-standing of dissenting positions on doctrines central to his faith.

This pose of sceptical disinterest often alarms his interlocutors, as it does the 'good doctor' of Isny who 'loudly denied the imputation [that his belief was similar to that of Zwingli] and defended himself against it as against a calumny'. Montaigne's powers of judgement are, the secretary notes, only strengthened in the process: 'In fact it seems to Monsieur de Montaigne that he [the doctor] did not defend himself very well' (*ibid.*). This note of disappointment – Montaigne perhaps wants to be persuaded he has misunderstood both the man and the doctrine – concludes the first stage of this encounter. The Catholic traveller and local Protestant divine then visit a monastery together, translating discussion into shared observation of each other's faiths and customs.

What the meeting in Isny demonstrates, then, is how 'prendre langue' is not only to acquire information but also to question terms, to compare and to draw distinctions. It is less to be sceptical about the worth of travel, in the manner of the old man in Lucca, than to travel as a sceptic: first suspend judgement, the better to tease out the complexities of the other's position, and then apply judgement to that position, suited to its time and place. This, in rhetorical terms, is to travel with decorum.

It also demonstrates how Montaigne is, strictly speaking, not a pilgrim, not least because of his addiction to discussion and digression. He neither follows pilgrim roads on his travels nor tells his stories along prescribed narrative lines. His travelling companions – all a good deal younger than him – complain that it is taking so long to reach Rome because he will keep wandering off the pilgrim route. His response is to compare them to 'people who are reading some very pleasing story and therefore begin to be afraid that soon it will come to an end, or any fine book' (p. 915). Their fear foreshortens their enjoyment of the journey, and they are so preoccupied with the end, the point, of a story that they miss the local pleasures of the narrative. Montaigne, by contrast, travels to affirm the worth of 'honest curiosity' against both the strictures of the pilgrim legislators and the secular handbooks. To do so is to rewrite contagion, figured in the manuals as occurring by accident and in spite of the traveller's best intentions, as willed hybridity. It is, finally, to affirm the worth of discussion over that of doctrine, to allow for the facts of change, and to argue for the deliberate rubbing up against the lives, bodies and narratives of others, even, or perhaps especially, on the pilgrim road.

IV

> Mixing with men is wonderfully useful . . . not merely to bring back, in the manner of our French noblemen, knowledge of the measurements of the Santa Rotunda, or the richness of Signora Livia's drawers, or how much longer or wider is Nero's face on some old ruin there than on some similar medallion . . . but to rub and polish our brains by contact with those of others. (p. 112)

If the rhetorical principle underlying travel and discussion in German lands is that of decorum, that of Italy is digression. As the *Essays* make clear, Romanesque Italianate digression is the mode in which the essayist feels most at home and is most able to question his own project.[20] In practical linguistic terms, Montaigne is restricted in Germany by his ignorance of the vernacular and irritated, for instance, that the revised Augsburg Confession – which sought among other things to resolve differences on the doctrine of ubiquitism – is published only in German: he cannot read it.[21] In Italy, by contrast, he is linguistically freer, being able to take every opportunity to 'prendre langue', not only with those who represent the voices of clerical and political authority but also with those who are more sceptical both of the value of change and of the worth of travel. It is this sense of freedom that takes Montaigne into the hills on his horse after lunch that afternoon in Lucca, where he meets the man who expresses doubts about the worth of the journey which made their meeting possible. The old man is sceptical, but Montaigne is able to recuperate the local sage's catalogue of reasoned doubts to the rhetoric of experience gained 'en chemin'. For it is the attention to the details of the dialogue with others – whether they argue for or against pilgrimage – that justifies Montaigne's own experiment in travel.

In so far as he is a pilgrim, Montaigne understands the significance of a place to be a function of its ability to generate narrative. And narrative is, Montaigne teaches us – even when it tells as it does here in Lucca, as in Isny, of difference, distance and disappointment – a socially symbolic act. The details of the encounter with the old man in the hills offer further, now vernacular, textual proof of the fact that the pilgrim traveller can usefully 'prendre langue' with living others, of other cultures, and not just with the learned and the dead who inhabit the sanctioned sites of sacred or educational pilgrimage. The point is reinforced by the form and the detail of the interlocutor's arguments:

He said he was very sorry about one thing, that for a number of years he had observed that the baths did more harm than good to those that used them. He said that the cause of it was this: that whereas in times past there was not a single apothecary in these parts, and you never saw a doctor except rarely, now you see the contrary; for those people who consider their own profit have spread the notion that the baths are of no value unless you take medicine, not only after and before the bath, but even mixing it with the operation of the waters. (p. 1021)

Montaigne here represents himself as questioner and then stands back from the scene. The traveller, as he had in Isny, gives his *Journal* over to the words of the 'native', reported in careful detail. He pays close attention to the old man's analogies as well as his arguments, the rhythms and the pace of his experience. Until, that is, those stones reassert their claim to his descriptive attention. The passage quoted above continues:

And they would not readily consent to your taking the waters pure. From this, he said, there followed this very evident result, that more people died from these baths than were cured by them. And he held it for certain that in a little while they would fall into universal disrepute and be abandoned.

Monday September 11th, in the morning, I voided a good quantity of gravel, most of it looking like millet, solid, red on the surface and gray inside. (*Ibid.*)

What is important here is both the juxtaposition of the old man's wisdom with Montaigne's own experience and the specific tenor of the old man's 'popular' critique of the twinned figures of pilgrim priests and medical doctors: 'look, there are more sick people – like you – around now that the doctors are here than ever there were before, it's as bad as it is at Loreto, and you can trust me, I'm a local, I know'. This is an argument that had been voiced throughout the century before him and will echo in Reformers' arguments against the institutionalization of pilgrimage for some time to come. Its focus is the mediation of experience by the authorities, the appropriation of the bodies of both pilgrims and patients by the professionals. To argue as the old man does is to argue against the mediation of pure piety or pain, to resist the claims of the institution. It is also to lament the discursive capture and commodification of the body, its surrender to the professional, prescriptive discourses of priests and doctors. It is, finally, to argue that things were once (and therefore, perhaps, could be again) otherwise. No one these days 'consents to your taking the waters pure', and it takes a local, unlettered 'very old man' to recognize what is going on.

Read in this way, the old man in Lucca seems to be a fantasy Montaigne. His experiential argument appears close to learned Humanist ventriloquism: Montaigne finally gets to voice his real doubts about the professionalization of the institution of pilgrimage and about the cure on which he is embarked, through the figure of the wise old man he fears he will never become. His stones may kill him before he attains to such wisdom in his own voice.

This is not quite to argue that this encounter never took place. We must be careful about the voices in play here, for to read rhetorically is not to deny the claims of the event – indeed the details of time, place, date and weather, and the age of the speakers are crucial to an understanding of the scene. It is rather to recognize that events take place in specific frames of historical and rhetorical reference and come to be narrated in particular voices. So, for instance, it is important to acknowledge that Montaigne's *Journal* arouses such interest largely because he is the consecrated Author of the *Essays*; and that the local oral argument against mediation is itself mediated by the writer on his travels.[22] But we do not have to move from there to arguing that no real dialogue occurs here, that this is Montaigne speaking to himself, or that recognition inevitably involves the erasure of otherness. Rather, the experience of encountering the old man's forceful expression of the argument against the professionals is itself proof of the rightness of travel undertaken as an experiment with identity, as a means towards an encounter with alterity, with others, and with oneself as other.

Each of the meetings on the road outlined thus far, together with the contexts in which we have placed Montaigne, has to do with bringing together place and knowledge so as to effect change as a measured consequence. They speak of travel in relation to epistemology; their procedural metaphors are negotiation, experiment and accommodation to the limits of explanation and understanding. But what of travel as miracle or cure, and the fear or the wonder which moves the traveller beyond the limits of knowing? The third and last narrative of transformation through travel to be read here tells of a miracle cure – one of a number in the *Journal* – associated with Loreto.

V

Like an access of free power, as if belief
Caught up and spun the objects of belief
In an orbit coterminous with longing.

But enough was not enough. Who ever saw
The limit in the given anyhow?[23]

Montaigne's journey to Loreto is undertaken under the sign of diversion, and his companions, like certain later readers, complain of his going there. But to travel to Loreto is also to move to the centre of early modern European pilgrimage. The Loreto house, believed to have been transported there from Nazareth by angels, is not simply holy ground, it is, many pilgrims will say – and Montaigne will not argue against them – itself part of, consubstantial with, the Holy Land. Montaigne's description of his time in Loreto seems at first to be utterly conventional, defined in terms of sanctioned sacred signs, concerned with determining the appropriate level of financial benefaction to those who run the house and with affixing his votive shield in the correct position. His account looks to conclude with a tally of days spent there and the saying of the mass: 'I stayed here Monday, Tuesday and Wednesday morning; after Mass we left'. But there then follows, as if by way of an afterthought: 'But to say a

word about my experience of this place, which I liked very much. . .'
(p. 973).

As we might expect from the other encounters discussed thus far,
Montaigne's 'word about [his] experience of the place' is actually a
story about someone else. Through the lens of another's experience,
as recounted by others still, Montaigne glimpses the pilgrim's sense
of the sacred and shares in the pilgrim's physical access to the effects of
miraculous change. In recounting the experience of another, this time a
fellow French noble pilgrim, Montaigne charts, by means of a narrative
structured through repetition and around an aporia, the coordinates of
his own experience. The sentence quoted above continues:

[T]here at the same time was Michel Marteau, seigneur de la Chapelle, a
Parisian, a very rich young man with a big retinue. I had him and some of his
attendants give me a very particular and careful account of the facts of the cure,
which he said he had derived from this place, of one leg of his; it is not possible to
represent better or more exactly the effect of a miracle. (*ibid.*)[24]

There follows the young man's story, which the *Journal* records without
sceptical comment. Marteau's knee had once been so horribly inflamed
'to the point of giving him a fever', and he had spent more than three
years and three thousand crowns on doctors, all to no avail. Having
'derived from that place' a cure, he has now returned to Loreto to give
thanks. A man whose experience would serve as a counter-example to the
doctrine of ubiquitism, the cured patient travels in time with the primary
principles of pilgrimage: those of repetition and specific location.

For Montaigne, these principles are also in play, but they operate rather
in relation to narrative than to the event or the place proper. By the time
the story is told in the *Journal* the rich young man is already cured:
Montaigne does not witness the cure itself, he travels in its narrative
wake. Montaigne consequently takes care to have the story told to him
several times, from several points of view, the better and more exactly to
represent the effect of the miracle. Repetition comes in threes, and the
cure occurs at the point of intersection of three coordinates: that of place
– the man has finally come to Loreto; that of time – he has been travelling
in search of a cure for three years; and that of the body – his knee is 'more
red and inflamed and swollen' than ever. The point of intersection is 'the
point of giving him fever':

[A]nd at that point . . . while sleeping, suddenly he dreams that he is cured and he
seems to see a flash of lightning; he wakes up, cries out that he is cured, calls his
men, gets up, walks around, which he had never done since his malady . . . Now

completely cured, he has returned to Loreto; for it was on another trip, a month or two before, that he had been cured, and he had meanwhile been in Rome with us. From his own mouth and from all his men that is all you can get for certain. (*ibid.*)

What was the shape of the young man's dream? Did he dream himself walking, running, riding on horseback, calling to his men and having them obey; did he dream his identity back by dreaming a mastery of mind and body at the point at which such mastery was most under threat? The breathless present tense of the narration above, like the urgency of the list of verbs of urgent action and command, suggests as much. On his own account, on waking, Marteau tested the dream against the reality, and they were the same.

But what of Montaigne, and what is the function of this narrative within Montaigne's *Journal*, his pilgrimage and search for a cure? What bearing does Marteau's experience have on Montaigne's sense of mastery over the contingencies of time, place and the body? In line with previous readings here, we might be authorized to see Marteau's story as offering the fantasy of cure for Montaigne's stones. This is to read the young French man as occupying a similar space to the old man from Lucca. He is another ventriloquized Montaigne, only this time closer to home: a Frenchman, a noble, afflicted himself. Less the sceptic lamenting the loss of unmediated experience and more a dreamer, the young Marteau is the more able to be read as a fantasized early version of the essayist in pain.

The *Essays* themselves offer some support for such a reading, at the point where Montaigne most explicitly discusses his stones and the force of his desire for a cure, in the essay 'Of the resemblance of children to fathers'. Here Montaigne stresses what seems to be his pride in maintaining his mental powers even in the midst of excruciating pain: 'I test myself in the thickest of pain, and have always found that I was capable of speaking, thinking and answering as sanely as at any other time, but not as steadily' (p. 577). The measured, careful reporting and observations of the *Journal* bear out Montaigne's self-description here. Yet what follows in the essay is a sudden burst of emotion, all the more anguished for the degrees of mediation, quotation and pun through which it passes into expression:

Oh, why have I not the faculty of that dreamer in Cicero who, dreaming he was embracing a wench [*une garse*], found that he had discharged his stone in the sheets! Mine diswench me [*me desgarse*], and extraordinarily, too! (*ibid.*).

The young Marteau is the anonymous wet dreamer to Montaigne's Cicero; what the parallel lives teach us is something about the connectedness of stories about others and ourselves. The dreamer is 'in Cicero' just as Marteau's experience says 'a word about [Montaigne's] experience of the place'. But questions remain as to the nature of the connections here revealed. If both the ancient example and the modern narrative can be read as fantasies for Montaigne, displaced versions of his own experience of a place, then their relationship to pilgrimage, and to the *location* of the possibility of change, is very different. We are not told where the young man with stones' dream takes place, other than 'in Cicero'. The important coordinates here are those which connect the two readers of others' experience: Cicero and Montaigne. Both are brought together through recollection and writing to meet at the time and place of reading the bodies and texts of others. From dream to the bed-sheets, and on to the page, the experience moves on across time and place to enter the dreams of Montaigne (and *his* subsequent readers). What this chain of narrative and experience renders sacred, mysterious, is not so much a time, nor a place, but an act: the agent both of continuity and change is the act of reading (with) the body.

Marteau's experience, of course, does belong to a particular place: Loreto. For the cure to be effected, the dream must happen in this place, and the rather gaudy, over-determined detail of the flash of lightning needs to be acknowledged. But can a dream really be said to *take place*; is it co-extensive with the location in which it is dreamed? Can a dreamed cure properly be said to 'derive from a place' of pilgrimage? And what does it mean to characterize as the 'perfect representation' of pilgrimage a tale of dreams and spectacular metaphors of mental illumination, mystifyingly curing the ills of the body? What, finally, is the relation of this dreamed cure, in this place, to Montaigne's text, to his account of his search for healing, to his body?

A number of approaches to these questions suggest themselves. The first is to subject Montaigne to a particular form of analysis. The miraculous is of the order of the imaginary; cure, which cannot be willed, but only dreamed of, is to be found in images of return to the mother's body. Christ's Mother's house, Loreto, represents one such image, one access to a pre-Oedipal stage of being, sanctioned by the discourse of pilgrimage. Montaigne is unable to reach this Loreto. He subjects the place rather to the technologies of mastery: he describes it, measures it, pays the priests the requisite sums of money, affixes his family shield to the building. All of these actions are of the order of the symbolic, in that they repeat gestures constitutive of the struggle with his father's legacy which determines Montaigne's sense of identity. Furthermore, our readings of earlier encounters on the journey suggest that his desire for contact with others finds expression in a recognition of similarity rather than an acknowledgement of difference: the cosmopolitan self sees itself everywhere reflected. Wanting to always imagine himself everywhere at home, Montaigne is unable to acknowledge the presence of the 'unheimlich', the uncanny, that which is irrecuperable to inherited forms of symbolic understanding.[25] So too with specific respect to Marteau's cure, it seems that Montaigne's attention to rhetoric, his sense of a 'perfect representation of a miracle', blocks his access to the imaginary, and so to the effects of the miracle itself. His insistence on the mental mastery of pain does not so much release him from his inheritance as confirm his inability to dream his way, by accident, to a cure or to death.

Such a reading is neat and fills in some of the gaps in explanation left by the *Journal* and the *Essays*. But such neatness comes at too great a cost, both to the texture of the writing and to the experience of reading. For Montaigne's account asks to be read at once more historically and with more of a sense of its own resistance to the mastery which comes of analysis. What is striking about the Loreto miracle story in the Renaissance context is the extent to which the experience escapes the master discourses which have articulated Montaigne's text thus far: that of the Humanist arts of travel, and those of the doctors of medicine and theology whom the old man in Lucca complains about, and who protected and policed Michel Marteau as he suffered through three years of increasing pain. None of their prescriptive arts proved adequate to the claims of the young man's body, any more than they fulfil Montaigne's every need or desire.

It is in the end a dream, the content of which is never elucidated except by way of something 'which seemed to be a flash of lightning', which wakes Marteau to the possibility of a cure. This seems to cut across the discourses of consequence – if you do this, your knowledge will increase, you will be healed etc – which the doctors had sold him so dear. And in a sense it does. But it also establishes its own narrative of consequence: he had to go to Loreto and dream the right dream, for the contiguity of dream and place is crucial. This is hard enough. But this is not all he had to do; the success of the dream also relies on a number of further tests. The first is that of being ready to maintain the sense that something uncanny has indeed happened. The man must test the dream against the waking reality and must find them to be identical. This is, furthermore, to read his own experience as that of a pilgrim, at once his own and not his own, at once a result of his having come to this place and an accident. He must, in other words, surrender the coordinates of his individual cure to those of the master plot of pilgrimage, must make of his experience a 'perfect representation of the effects of a miracle' and nothing more.

It is, I think, this surrender of the traveller's story to the formal perfection of the miracle cure narrative that Montaigne finds so arresting. This is why he questions the man, repeatedly, and questions those of his train, too, and is stunned to find them all tell exactly the same story. It is this submission of self to form that Montaigne at once admires and cannot quite accept. This is why the story troubles him, why he reproduces it in detail, and why he does so without comment. Thoroughly recuperated to the plot of pilgrimage, the young man's experience hovers on the edge of intelligibility for the older, sceptically-minded Montaigne. For all his assiduous attention to the details of transformational tales throughout his journey and his painstaking recollection of this particular story in his *Journal*, Montaigne is less a pilgrim, himself, than a careful reader of the pilgrim plot.

That he does not fully embrace pilgrim identity is clear; it is important that he cannot, and we should not try to 'bring him home' to pilgrimage to stay. Not least since the suffering traveller leaving his stones along the route seems at first to bear only a cruelly parodic relationship to the pilgrims in his text who travel to see parts of *others*' bodies scattered across Christendom, or find themselves cured by means of dreams. And yet these stones, which are both Montaigne's own and his father's, like the 'experience of the place' which is both Marteau's and Montaigne's, do indeed relate to relics and the technology of pilgrimage in ways other than those of parody. For the structure of the pilgrim journey allows for each measured stone to be described with the kind of attention normally reserved for a relic. The collocative structure of pilgrimage narrative is exploited by Montaigne in such a way as to allow him to place the details of the movements of his own body, his own story, alongside those of others he meets, or hears tell of, in the course of his travels.

Through the crowded house of the *Journal* weaves the host Montaigne, collecting to himself the voices, stories and views of leading Humanist men of learning as well as local, unnamed ministers, priests and storytellers. The details of how a girl turned into a boy when she jumped over a ditch one afternoon are accorded as much room as those which distinguish Lutherans from Calvinists and Calvinists from Zwinglians, or those which distinguish a reddish-purple stone the size of a pea from one which takes six hours to pass and has the shape of a small man. It is these details, these bodies, and the narratives of encounter, cure and futility that they generate which have been our focus here. For they act both as literal road-markers on a particular journey and as indices of shared cultural continuity, physically expressed. As such they teach us much, both about the journey of this particular man, looking, as the *Essays* have it, to 'go die' among strangers, and about the material and narrative conditions of Renaissance pilgrimage.

Montaigne's account of how travel changes us is thus both a series of historically bound observations and the record of one man's persistent fantasy that he might escape his own observation. The manner in which he collects stories and measures stones in the *Journal* suggests that to travel is to account for, to measure, to distinguish and to judge. It is a movement so central to our models of epistemology that knowing and travelling can become confused, in such a way that we are sometimes unsure as to whether we can ever really move beyond ourselves, to some 'païs au-delà' – some place beyond our knowing – at all.[26] It remains difficult not to argue that Montaigne no more fully escaped his writing self than he escaped the reach of the letters of the officers of Bordeaux who call him home from the hills above Lucca where he might have lived.

But the *Journal* does also project the hope that sometimes we might surprise ourselves: at the turning of a road, in the corner of a garden, while watching other people pray, or while recounting the shape of these and other experiences. Here, as in the *Essays*, Montaigne argues – or suggests – that in reading, writing and travelling we might not only fulfil our stated wishes but also discover needs and desires we never knew we had. This is to figure reading and travel neither as preludes to an event, nor yet as retrospective modes of alienation from experience. Rather, it is to assert their worth, with all the ruses and the rhetoric, as connected, and changing, forms of experience in themselves. Connected, because it seems we can no more travel without narrative than we can narrate without reference to some form of journey. Changing, because at times we want to return, as if from the dead, to 'tell all'; while at other times we may find that our journeys, and the encounters they present to us, affect us in ways we can only speak of by recording, with care, the dreams of others we meet on the road.

4

The Philosopher as Traveller: Bernier's Orient[1]

PETER BURKE

Historians of travel, aware of the importance of travellers' stereotypes of the 'other', are more and more likely to sympathize with G. K. Chesterton's claim that travel narrows the mind. They should not assume that travel encourages the belief in cultural relativism. It is equally possible to argue that cultural relativism encourages the desire to travel. In any case, it is only prudent to distinguish types of traveller, not only by profession and gender but also by motivation and by the amount of time he or she spent abroad. One type might be described as the 'philosophical traveller', remembering that Voltaire's *Lettres sur les Anglais* (1734) are also known as *Lettres philosophiques*. The description of a foreign country served Voltaire as a way of criticizing his own.[2]

A case study of the career and writings of François Bernier may illuminate these issues, as well as serving to illustrate connections between the revival of ancient scepticism, the increasing interest in other cultures, and the 'crisis of European consciousness', as Paul Hazard called it two generations ago in his classic study of late seventeenth-century European thought.[3]

The example of Bernier might also be used as an empirical test of some of the ideas about the 'construction of the Orient' put forward by Edward Said (and, in the case of India, by Ronald Inden).[4] Said's essay, now a classic, is not only a devastating exposure of Western prejudices but one of the most brilliant attempts to work with the ideas of Michel Foucault. However, its reconstruction of the Western construction of the Orient suffers from certain weaknesses, three in particular.

In the first place, the author is curiously reluctant to discuss what he admits to be the variety of responses to 'the Orient' to be found in the work of an 'almost uncountable' number of individual writers.[5] Following in the wake of Foucault's assertion of the death of the author, Said presents an Orientalism virtually without Orientalists. He discusses Western

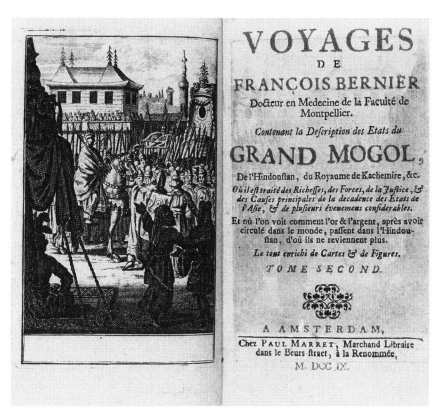

Frontispiece and title page from *Voyages de François Bernier . . . Contenant la Description des Etats du Grand Mogol . . .* (Amsterdam, 1709).

assumptions of superiority, but not the Western use of the East to question these assumptions. In the second place, he does little to place specific texts, even texts he uses again and again, in any sort of social or cultural context. In the third place, asserting that the late eighteenth century marks the rise of Orientalism in the sense of 'a corporate institution for dealing with the Orient', he passes over centuries of Western writing about the Middle East, India and China.[6]

The three points may well be related, since it appears that the social gulf between Europeans in Asia and the indigenous inhabitants was less wide in the seventeenth and eighteenth centuries than it became in the age of colonialism. The case of the British in India in the nineteenth century offers a vivid illustration of withdrawal or separation from local society and culture.[7] In any case, the most famous examples of philosophic travellers who use the Other to criticize their own culture, rather than the other way round, date from France in the early modern period: Montaigne, Montesquieu and Voltaire. This essay was conceived as part of a possible response to these three weaknesses of Edward Said's *Orientalism*. It focuses on a Frenchman who learned something from Montaigne and taught Montesquieu something but, unlike either of them, lived for some years in Asia. The aim is to replace him in his milieu, or better his various milieux, in Paris as well as in Delhi.

François Bernier was born near Angers in 1620.[8] He studied philosophy and medicine, but he is best known as a traveller. He visited Italy, Germany and Poland, and he spent about fourteen years of his life in Asia, mainly in India, between 1655 and 1668. He is the first European known to have visited Kashmir. If we divide travellers into 'short stayers' and 'long stayers', Bernier unquestionably belongs to the second category. He travelled widely. He learned to speak at least one major Asian language, Persian, which was a kind of *lingua franca* in India under the Mughals. He also seems to have been a good listener and a keen observer. He has been well described as having an unusual capacity to enter into another culture.[9] He certainly claimed to have made diligent enquiries among the indigenous inhabitants (*les gens du pays*) as well as among foreign merchants.[10] It would be interesting to know how many of his opinions about India were derived from his friends and acquaintances there, men such as his 'aga' Danishmend Khan, for whom he translated works by Pierre Gassendi and René Descartes into Persian, or Danishmend's secretary Bendidas, or Rustam Khan, a cultivated man who knew Portuguese and Latin.[11]

Bernier's various accounts of his travels, if occasionally inaccurate, are among the fullest, the most vivid and the most philosophical descriptions of seventeenth-century India under Western eyes at a time when such descriptions were becoming increasingly common.[12] The Venetian Nicolao Manucci, who was active both as a physician and as a soldier, wrote a detailed history of the Mughal empire, while his fellow Venetian and fellow physician Angelo Legrenzi published an account of his travels.[13] The German Jesuit missionary Heinrich Roth produced a Latin description of the empire with special reference to religion.[14] The Dutch Calvinist minister Abraham Rogier, who worked in the south, on the Coromandel coast, opened the door, as he put it, on the customs of the Brahmins there.[15] English travellers to India at this time included the diplomat Sir Thomas Roe, who lived at the court of the emperor Jahangir from 1615 to 1618; the clergymen Henry Lord, John Ovington and Edward Terry, all chaplains to the East India Company; and the physician John Fryer, who published his *New Account of East India* in 1698.[16] Among non-travellers, the Jesuit Pierre Du Jarric, who never left France, described the East Indies on the basis of reports from his colleagues in the mission field, while Johannes de Laet, who had access to Dutch commercial sources, produced a thorough general survey of the Mughal empire.[17]

In French, besides Bernier's descriptions, published accounts include those written before him by François Pyrard de Laval and François La Boullaye le Gouz. After him, they include accounts by Jean de Thévenot, who passed over Delhi briefly because Bernier had already described it; by the Abbé Carré, a secret agent of Jean-Baptiste Colbert; and by Bernier's acquaintance, the Protestant jewel-merchant Jean-Baptiste Tavernier (it should be clear enough why jewellers were travellers in this period just as travellers often carried jewels with them).[18] Jean Chardin, another Protestant jeweller, whom Bernier met in Surat in 1667, omitted India from his description of the East because, as he put it, 'I only spent five years there', a classic put-down of short-stay travellers like the Italian Gianfrancesco Gemelli Careri, who went round the world in five years and wrote on India (among other places).[19]

Bernier himself learned something about India from books. He cited Roth, whose observations were used by the Jesuit scholar Athanasius Kircher; Rogier, whose description was published in French in 1670; and Lord, whose *Display of Two Foreign Sects* (1630) was translated into French in 1667.[20] In any case, he had the good fortune to arrive in Delhi at the time of the famous *coup d'état* of 1658 in which Aurangzeb, third son of Shah Jahan, displaced his father from the Peacock Throne and crowned himself emperor. Bernier's privileged position for observation gives the *History of the Late Revolution in the States of the Great Mogul* (like Manucci's history) particular value as a more-or-less eyewitness account.[21] Bernier used the term *révolution* in its normal seventeenth-century sense (employed by other French travellers to the East in the seventeenth century, including Chardin and Thévenot) to mean an important event. Like *révolution*, *coup d'état* is not an anachronism. The phrase is to be found more than once in Bernier's text and was apparently coined by a French writer earlier in the seventeenth century, the sceptic Gabriel Naudé.[22]

Even more interesting than the eyewitness accounts of political events, however, are Bernier's observations on Indian customs. These observations were, at least on occasion, systematic rather than casual. For example, he tells us (in his ninth letter on Kashmir) that in Lahore he was able to enter a harem, acting the role of a young and marriageable relative of his Persian teacher. He not only saw widows burned on their husbands' funeral pyres (the practice known as *sati*) but also spoke to one of them in order to dissuade her, as Pietro della Valle had done before him. In Benares, his discussions of religion with the local pundits might almost be described as interviews.[23]

The focus of this essay is not the reliability of these observations but the problem of what may be called the 'uses' of India for Bernier. It would be unwise to make any simplistically utilitarian assumptions about a man who spent nearly a fifth of his life in Asia and came to feel almost at home in Indian society (he wondered on occasion whether his tastes were not a little too Indian ['je ne sais bien . . . si je n'aurais pas le gout un peu trop indien']).[24] Yet, when he came to write about India, Bernier chose to address himself to certain friends and acquaintances in France. Despite his relatively deep knowledge of the culture, he was presenting it to readers, however open-minded, who had never left Europe. To explore this literary strategy involves investigating Bernier's somewhat complex relation to his own culture, from two points of view in particular, philosophical and political.

BERNIER THE PHILOSOPHER

Bernier probably attended one of the best grammar schools in France, the Jesuit College at Clermont, and he certainly studied medicine at the University of Montpellier. Thinking of Manucci and Fryer as well as Bernier, it is tempting to argue for the significance in the history of travel of the physician, a man trained to observe small details as symptoms of general states of affairs. However, the most important feature of Bernier's intellectual biography was that he belonged to a circle of so-called 'sceptics', 'pyrrhonists' or 'libertines'. In a volume concerned with cultural relativism, as a cultural history of travel has to be, it is impossible to pass over the last term without comment.

Historians still talk about certain seventeenth-century men of letters as 'free-thinkers' or *libertins*, notably a Parisian circle which included Gabriel Naudé, who was librarian to Cardinal Richelieu, and the physician Guy Patin.[25] The term *libertin* was often employed in the seventeenth century itself. The modern scholars who use the label do not assume that all the individuals to whom they apply it had exactly the same beliefs. They are aware that the term is no more than a convenient abstraction. All the same, I should like to argue that (unlike the term 'sceptic', for example) 'libertine' should be eliminated from the historian's vocabulary.

The problem is that the term functioned in the sixteenth and seventeenth centuries, rather like the word 'atheist', as a means for the more orthodox to smear the less orthodox.[26] It was always the other who was a libertine, as in the case of Calvin's pamphlet *Contre la secte phantastique et furieuse des libertins* (1544). The smearing worked by associating the religious and philosophical views of the accused with sexual promiscuity, in a manner which will be all too familiar to historians of heresy and witchcraft.[27] Free thought was linked to free love, the free spirit, antinomianism and so on. One is reminded of the cultural construction of the anarchist or the 'nihilist' in the nineteenth century.

It might be more precise and more illuminating to describe Bernier by two further adjectives current in his culture: *curieux* and *sceptique*. Someone who was 'curieux' was someone of many interests, pursuing knowledge primarily for its own sake. Descartes employs the word on occasion. The term expresses a new and more positive valuation of curiosity, so often condemned by Christian thinkers from Augustine to Calvin.[28] Bernier used the term about Thévenot, and it might equally well be applied to himself. He travelled, so he tells us, out of 'the desire to see the world'.[29] The phrase was a literary commonplace, but Bernier's life suggests that he meant it. His friend Chapelain described him as going to India not from 'sordid gain' but only from the desire to know ('la seule passion de savoir').[30] A contemporary made the point with still more force – and some echoes of Montaigne's essay on vanity – in a letter about Bernier to the secretary of the Royal Society. Unlike Bernier,

we ordinarily travel more out of unsettledness than curiosity, with a design to see towns and countries rather than to know their inhabitants and productions; and we stay not long enough in one place to inform ourselves well of the government, policy, interest and manners of its People.[31]

As for scepticism, Bernier was at one time both the disciple and the secretary of the philosopher Pierre Gassendi, whose work he helped to popularize and even translated into Persian.[32] Gassendi, a critic of Aristotle and Descartes, and an admirer of Epicurus and Montaigne, followed a middle way between the extremes of scepticism and dogmatism, arguing that experience is the source of all knowledge and that knowledge is therefore restricted to the appearances of things. Other members of Bernier's circle were Samuel Sorbière, Jean Chapelain and François La Mothe Le Vayer, all three followers of Gassendi. Sorbière was a physician, an enthusiast for Montaigne, a friend and translator of Thomas Hobbes, and the author of a *Relation d'un voyage en Angleterre* (1664), describing the curious manners and customs of the English.[33] Chapelain was a poet, critic and literary adviser to Louis XIV's minister Jean-Baptiste Colbert.

As for La Mothe Le Vayer, another enthusiast for Montaigne and himself a man of wide curiosity, his works included an essay on the uncertainty of historical knowledge and a discussion of the ideas of Confucius (a subject on which Bernier would also have something to say on a later occasion).

In close touch with Chapelain and La Mothe and encouraged by them was another philosophical traveller, Isaac de La Peyrère, notorious in his own day and best known today for his claim that there were men before Adam. On the basis of a visit to Denmark, La Peyrère published a *Relation du Groenland* (1647), including a description of the customs of the Inuit, and a *Relation de l'Islande* (1663). His concern with the Inuit originated from the current debate on the origins of the American Indians.[34] All the same, the richness of detail in the *Relation* suggests that La Peyrère had become interested in this people for their own sake.

While he was in India, Bernier kept in touch with his friends in France. He wrote to Chapelain, for example; to François Boysson, Seigneur de Merveilles, his former travelling companion in Germany; to Claude-Emmanuel Chapelle, another member of Gassendi's circle; and to Gassendi's protector, Henri-Louis Habert de Montmor, who organized an academy in his house which Chapelain and Sorbière attended.[35] These letters were not treated as private but were passed around the circle, some of them being read aloud in 'our assembly' in the house of the chancellor (Pierre Séguier, 1588–1672, one of the leading advisers of the king).[36] In return Bernier's friends provided him with books and news from Europe and plied him with questions about the Orient. Chapelain, for example, asked him about religion, the position of women, and Persian poetry, while Thévenot sent five questions about the fertility of Bengal and other topics.

In addition, Chapelain wrote Bernier a long letter of advice, suggesting that he spend more than two years in India, observe with care the political system, nature and the arts insofar as they are 'different from ours', and finally write an account of the country which would be the equivalent of Olearius on Persia or Martini on China.[37] Whether or not he needed this advice from a stay-at-home, Bernier did all these things. His letters to Colbert, La Mothe Le Vayer, Chapelain and Merveilles add up to a substantial description of India.

On reading his account, Chapelain praised the author as a practitioner of 'non-academic philosophy' (*cette philosophie qui n'est point de collège*), which aspires to usefulness to the public' (*l'utilitè publique*).[38] Whether or not Chapelain had Gassendi in mind when he made this observation, the stress on experience in Gassendi's work was extremely appropriate for a philosophical traveller such as Bernier. The importance of philosophy for Bernier's descriptions of India is revealed most clearly in his cultural relativism.[39] The most famous classical text expounding sceptical thought, the *Hypotyposes* of Sextus Empiricus, supports these ideas by referring to the diversity of human customs; what is regarded as right in Greece is viewed as wrong in India, and so on. That this diversity was familiar in Greek culture is suggested by the discussion of alien customs in Herodotus and also in the Hippocratic corpus, where customs are related to climate. The idea of the diversity of customs was also a commonplace among early modern travellers. To take an example from India, the clergyman John Ovington quoted Herodotus on the subject and reflected on funerals in Surat that 'Custom is the spirit and genius of a man's actions, and introduces a nature and religion itself: and were the prejudice of that removed, other civilized nations might doubtless be as zealous for burning their dead friends, as the Bannians are nowadays'.[40]

What was relatively rare, however, was the exploration of the intellectual implications of this diversity. Montaigne did so when he used his wide reading about other cultures, from China to Brazil, to undermine what his contemporaries thought was knowledge.[41] A remark by Bernier, 'Plutarch claimed that little things are not always to be neglected. . .', virtually paraphrases a sentence in one of Montaigne's essays (*Essays*, Book 2, chapter 10) on the importance of the intimate detail.[42]

FRACTURES

Montaigne was not a consistent cultural relativist. In his *Essays* he tends to fluctuate between two incompatible positions. On some occasions he espouses the view that 'everyone calls barbarous whatever is not his own custom' (*chacun appelle barbarie ce qui n'est pas de son usage*) and that 'we are Christians by the same title that we are either Perigordins or Germans'. In the famous essay on cannibals, however, he also argues that it is the Europeans who are the true barbarians.[43] His text reveals what Pierre Macherey has called 'fractures', the kind of contradiction which Jacques Derrida has explored so brilliantly in the case of Plato (for example).[44] However, it should be added that Montaigne was more concerned to persuade his readers, by whatever means, to take a detached look at their own culture than he was to achieve consistency. His genre was, after all, the essay, not a formal treatise.

Bernier, too, tends to fluctuate in this way. On occasion (especially when writing to Colbert and Colbert's follower Chapelain), he will assert the superiority of European culture to that of India, noting, for example, the corruption of justice there, the large number of beggars in the streets, or the 'unfortunate custom' of leaving the succession to the throne un-regulated 'for lack of good laws like ours establishing primogeniture'. He described Paris as offering 'the most beautiful and the most magnificent view in the world'.[45] His comment on *sati* is to express his detestation of the 'horrible religion' which required such 'barbarous and cruel' prac-tices.[46] He makes a similar comment on the juggernaut. 'When this infernal triumphal chariot gets under way . . . there are people so mad and so deep in false beliefs and superstitions that they throw themselves in its path. . .'[47] He also speaks of the 'extravagances' of Hindu beliefs.[48]

Elsewhere, however (especially when writing to his fellow sceptic La Mothe Le Vayer), Bernier is concerned to combat his Western readers' assumption of superiority, to express his surprise at the way in which his fellow Europeans despise Indian cities, for example, arguing for his part 'that Delhi does not lack truly beautiful buildings, although they are different from European ones' and fail to obey 'those rules and orders of architecture which we believe should always be followed'.[49] The addition of the phrase 'we believe (*nous croyons*)' should be noted. Again, he describes the Taj Mahal as 'marvellous, superior to the much-vaunted Egyptian pyramids'.[50] Bernier also argues that Indian music has its rules and indeed beauties which habit makes perceptible.[51]

As in the case of Montaigne, it would surely be mistaken to conclude the analysis of these texts at the point at which fractures or inconsisten-cies in them have come to light. It would be more prudent to take apparent contradictions in the text as invitations to explore further, to identify the author's aims and strategies and – in particular – his views of his own culture, from politics to religion.[52]

BERNIER AND POLITICS

Besides his history of the 'revolution' of Aurangzeb, Bernier published a number of letters about India written to his friends in France. One, on Delhi, was written to François La Mothe Le Vayer, who had frequently expressed interest in India. A second letter, on religion, was addressed to Chapelain. A series of letters on Kashmir were addressed to the Seigneur de Merveilles.

Bernier also addressed a letter to Jean-Baptiste Colbert, with whom he had already corresponded about the possibility of trade between France and India. At this time Colbert was not only Superintendent of Finance but a kind of minister of trade, industry and culture. He seems to have been extremely interested in developing economic and political relations with the East, especially the Middle East, the 'Levant' as contemporaries called it, but also further afield. For example, he asked the writer François Charpentier to write a proposal for forming a French East India Company (Compagnie des Indes Orientales), which was duly founded in 1664 to compete with the English and Dutch for the Indian trade. He sent Abbé Carré to India in 1668.

Despite his and other people's references to his disinterested curiosity, Bernier probably wrote to Colbert because he wanted employment. At all events, when he returned to France he tried to approach Colbert via Chapelain with a view to an audience with the king.[53] A memoir of his to Colbert was discovered in the French archives in the late nineteenth century. Among other things, it recommended French envoys to greet the Great Mogul with a salaam in the Indian style.[54] Bernier's letter to Colbert, unlike those to Chapelain and La Mothe, was in the style of a diplomatic report about the Mughal empire, its economy, its military forces and its administration.[55] On the surface, Bernier's message to Colbert is complacent and flattering. 'It is in India, Sir . . . that I have learned of the good fortune of France and how much it owes to your efforts.' The comparison between the political systems of Europe and India (or more generally the three great empires of the Ottomans, the Safavids and the Mughals) reveals the great advantages of the West.[56]

Like some sixteenth-century Europeans describing America (Peter Martyr, for example), Bernier has recourse to the traditional topos of the absence of private property, *meum* and *tuum*. These empires 'have abolished this Mine and Thine so far as land and other property is concerned'. However, he does not see this absence as evidence of a golden age: quite the reverse. Under the Indian system the emperor gives land to the *jagirdars*, who have 'virtually absolute power' which they exploit in a tyrannical manner. If the monarchs of Europe owned all the land, like the rulers of India, Persia and the Ottoman empire, Bernier claims, their kingdoms would not be 'so well cultivated, so populous, so rich, so civilised and so flourishing as they are'.[57]

This passage is of course one of the most famous Western discussions of 'oriental despotism'. Not the first. After all, the Greeks had already perceived the rulers of Persia as Oriental despots around 400 BC.[58] The government of Charles V regularly referred to the sultan as a 'tyrant'. In 1576, the French theorist Jean Bodin had described the Ottoman empire as a 'monarchie seigneuriale' in which the prince was the the owner of all property ('proprietaire de toutes choses').[59] The Venetian ambassadors of the period also saw the Ottoman empire in these terms.[60] Sir Thomas Roe,

British ambassador to Jahangir in 1615, also noted the custom of the ruler 'inheriting all mens goods' and described the government as 'uncertayne, without written law, without Policye'.[61]

Bernier's account is at once one of the most important and one of the most opaque early modern Western accounts of the Orient as 'other', indeed as the opposite of 'us'. How are we to understand it? As we have seen, Bernier was far from regarding Indian culture as necessarily inferior to that of the West. He employs the topos of the absence of private property to criticize India, but he must know that readers associate this topos with the presence of a golden age. It is also, to put it mildly, a little ironic to find him writing to the centralizing minister of a monarch who claimed 'absolute' power (*pouvoir absolu*, a term used at the time before it was taken up by historians), praising the French system precisely for its distance from absolute power and despotism.

It is also interesting to discover that in the so-called 'memoirs' of Louis XIV, texts written by his secretaries in the 1660s to instruct the Dauphin in the art of kingship, the king is made to claim 'the full and free disposition' (*la disposition pleine et libre*) of all the goods of his subjects.[62] Bernier would not have had access to this confidential document, but it was no secret that the government was thinking in these terms. Hence there would seem to be a subtext underlying the surface of this letter, a suggestion that the author was not altogether happy with the political changes which had taken place in France during his absence, during the early years of the personal rule of Louis XIV, and a recommendation to the government to proceed along more traditional lines. As Sylvia Murr neatly puts it, Bernier may have offered 'a criticism, via the Mughals, of the system of government currently under construction by the king and his Vizier Colbert'.[63]

Whether or not Colbert was aware of this subtext, Bernier did not obtain official employment. Instead, he became a well-known figure in the famous salon of Marguerite de Sablière.[64] One of his companions there was La Fontaine, a poet whose career would have been more successful had he not insisted on maintaining a certain critical distance from the Colbert regime. It was for Madame de Sablière and her circle that Bernier wrote an 'abridgement' – in eight volumes – of the philosophy of Gassendi (although the book was dedicated to Colbert). Bernier's last work was an introduction to Confucius, or more exactly to Chinese culture, written for Madame de Sablière, which offers China as a model revealing the defects of Europe and suggesting how they may be remedied.[65]

BERNIER AND RELIGION

With the problems of interpretation raised above in mind, we may turn to Bernier's discussion of Indian religion, remembering that, given the seventeenth-century 'moral panic' concerning libertines discussed above, sceptics had good reasons for expressing themselves in an indirect fashion. At times Bernier offers a sociology or even an ecology of customs, suggesting, for example, that the founders of Hinduism emphasized ablutions for reasons of hygiene in a hot climate.[66] He might even be described as a 'medical relativist' in the tradition of Hippocrates. All the same, I should like to suggest that the discussion of Hindu 'superstition' in the letter to Chapelain should be read as if the author's true subject was the religion of his own country. India functions for Bernier as a convenient means of defamiliarization – as the Brazilians were for Montaigne and the Persians would be for Montesquieu. Bernier hints as much by opening his letter with a comparison of two eclipses he has seen, one in France and the other in India, noting what he calls the 'panic' and the 'infantile credulity' he had witnessed at home (this letter of 1667 deserves to be juxtaposed to Bayle's more famous letter on comets).[67]

Thus, when Bernier writes of the Brahmins that they encourage the people in their 'errors and superstitions' and that they do this 'in their own interest and for their own profit', he is not necessarily assuming Western superiority. He may, like some of his contemporaries in England, be concerned with the dangers of what was coming to be known as 'priestcraft', Christian as well as pagan.[68] After all, he once wrote an article on what he called 'le quiétisme des Indes', explicitly comparing Hinduism with the controversial Quietist movement in the Catholic Church in France in his time.[69]

Again, irony should not be excluded from our interpretation of the central passage in Bernier's letter in which he tells the reader that the Hindus told him – like good cultural relativists – that God had made their law for them alone and 'refused to see that, since our religion is universal, theirs must be nothing but myth and pure invention'. The implication is that – to return to Montaigne – 'we are Christians by the same title that we are either Perigordins or Germans'.

BERNIER'S LEGACY

Bernier may have exercised some influence on later constructions of the Orient. When his book was published in 1670, a French scholar, André de Monceaux, sent it to the secretary of the Royal Society of London in the hope that the society (which in those days defined its scope more widely than it does today) would give its opinion on the book. Whether or not they did so, the book was rapidly published in English, in 1671–2, and by 1675 it had been translated into three more languages (Dutch, German and Italian). It was read by Fryer, for example, and also by John Dryden, who made it the basis for his play *Aurang-Zebe* (1675).[70] In its original language the book reached its eighth edition in 1725. Among its readers was Bernier's fellow sceptic Pierre Bayle (with whom he corresponded), who made use of the text in his famous *Dictionnaire*.[71]

Bernier also has his place in the long tradition of using the Orient to criticize Europe, a tradition mentioned at the beginning of this essay. In a mild form, many people contributed to this tradition. To take a minor example from India, the English clergyman Edward Terry declared that the morals of 'pagans and Mahometans' there put Christians to shame.[72] A more famous example is that of the expatriate Italian journalist Gianpietro Marana. A few years after Bernier's book, Marana published his *Espion Turc* (1684), a description of France (duels, Jesuits, science and so on) purporting to be written by 'Mahmut the Arabian'. Marana's book was quickly translated and imitated, and it gave rise to a whole genre of 'spy' literature.

It is of course in this tradition that we should place Montesquieu. His *Lettres Persanes*, inspired by the visit of the Persian ambassador Mohammed Riza Bey to Louis XIV in 1715, made brilliant use of the Persian 'other' as a means of defamiliarizing French readers with their own institutions. The Persian comment on the royal touch, for example, is that 'Ce roi est un grand magicien'.[73] Montesquieu made good use of Bernier in his *Esprit des Loix* (1748), drawing on him for ideas as well as for information.[74] His famous discussion of Oriental despotism – *despotisme asiatique*, as he called it – in Book 3, chapter 9, implies a critique of the Western absolute monarchies of his day. Montesquieu was of course a defender of the privileges of the parlements against centralization.[75]

In this essay I have tried to make two main points about Bernier as a philosophical traveller, without (I hope) giving the impression that he was a twentieth-century intellectual in disguise. The argument is not that he was an atheist, nor an outright opponent of Louis XIV's regime, despite his implicit comparisons between the king and Aurangzeb. My point is rather that both his education in scepticism and his years in India enabled (indeed, encouraged) Bernier to view the conventional religious and political views of his own society with a certain detachment. For Bernier, one of the principal uses of India was to encourage that detachment in others. In his sympathy for Indian culture and his use of India to criticize France he offers an important counter-example to the instances of ethno-centrism and prejudice described so vividly by Edward Said. Did the rise of colonialism silence travellers like Bernier? Or would it be possible to write a history of 'anti-Orientalism', of European sympathy for Asian cultures, even for the nineteenth and twentieth centuries?

5

Looking for Virgil's Tomb: The End of the Grand Tour and the Cosmopolitan Ideal in Europe

MELISSA CALARESU

In the eighteenth century, as in the twentieth, the writers of guidebooks to Naples urge the traveller to visit the tomb of Virgil. The object of this pilgrimage was the contemplation of the glory and spirit of the Augustan age, which the Roman poet so powerfully represented. For the twentieth-century visitor, contemplation is a difficult enterprise beside a traffic tunnel roaring with cars. While today this juxtaposition of an increasingly remote ancient world and the pungent reality of the modern world is particularly alienating, in the eighteenth century the bucolic setting of the tomb, as depicted in many contemporary paintings and engravings, conformed nicely to the visitor's image of the city which had once been the summer residence for the world-weary ancient Roman elite. And, no matter how far the visitor had travelled, from Lutheran Sweden or from Catholic Poland, this setting would have been strangely familiar – recalling the childhood study of ancient history and literature, a memory heightened by reading Virgil's poems in Latin in front of the tomb. This familiarity would, however, be broken once the carriage made its way back to the centre of the chaotic city – where the visitor would be confronted with its noisy barefoot inhabitants. The old adage, repeated in the guidebooks, that Naples was 'a paradise inhabited by devils' seemed to most visitors in the eighteenth century perfectly accurate, and, while the pleasures of paradise continued to be enjoyed, there grew by the end of the eighteenth century an interest in the devils who inhabited it.[1] It was this new interest which, as we shall see, reveals a number of fault lines in the enlightened rhetoric of cosmopolitanism.

The descriptions of the Neapolitan people as touristic curiosities became increasingly common in eighteenth-century travel accounts, and it was these stereotypes which provoked a response among Neapolitan critics. As Pietro Napoli-Signorelli, a Neapolitan *cosmopolite*, wrote near the end of the century:

When one sees travel writers repeating always the same things by copying their predecessors without further examination, one has good grounds to suspect that they compile their books before seeing Italy and that they then descend here to verify, if they can, that which is outrageous, for the rest not caring to scrutinise the evident truth whenever it does not fit with what they read before crossing the Alps.[2]

As Napoli-Signorelli's remark exemplifies, Neapolitans were not simply passive objects of the travellers' interest but also responded to the stereotypes projected of them in ways fraught with complexity. I will attempt to disentangle the contradictions of an intellectual culture which was simultaneously participating in the language and ideals of the Enlightenment and defending the local particularities of Neapolitan society and traditions. The case of the French guidebooks, and, more importantly, the response to the stereotypes found in these guidebooks, reveals one thread by which we can see that process of exchange and response within Enlightenment culture.

Vuë du Tombeau de Virgile, près de Naples, dessiné d'après Nature par M. Robert peintre du Roy, from Abbé de Saint-Non, *Voyage pittoresque. . .* (1781–5).

Travel, as well as the reading of travel accounts, by the European elite, are often seen as having made an important contribution to the founding principles of enlightened thought, in particular, toleration, by having extended not only the perimeters of human knowledge but also by testing the moral certainties of an expanding world. In practice, the European elite placed increasing importance on the value of travel as an educational tool, which became institutionalized as the Grand Tour. By the eighteenth century, however, the educational value of the Grand Tour, especially to Italy, was mostly limited to the illustration of ancient history rather than the confrontation with new moral worlds. Nonetheless, the Grand Tour did assure a commonality of experience among the sons of the European elite, reinforced by the sharing of a humanist education based on reading ancient Latin and Greek texts, and by the uniformity of itineraries as laid out by the guidebooks. The commonality of this experience, some have argued, also contributed to the sharing of cosmopolitan values by these travellers. Cesare de Seta confidently states that 'The Grand Tour was essentially cosmopolitan'.[3] However, the case of Naples – as a place to which Europeans travelled and, in particular, as a place which harboured its own enlightened community – shows the limits of this rhetoric of cosmopolitanism within the principles and practice of the Grand Tour.[4]

The claim to cosmopolitanism in enlightened discourse is, in part, proven by the vast community of intellectuals who participated in enlightened debates as readers, writers and commentators. What had been a fragile network in the Renaissance, often broken by the difficulty of travelling long distances and by religious and political divisions, had become by the eighteenth century much more consolidated and had a wider social base. The growth of the publishing industry testifies to this expanding network, as access to the printed word was made easier by better transportation and the lowering of book prices to meet the needs of an increasingly literate and prosperous society. As indicators of the expanding boundaries of the enlightened community, one need only think of the publishing houses which sprang up along the French–Swiss borders during the eighteenth century and the growing number of literary and political journals which published articles and reviews of books from all over Europe, articles which in turn were translated in journals in other languages.[5] Polish noblemen read Montesquieu, Belgian lawyers commented on the events of the American revolutionary wars, and Florentine administrators implemented agricultural reform based on their readings of English economic writings.

This exchange of ideas across national boundaries was matched by social networks, which were reinforced through travel. Visiting members of national academies as well as members of sister Masonic lodges were welcomed in salons as they travelled across Europe on their Grand Tour.[6] Some cities harboured large communities of foreigners who congregated there for months at a time; many British, French and German Grand Tourists stayed throughout the winter in Rome and Naples. In turn, a resident population of painters, musicians and guides established itself to serve them. The cosmopolitan make-up of such communities and the exchange between travellers of various nationalities testifies to the increased popularity of the Grand Tour and the widening of the social and geographical base of those who participated. By the eighteenth century, the Grand Tour had become not only a requisite part of a wealthy young man's education, whether he was aristocratic or not, but also an experience which identified him as a member of the cosmopolitan community of enlightened Europe.[7]

The sharing of this experience among the European elite often extended to the use of the same guidebooks in their travels. The development of the guidebook had accompanied the growth of an entire industry designed to meet the needs of the increasing numbers of Grand Tourists in the eighteenth century. By the end of the century, a network of safe routes with inns and a change of horses along the way had been established. And, in each of the major cities visited, the Grand Tourist found *ciceroni* in place to show him the sites, painters to sell him views and sculptors to make copies of the antique sculptures he had seen in the museums. The development of the guidebook formed part of this process by providing not only the necessary practical information but also a kind of cultural convenience of travel. In the eighteenth century, it was not simply the physical discomforts of travel which were lessened, but the cultural ones too.

The letters and diaries of Grand Tourists follow a predictable monotony of sites seen, experiences had and classical quotations contemplated. Many guidebooks included introductory letters to the reader, often claiming exclusive knowledge of new sites or routes. Despite these claims, the information and opinions in the guidebooks most commonly used by travellers are very similar, reflecting in part the common practice of wholesale lifting of passages from earlier guidebooks.[8] This uniformity created by the guidebooks demanded little from the traveller, a passive assent at most by which what he saw conformed simply to what he read. In this way, travel became largely a passive experience, mediated by the guidebook, in which new worlds were rarely confronted and old prejudices effectively confirmed.

While the guidebooks reinforced similar cultural prejudices, most travellers already shared a common educational background with the history and literature of ancient Rome and Greece at its centre. The travellers, even before setting off, carried this cultural baggage which included an existing image, in particular, of Italy.[9] Much of the Grand Tour was, in fact, taken up with visits to the sites and cities of the ancient world, and it was not unusual to include in the guidebooks a map of the Italian peninsula with the Latin names of ancient Roman cities. Visits to sites such as Virgil's tomb gave a physical reality to a world which they had imagined while reading the Latin texts at home. The Grand Tour extended the literary boundaries of the classical world by these prescribed visits to the cities and architectural monuments of the ancient Romans.[10] After the discovery of the ancient cities of Herculaneum and Pompeii, that world became even more familiar to visiting Grand Tourists through the display of objects of everyday life from an ancient Roman city.[11]

Thus ancient Roman sites and the nearby natural attractions of the active volcano Vesuvius, which itself had classical connotations, brought most travellers to Naples. They arrived in anticipation of all the delights which they had read about in the guidebooks or seen in the engravings of books such as Abbé de Saint-Non's *Picturesque Voyage, or Description of the Kingdoms of Naples and Sicily*.[12] Roman baths, tombs of dead poets, and smouldering craters were not, however, the only sites which visitors wanted to see. In the city of Naples itself, visitors went to see the paintings and interiors of various churches and convents during the day and in the evenings went to the opera.[13] The visit usually lasted a few weeks, several months at most, and almost always during the winter, after which they either returned to Rome for Carnival or began their journey home.

All travellers went first to Rome, and comparison with the city was often in the mind of the traveller when approaching Naples (it was often this comparison in the guidebooks with their Roman rival of centuries which aroused the ire of the Neapolitan critics).[14] The first sight of Naples and the bay in which it lies was often seen from the hills above the city, a sight that all guidebooks describe as one of the most beautiful views in the world (and so different from the mosquito-infested plain on which Rome lay). The image of the theatre provided the metaphorical framework with which to visit the city, for what travellers found upon entering the city was a theatre of contrasts, in which its beauty was set against the misery of many of its inhabitants, in which Misery and Luxury played

As Luxury and Misery, sophisticated aristocrats and naked fishermen occupy the
same theatrical space: *1ere Vue de la Ville de Naples, prise du Faubourg de Chiaja*,
from Abbé de Saint-Non, *Voyage pittoresque. . .*

opposite roles.[15] It was through these extremes established in contemporary guidebooks that the Grand Tourist experienced Naples.

The guidebook in French which was read and cited most often by
European travellers to Italy in the last decades of the eighteenth century
was Joseph-Jérôme Lefrançais de Lalande's *Voyage of a Frenchman in
Italy*, first published in Paris and Venice in 1769 after his 1765–6 trip to
Italy.[16] It was also the guidebook which provoked the strongest reaction
from Neapolitan critics. Lalande (1732–1807) had entered the Académie
des Sciences in 1753, and while his writings on astronomy were well
known in Europe, it was the guide which was recognized as his greatest
accomplishment by contemporaries and later generations.[17] The success
of Lalande's guide lay in the systematic way in which both practical and
erudite information was provided.[18] The traveller found, on the one hand,
bibliographies of historical works and translations of Roman inscrip-
tions and, on the other, instructions for time-keeping from one region to
the next, the distances and routes between various cities, and even a short
essay on the kinds of cheese available in Italy. The number of pirated
editions testify to its contemporary popularity.[19] Lalande's themes and
opinions were also echoed in later guidebooks.[20] While Lalande's account
was the most popular of its genre throughout the 1770s and 1780s, it
also reflected many earlier descriptions of Italy. Passages were copied, for

example, from Misson's account of his trip to Italy in 1688 – a work
which had had a similar success to Lalande's in the first decades of the
century. An important difference from this earlier book was Lalande's
lengthy description of the people of Naples. This greater attention to the
'ethnology' of the city reflected the increasing curiosity for the realities of
modern Italy, and it was the descriptions of this 'reality' which provoked a
response from the community the guidebook was describing.

Brief descriptions of the people of Naples, like Virgil's tomb, had always
appeared in the accounts of the city. Already in the travel compendia
popular in the sixteenth and seventeenth centuries, the people of Naples
appear as wicked, indolent and especially inconstant.[21] The people's role
in the revolt of 1647 in Naples simply proved that which travellers had
noted for centuries – that the city was indeed inhabited by devils – and
the leader of the revolt, the fisherman Masaniello, came to represent the
particular characteristics of the Neapolitan people.[22] The late eighteenth-
century ethnological interest in the Neapolitan people stemmed from a
new interest, at least outwardly, in the social and economic conditions of
the city, prompted by Enlightenment philanthropic attitudes. This interest,
however, when translated to the format and limits of the guidebook,
served simply to confirm the stereotypes of the earlier accounts. More
importantly, guidebooks such as Lalande's tried to give these stereotypes
a rational basis through which the Grand Tourist could understand the
obvious indolence of the Neapolitan people and the consequent economic
problems of the city.

Thus Enlightenment both created interest in the people of Naples and
a way of rationalizing their 'otherness'. In order to understand fully the
interplay between representation and self-representation in the voluminous
literature of the Grand Tour in Naples, one needs to look to the origins
of this interest in the people, as well as to the rationalization of cultural
differences through climatic determinism on the basis of the influential
ideas of the French writer, Montesquieu.

In the later eighteenth century, the prominence given to the actual state
of Italy on the frontispieces of guidebooks marked a growing change
in the perception of the peninsula as not simply an enchanted land of
happy-go-lucky peasants dancing among abandoned Roman ruins and
sun-drenched olive groves – an image which continued in contemporary
paintings for tourists in the period.[23] Franco Venturi places this change in
the 1760s, with news of the Italian famines of 1763–4 and with the translation of books into French such as Carlantonio Pilati's *On the Reform of
Italy*.[24] It was through these events and works that European debates, led

Danse de la Tarantele à Capo di Pausilipo près de Naples,
from Abbé de Saint-Non, *Voyage pittoresque. . .*

by the French, concerning political and economic reform in the Italian peninsula were discussed in the journals and books of the period.[25] This new interest in contemporary Italy filtered down to the French guidebooks as an interest in, or rather curiosity about, the people of the city of Naples, particularly the poor.

The city of Naples was the most populous city in Europe, after Paris and London, in the eighteenth century.[26] Guidebooks did not fail to mention this and estimated that the *lazzaroni*, or the poorest inhabitants of the city, made up at least a tenth of the population, a figure that Neapolitans often denied. It was this section of the population that fascinated travellers and that came to typify the Neapolitan character. In an earlier guidebook (which was most frequently compared to Lalande's by contemporaries), Jerome Richard's *Historical and Critical Description of Italy* (1766), Naples is the only city which merited a separate extended section specifically on the customs of its inhabitants.[27] The *lazzaroni* appear as ready to revolt, like Masaniello, and willing to sell their wives and daughters as prostitutes.[28] For Richard, it is their laziness and greed which make them 'devils'.[29] In Lalande's chapter on the customs of the Neapolitans, the *lazzaroni* are similarly described as idle and noisy people

who can only be held in check by '*farina, furca*, and *festini*, by the provision
of food, examples of severity, and great festivities'.[30] In a later guidebook,
which was also compared to Lalande's, Richard de Saint-Non's *Picturesque
Voyage*, the author places particular emphasis on the *lazzaroni* as the
essence of the Neapolitan character. Saint-Non writes:

> One can say that idleness is the trait truly characteristic of the Neapolitan
> Nation, but it manifests itself most clearly among the common people, where
> one always finds the vices and virtues more pronounced with greater force and
> energy [. . .].[31]

While guidebook writers would all agree that idleness was the defining
characteristic of the *lazzaroni*, Saint-Non pushes this farther, suggesting
that idleness was inherent in the Neapolitan nation as a whole. It was,
as we shall see, a characterization linked to climate and against which
Neapolitan intellectuals necessarily had to distance themselves (in order
to claim membership of the community of the enlightened industrious).

The idleness of the *lazzaroni* was often linked to other defining characteristics of southern peoples such as immoderation and debauchery.[32]
Only the moral corruption characteristic of such a society, it seems, can
explain the castration of young boys for operatic careers (as *castrati*). No
guidebook fails to mention this 'Neapolitan' practice.[33] There are other
'characteristic' practices which appear in most accounts of Naples. The
rituals surrounding the cult of San Gennaro, for instance, are also used as
examples of the superstitious character of the Neapolitans.[34] And, when
not observing the religious processions of the Neapolitans, the Grand
Tourist is urged not to miss the presentation of the *cuccagna* by the
king, a scene which is often depicted in the engravings and paintings of
the period.[35] The savagery with which the hungry multitude attacked the
enormous float made up of food and live animals was curiously savoured
by the guidebook writer, and certainly his readers. The example of the
Neapolitan mob in front of the *cuccagna* provoked the indignation of
the travellers and served to confirm the stereotype of the *lazzaroni*, which
was becoming increasingly elaborate.

For the eighteenth-century writer and traveller, the characteristics of
the *lazzaroni* outlined above, in fact, corresponded to those shared by all
peoples of a southern climate. Making a connection between climate and
particular human characteristics was not new – one need only think of
Hippocrates or Bodin – but in the eighteenth century it was given greater
weight in order to explain national differences, in particular in relation
to kinds of government.[36] The enormous influence of Montesquieu's *The*

Spirit of the Laws, first published in 1748 and one of the most influential books of the Enlightenment in Europe, contributed to the popularization of the climatic theory in relation to the development of different societies.[37] Montesquieu claimed that people of a colder climate tended to be industrious and orderly while those of a hot climate tended to be lazy and chaotic. These characteristics determined by climate had obvious political consequences, for example the need for strong government in hotter climates, and this theory contributed to Montesquieu's general premise that laws and institutions should be relative to these differences in character created by the natural effects of climate.[38]

This climatic theory incorporated a strong determinist component which allowed little room for the possibilities of change in societies, other than that determined by physical factors.[39] In fact, Montesquieu found it difficult to see beyond the limits of his theoretical framework in his description of the *lazzaroni*, during his two-week stay in Naples while travelling in Italy in 1729 and almost twenty years before the publication of *The Spirit of the Laws*.[40] While recognizing the beauty of the Bay of Naples, he had little positive to say about the city, especially when compared to Rome.[41] The *lazzaroni*, he wrote, 'have nothing in the world,

Vue de l'intérieur de l'Eglise Cathédrale de St. Janvier à Naples, prise dans le moment du Miracle de la Liquefaction du Sang, from Abbé de Saint-Non, *Voyage pittoresque. . .*

Fleuron *depicting 'La Fête de la Cocagne'*, from
Abbé de Saint-Non, *Voyage pittoresque. . .*

neither land nor skills (*industrie*); they live on grass; they are not dressed,
wearing only trousers (*culottes*)'.[42] Like most visitors, he also did not
fail to mention the superstitious nature of the people, after having gone
twice to see the liquefaction of the blood of San Gennaro.[43] To be fair,
Montesquieu made some attempt to understand the economic conditions
and the historical circumstances which had brought such a large proportion of the population to such misery.[44] Nonetheless his description
of the *lazzaroni* fell into the usual stereotypes of laziness and languor.[45]
Montesquieu concludes that the people of Naples are 'more like the
people than any other':[46] the *lazzaroni* of Naples did not simply represent
the essence of the Neapolitan nation, but the distillation of the defining
characteristics of the common people in any society.

Naples was as far south as Montesquieu would ever actually travel in his lifetime. While he had read about other hot climates, like the Indies, his experience in Naples is of special significance. When he was writing *The Spirit of the Laws* years later, the people of Naples must have served as his model not only of the common people generally but, more importantly, of people in a southern climate where a strong authoritarian government would be necessary to curb the natural instincts of its populace.[47] It was the vulgarization of this theory which made its way into the guidebooks of the later eighteenth century. In this way, travellers' views informed theories and then the theories substantiated prejudiced observation.

One example of how the effects of a hot climate increasingly acted as an interpretative framework for the state of the *lazzaroni* was Richard de Saint-Non's *Picturesque Voyage*.[48] A well-known account of the 1780s, it did much to introduce Europeans to the rest of the kingdom outside of Naples, while hardly straying from previous interpretations of the poorest inhabitants of the capital. This geographical expansion for the Grand Tour was barely accompanied by a corresponding interest in understanding the political and economic background to the kingdom's problems. Using the scientific language of the time, Saint-Non wrote of dilating nerves and fermentation of the blood to explain the violent passions and indolence of Neapolitans. While careful not to deny the universal nature of man, much proclaimed by enlightened writers and to be revealed by travel, Saint-Non admits that climate does have indirect repercussions on character.[49] For Saint-Non, the most characteristic trait of the Neapolitan nation, laziness, could be explained by the hot climate of southern Italy.[50] While most clearly manifested in the *lazzaroni*, this characteristic was shared in varying degrees by all Neapolitans, and the nobility served as a perfect example for guidebook writers.

The inconsequential and disinterested lives of the Neapolitan nobility in their luxurious palaces were a perfect contrast to the way the poor lived in the streets of Naples. The juxtaposition of these two extremes, embodied by the *lazzaroni* as Misery and the nobility as Luxury, made the city even more compelling as theatre. Like the misery of the poor, the excesses of the nobility appear in all accounts and are seen as symptomatic of a southern society.[51] The indolence of the poor corresponded to the indifference of the ruling elite and with obvious political consequences. Furthermore, the consequences for the intellectual life of the city were also clear to writers such as Lalande – and, once again, the determining factor of climate plays a part. Lalande writes:

There are not as many men of letters in Naples as in Rome or in other cities of Italy; there is not enough emulation. This city has been nicknamed *Otiosa* [or idle], because the effect of the climate, the fertility of the soil, and the indifference of the government have always contributed to making the Neapolitans indolent. Nevertheless there would have been greater activity if the heat of the climate had not prevented more application and work.[52]

This passage clearly reflects the extent of the interpretative force of climatic theory in late eighteenth-century guidebooks, and it was this attitude which particularly riled critics in Naples who were desperate to distance themselves from the stereotype of the indolent Neapolitan, a response which reveals the ambiguities and contradictions of being Neapolitan and being part of a cosmopolitan elite in the eighteenth century.

While contemporary interest in Italy was reduced to what were to become commonplace descriptions, Neapolitan intellectuals were becoming increasingly aware of, and writing about, the need for reform in the Kingdom of Naples.[53] For most travellers the existence of the *lazzaroni* was conventional confirmation of the characteristic indolence of a southern climate. For Neapolitan reformers, they were symptomatic of the economic and social problems of the city. In 1763, the same year that Pilati's book on the reform of Italy was published, Naples and outlying provinces were hit by a famine, the extent of which reinforced the need to address urgently the social and economic problems of the city.[54] The call for reform was led by Antonio Genovesi, who had consistently urged practical solutions to the problems of the kingdom in the 1750s and 1760s, and who was teacher and mentor of the later generation of Neapolitan reformers.[55] While the famine may have brought these problems into sharper focus, there was a long-standing intellectual tradition which had identified a history of weak government as the origin of many problems in the Kingdom of Naples. For many political writers, even before the arrival of the new king Charles of Bourbon in 1734, which is the conventional starting point of studies of the Neapolitan Enlightenment, the absence of a resident king under the Spanish viceregal government for two centuries and the competing powers of the Church and the feudal nobility within the kingdom were the keys to this political weakness. And, by the last half of the eighteenth century, enlightened programmes for reform were particularly critical of the role of the feudal nobility in hindering the development of effective government in the kingdom.[56]

Not surprisingly, the effects of climate which were so central to the interpretations of guidebook writers hardly entered contemporary

Neapolitan works of jurisprudence and history dedicated to reform in the kingdom. The disparity between how travellers saw Naples and how Neapolitans understood the city are clear in the response of Neapolitans to the interests of travellers and to the guidebooks which had determined those interests. Ferdinando Galiani, a Neapolitan who observed the arrival and activities of the travellers and who later, more than any other Neapolitan of the eighteenth century, would bridge the worlds of Paris and Naples, wrote to a friend in 1753 'on the manner in which most foreigners travel' to Naples.[57]

They come to a city in which the government, its characteristics, and the political system are the only interesting things which merit study, and yet they do nothing but see a few bricks and bits of marble at Pozzuoli and Portici, a few smouldering rocks at the Solfatara and the Vesuvius, a day at San Martino, a night at the theatre and in eight days they have dispatched with everything. In this way they inform themselves of a city of four hundred thousand souls, which is unique in Italy, and perhaps in the world, which for two thousand years has never breathed the air of liberty, and which has changed its master more often than any other city on this earth [...].[58]

Galiani wrote this letter when the reform movement under Genovesi's leadership was at an early stage. Nonetheless, it clearly reflects the native intellectual tradition which had recognized the need for political reform. Above all, it represents the concern of Neapolitans about the way in which Naples was seen and experienced by foreign travellers. While Galiani had expressed his concerns in a private letter to a friend, by the 1780s similar sentiments were expressed publicly in printed works by Neapolitan critics.

Very few studies of the Grand Tour in Italy have considered the reaction and response of those communities which were 'travelled to' in the eighteenth century. Most have tended to focus on the travellers, mainly French and British, their guidebooks and changing vision of Italy.[59] The first half of this article outlined the framework through which travellers 'saw' Naples, in order first to establish what Neapolitan critics were responding to, but also to show how their response shared many of the same cultural assumptions and even aspirations of the guidebook writers, particularly in relation to the *lazzaroni*. The second half of this article will show the native writing back, a process which Marie Louise Pratt has described as 'autoethnography', by which 'the colonised subjects undertake to represent themselves in ways which *engage with* the coloniser's own terms'.[60] Although the colonial contexts she describes are fraught with different kinds of moral anxieties, a comparison with European travellers to the southern edge of Europe offers an important insight into the existence of a centre and periphery, between north and south, in Europe.[61]

French travellers and the Neapolitan intellectuals shared ostensibly the same culture – with Christ and the Romans at its centre and the language and arguments of Enlightenment at its edge. But, despite the shared cultural framework, the Neapolitans are 'orientalized', depicted as the Other, (to use a contemporary expression) in the guidebooks. The Neapolitans as southern Europeans become an Other within Europe, but interestingly one with the means to reply. The Neapolitan response to this northern European representation could not but be written from within the same culture which was busy framing them as lazy and debauched. Neapolitan critics had to manoeuvre carefully between the language and concepts which they shared with the travellers who 'orientalized' them and their desire to represent themselves accurately to the northern European. The Neapolitan response was at once tempered by indignation at perceived misrepresentation and by the need to portray Neapolitan society as different, with particular problems which had developed from particular political and social contexts. The need to recognize these differences, encouraged by Genovesi and incorporated into the later reform programmes, in fact strikes at the heart of the universalist assumptions of enlightened cosmopolitanism.

So, while ever greater numbers of Grand Tourists flocked to Naples, accompanied by the second and various pirated editions of Lalande's guidebook of the 1780s, Neapolitan intellectuals – students of Genovesi such as Gaetano Filangieri, Francesco Mario Pagano and Giuseppe Maria Galanti – participated in the debates of enlightened communities across Europe, writing critiques of and reformulating ideas from works such as Montesquieu's *Spirit of the Laws*, publishing their own works and translating French, British and German works into Italian. It was this kind of dialogue or exchange of ideas, in journals, academic discourses and books across national and linguistic boundaries, which characterized the cosmopolitan nature of the enlightened movement in Europe. This dialogue extended to the critiques of the French guidebooks, at a time when Neapolitans themselves were addressing the very political and social problems of the city identified by the guidebooks.

A reader of the many journals published in Naples in this period cannot fail to notice the name of Michele Torcia (1736–1808), an archivist and librarian for the Bourbon government as well as a member of the Royal Academy. Most of his articles are reports about various archaeological findings in the Kingdom of Naples – a coin in Calabria, for instance, or traces of a Roman cult of fertility in popular festivals in Apulia.[62] While these writings reveal a provincial antiquarian at work at the end of the eighteenth century, Torcia's interests were in fact much wider as he actively participated in the central debates of the enlightened movement.[63] Less well known outside Naples than his more gifted contemporary, Filangieri, Torcia had in fact travelled much more, having been appointed as secretary to the Neapolitan Legate to Holland in 1762 and having spent some time in London several years later.[64] Torcia returned to Naples in 1770, convinced of the importance of the particular historical and cultural identity of the Kingdom of Naples and critical of the way in which foreigners had depicted its inhabitants. This patriotism, as Anna Maria Rao has shown, did not represent a close-minded provincialism, but rather, after years of residence in two of the most intellectually stimulating communities in Europe, an awareness of the need to address the particular problems of the kingdom combined with an openness to foreign models for reform, such as the government of Maria Teresa of Austria.[65] Torcia expressed this patriotism, above all, in his critique of contemporary guidebooks to Naples.

In 1783, Torcia published anonymously a 300-page work entitled *Appendix Containing a Brief Defence of our Nation against the Accusations of Several Foreign Writers*.[66] Although at times almost unreadable for its chaotic organization and difficult rhetorical style, the *Appendix* was the first comprehensive contemporary criticism of French, English and German guidebooks to Naples, including the works of Richard and Lalande. In the annotations to his translation of an English work on commerce in 1775, Torcia had already signalled his displeasure with the role foreigners assigned to climate in accounting for the problems of Naples.[67] For Torcia, as for his Neapolitan contemporaries, it was above all the particular history of the kingdom which had brought its government to such political and economic weakness, and, in the *Appendix*, he berates those writers who could not see beyond the effects of climate as an interpretative framework.[68]

In defence of Italians and in particular Neapolitans, Torcia answers many of the charges made against them by guidebook writers as 'ignorants, assassins, . . . traitors, pederasts, . . . predatory charlatans, . . . [and] buffoons'.[69] It was in part the writers' lack of direct experience in Naples which allowed them to fall into the interpretative trap of such stereotypes. He ridicules, for instance, Lalande's account, as an example of Neapolitan barbarity, of the castration of young boys which, he thinks, implies that in Naples there are shops with signs outside advertising, 'Here we do castrations'.[70] Such an obvious exaggeration could not have come from direct observation of the native inhabitants and Torcia, in response, expresses his doubts about the length of Frenchman's stay in the city, a common criticism which was usually followed by accusations of writers simply copying other accounts of places they had not visited themselves.[71] Lalande, he concludes, may be a great astronomer but he is not much of an observer of the customs of Italy.[72] And, even when writers such as Lalande have travelled to Naples, they fail to see parallels with their own countries. For example, on the renowned superstition of the Neapolitan people and their veneration of San Gennaro, Torcia asks whether the Parisians' devotion to their patron saint is any different.[73] What makes Torcia's critique interesting is his recognition of the guidebooks writers' desire to differentiate themselves from the Neapolitans and in order to do so, their need to emphasize those characteristics of the people – passion, indolence and ignorance – which more effectively portray the Neapolitan as less civilized. In this way, they also have to deny the existence of intellectual activity in Naples. It was this misrepresentation in particular which Neapolitan intellectuals such as Torcia attempted to rectify.

Torcia described the 'literary intolerance' of foreign guidebook writers, contrasting the supposed 'enlightened' reputation of many of the authors with the obvious prejudices of their accounts.[74] And it was the enlightenment of the Neapolitans which Torcia and others had to defend. The guidebook writers had failed to recognize not only the validity of the activities of the intellectual community in Naples but also the contribution of Neapolitans to the enlightened movement in Europe.[75] In this defence, Torcia was not alone. Pietro Napoli-Signorelli, in his *On the Culture of the Two Sicilies* of the 1780s, dedicated five volumes and various supplements to the intellectual and artistic accomplishments of Neapolitans in the past as well as in his own century.[76] Napoli-Signorelli, like Torcia, had spent many years abroad in Madrid, where he translated French plays into Spanish, including the works of Voltaire, and where he wrote his own plays.[77] On his return to his native city in 1784, he became the secretary of the Royal Academy in Naples and continued to correspond with Enlightenment figures across Europe. Napoli-Signorelli's work therefore reflected the heightened patriotism of Neapolitan writers of the period, which in turn demanded the recognition of the unique qualities of Neapolitan history and culture – what Napoli-Signorelli and others described as '*napoletanità*'.[78] His work was not simply a local history but an attempt to weave the achievements of Neapolitans within a broader European context beyond the confines of the city. Napoli-Signorelli expected the same approach from contemporary foreign writers – to acknowledge the distinctive qualities of Neapolitan culture and history while recognizing the sharing of a common cultural foundation.[79] When discussing Lalande's guidebook, Napoli-Signorelli asks, 'Why is it that even the most ENLIGHTENED foreigners when confronted with their own knowledge and evidence maintain constantly the same national prejudices which they acquired in the milk of their wet-nurses?'.[80] For this Neapolitan writer, it is above all their enlightened condition that should allow foreigners to see beyond the static frameworks handed down to them by their particular national perspectives.

While Napoli-Signorelli's belief in Enlightenment led to disappointment, another Neapolitan writer, Carlo Vespasiano, saw through the veneer of enlightened rhetoric to reveal chronic cultural intolerance, particularly among the French. Vespasiano, provoked by the misrepresentation of Naples and encouraged by the patriotism of his contemporaries, extended his critique of French travel writers over two decades, choosing the most famous of them, Lalande, as the focus of his ire. Vespasiano, who had been secretary to the Neapolitan embassy in Paris and who had written an essay in defence of Italian poetry in 1769 in the influential *Journal des Scavans*, returned to an attack against Lalande fifteen years later in Naples.[81] Vespasiano's criticisms were published in a series of four letters (two of which were addressed to the guidebook writer) in the *Scelta miscellanea*, a Neapolitan journal edited by a group of prominent young intellectuals which during its short but vibrant life reflected the enlightened patriotism of the reform movement in Naples.[82]

While Torcia's work had discussed many of the guidebooks written in the period, Vespasiano focused his attention on the sixth volume of Lalande's *Voyage*, the one specifically concerned with Naples or, as Vespasiano remarks, *mia patria*.[83] The first two letters by Vespasiano on modern travellers describe with humour the disparity between Lalande's account of the city and the reality. The later letters, addressed to Lalande, highlighted more seriously the paradox that a city which most travellers saw simply as a paradise of earthly delights or a hellish vision of popular anarchy also harboured an active intellectual community. Vespasiano's critique, in particular, then centred around the French writer's observations on the paucity of intellectual life in Naples.[84] In response to Lalande's highlighting of the ancient nickname of *otiosa*, or idle, for Naples, Vespasiano writes that the city should in fact be called *dotta*, or scholarly, for all the important intellectuals who reside there.[85] As proof, Vespasiano concludes his letters with an account of the accomplishments of Neapolitans in history and suggests that Lalande himself could have consulted Napoli-Signorelli's work in order to write a more accurate account of contemporary Naples.[86]

For Vespasiano, Lalande's account reflected generally the attitudes of French travellers to Naples. In the *Scelta miscellanea*, he specifically rejected the climatic determinism popularized by Montesquieu, through which Lalande and his readers 'saw' and understood the city and its inhabitants. He ridiculed the suggestion that the hot climate had prevented intellectual excellence in Naples and noted that it was as hot in southern France (where Montesquieu had his estate) as it was in southern Italy.[87] Although the climatic theory provided French travellers with a scientific rationality for the apparent chaos which surrounded them, Vespasiano recognized that there was something else which prevented the French from seeing beyond these stereotypes. Their ability to see and understand was also limited by contemporary French cultural prejudices, reflected in the guidebooks, which placed the Neapolitans on the edges of Europe of which the centre was undoubtedly Paris. Vespasiano accused French travel writers, above any other nationality, of fables, falsehoods and insults when writing about Naples. Paraphrasing Rousseau, he wrote: 'Of all the people of the world, the Frenchman travels the most, but full of his own customs, he confounds and looks down upon that which is not similar.'[88] Once again the supposed association of travel and Enlightenment is contrasted with the obvious cultural intolerance of the French – a continuing theme in the Neapolitan critiques.

It was this sense of cultural superiority which Vespasiano was targeting, now as fifteen years earlier. Italians and Frenchmen alike had recognized the pre-eminence of Italian culture in the Renaissance (although ancient Rome was often considered a common heritage for all Europeans and not particularly Italian, except for the Italians), but French writers claimed the eighteenth century as their own. Italian critics like Vespasiano and Torcia were pushed to defending the 'national genius' of their own countrymen and had to respond in kind, that is, with more accusations of plagiarism. A common riposte by Neapolitan critics was to accuse Montesquieu of having read and been influenced by the work of the Neapolitan philosopher Giambattista Vico, the *Scienza nuova*, or *New Science*, without acknowledgement.[89] This Neapolitan accusation of French plagiarism struck at the very heart of the corpus of the French Enlightenment. (In fact, this accusation has remained in Italian historiography until the twentieth century. When Montesquieu's diaries of his travels to Italy were found and published in 1894, Italian historians were not surprised to find a short note reminding himself to buy a copy of the *New Science* on his arrival in Venice. Although it is almost certain that, in the end, Montesquieu never had access to Vico's book, the accusation of plagiarism has not disappeared entirely.)[90] The nature of this debate only reinforced ideas of national difference and polarized the enlightened cultural community.

Significantly, this dialogue of difference took place within the enlightened forum of the literary journal. So it was through one of the central mechanisms in the construction of a wider cosmopolitan community from the seventeenth century in Europe, the literary journal, that the ideology of cosmopolitanism was challenged and began to fracture at the end of the eighteenth century. It was also through the literary journal that Vespasiano's voice was heard, getting a direct response from the object of his criticism. When the *Scelta miscellanea* letters were published in 1784, the editor claimed that Lalande had taken into account Vespasiano's criticism and would include the corrections in a new edition.[91] The second edition appeared two years later in 1786 and Lalande thanked Vespasiano, among others, in the new preface for his suggestions.[92] Lalande responded to Vespasiano's criticisms with twenty pages of additions and corrections in the second edition. In fact, Naples was the only Italian city in the seven-volume *Voyage* to merit such revision. This demand for 'correction' of the vision of the French when writing of Naples was not unique – although such a response certainly was.[93] These criticisms also extended to the *Encyclopédie* itself, one of the central vehicles of the Enlightenment in Europe.[94]

Thus Neapolitans actively criticized the conventional and seemingly irrepressible representations of Naples, criticisms which were often incorporated into later accounts. Critics on the 'edge' of Europe were speaking out and to the 'centre' through the central mechanisms of the Enlightenment – often in French – as participants in the cosmopolitan enlightened community of the eighteenth century. Increasingly, however, Neapolitans were not only responding to the centre but attempting to construct their own centre from which they questioned the cosmopolitan underpinnings of the Enlightenment in Europe and from which, more importantly, they addressed the particular problems of the Kingdom of Naples.

The cultural revival at the end of the century brought the writing of new histories, such as Napoli-Signorelli's work, with Neapolitans and their achievements at the centre.[95] These new histories brought a historical awareness of the origins of contemporary problems, an awareness from which reform programmes could be implemented. One of the most ambitious contributions to this reform project was Giuseppe Maria Galanti's *New Historical and Geographical Description of the Two Sicilies*, which was published between 1786 and 1790.[96] Galanti, a follower of Genovesi, had been funded by the Bourbon monarchy to do his own 'Grand Tour' and to describe each of the regions of the Kingdom of Naples.[97] Galanti was one of the fiercest and most active critics of the feudal system in the kingdom, and the geographical, demographic, economic and political information collected was to be the basis for a new programme of reform.[98] Although it could have been used to travel in an area little known by most Grand Tourists, the function of Galanti's *Description* was very different from that of guidebooks such as Lalande's.[99] The *Description* described in detail the actual state of this region of the kingdom and its inhabitants and attempted to go beyond the stereotypical descriptions of the French accounts (and also beyond the defensive claims of national genius of the Neapolitan writers). Although the *Description* lay outside these debates, only a few years later, in 1792, Galanti wrote his own guidebook to Naples, employing the kind of rhetoric and arguments found in his earlier works advocating reform.

The preface to Galanti's *Brief Description of Naples and Surroundings*, originally published as an appendix to the *Description*, places it clearly within (and against) the tradition of travel guides to the city.[100] The editors accuse previous guidebook writers of inaccuracy when describing the city. Lalande's *Voyage*, they write, is the book of a 'philosopher' and not an accurate writer; in any case, he relies on the descriptions of others, like most foreign writers, copying passages out of previous accounts and ensuring 'extreme inaccuracy'.[101] This guidebook, they promise (as most do in the introductions), will be different.

This certainly does not seem to be the case in the first few pages of Galanti's guidebook in which he describes the beautiful setting and mild climate of Naples and the bay (using such tired expressions as '*ridente cielo*'). Galanti goes even further than this, establishing once again the connection between climate and the character of Neapolitans as inescapably pleasure-loving.[102] If the first four pages of the guidebook were all the traveller had time to read, his or her immediate impression of Naples would have been much like that created by contemporary paintings and engravings of Neapolitans dancing under the warm sun. On further reading, however, this guidebook offered an alternative

Pietro Fabris, *Napolitani mangia Macaroni*, from *Raccolta di
varii Vestimenti ed Arti del Regno di Napoli* (Naples, 1773).

version of Neapolitan society rarely depicted in contemporary guidebooks. The usual descriptions of sites to see were included, but interspersed
between them were invectives against the Church, the Spanish and the
nobility.[103] Although the first few pages may be misleading, Galanti
manages to translate some of the central concerns of the reform movement in Naples into the format of the guidebook (and consequently to a
much larger audience).[104]

The characters of Luxury and Misery have a role in Galanti's guidebook but not as the exaggerated and lifeless caricatures of other accounts.
He not only links them (rather than just simply contrasting them) but
places them within the specific historical and social contexts of the
Kingdom of Naples. The lifestyle of the nobility, for instance, can only be

understood within the context of feudal system and linked clearly to the misery of the poor. Galanti writes: 'All is decorated with opulence and all is sustained by the hands of the miserable and sad cultivator'.[105] The political problems of the kingdom, often noted by observers, are similarly linked in Galanti's guide to specific contexts and traditions – in particular, the frequent changes of government over the centuries had brought overlapping and contradictory legal systems and, in turn, weak royal government.[106] These were the themes which dominated the debates of Neapolitan reformers in this period, the writings of whom he includes in a long section on intellectual traditions dealing with these problems (certainly in response to Lalande's depiction of the poverty of intellectual life in Naples).[107] Galanti recognized that the tourist, or, in his words, the 'spectator', was probably more interested in the customs of the Neapolitans (and in particular the *lazzaroni*) than in the political problems of the kingdom and any attempts to solve them. For Galanti, however, the political and historical background which he provided was essential to understanding that customs 'are as much the work of constitutional laws as of the climate'.[108] While not entirely breaking the force of the climatic theory as the explanatory framework from which to understand the social problems of the Kingdom of Naples, Galanti incorporated one of the primary concerns of contemporary Neapolitan debates – the need for legislative reform – into his guidebook for tourists.[109] In this way, Galanti satisfied a foreign interest in the actual conditions of southern Italy with a guidebook which reflected, more accurately than French guidebooks, both the intellectual vitality and the social complexity of Naples.

Galanti's place was problematic, on the edge of Europe in a cosmopolitan century – trying to find solutions to the problems of Naples, but within a culture of reform dominated by the French. His desire to go beyond the commonplace descriptions of Naples and Neapolitans found in the guidebooks carried by French travellers was in part limited by his need to distance himself from those Neapolitans, the *lazzaroni*, who defined *napoletanità* for foreign observers, both positively and negatively. He understood the language of climatic determinism – in fact, he could not escape it entirely when describing his poorer *concittadini* – but at the same time was well-versed in the intellectual traditions of Naples, which identified the poverty of the *lazzaroni* as a long-standing historical problem. Galanti was struggling to remain cosmopolitan in an increasingly patriotic age. His criticism of Lalande, for instance, included the accusation that he was in the end 'too patriotic' – confirming Napoli-Signorelli's suspicious attitude towards the self-proclaimed cosmopolitan credentials of the French.[110] However, the Neapolitan elite was caught, in particular, between their refusal to be travelled to as the Other of the Enlightenment and the necessity of recognizing the economic and political gap that separated their nation from France and England, a recognition which in effect was implicit in their very desire to be part of that Enlightenment.

Observations coloured by what was perceived as French prejudice, such as those found in French guidebooks or the *Encyclopédie*, provided Neapolitans such as Torcia, Napoli-Signorelli and Vespasiano with the opportunity to trumpet the accomplishments of Neapolitans and to place Naples and Neapolitan intellectuals within the European Enlightenment. Each of these writers had participated in the enlightened community as translators of foreign works, as travellers themselves, through their acquaintance with foreign visitors, and through their membership in academies outside of Italy. Their attempts to correct the vision of European readers about Naples also corresponded to a cultural revival in the city in the same period. The new sense of patriotism or *napoletanità* in the last decades of the eighteenth century revealed a fundamental contradiction within the cosmopolitan ideal of Enlightenment. While Lalande was able to recognize his mistakes and even correct them as part of a cosmopolitan exchange, the intolerance of French travellers towards other cultures such as southern Italy did not disappear. This period instead saw the emergence of the study and celebration of differences between cultures within Europe.[111] It is then paradoxical that the increasing popularity in the eighteenth century of the Grand Tour, which at one time was considered an important vehicle for the sharing of cosmopolitan culture in Europe, contributed to the breakdown of the cosmopolitan vision which it had helped to create.

6

Precision and Curiosity in Scientific Travel: James Rennell and the Orientalist Geography of the New Imperial Age (1760–1830)

MICHAEL T. BRAVO

> Those to whom the King had entrusted me, observing how ill I was clad, ordered a tailor to come next morning, and take my measure for a suit of clothes. This operator did his office after a different manner from those of his trade in Europe. He first took my altitude by a quadrant, and then with a rule and compasses described the dimensions and outlines of my whole body, all which he entered upon paper, and in six days brought my clothes very ill made, and quite out of shape, by happening to mistake a figure in the calculation. But my comfort was, that I observed such accidents very frequent, and little regarded.
>
> J. Swift, *Gulliver's Travels*, 1735
> (Penguin edn,1994, p. 175)

Jonathan Swift's satirical assault on the cultural assumptions of the eighteenth century takes aim not only at human and state corruption but also at the pretensions of the scientific spirit of his age. The tailor who takes Gulliver's altitude with a quadrant but produces very ill-fitting clothes reminds us that precision, as a means of describing and representing the world, is simultaneously rhetorical and open to irony. Swift's Gulliver is 'first and foremost a Scientific Traveller'.[1] As such he is both the vehicle of authorial criticism and an object of satire. In this guise he is the anti-hero to Captain Cook, whose training as a maritime surveyor underpinned his subsequent apotheosis as the god of explorers in the face of his encounters with the 'Other' in the Pacific: precise in his habits, calm in his judgment, dispassionate in temperament. Gulliver, like Orou, the priest in Diderot's satirical *Supplement to the Voyage of Bougainville*, challenged readers to question the judgments of monarchical, parliamentary and scientific authorities. These fictional characters, construed as a dissenting traveller and a Tahitian priest, respectively, used irony to expose the pretensions to certainty of enlightened travellers and their patrons.[2]

Swift and Diderot used the discourse of travel with its various appeals to curiosity, novelty, utility and natural law to invite their readers to question political authority. Today, they invite us to meditate on the conditions which enabled the many idioms of travel to resonate powerfully in eighteenth-century culture. Recently, for example, the received psychological portrait of Captain Cook has come in for close scrutiny: the Cook inhabiting our imaginations is a quiet, perceptive, perhaps even stern man, proper in conduct, unflinching in conflict, and yet humane in his leadership. What is the substance of this image of the heroic eighteenth-century explorer? Greg Dening and Gananath Obeyesekere have each recently shed light on the mythical construction of the explorer, the former bringing out the self-conscious conventions of theatre governing the stages of encounter, warfare and exploration, while the latter's fine-grained reading of the officers' journals reveals a level of violence which should cause us to question the longstanding reception of Cook as an icon of benign imperialism, enlightened rationality and 'the white man as god'. Similarly, the completeness of the received portrait of Sir Joseph Banks as Cook's heroic naturalist, typified by his passion for voyaging, collecting new plants and placing botany at the heart of gentlemanly science, has also been tempered by significant revisionist studies. Recent studies discussing Banks's place as a centrepiece of scientific imperialism, his cautious (if qualified) approval of slavery and his autocratic methods of running the Royal Society contribute to a much more complex picture of the man and, more generally, of late eighteenth-century science in Britain.[3] It is now plausible that his commitment to faithful pictorial representations of plants, to the institutional support of the learned scientific societies and to imperial networks makes him as much a champion of precision as Cook, though in a different sphere of expertise.

A history of precision and travel in the eighteenth century is nothing less than a history of the formation of the judgment of travellers and their patrons during the Enlightenment. Precision, I suggest, added a new, critical, and sometimes polemical, dimension to the language of travel; it made space for making differential judgments about the reliability of observations. In the eighteenth century, one sees the communities of naturalists, travellers, publishers and reviewers addressing this in part through the vocabulary of precision. This focuses our attention on the relationship between scientific curiosity on the one hand and precision on the other. These two qualities, inextricably associated with

Enlightenment, do not sit easily together. One reason is that we, as moderns, may be inclined towards a more trivial notion of curiosity, to oppose the creativity and serendipity of curiosity with the self-disciplined, narrow focus of precision. And looking back in time, they seem to possess substantially different social origins. Curiosity was a gentlemanly virtue, to be displayed in the natural history cabinets of collectors and in the salons of Royal Society gentlemen, for example. Until Banks made botanical recording the province of accuracy, this belonged more squarely in the world of instrument-makers, engineers, architects, artisans and astronomers.[4] The witnessing of experiments at the Royal Society in the time of Robert Boyle (who also wrote instructions for travellers) was carried out according to a strict division of labour between gentlemen witnesses and artisanal demonstrators, between the visible and the hidden. Perhaps the shared intellectual strand which binds us most forcefully to the image of Cook is precision, its association with advanced navigational tools, and its archetypal visual representation, the map.

The meanings of precision varied according to usage. Different meanings invited different kinds of comparison and, arguably, licensed multiple possible terms of reference. The terms 'precision' and 'accuracy' could refer to a person's habits of observation, their care and trustworthiness. Alternatively, if a traveller corrected the description of a place made by a previous traveller, the new description could be said to be more precise. Likewise, a measurement could be described as precise in contrast to a verbal description or another measurement. Moreover, the instruments with finely graduated scales used to make such measurements were evaluated as more or less precise. The authority of 'precise knowing' certainly owed much to the design and construction of the quadrants, sextants, chronometers and repeating circles in which materials were ever more finely harnessed towards perfection in their geometric division and measurement. The capacity of the term 'precision' to sanction authority in these multiple contexts provided it with considerable rhetorical force. Small wonder then that Swift found such delight in parodying those gentlemen who clothed themselves in the language of precision. The elasticity of the term lent itself to excessive usage. And yet it still retained specific, tangible meanings. For the scientific traveller, this rested on reliable habits of work.[5] For surveyors like Cook and his officers, the ability to hold an instrument steady – for example, steadying one's body to read the sun's altitude on a ship's deck driving through heavy seas – was acquired over many years of practice, as was the care to wind the chronometers regularly and evenly, to keep them at a near-constant temperature. Precision figured equally importantly in other kinds of work. The writing of a traveller's journal, attention to the conventions of description and expression, the invocation of appropriate critical terms such as 'accuracy', attested both to the credibility of observation and to the traveller's own credibility as a witness. In Cook's case, 'precision' served as an excellent epitaph both because it paid homage to the calibre of his specialized skills and because it testified to the moral virtue of his heroic apotheosis. In other words, precision had allusions to universal values, as well as personal qualities. For that reason, it played an important role in legitimating imperial travel, a theme I shall explore further below in my discussion of James Rennell, the surveyor–geographer whose dedication to precision placed him alongside Cook and Banks as icons of the British Empire.

These voyages of discovery raise some fascinating questions about the relationship between precision and cultural relativism. Was it necessary to possess accuracy in order to discern it among other cultures? Were Europeans gifted with precision as a unique instrument of Enlightenment and commerce, or was exactitude (as the Europeans conceived the term) discernible in the manners, customs and habits of other societies? Here travel literature as a collective European enterprise revealed the existence of other traditions of number systems, time, building and astronomy. The recognition that the artisans of Europe had furnished it with superior means to measure, describe and understand the globe was tempered by the classic Enlightenment doubts about the moral, economic and political price of this knowledge: corrupt monarchs and governments, the loss of innocence and, more bluntly, the draining costs to the treasury of maintaining empires. The recognition that accurate cartographic knowledge could be forthcoming from native informants, and that local navigational systems (e.g. those of the Polynesians) predicated on different principles could rival those of His Majesty's Royal Navy, contributed to the ferment of travel literature in overlapping with political discussions about a wide range of topics such as liberty, empire or colonialism. For travellers, the idiom of 'encounter' became widespread as a cultural means of framing the meeting between Europe and the rest of the world. The prominence given to travellers in the mythical image of a series of face-to-face encounters was a theatrical device for staging Europe's place in the globe.

Just as precision can be understood as a series of dispositions or attitudes, it is tempting to see it – especially in the context of Banks and the Royal Society – as a powerful force for domesticating 'Otherness', reigning in the thousands of newly discovered species of plants and animals, bringing the indigenous peoples of the Pacific into the regulated trading empires of European commerce. While that much is true, the institutions, techniques and conventions of precision in natural history and travel were diverse and varied, rather than homogeneous. The language, values and uses of precision were incorporated into travel literature as a revised set of standards, enlarging and reshaping the gentleman's critical language of veracity and propriety: they were sometimes implicit in the author's self-presentation and, in other instances, explicit in the form of objective judgments. This points to what may be the key problem of travel literature: to understand how knowledge is described, translated and transmitted across culture, time and distance. Clearly narrative techniques, ways of organizing and presenting data and statistics, were part and parcel of the use of the travelling experimental apparatus and the classificatory systems of natural history.

In the same period the conventions of travel literature change to accommodate new realms of observation. On the one hand there is no simple correspondence between what is written and what is observed. Absence in travel writing is a poor indicator of absence in fact. Certain topics, such as politics, were taken to be 'off limits'. Observations which were either too familiar or banal were also likely to be excised by the editor. On the other hand, it was increasingly common to find observations qualified using techniques of precision. For example, closer attention to aesthetics in journals owes much to the emerging patronage relationships in this period between artists (e.g. Paul Sandby) and surveyors like David Watson or naturalists like Joseph Banks, both of whom took artists on their northern tours of the British Isles. The place of tables of measurements in travel accounts was a sign not only of the possession of instruments but also of the serious scientific traveller. This triumvirate of surveyor, naturalist and artist (and its variations) laid the ground for future models of scientific travel and expeditions. Techniques of measuring, drawing and describing contributed to a common vocabulary of precision, a technology applicable throughout all the reaches of the empire. Where a traveller's narrative had once been a vehicle of witnessing other peoples and places, increasingly it became a key instrument of empire for describing, categorizing and mapping the world which it aspired to possess. In order to justify this claim, it is necessary to make some reference to the proliferation of forms and geographical contexts of travel. The need of imperial bureaucracies for experts like Rennell to oversee the use of a critical instrument such as (cartographic) precision, to function as an all-embracing meta-language to give or withhold sanction to information on different scales in different places, will then become more clear.

The relationship between curiosity and precision changes fundamentally in the course of the eighteenth century, and this is crucial for making sense of changes in the production and conventions of travel literature. Learned travel, once restricted to those aristocrats who could afford the Grand Tour, could be undertaken much more widely. In part, this was because it could be justified in terms of the disinterested value of scientific collecting, without the pretensions to gentlemanly status. All the same, travelling, collecting and participating in a growing range of natural history correspondence networks presented opportunities for acquiring social credit and social mobility. A corollary of this is that in thinking about natural history writers and their readers, one finds that the period eye of *virtuosi*, *curiosi* and *savants* acquired overlapping, but different, currencies.[6] Just as one can speak of different currencies of curiosity in the eighteenth century, so one can also differentiate new contexts of precision as a language of qualification and criticism in travel writing. Undoubtedly the rising popularity of travel in the eighteenth century and the growth of a variety of genres of travel literature are important. There are a number of factors at play here. The Grand Tour as a topic of writing became 'old hat'. New contexts of travel offered refreshing sources of novelty, particularly in the latter half of the eighteenth century. The tremendous growth of the travel literature industry accompanied the emergence of many new forms or styles of travel: Thomas Pennant's natural history 'tourist' travels through England and Scotland; Joseph Banks's inauguration of the naturalist's 'northern tour' beyond Staffa and the Highlands with his expedition to Iceland (1773); Edward Daniel Clarke's extension of a liberal education for his student Thomas Malthus, from the Grand Tour to the northern tour through Scandinavia and Russia; Ferdinand de Saussure's 1787 ascent of Mont Blanc equipped with a barometer – an expressly philosophical pursuit; the voyages of Cook, Malaspina and Bougainville, which institutionalized large-scale collaboration between gentlemen of science (botanists, mineralogists, astronomers and their artists) from the Royal Academies and the explorers and surveyors of the navies; Napoleon's integration of an army of scientists in his occupation of Egypt (*c.* 1800); the journey of Alexander von Humboldt (and Aimé Bonpland) to New Spain (1799–1803), during which he sought to redefine the relationship between the aesthetics of travel, guided by a vast array of portable precision instruments, and visual representations of natural history; Edward Sabine's voyages in the 1820s under the patronage of the Admiralty, chauffeured to the Greenland Seas and around the Atlantic Ocean to swing his seconds pendulum in the service of elite precision science.[7]

More recent studies of the techniques and conventions of eighteenth-century travel are no small way indebted to Bernard Smith's classic study *European Vision and the South Pacific* (1960), and it is worthwhile returning to it to recall the place of precision in his wider thesis. In addressing the century between 1760 and 1860 Smith set out to show the importance of collecting, measuring, drawing and painting in the course of voyaging to the South Pacific for the accumulation of a specifically, empirically based body of knowledge, which could provide a kind of evidence used by Darwin in his *Origin of Species* (1859). In suggesting that certain techniques of voyaging (including those of precision) were crucial in this regard, he was drawing attention to an emerging appreciation of empiricism on an unprecedented scale. Rather than linking this to similar developments in previous centuries, Smith chose instead to present it as a break with the past and put forward his argument in terms of Thomas Kuhn's notion of a paradigm shift with new flora and fauna from the South Pacific producing an ever-growing set of anomalies.[8] This realist part of his argument is often forgotten in the light of his skilful handling of the question of the 'noble savage' and issues of cultural relativism. Although we need not agree with Smith's commitment to Kuhn's model of the transformation of the physical sciences, three of his ideas in particular stand out for my argument: the role of Banks as a champion of accuracy in natural history, the growing accuracy among voyaging artists who drew and sketched for scientific purposes, and the importance of the South Pacific as a model theatre of enlightenment. Because of the relative efficiency and safety of oceanic navigation, it is here that Smith locates the crucial laboratory of precision. He shows for example how Alexander Buchan, the topographical artist, and Sydney Parkinson, the botanical artist, learned from each other's aesthetic conventions, each thereby acquiring new standards of accuracy and sophistication.

Perhaps one consequence of Smith's own scholarly preoccupation with the Pacific is that Cook's 'land-travelling' scientific colleagues have yet to receive comparable scrutiny from historians of science and travel. To argue that the great continents remained virtually unknown is to overstate the case. The reach of a global network of botanical gardens extended into 'continental' interiors, as for example in India and Nepal, or the

American colonies and Upper Canada. In this essay, I wish to take up Smith's thesis and examine it in the context of the continents where fundamentally different institutional forces were at play in the cultivation of the sciences in the same period. To make the question more manageable, I will focus primarily on the work of one individual, James Rennell (1742–1830), who played a key role in the expansion of geographical knowledge about Asia and Africa. Rennell's training as a maritime surveyor under Alexander Dalrymple (a rival candidate to Cook for the command of the *Endeavour* expedition) and his adaptation of maritime techniques to continental rivers provide an important link to Smith's study of the Pacific. Moreover, Rennell's reputation for accuracy eventually brought him into the company of Joseph Banks and the Fellows of the Royal Society, where he acquired a place in Banks's inner circle. In the course of discussing Rennell, I will show how his geographical work was interwoven with maritime science and Banks's 'learned empire' throughout his life. This may illuminate his understanding of precision, shed some light on its different forms and suggest further lines of enquiry provoked by Smith's insightful analysis of Pacific travel.

Rennell was Banks's contemporary and eventually became his *de facto* right-hand man in matters of travel. Their backgrounds however presented a striking contrast. Banks, born into wealth, used his fortune to finance and build his career as an elite naturalist around Cook's *Endeavour* expedition (1766–9); Rennell, raised by his mother in financially poor but otherwise supportive circumstances, began his career as a captain's servant in the Navy at the outset of the Seven Years' War and used his survey expeditions over the next fifteen years to acquire whatever financial security he could by saving. Banks encountered the peoples and flora of the Pacific and rewarded himself with extraordinary rich and diverse collections, whereas Rennell found himself, like many others, on station in India, searching for patronage in an empire awash with corruption. Banks, intellectually, could afford to look to Sweden in cultivating the disciples of Linnaeus (e.g. Daniel Solander) and adopting his bold, practical, taxonomic system for botany, whereas Rennell looked to Alexander Dalrymple, his hydrographer mentor in the East India Company, and later to France in adopting the systematic principles of criticism for ancient cartography used by the established and respected school of Guillaume Delisle (*d.* 1726) and, later, Jean Baptiste Bourguignon D'Anville (*d.* 1782).[9] Curiosity as experienced by Banks in the Pacific context was epitomized by a plenitude of new plant species and a moral freedom in the sexual mores of the Tahitians, whereas Rennell's curiosity took the form of self-discipline, the energy he put into his cartographic productions, and his political consciousness of anti-corruption and benign colonial administration, formulated during his formative years surveying in the East India Company's Bengal Engineers (1764–77).[10] Given that Rennell rose to the position of an authority on travel, first as Surveyor-General in the Bengal Engineers and subsequently in the Royal Society, it is worth exploring the basis for his inclusion in Banks's circle of *curiosi*. Rennell's life also has much to instruct us about the emergence of maps and cartographic criticism in travel and in the critical principles applied to reviewing the published works of travellers.

The cartographic memoir was Rennell's keystone for putting his ideas about precision into practice. This document's purpose was to bring accountability and transparency to the processes of digesting information. It made visible cartographers' 'rough work' and demanded that they disclose their sources, explain their rationales and distinguish between those aspects of a map which were demonstrably true and those interstitial spaces which were merely coincidental and empirically unsubstantiated. This required the adoption of a high standard of cartographic conventions of toponymy and source citation which learned travellers, armchair geographers and reviewers incorporated (some more, some less) into their repertoires. Rennell's cartographic procedures for precision and accuracy can therefore be seen as one particular solution to the long-standing, vexing problem of reliable communication between travellers and *savants*. Ignoring conventions of accuracy could invite censure from other travellers, editors, publishers and reviewers. Likewise travellers, surveyors and geographers could make judicious use of the vocabulary of accuracy to draw attention, if warranted, to a set of observations or to stress the singular care, methodical fidelity or certainty of the traveller.[11]

Of course Rennell's use of the cartographic memoir was not without precedent. Its didactic rhetoric and its expression of ordering the procedures of travel, rather than an unprecedented epistemological break, had roots in the tradition of 'Instructions to Travellers' which emerged in the course of Humanist reforms of the fifteenth century, spreading from Mediterranean countries to Germany, the Netherlands and Elizabethan England.[12] These 'Instructions to Travellers' were much more than a mere set of directions. They were 'in fact a new genre through which a new intellectual elite sought to teach Europeans how to see the world'.[13] Like contemporaneous discussions of method in subjects such as history, 'Instructions to Travellers' also marked 'the development of a meta-cultural discourse – a discourse on a discourse – by which the older

An engraving of James Rennell by A. Gordon.

practice became methodised – and *method* was, indeed, a key concept of this period'. [14] Between the time that Bacon wrote his essay of instruction *Of Travel* (1625) and Robert Hooke, the Secretary of the Royal Society, wrote his analysis of Knox's *Historical Relation of the Island of Ceylon* (1681), this distinctive rhetorical genre had been firmly established. These essays provide a common thread between maritime exploration and land travel. Bernard Smith cited Bacon's essay, with its emphasis on procedures such as keeping a journal and making topographical sketches, as a significant antecedent for European expansion in the Pacific 150 years later. [15] In this respect Rennell's surveys, his use of a basic set of navigation instruments, his topographical sketches and his journals were not unlike those of his brother officers on the oceans. One should recall that the Indian Ocean was his first school and that he effectively treated the river systems of India as special cases of mapping continental coastlines. To understand why Rennell was in a uniquely privileged position to survey the interior of India in this way, we must turn our attention to the political expansion of the East India Company in the decade preceding Cook's first voyage (1768–71).

EMPIRE AND COLONIAL ADMINISTRATION

The East India Company's significant role in the maritime exploration of the East Indies has been overshadowed by the acclaim granted to the grand voyages of the Royal Navy. Alexander Dalrymple, acknowledged as the most informed hydrographer in the British Empire, planned many of these lesser-known voyages in search of geographical knowledge and new markets. The Company's need to gather and collate information took on a new dimension with the advent of its territorial acquisition of Bengal following Clive's decisive victory at Plassey in 1757. This began the transformation of the Company from a trading empire whose operations were primarily located at ports on coastlines into a regional power-broker and policy-maker manipulating indigenous elites through a series of treaties and alliances. The Company's move from the littoral into the interior of India was mirrored by the deployment of its surveyors. They employed a team of Bengal Engineers to survey the principal river (and road) trade routes to secure information and to prepare the way for revenue surveys.

Rennell, instead of following coastlines, charted the interior littoral – the banks of the great rivers Ganges, Brahmaputra and Indus. Rivers and roads, the major inland trade routes, were mapped with a zeal commensurate with the Pacific voyages of discovery. During his time in India (1764–77), Rennell acquired the materials and experience for the works which he later published and used to establish his reputation: the *Bengal Atlas* and the *Atlas of Hindustan*.[16]

The demand for precision as a tool of colonial administration accelerated during the 'imperial meridian' (1780–1830), a term coined to describe a period in which the British repeatedly attempted to 'establish overseas despotisms which mirrored in many ways the neo-absolutism and the Holy Alliance of contemporary Europe . . . characterised by a well-developed imperial style which emphasised hierarchy and racial subordination, and by the patronage of indigenous landed élites'.[17] Journeys of exploration into the interior of the continents, riding the crest of the wave of colonial expansion, offered a select group of self-motivated individuals an opportunity to capitalize on new knowledge. Making striking and singular observations, collecting rare species, surveying new territorial acquisitions and codifying local knowledge held out the hope of further prospects: fortunes made in trading and the converting of expertise into an elevated social standing.[18] This reciprocal desire, either to return to Britain to settle in comfort or to accumulate wealth for a privileged life in the colonies, was an important feature of demographic and social mobility in this period. Rennell's career fits the former pattern of accumulating useful knowledge to petition the Company for a substantial pension. His honing of precise topographical analysis, knowledge and judgment placed his talents in great demand long after his retirement from official service.

AMONG ROYAL SOCIETY GENTLEMEN

Rennell eventually succeeded in his bid for a special Company pension and at the age of 35 settled in London. While exploring the Company's frontiers, his imagined community of travellers, surveyors and geographers sharing democratic, precise attitudes and practices had remained little more than imagination. His belief in benign imperialism and a free commerce in geographical knowledge, devoid of corruption, was at odds with the reality which confronted his surveys and brought him within a hair's breadth of losing his life. His correspondence from this period reveals that his survey team was widely regarded with hostility by the people inhabiting the peripheries of the company's territory and that he generally took a military escort for protection. While surveying Baar, a small province near Bhutan, Rennell was called away to assist a fellow officer in quashing an uprising. They soon found themselves surrounded (by Snyasi Fakirs, according to Markham), ambushed by 'two lines of them drawn up in the market place' [1766, Aug. 30], 'with not the least prospect of escaping'.[19] Rennell described the wounds which led to his permanent disability with characteristic precision. A sabre stroke through his right shoulder bone 'laid me open for near a foot down the back, cutting thro' and wounding several of the ribs'. At the left elbow, the 'muscular part was taken off to the breadth of a hand'. A 'stab in the same (left) arm and large cut on the hand . . . deprived me of the use of my forefinger', (a crippling injury in his profession).[20] In spite of his injuries, he stayed in India for ten more years, working with one or sometimes two assistants at his disposal, trying to accrue sufficient wealth to return to England.[21]

After he settled in London in 1778, Rennell's house in Suffolk Street became something of a landmark for travellers and geographical *savants*, effectively an annex to Sir Joseph Banks's study in Soho Square. He received visits and gave advice to such intrepid explorers as the Scottish surgeon Mungo Park, who went in search of the source of the Niger, and the English naval officer Thomas Ledyard, who some years after having accompanied Cook on his third voyage set out to walk across the Russian empire to the Pacific. Rennell and Banks together plotted many of the journeys that have since acquired the legendary, 'Boys' Own', status of British imperialism. This metropolitan position enabled Rennell to construct cartographic memoirs on a global scale by coordinating and delegating geographical research to other travellers. Never far away, whether in the context of his work with the African Association, his antiquarian activities in the Royal Society or his consultancy for the Navy Board, was the guiding hand of Banks, managing the machinery of science and empire.[22]

In an exploration of Rennell's position as an icon of precision, his work on antiquarian geography might seem out of place. It is worth keeping in mind the prestige enjoyed by Oriental scholarship and the comparative study of ancient and modern knowledge in language, mathematics, astronomy and law, as well as geography, in this period. Rennell, like William Jones (founder of the Bengal Asiatic Society, 1784), Charles Wilkins and Henry Thomas Colebrooke, went to India on colonial service. Through guidance from learned Hindu pundits, they discovered their primary sources. In the years following his move to London, Rennell came into contact with other Orientalist scholars and travellers whom he had rarely if ever encountered during his colonial service but who, like Rennell, had retired to the mother country. This movement from the colonies back to London created a concentration of scholarship which was specifically Asian, antiquarian, colonial and corrective. This last feature, the corrective or reformist quality of the work, links Rennell, Colebrooke, Jones and, more generally, the Calcutta scholars of the Royal Asiatic Society and illustrates the mutual attraction and common purpose of the circle in which Rennell moved. The Sanskrit studies of William Jones and Henry T. Colebrooke, for instance, were part of a wider administrative project to produce a carefully unified, precise digest of Hindu law from the many sources, historical and contemporary, available to them, as a conservative reform to the contemporary heterogeneous blend of Muslim and Hindu law.[23] Rennell's project was similarly situated among the moderns and the ancients and possessed a common spirit of accountable bureaucracy. Precise attitudes were implicitly prescriptive. In each case, the commitment to precision was a response to cope with a political environment in which contemporary life in India, whether the relations of Hindus to Muslims or the role of the Company, was perceived to be in need of some form of correction and regulation. In practice the Orientalists' advice was indispensable to Rennell, not least because he was unschooled in classical languages and relied for the most part on translations.[24]

Corrective and regulatory scholarship was however not limited to such colonial contexts as India. Although Bernard Smith rightly emphasized the novelty of Pacific flora, fauna and landscapes for European artists and audiences, he understandably took for granted the reliability of the sciences of navigation and astronomy. Government-sponsored precision projects such as measuring the transit of Venus with the aim of constructing more definitive longitude tables, or offering the Longitude Prize of £20,000, directed towards the improved keeping of time, are but two of the most famous examples. The longitude problem was not solved by triumphant discovery – that is only the popular myth of the story about the clockmaker John Harrison.[25] Instead it was a story of an enduring problem solved by a combination of incremental technical change and institutional reform: changing materials and constructions, restricted opportunities for official trials, and a Royal Navy fundamentally suspicious of carrying out research under its own auspices. Even in 1800, precision instruments such as charts were purchased privately at the expense of individual officers and were not included as a part of the Navy's commission.

The discourse of precision and standardization of measurement developed through the eighteenth century, most notably in the context of colonial and imperial surveys. Surveyors, bureaucrats and imperial elites such as Rennell and the East India Company could claim to possess a technology which surpassed anyone else's as a geographical measure. What had once been the traveller's narrative, witnessing and reporting, had become the precise instrument of imperial institutions for describing, categorizing and mapping the world. This impetus towards systematic mapping brought together gentlemen of science and military men in new institutional configurations. Some of the imperial doyens of precision in the outposts of empire returned to London to place their experience at the service of metropolitan science. Such institutions as the Royal Artillery School at Woolwich employed and trained men in the arts of precision and surveying. Following the conclusion of the Napoleonic Wars, the Royal Navy caught wind of scientific reform and increasingly offered its services in support of the Royal Society and, eventually, in cooperation with the British Association for the Advancement of Science (*f.* 1831)and the new scientific disciplines. This alliance between science and the state was consolidated, so that precision as a tool for the reform of navigation, weights and measures acquired value for the growing state's authority to

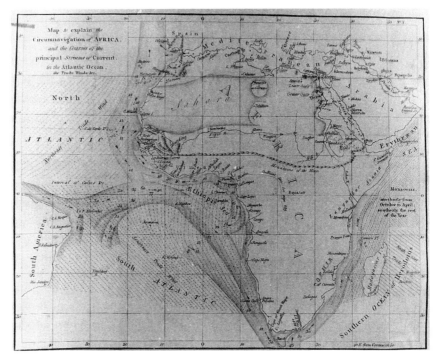

J. Walker, *Map to explain the Circumnavigation of AFRICA, and the Curses of the principal Streams of Current, in the Atlantic Ocean, the Trade Winds &c.*

represent the nation. As the possession and use of instruments became much more widespread, the elite carved out a niche for themselves as regulators of measurement. Whereas Rennell had made himself a regulator of cartography, the elite of nineteenth-century scientific officers distanced themselves from what they perceived to be ordinary or 'mere' geography, preferring internationally coordinated surveys using new and difficult kinds of precision measurement. In this era, the assumption that precision was guaranteed by instruments of measurement became much more pervasive, as did a certain arrogant disdain for qualitative judgments in general, and this has remained the case down to the present day.

THE PROCEDURES FOR ACCURATE TRAVEL

Thus far I have suggested that precision provides a common link between the settings of India and the South Pacific for understanding the relationship between science and European expansion. It worked as a vehicle for distilling knowledge in the diverse arenas of British imperialism, boiled down and represented through the essential sameness of the survey reports, the maps and the memoirs. For example, the precise techniques of maritime surveying and navigation were pivotal both in the development of the artists' techniques of sketching and painting on Pacific voyages and in the rigorous construction of cartographic representations in the course and the wake of Rennell's Indian surveys. Moreover, just as accuracy was encouraged to set new standards and techniques of representation when naval draughtsmen and botanic and ethnographic artists rubbed shoulders, so it was also productive when such surveyors of India as Rennell or Kater teamed up with such Orientalist *virtuosi* as Marsden (an expert on the Sumatran language) and Young (of Rosetta Stone fame) as experts on the national reforms to weights and measures. The reader may rightly feel that the meaning of precision and accuracy is being stretched to the limit by applying it to such different contexts as surveying and philology. Yet the term 'precision' acquired widespread usage in diverse branches of knowledge from the 1770s onwards. Whether or not these amounted to different meanings or merely different applications of some shared meaning is open to debate. The power of terms like 'accuracy' and 'precision' is really only comprehensible in the overall context of imperialism, by acknowledging the apparent contradiction between their widespread applicability to radically different contexts and their rhetorical specificity. The malleability of these terms was in part what permitted artists, surveyors and Orientalists, among others, to share a common language.

One area of ambiguity which can be clarified is the attribution of precision on the one hand to individual travellers' habits and on the other hand to a set of systematic principles. Or, in terms of travel literature, the appellation of accuracy might equally well be applied to an author as to the layout and organization of a travel narrative. Rennell's work was in part specifically aimed at showing how procedures for travel could be used to link personal habits to systematic knowledge. Rennell wrote and occasionally published treatises on techniques of travel to provide such a bridge. His essay on travel by camel published in the *Philosophical Transactions* (1791) of the Royal Society is a good example, but before examining it more closely I wish to show how Rennell's accuracy has been described both as a personal quality and as an attribute of his geographical system.

In the thirty years preceding his death in 1830 Rennell was widely regarded as Britain's foremost geographer, a claim made by Clements Markham, his principal (late nineteenth-century) biographer, and supported by my reading of his contemporaries' views of him. Rennell had earned the Royal Society's Copley Medal (1791), had enjoyed the esteem of Banks and other Royal Society luminaries and had been nominated, at the age of 88, to hold the first presidency of the Geographical Society (1830). Bearing in mind the characteristically Victorian (much more than eighteenth-century) tendency of biographers to credit intellectual labour to personal qualities, Markham's description of Rennell as the 'first great English geographer' is significant. It reflects a parallel between Rennell's social and intellectual mobility and the emergence of a coherent ideology of imperial geography in which systematic criticism and precision were central features. Markham eulogized Rennell thus:

James Rennell may not have been the father of English geography, but he was undoubtedly the first great English geographer. Much laborious work had to be done before geography became a science in this country. Materials had to be collected, instruments and projections had to be invented and improved, correct methods of criticism and accurate habits of thought gradually had to be established, before the work of the scientific geographer could commence.[26]

A command of the methods of precision was the valorization of imperialism: it justified the British Empire insofar as it could manage copious 'facts', to the extent that it could succeed in insulating questions about the legitimacy of precision from its everyday application. Again this begs the wider question: what conditions gave rise to precision being the mark of an imperial role model? The role of the cartographer or geographer, as Rennell saw it, was to fix the facts recorded by travellers within the framework of a system. Fixing facts required justification or qualification as to their source and reliability. Rennell introduced methods of criticism from his own field experience to establish rigorous cartographic principles, a meta-discourse governing the preparation of maps and charts. Applying these rules of precision to geographical domains beyond the application of instruments accorded them some generality, especially at those margins of empire where sources of information were least standardized and culturally most diverse. Implicit in this was an awareness that systems of geographical knowledge were open and subject to correction. The job of the geographer was not to have the final word or to close the complete system. Accuracy was not therefore a statement of closure, but rather an endorsement of the specifications of the sources and the relations between them. Accurate work was necessarily both historical, at least so as to be cognizant of previous observers, and forward-looking or progressive, in the sense of anticipating that future cartographers would require detailed memoirs in order to integrate, re-evaluate or calibrate new material.

The demand for transparency also implied an openness in terms of possible audiences. Rennell was concerned to lay bare the conditions of scientific travel, to make them as visible and accessible as possible to his audience of readers, navigators and cartographers – as well as to his patrons.[27] This reinforced certain wider developments in travel literature in the course of the 'imperial meridian': the importance attributed to criticism of travel literature in the popular reviews; the proliferation of maps to accompany travel narratives; the emergence of many new kinds of thematic distribution maps; and the gradual separation of travel narratives *per se* from ethnographic and commercial information, which was increasingly organized along encyclopaedic lines and moved into appendices.

The beginning of what was to become the Victorian 'imperial archive' had an important ideological component.[28] The introduction of critical methods of organizing ethnographic and cartographic information re-inforced the deracination of the landscape in travel literature. The absence of human activity, or culture, in the landscape as described in travel journals, such as John Barrow's *Travels in the Interior of Southern Africa*, served to reify the traveller's all-seeing, surveying eye. This com-plicity by absence has been called 'anti-conquest', although it may owe more to changing literary conventions and the reorganization of the contents of travel narratives than to the specific ideologies of imperialism. Nevertheless the identification of an 'imperial eye' takes in Rennell just as much as Barrow, who rose to become one of the chief reviewers of travel literature for the *Quarterly Review*.[29]

The paradigm of precision for Rennell lay at the intersection of the field and the library, or at the cross-roads of the habits of the individual traveller in foreign lands and the systematics of the cartographic memoir.[30] Rennell's treatises on techniques of travel can be seen as a continuation of the tradition of 'Instructions to Travellers' begun centuries earlier. The main distinction in the case of a treatise like the one on camel travel is its concern with precision itself: the methodology of travel rather than its actuality, its didactic and illustrative tone rather than an emphasis on the particular objects of description, and its dependence upon the imperial organization of travellers superseding the traveller's own narrative of his journey. In his essay 'On the Rate of Travelling, as Performed by Camels; and its Application, as a Scale, to the Purposes of Geography' (1791),[31] Rennell noted that the journals of desert travellers suffered from a general lack of astronomical observations with which to fix their routes, unlike scientific travellers on the oceans, for whom – given fair weather – measurements of latitude and longitude were comparatively routine. Quite simply, it was still more common and practical to carry instruments for great distances over sea than land. To understand why the speed of camels should deserve a place in the *Philosophical Transactions* is to recognize the importance attributed to the exploration and development of inland trade routes. In the absence of astronomical instruments, Rennell turned his attention to a mechanical system far more appropriate for the desert environment, namely the caravan.

Question: When is a camel like a well-lubricated machine? In the case of 'light and heavy caravans', concluded Rennell, 'in which the camels are left to pursue their journey quietly and at leisure; and with the regularity of a machine: and not that of the light camels, which are not only freed from encumbrance but are also urged on'.[32] Precision lay not in the constitution of the camel itself, but rather in its harnessing in the caravan system. Rennell's aim was to translate the speed of camels into reliable displacements for a map as part of his work on African geography. Travellers commonly described desert travel in terms of the elapsed time: some number of hours or days. Knowing the average speed of camels, together with their direction of travel, as well as their average variation from a straight line, would enable one to convert time into displacement. Camel travel

... serves to furnish a remarkably equal scale: the rate of the camel's movement appearing to be, beyond all others, the least variable; whether we examine it by portions of days, or of hours. In the present state of things, the former mode alone can be used; because few or none of the African travellers carry watches with them: but it may be hoped that at no very different period, the time employed on the road may be obtained with such a degree of exactness, as to furnish the geographer with materials of a far better kind.[33]

In this treatise, Rennell generalized about method on the basis of several of the many journals and records he had perused. He displayed the evidence, clearly identifying the sources, making his inferences verbally and graphically, and evaluating the degree of confidence that should be placed in their accuracy. Typically, he also singled out particular travellers, in this case giving 'Mr. Carmichael credit for much general accuracy',[34] because he has understood the circumstances in which camels behave with the regularity of machines, he has documented his measurements reliably and clearly in his journal, and he has shown foresight in taking steps to calibrate his journey between Aleppo and Bussorah in 1757. He 'determined to keep a register of the courses by a compass, and to compute comparatively, if not absolutely, the intermediate distance on each course; by counting the steps of the camel he rode, during a certain interval of time; and afterwards measuring a number of them on the ground'.[35]

TAKING PRECISION FULL CIRCLE

Precision and accuracy are generally recognized as crucial features of scientific travel in the eighteenth century, developing out of a long tradition of empiricism set out in earlier essays in this book. Some of the ingredients of precision are quite familiar: the use of exact instruments, the keeping of meticulous records, the development of new techniques of sketching, and the emergence of new forms for organizing substantial amounts of information in travel narratives. The historian's challenge may lie not in identifying instances of precision as much as in accounting for the ubiquity of precision, its valorization and its widespread acceptance as a meta-discourse. Explaining the meaning and significance of precision is necessary to understand scientific travel in the eighteenth century and should not simply be dismissed as a characteristic of 'the Enlightenment'. The relationship of precision to economics and politics deserves further attention from scholars of European imperialism and the sciences in the eighteenth century. A tendency to focus exclusively on precision in terms of the use of instruments has left the imperial context largely ignored and, as a result, has masked the importance of precision as a key issue in the history of travel: how to account for the representation and communication of a truly diverse range of places, sights, artefacts, dangers and methods of travel.

Instead, I have picked up on Bernard Smith's lead by emphasizing the cross-fertilization of ideas and techniques between travellers with different backgrounds and training to show how the language of accuracy and precision could be used in new genres of memoirs and treatises to scrutinize, combine, discard, evaluate, praise or criticize the scientific conduct and observations of travellers. Although this has not provided the final word on the meanings, uses or values of precision, it has allowed me to explain a wider range of meanings of precision, to connect them as cultural phenomena, and to relate the surveys and Oriental scholarship in India to the better-known voyages of discovery and botanical expeditions to the Pacific. Having emphasized the importance of maritime science for conceptualizing continental interiors, as for example with the great rivers of India, which Rennell based on modified ocean coastal survey techniques, it is appropriate to conclude by bringing the argument full circle, illustrating how continental river travel came to play a role in the mapping of the oceans.

Modelling a current 'as an ocean's river', Rennell hypothesized that such a river of water flowed from elevated ocean sources down its gradient to a lower part of the oceans, the river's mouth. This reversal of the direction of modelling between ocean and continent is of course a good example of metaphorical borrowing. More importantly still, it draws our attention to the limits of precision and its dependence on institutionalized cooperation. Although this pioneering imperial accomplishment – charting currents as though they were the oceans' rivers or canals – occupied Rennell on his return journey from India, the institutional conditions of sufficient cooperation between the Royal Society and the Navy only materialized during and after the Napoleonic Wars. By the early nineteenth century, the introduction of institutional reforms, including a certain amount of open debate in such sciences as geology, had left Rennell feeling remarkably despondent about the state of maritime science: 'there is no one department of practical Science that calls more loudly for reform, and this consideration ought to stimulate those whom it may concern; *that the lives of so many brave and useful men often depend on the mechanical perfection of this heavenly gift'.*[36] Opportunities for naval officers to carry out and publish hydrographical research were few and far between. Precision implied criticism and publishing implied public criticism. The Navy Board was adamant that scientific work should not interfere with prescribed survey duties. Some officers eagerly undertook current measurements, at Rennell's request, in what little spare time they had. Contributors to the *Naval Magazine* could voice their criticisms of navigation methods and regulations, and take broadsides at the Navy bosses, with less fear of censure where they published under pseudonyms. The resolution of the conflict between carrying out research into precision itself and the more immediately military priorities of mapping and fighting was worked out through a series of fundamental reforms to scientific and military institutions. That story belongs to a history of the construction of military-industrial states in the nineteenth century and the marshalling of scientific travellers in their service.

Rennell's position at the beginning of the nineteenth century was in this regard exceptional. Unconstrained by any commission from the Navy, and yet lacking any official access to their fleet and officers, he was granted special limited access to inspect log books (which complemented

his informal correspondence with the more scientifically oriented officers).
His methods of inspecting the logs were those of an antiquarian, using a
fine-toothed comb to search through thousands of pages of log books in
search of new traces of currents. To my taste, a most telling example of
the limits of precision at this time is that the most elegant and informed
description of the course of the Gulf Stream was to be found in Rennell's
comparative study of the ancient geography of *Herodotus*, corrected and
judged against his own, that of the moderns, as revealed through a minute
analysis of Navy logs.

7

'The Ghost in Chapultepec': Fanny Calderón de la Barca, William Prescott and Nineteenth-Century Mexican Travel Accounts

NIGEL LEASK

I

In April 1840 the historian William Hickling Prescott dispatched a new daguerreotype machine – one of the first batch to arrive in the United States from France – from Boston to his friend Fanny Calderón de la Barca in Mexico City. The 44-year-old, nearly blind historian had already been working for two years upon his *magnum opus*, *The Conquest of Mexico*, which was published three years later in 1843. Debarred from libraries and archives by his handicap, he had devised a writing machine or 'noctograph' which enabled him to write 'in the dark' without using up his scanty reserves of eyesight. Confined to his New England study, Prescott's access to the enormous body of scholarship relating to the conquest was in part dependent upon his correspondents in Spain, Italy, France, England and Mexico. The daguerreotype, as we shall see, was intended to open a window upon his exotic Mexican setting for the crepuscular historian, providing a form of collateral documentation for his evocative, romantic historiography.

The recipient of Prescott's daguerreotype machine, Fanny Calderón de la Barca, was the Scottish wife of the Argentinian-born Ángel Calderón de la Barca, first Spanish ambassador to the young Mexican republic, which had thrown off the Spanish colonial yoke in 1820 after a decade of bloodshed. Ángel's appointment as Spanish Ambassador to Mexico, the year after the couple's marriage, was a token of Spain's long-deferred official recognition of her former colony. Prescott had met the Calderóns while Ángel was serving as Spanish minister to the USA, and he had already assisted the historian in procuring documentation from the Spanish archives. Ángel had married Fanny Inglis in 1838; the daughter of a wealthy Edinburgh Whig lawyer who had been financially ruined in 1828, she had been forced to emigrate to the USA with four other female members of the Inglis family. There they had opened a school for girls in Boston and later in Staten Island, where she first met her future husband. Fanny and Ángel set off for Mexico via Havana in October 1839, returning to the United States in April 1842, when Ángel's successor was appointed after the fall of his political patrons in the Spanish Moderate party.

After the Calderóns' return to Staten Island, Prescott persuaded Fanny to shape the letters she had written to friends and relatives during her two-year Mexican sojourn into a travel book, published in 1843 (the same year as Prescott's *Conquest*) with the title *Life in Mexico*, with a preface by Prescott himself. Although there had been massive British and American capital investment in the newly independent republic, there were surprisingly few English-language precursors to Fanny's Mexican travel book, partly as a result of the fact that pre-independence Spanish America, including New Spain (Mexico), had been long closed to foreign, and particularly British, travellers. A notable exception was the Prussian *savant* Alexander von Humboldt, who had spent a year in New Spain in 1800 on his return from South America: John Black's English translation of Humboldt's seminal *Political Essay on the Kingdom of New Spain* had been published in 1811, but the book was more of an assemblage of statistical and naturalistic data relating to pre-independence Mexico, and particularly its lucrative mining industry, than a travel book proper.[1] All subsequent travel accounts of Mexico, Fanny's included, were indebted to Humboldt's encyclopaedic *Political Essay*. The generic differences between Humboldt's *Political Essay* and Fanny Calderón's *Life in Mexico* however aptly illustrate the polarization of the eighteenth-century travel account (as described by Charles Batten and Barbara Stafford) into 'objective' observation and 'subjective' reflection, a distinction which, as we will see, was often represented in terms of gender.[2] In Humboldt's case, the personality of the traveller and his itinerary/plot survive only vestigially beneath the systematic presentation of statistical and geographical information, whereas in Fanny Calderón's book they both inform and structure the narrative.

The major British precursors to *Life in Mexico* (there were several other French, German and US accounts of Mexico which I will have to pass over here) were William Bullock's *Six Months' Residence and Travels in Mexico* (1824) and H. G. Ward's *Mexico in 1827*, updated and republished in 1829. Like the British travellers in South America discussed by Mary Louise Pratt in *Imperial Eyes* under the rubric of 'the Capitalist

Vanguard', both Bullock and Ward travelled 'in search of exploitable resources, contacts, and contracts with local elites, information on potential ventures, labour conditions, transport, market potential, and so forth'.[3] Like Humboldt, both were mainly concerned with the Mexican mining industry, which had been virtually taken over by foreign – mainly British – capital in the 1820s. Bullock the garrulous, Pickwickian entrepreneur represented Mexican independence as a commercial opportunity for his countrymen:

> . . . the liberality and wisdom of her councillors, under the new order of things, will enable her to break the trammels in which she has been so long confined, that intelligent strangers may be induced to visit her, and bring with them the arts and manufactures, the improved machinery and great chymical knowledge of Europe; and in return she can amply repay them by again diffusing through the world her immense mineral wealth.[4]

The Harrow-educated career diplomat Ward on the other hand assumed a more grandiose, pro-consular attitude to his mission; pompously proclaiming that 'a new epoch in the history of America . . . commenced with our arrival', adding that 'many of the [Mexicans] termed the commencement of a more unrestricted intercourse with Europe, "the second discovery of the New World"'.[5] It is against this rhetoric of 'unofficial' British imperialism – and, as we will see in the second part of this essay, the more tangible pressure of US political intervention in relation to Prescott's history – that I want in this essay to measure the qualities of Fanny Calderón's *Life in Mexico*.

Although Bullock's and Ward's travel books (to a greater extent than Humboldt's *Political Essay*) sought to entertain their readers at the same time as purveying useful information, both authors wrote as outsiders: the poorly educated Bullock at least (Ward had spent four years in Spain) had a very shaky command of the Spanish language. Fanny Calderón's knowledge of Mexico was of a completely different order. In 1842, Prescott wrote to Charles Dickens (who would oversee the publication of the London edition of her book) that, as a consequence of the Calderóns' diplomatic mission, they had known Mexico as no other foreigner had before: 'the English and Americans who visit those countries are so little assimilated to the Spaniards [*sic*] that they have had few opportunities of getting into the interior of their social life. Madame Calderón has improved her opportunities well, and her letters are those of a Spaniard writing in English'.[6] The cultural inversion to which Prescott here refers marked off Fanny Calderón from other (particularly women) travel writers who remained outsiders in the countries they described, although it also left the integrity of her 'original' cultural identity open to question.

Fanny Calderón seems to have been the first Anglophone woman to have written about Mexico; as such her cue, according to the generic conventions of nineteenth-century female travel writing typified by Lady Morgan and Frances Trollope, was to 'get into the interior of [Mexican] social life'. By 1828 female travel writing was already a sufficiently well-defined genre for male critics to grumble about 'romantic females, whose eyes are confined to some half a dozen drawing rooms and who see everything through the medium of poetic fictions'.[7] In a long review of twelve travel books by women writers (including Calderón's *Life in Mexico*), published in the *Quarterly Review* in June 1845, the (female) reviewer sought to counter these misogynistic accusations by defining a sort of contract for women travel writers based upon a sexual division of intellectual labour between the public and the private spheres. 'Every country has a home life as well as a public life,' the reviewer asserted, 'and the first [is] quite necessary to interpret the last'. Every country thus required 'reporters of both sexes'; the observant woman, her eyes trained to detail by years of 'counting canvass stitches by the fireside', her unschooled descriptions of men and manners full of freshness and spontaneity, balancing the preoccupied, purposive male traveller, who 'either starts on his travels with a particular object in view, or, failing that, drives a hobby of his own the whole way before him'. The *Quarterly* approved a 'kind of partnership . . . between books of travel [on the model of matrimony] . . . to supply each other's deficiencies, and correct each other's errors, purely for the good of the public'. [8]

Fanny's book broke these rules of divided labour by its refusal of domesticity and its very full account of public as well as private life in Mexico. Her husband Ángel, preoccupied with his diplomatic duties, his antiquarian and geological researches and his scholarly translations into Spanish, is a virtual absence in her text.[9] As I will argue below, it is not Ángel but the Harvard historian Prescott himself who assumes the role of the male foil to Fanny's travel book. In one respect, however, *Life in Mexico* does conform to the more domestic focus of women's travel texts, namely at the level of narrative structure. Mary Louise Pratt has compared the 'goal-directed, linear emplotment of conquest narrative' in male travel accounts with the South American travelogues of María Graham and Flora Tristan; these latter being 'emplotted in a centripetal fashion around places of residence from which the protagonist sallies forth and to which she returns'.[10] Whereas Bullock and Ward selfconsciously map

A. Agilo, *Exhibition of Antient Mexico at the Egyptian-Hall Piccadilly*, from
William Bullock, *A Description of the Unique Exhibition called Antient Mexico*
(London, 1824).

their route from Vera Cruz to Mexico City (and thence onwards to their
ultimate 'goal', the silver mines of Temascaltepec and Real de Monte)
in terms of the Spanish conquest, Fanny Calderón shies away from
representing her travels in terms of a second 'discovery' or 'conquest'
of Mexico. *Life in Mexico* is framed by the long journey to and from
Mexico City, but for most of the narrative Fanny is firmly situated in the
Calderóns' diplomatic residence in the capital, 'getting inside' Mexican
polite society. Short excursions in the environs of the city (to Chapultepec park, the shrine of the Virgin of Guadalupe and the pyramids of
Teotihuacán) are punctuated by longer expeditions, to the mines of Real
de Monte, to Cuernavaca and the cavern of Cacahuamilpa, Puebla, and,
as the book's climax, 'five weeks on horseback in Michoacán'.

Ironically, the quality of *Life in Mexico* which Prescott had singled out
for praise, the book's conventionally feminized achievement of 'getting
inside' Mexican society, caused deep offence in Mexico itself, where
Fanny was denounced as the 'Frances Trollope of Mexico'. Frances
Trollope had published *Domestic Manners of the Americans* in 1832 in
which she had notoriously concluded 'I do not like [the Americans]. I do
not like their principles. I do not like their manners. I do not like their
opinions'.[11] For all her fascination with the Mexican picturesque, Fanny
Calderón's view of contemporary Mexican society was, on the surface at

least, largely negative. Although Fanny is mentioned only fleetingly in Antonello Gerbi's authoritative study *La Disputa del Nuovo Mondo* (1955), her jaded view of post-colonial Mexican society, both patrician and plebeian, drew upon the common European Enlightenment notion discussed by Gerbi and represented by the writings of such eighteenth-century *savants* as Buffon, De Pauw and William Robertson. According to this argument, the inhabitants of colonial America, of both Spanish (*criollo*) and native stock, were a degenerate race, greatly inferior to purposive, progressive northern Europeans. In conformity with this notion, Fanny frequently lumps together Mexican *criollos* and *indígenas* in the same category. Of the patrician family of the Countess Cortina, for example, she wrote: 'These people would be just as happy in an Indian hut. All seems of very little use or pleasure to them. To sit smoking in an old *rebozo*, any room is good enough'.[12] Like Buffon and De Pauw, she blames climate; 'since enough to support life can be had with little trouble, no trouble is taken to procure more . . . Great moral energy would be necessary to counteract the physical influence of the climate and neither education nor necessity teach or impart it'.[13] Fanny's role as wife of the Spanish ambassador clearly influenced her negative picture of Spain's ex-colony, but this was built upon pre-existing foundations of a stadial Scottish theory of history as social progress and a Protestant, capitalist work ethic.

Like Fanny Trollope, and in line with the allowable conventions of female travel referred to in the *Quarterly* article, Fanny Calderón was particularly interested in the condition of Mexican women of all classes and stations; chapters with titles like 'A Convent from the Inside', 'On the Subject of Mexican Servants' and 'Mexican Woman Appraised' are characteristic of the genre of nineteenth-century women's travel writing. Her Radcliffean horror and fascination with convents as sites of female confinement and autonomy has its equivalent in the common focus upon the harem and zenana in nineteenth-century European women writers on the Middle East and India. Fanny Calderón is at her most Trollopean when describing Mexican society women: 'Upon the whole, I saw few striking beauties, little grace, and very little good dancing. The Mexican women are decidedly neither pretty nor graceful, and their dress is *awful*'.[14] She regrets the passing away of the old viceregal aristocracy and its replacement by republican social climbers – 'wives of military men, sprung from the hot-beds of the revolutions, ignorant and full of pretension, as parvenus who have risen by chance and not by merit must be'.[15] She finds 'much more beauty amongst the lower classes, only they are too

dirty to admire very close'. Any suspicion that this might be a prelude to a
favourable view of indigenous Mexicans as romantic exotics is soon dis-
solved, however, as it becomes clear that this judgement is confined to
mestizos: 'I do not speak of the unmixed Indian women, who are as ugly
and squalid as possible'.[16] Fanny's negative attitudes here contrast with
Bullock's idealized, ethnographically inept representations.

In her remarks on Mexican Indians or *indígenas* Fanny draws upon
a long tradition of racist denigration which stretched uninterruptedly
from sixteenth-century Spanish chroniclers like Sepúlveda, Oviedo and
Gómara to the 'enlightened' works of De Pauw, Buffon, Robertson and
even Humboldt; 'under an appearance of stupid apathy they veil a great
depth of cunning. They are grave and gentle and rather sad in their
appearance, when not under the influence of pulque'.[17] Lack of facial hair
in the men emasculates them, so there is 'scarcely any difference between
the faces of men and women'.[18] Devoid of imagination or creativity, the
Indians excel only at imitation, which Humboldt had speculated would
be a useful propensity 'when mechanical arts are introduced into the
country'.[19] To Humboldt, the deterritorialized *indígena*'s slavish imita-
tiveness seemed the perfect quality to make him a serviceable member of
a capitalist work-force, although subsequent foreign observers were less
confident on this point.

The relationship between the contemporary *indígena* and the Aztec
past was a problem that had to be negotiated by all commentators on the
post-independence Mexican scene. In the Mexican Wars of Independence,
the heroic, martial Aztec past had been an important element in *criollo*
self-fashioning, replacing the Spanish colonial heritage with a Mexican
national myth. During the anti-Spanish war, Fanny's friend the conservative journalist and historian Carlos Bustamante (not to be confused with
President Anastasio Bustamante)[20] had saluted the insurgent leader José
María Morelos with the stirring words:

Go with God, favoured son of victory. The guardian angels of America guide
you; and in the silence of the night Moctezuma's shade ceaselessly demands that
you exact vengeance for his gods and for those innocent victims whom Alvarado
sacrificed in the temple of Huitzilopochtli.[21]

But as both Anthony Pagden and David Brading have pointed out, this
romantic nationalist identification with the Aztecs by the white *criollo*
descendants of Cortés was largely rhetorical, disguising a practical terror
of indigenous uprisings like the rebellion of the Andean peasantry in 1781
led by the Peruvian cacique José Condorcanki (Tupac Amaru II).[22] If the

Nahuatl-speaking Indians of the central highlands had long accepted their subjugation, other native groups were far from pacified at the time of Fanny's Mexican sojourn: the Mayas rose against the Mexican republic in 1847, fighting continued in the Sierra Gorda de la Huasteca until 1849, and the heavily armed Yaquis of the northern frontier remained a serious military threat until the end of the century.[23]

In contrast to the *criollo* polemicist Bustamante, North American historians like Washington Irving in his *Life and Voyage of Columbus* (1828), or Fanny's mentor William Prescott, had little use for an indigenist historical myth. Irving dismissed the Indians of Hispaniola as 'a singularly idle and improvident race'[24] and, although Prescott compared Aztec institutions to those of the Anglo-Saxons under Alfred and the ancient Egyptians,[25] their cannibalism and human sacrifice proved that they had never really evolved beyond savagery. Both writers represented the discovery and conquest of America as a primordial struggle between savagery and progress, recasting their Hispanic Catholic heroes in the mould of the Anglo-Saxon empire-builders of the nineteenth century.[26] Like Prescott, Fanny Calderón consciously side-tracked the *criollo* Aztec myth, although her sympathetic reading of the expatriate Mexican Jesuit historian Francisco Clavigeros's *Historia Antigua de Mexico* (1780–81) would have offered her a more balanced and favourable view of the subject than Prescott's strongly prejudiced view of the Aztecs. I will be suggesting below that Fanny's negative image of the feminized, degraded *indígena* is not the whole story, however, and that in contrast to Prescott's heroic depiction of Cortés, Fanny's subversive landscape descriptions and her identification with Cortés's indigenous mistress and interpreter 'Doña Marina' as a hybrid, undomesticated woman in the political sphere problematizes her own ideological affiliation with the 'capitalist vanguard'.

Fanny's negative strictures on Mexican culture and the uproar which greeted her book in Mexico itself might seem to have been sufficient to redeem her own cultural hybridity and ensure her a place within the pale of cultural acceptability at home. This was however far from being the case. The *Quarterly Review* for June 1845, for example, objected to her book's 'unEnglish' and 'unladylike' qualities. In contrast to the 'gung-ho' English travel authoresses praised in the rest of the review, Fanny was represented as a cultural and sexual apostate who had on both counts 'gone over to the Other side'; 'Madame Calderón was a Scotchwoman – and a Presbyterian . . . she is now a Spaniard, and a Catholic, we have more than reason to suppose' (wrongly, as it turned out: she didn't convert to Rome until 1847). Moreover, the article continued, we feel that it is not only tropical life we are leading, but, with the exception of an occasional trait of Scotch shrewdness, and, we must say, of Yankee vulgarity, a tropical mind is addressing us . . . It is a brilliant book, and doubtless very like life in Spanish Mexico; but we may save ourselves the trouble of looking for anything domestic in it.[27]

The *Quarterly* unknowingly put its finger on the complexity of Fanny's *Life in Mexico*, which, despite the reviewer's condemnation, was quickly recognized as a classic of nineteenth-century travel literature. If Fanny transgressed the allowable limits of gendered writing, she also transgressed the recognized boundaries of nation and culture.[28]

No writer on Mexico in the years 1839–42, male or female, could have ignored politics. The Calderóns' years in Mexico saw two revolutions or *pronunciamientos*, the second of which (in September 1841) resulted in the collapse of the conservative government of General Anastasio Bustamante and its replacement by a radical/federalist coalition led by the veteran General Santa Anna. Fanny painted a jaded picture of Mexican political life ('I fear we live in a Paradise Lost, which will not be Regained in our day'),[29] which mingled the pro-Spanish bias of her husband with the common Anglo-Saxon prejudice that Latin Americans were incapable of developing an autonomous political culture. Fanny was of the opinion that the power struggle between rival *caudillos* which had marked Mexican politics since independence 'may produce an Iturbide [the liberator and, briefly, self-proclaimed 'Emperor of Mexico' in 1820–22] but a Washington never'.[30] Yet if Fanny's picture of Mexican politics in 1841 is much more negative than William Bullock's had been in 1824, it was not simply because she was more prejudiced. Her strictures must rather be put in the context of the beginning of the severe political crisis which David Brading has called the 'tragic [Mexican] decade of the 1840's'.[31] After the disastrous US– Mexican war of 1845–6 and the US occupation of vast tracts of Mexican territory, Mexico ceded all her possessions north of the Río Bravo including New Mexico and California – about half of her total land surface – at the Treaty of Guadalupe Hidalgo in 1848. Writing on Mexico in 1840, Fanny found herself situated in an uneasy power vacuum between an exploded Spanish colonialism, contemporary political anarchy and an imminent US invasion. It is hardly surprising if we find the *independentista* Mexican present vanishing in Fanny's narrative, or at least assuming a strangely evanescent quality. Quoting from Byron's poem 'Parisina', she wrote ominously: '"The Past is nothing; and at last, / The Future will but be the Past", . . . Here the Past is everything; and the Future – ? Answer it who can. I suspect that it will be utterly different. Amen'.[32]

II

Fanny's comments on Mexican politics and society show how easily a racy satirical style, at its best piquant and insightful, can easily degenerate into arrogance and ethnocentrism. At one level *Life in Mexico* constitutes what Pratt has called – in relation to Flora Tristan in nineteenth-century Peru – 'a form of female imperial intervention in the contact zone'.[33] And yet this is not the whole story, and in most of what follows I want to concentrate on Fanny's text as *picturesque* travel narrative, taking picturesque discourse in the contact zone to represent an exemplary site of colonial ambivalence, susceptible to a variety of differing interpretations. Fanny seems to have felt that a combination of romantic and satirical styles was necessary to do justice to her Mexican experience, and that both could be subsumed within the terms of a picturesque aesthetic, for 'nothing in Mexico ever appears commonplace. Everything is on a large scale, and everything is picturesque'.[34] During her bumpy journey by diligence from Vera Cruz to Jalapa, she observed of the country and people through which she passed:

There is not one human being or passing object to be seen that is not in itself a picture, or which would not form a good subject for the pencil . . . Salvator Rosa [seventeenth-century Neapolitan painter, one of the inaugurators of the taste for picturesque landscape] and Hogarth might have travelled in this country to advantage, hand in hand; Salvator for the sublime, and Hogarth taking him up where the sublime became the ridiculous.[35]

Like many other contemporary travel writers, Fanny reaches for aesthetic, and in particular painterly, conventions in order to structure her experience of contradictory and ambivalent responses to the social experience which she sought to describe.

I have already dwelt on the 'Hogarthian' aspects of Fanny's Mexico, which I have equated with her satirical and bathetic view of the post-colonial, *independentista* present. What about the 'Salvatorean' aesthetic of the sublime and the picturesque? In a similar context Sara Suleri has remarked of the nineteenth-century British 'memsahib's' view of colonial India, which she describes as the 'feminine picturesque', that it is 'synonymous with a desire to transfix a dynamic cultural confrontation into a still life, converting a pictorial imperative into a gesture of self-protection that allows the colonial gaze a licence to convert its ability not to see into tudiously visual representation'.[36] Fanny's narrative is frequently in dialogue with the conventions of the female picturesque, to which she seldom succumbs in uncritical fashion. Writing of the bustling Viga promenade in Mexico City, she says:

... could you only shut your eyes to the one disagreeable feature in the picture, the innumerable *leperos* [the Mexican urban *Lumpenproletariat*] ... you would believe that Mexico must be the most flourishing, most enjoyable and most peaceful place in the world, and moreover the wealthiest.[37]

It is precisely her refusal here to 'close her eyes' that qualifies and undercuts the purely aesthetic possibilities of the scene. Despite her negative remarks on Mexican society and manners, Fanny often employs the conventions of the feminine picturesque to construct a vision of Mexico which refuses to see *appropriatively*, with the colonizing eyes of the new Anglo-Saxon 'conquerors'. This is not to say that her critical seeing necessarily represents solidarity with the oppressed so much as a kind of Byronic pathos, a political agnosticism which seeks to sublimate the negativity and ideological ambivalence of her sense of modern Mexico into a powerful imaginative experience at odds with the discourse of conquest.

This romantic sublimation finds an alibi in the conventionally anti-utilitarian bias of the picturesque, one of the elements which rendered it suitable as a specifically feminized discourse. This is illustrated by Fanny's description of her visit to the silver mines at Real de Monte in May 1840. Her initial account of the mine reads like something out of Bullock or Ward, with its admiration for 'all the great works which English energy has established here: the various steam engines, the buildings for the separation and washing of the ore, the great stores, workshops, offices, etc.'.[38] The description suddenly shifts into the conditional mood, however: 'I might give you a description ... I might tell you ... I might repeat the opinion. . .'. 'But', she continues, 'for all these matters I refer you to Humboldt and Ward, by whom they are scientifically treated, and will not trouble you with superficial remarks on so important a subject'.[39] Fanny's conditional clauses have the effect of parading her considerable knowledge of British technological intervention in Real de Monte *before* her conventional gendered disclaimer. If she truncates her discussion of mining technology, it is not because she lacks competence as a female subject, but because she *chooses* not to participate discursively in a foreign, male expropriation of Mexican natural resources. This display of 'unfeminine' knowledge *sous rature* has the effect of qualifying her shift into the register of the feminine picturesque, from culture to nature, in the next paragraph:

In fact, I must confess that my attention was frequently attracted from the mines, and the engines, and the works of man . . . to the stupendous natural scenery by which we were surrounded: the unexplored forests that clothe the mountains to their very summits, the torrents that leaped and sparkled in the sunshine, the deep ravines, the many-tinted foliage, the bold and jutting rocks.[40]

In this passage Fanny as it were transforms the conventions of the 'feminine picturesque' by employing it not as a discourse of female suffering and resignation, but rather as an implicit rebuke to the 'busy' expropriation of natural resources going on at Real del Monte.[41]

Elsewhere, and more characteristically, Fanny hijacks the conventions of female travel-writing in quite a different direction by evoking history – and particularly an unresolved Mexican history of colonial domination – in order to disturb the melancholy composure of picturesque description. In these moments, as the *Quarterly* put it, Fanny shows herself at her most 'tropical', un-English and unladylike in refusing the other-worldly escapism of the conventional feminine picturesque. Generically, the picturesque is profoundly involved with history as an aesthetic of absence, although the extent of this involvement had been a matter of considerable dispute amongst critics. In 1794 Sir Uvedale Price, one of its most influential theorists, had defined the meaning of the term 'picturesque' as not merely referring a landscape view 'to the art of painting' but rather to the ruinous effects of time upon nature or culture: 'a temple or palace of Grecian architecture in its perfect state, and with its surface and colour smooth and even . . . is beautiful; in ruins it is picturesque'.[42] Ángel Calderón had employed a similar notion of the picturesque to describe modern Mexico in a letter of 1840 in which he invited the historian Prescott to come and visit in order to study 'the effects of time on the ancient Spanish race and the Indians, of which you must give the world an understanding'.[43] Fanny also at times employs the figure of the ruin as synecdoche for her Mexican experience: 'ruins everywhere – here a viceroy's country palace, serving as a tavern . . . there a whole village crumbling to pieces; roofless houses, broken down walls and arches, an old church, the remains of a convent'.[44] From one point of view ruins in colonial space betoken political neglect and, as Pratt has argued, 'neglect became the touchstone of a negative aesthetic that legitimised European interventionism'.[45] The conventional picturesque aesthetic might *empty* the Mexican landscape of present inhabitants, as it were naturalizing history (including the defeat and wished-for occlusion of indigenous culture) in the emblem of the crumbling ruin. And yet Fanny's picturesque landscape is not entirely empty, waiting to be appropriated and modernized by foreign capital intervention, given that it is haunted by ghosts of an unresolved indigenous past which refuse to lie still in its grave.

I want to argue that the indigenous 'ghosts' which haunt Fanny's picturesque Mexican landscape – in particular the 'ghost in Chapultepec', which I will address in the next section – represent the 'colonial unconscious' of her text. They figure that large (and in fact ever-increasing) indigenous population which, in her Trollopean register, we have seen her dismissing with ethnocentric repugnance and racial disdain. At least twice, when evoking the 'indescribable feeling of solitude' of 'being entirely out of the world'[46] characteristic of her Mexican aesthetic, 'alone with a giant nature, surrounded by faint traditions of a bygone race',[47] Fanny is disturbed by the living 'ghosts' of the *indígenas*. Once she is startled by 'the passing Indian . . . certainly as much in a state of savage nature as the lower classes of Mexicans were when Cortés first traversed these plains'.[48] In another passage, 'the silence is broken by the footstep of the passing Indian, the poor and debased descendant of that extraordinary and mysterious people who came, we know not whence, and whose posterity are now "hewers of wood and drawers of water"' on the soil where they once were monarchs'.[49] What makes these 'much-enduring',[50] abject Indians different from Wordsworthian leech-gatherers or beggars – whom at one level they resemble as resilient figures of solitude and self-containment – is the degree to which they make explicit a narrative of colonial dispossession and deterritorialization that has failed to tame and 'civilize' them. Moreover, they are conjured up to haunt her picturesque landscape at precisely those moments when her own cultural self-presence seems at a particularly low ebb, as if they in some way figure her own sense of female abjection and marginality as a counterpoint to the triumphalist historical narrative of Anglo-Saxon providentialism.

In his account of 'locodescriptive moments' in the Wordsworthian picturesque, Alan Liu describes 'antithetical moments [which] mark the boundaries of descriptive scenes when a residual feeling for narration daemonizes description, even as description contains the chthonic spirit and smoothes over the metamorphic ground once more'.[51] The Claudean composure of the picturesque scene contains what Liu calls the 'trembling' of historical narrative, in which historical anecdote is present to the scene only vestigially, offset by the formal unity of the description. Although the picturesque moment is marked by a melancholy and reflective stasis, it is precisely this 'trembling' historical allusion which makes the scene picturesque rather than beautiful, given that a purely formal unity without anecdote is already a sufficient condition for the aesthetic of beauty. The simultaneous absence and presence of history *consecrates* the present with the aesthetic value of the picturesque, in contrast to either the sublime or the beautiful.

This is illustrated in Fanny's description of her 'first sight' of Mexico City as she crosses the threshold of mountains on the road from Puebla. Nearly all Mexican travel accounts make much of this 'first sight', the sublime *coup d'œil* with its submerged allusion to the *conquistador* Bernal Díaz's famous description in *Historia Verdadera de la Conquista de la Nueva España*:

These great towns and *cues* [temples] and buildings rising from the water, all made of stone, seemed like an enchanted vision from the tale of Amadís. Indeed some of our soldiers asked whether it was not all a dream . . . it was all so wonderful that I do not know how to describe this first glimpse of things never heard of, seen or dreamed of before.[52]

As I mentioned above, nineteenth-century Anglo-Saxon travel writers of the 'capitalist vanguard' followed the route of the conquerors from Vera Cruz up into the central highlands of Anahuac, the climactic moment of which was the 'first view' of Tenochtitlán, in a *ricorso* of the original conquest. But nineteenth-century British travellers refigured Bernal Díaz's description of the valley of Mexico (with its conventional relapse into the verbal inarticulacy of wonder) as *disappointment*, transforming the sublime of the Spanish conquest into the bathos of centuries of Spanish colonial neglect, from which independent Mexico will be only be redeemed by northern capital. William Bullock's 1824 version is paradigmatic, evoking

. . . the celebrated and splendid capital of New Spain, which first seen is discovered to be situated in a swamp . . . all is dismal and solitary . . . resembles the worst parts of Lincolnshire . . . And can this, I thought to myself, be Mexico? – have I then for such a place left my home and all that is dear to me? . . . what have I gained in exchange?[53]

In Henry Ward's 1827 account, bad weather obstructs the *conquistador*'s view: 'we were gratified almost immediately with a view of the Valley of Mexico, but the day being unusually cloudy, neither the Lakes, nor the town, were distinctively visible'.[54] Compared with the picture painted by Humboldt, Ward found the reality a 'considerable disappointment'.[55] Fanny Calderón's version follows her male Anglo-Saxon precursors with respect to the murky, anticlimactic weather, but already she moves from bathos towards the picturesque by evoking the historical resonance of the vista:

At length we arrived at the heights on which we look down upon the superb valley of Mexico, celebrated in all parts of the world, with its framework of magnificent mountains, its snow-crowned volcanoes, great lakes, and fertile plains – all surrounding the favoured city of Montezuma, proudest boast of his conqueror, once of Spain's many diadems the brightest. But the day had overcast, nor is this the most favourable road for entering Mexico. . .[56]

But in contrast to Bullock's bad-tempered 'what have I gained in exchange', Fanny steps out of her diligence for a moment in order to travel back three centuries to identify with Cortés's first view. This picturesque impulse ushers in the 'trembling' of historical narrative, drawing attention away from the overcast present vista and Bullock's 'modern bathos'. Its picturesque quality is very much that of Prescott's *Conquest of Mexico* with its heroic identification with Cortés (in Suleri's terms, converting 'the ability not to see into a studiously visual representation'):

But as we strained our eyes to look into the valley, it all appeared to me rather like a vision of the Past than the actual breathing Present. The curtain of Time seemed to roll back a few centuries, and to discover to us the great panorama of Mexico that burst upon the eyes of Cortés when he first set foot upon these shores and first looked down upon the tableland . . . The great city of Tenochtitlán, standing in the midst of the five great lakes, upon verdant and flower-covered islands, a western Venice, with thousands of boats gliding swiftly along its streets and its long lines of low houses diversified by the multitude of its pyramidal temples, the *teocalli*, or houses of [the gods] . . . what scenes of wonder and of beauty to burst upon the eyes of these wayfaring men![57]

Fanny's spectral evocation of the historical Tenochtitlán also echoes Southey's description of the Aztec capital Aztlán in his imperialist epic of 1805 entitled *Madoc*; Fanny in fact quoted four lines from Part II, book 24, of *Madoc* as an epigram to the first edition of *Life in Mexico*: '. . .Thou art beautiful / Queen of the Valley! thou art beautiful, / Thy walls, like silver, sparkle to the sun; / Melodious wave thy groves. . .' It is perhaps significant that this feminized description ('Queen of the Valley') occurs at the moment in Southey's poem when Aztlán has been conquered and converted to Christianity; a few lines further down, Southey writes 'Against the clear blue sky, the Cross of Christ / Proclaims unto the nations round the news / Of thy redemption'.[58] But the picturesque description of Mexico City as it occurs here in *Life in Mexico* ultimately serves to question rather than legitimize Cortés's *conquistador* gaze. Fanny deleted the following sentences printed in italic (following immediately from the above paragraph) from the journal which she used as the basis for this passage in *Life in Mexico*. Reinstated, they disrupt the picturesque resolution by introducing a note of historical contention into the formal repose of the scene:

[Cortés] is blamed for cruelty – for injustice – but the first cruelty and the first injustice consisted in his entering these unknown lands, and disturbing an inoffensive people. Once considering it his duty to God and his King to subdue them, where was his alternative? And how forcibly [these pictures] return to the mind now when, after a lapse of three centuries, we behold for the first time the city of palaces raised upon the ruins of the Indian capital.[59]

Sought-for picturesque expectations are displaced from the obscured modern city to the bustling historical Tenochtitlán, described in the first passage quoted above as 'a western Venice'. In place of either the modern 'city of palaces' or the picturesque 'ruins of the Indian capital', Fanny's view of Tenochtitlán is of an intact, bustling, unruinous city (like Diego Rivera's mural of pre-conquest Tenochtitlán in the National Palace in Mexico City). Both the sublime and the picturesque – the aesthetic of ruin – are replaced here by the *beautiful*, a shift of aesthetic register tantamount to a historical and cultural recovery of the indigenous past. (By contrast, Southey could only describe 'Aztlan' as 'beautiful' after its conquest and conversion to Christianity.) Not time, but the Spaniards, will ruin this city, so that nothing will be left of the original vision which 'burst upon the eyes' of the conquerors. Fanny's brief identification with – and rejection of – the *conquistador* picturesque in favour of the beauty of the unconquered Aztec city thus ultimately leads to a disturbing consideration of the ethics of conquest, even if this is suppressed in the published version of her journal. This ambivalence, mapped out in a complex substitution of aesthetic registers, seems to be linked to Fanny's own particular subject position as a cosmopolitan foreign woman, unable or unwilling to identify with the *criollo* nationalist myth of the Aztec past, but still less with the symbolic appropriation of Mexican land and history by her Anglo-American male interlocuters Robert Southey and William Prescott.

III

I want in this concluding section to return to William Prescott in Boston and the gift of the daguerreotype machine with which I began my essay. In contrast to the generally pro-Aztec historiography of such *criollo* patriots as Francisco Clavigero and Carlos Bustamante, Prescott preferred to identify with Hernan Cortés, the 'knight-errant' of *The Conquest*, whom he described as possessing 'a spirit of enterprise that might well be called romantic'.[60] As I mentioned above, Prescott tended to describe Aztec

society as a static, 'oriental' despotism which could not be placed in the
same 'progressive' historical timescale as Europe, particularly Protestant
Europe.[61] Unlike the repetitive, imitative nature of Aztec civilization,
Prescott confidently asserted that 'far from looking back, and forming
itself slavishly on the past, it is characteristic of the European intellect
to be ever on the advance'.[62] In the course of this inexorable material
advance, the northern imagination gathered up and as it were 'consumed'
the past: Prescott sought to incorporate the conquest of Mexico into the
liberal, progressive model of Anglo-Saxon imperialism, a literary task
that had already been in part performed for him by the English laureate
Southey. Southey's epic *Madoc,* from which we have seen Fanny quoting
her epigram to *Life in Mexico,* reworked the historical record of the
conquest of Mexico, replacing Spaniards with medieval Welsh/British
conquerors. When Prescott wanted to intensify particularly poignant
moments of his prose narrative, he too was in the habit of quoting copious
passages from *Madoc* in his footnotes.[63]

Southey's imperialist fantasy seemed to be realized when in 1845, only
two years after the publication of Prescott's *Conquest of Mexico,* the US
army swept into Mexican territory in the biggest land grab in US history.
Ironically, invading US officers used Prescott's book as a guide as they
pushed inland from Vera Cruz to Mexico City on the trail of Cortés.[64] (By
a further irony of history, many of the US conscripts were poor Catholic
Irish immigrants, some of whom changed sides and were executed for
treason.) While Mexico City was still in US hands, Bustamante published
a shamefaced comparison between the Spanish and the American invasions
of Mexico entitled *El Nuevo Bernal Díaz del Castillo* (1847), playing
on the Anglo-Saxon rhetoric of historical conquest. As David Brading
comments, 'the [Mexican] patriotic identification with Moctezuma and
Cuauhtémoc, which Bustamante had deployed so vehemently against
the Spaniards, thus acquired a deeper, more bitter resonance'.[65] *Criollo*
abjection in the face of US invasion furthered the romantic identification
with the indigenous victims of the original Spanish conquest.

Appropriately enough, Prescott's letters describe the research and
writing of his *Conquest* as a scholarly replay of the conquest itself. His
strong identification with Cortés (wrested by Prescott from Catholic
backwardness and transformed into a symbolic precursor of the Anglo-
Saxon hero of empire) and his lack of sympathy with the Aztecs made
the preparation of the first book of his history, the 'View of Aztec
Civilization', an irksome task. 'I have yet been wholly taken up with the
Aztecs – a confounded hard and bothersome subject', he wrote to Ángel

Calderón de la Barca in 1840. 'This half-civilization breed makes a sort of mystification like twilight . . . I have now nearly disposed of them and shall soon be on my march with the great *Conquistador*'.[66] Nearing the completion of book , the siege and capitulation of Tenochtitlán, he wrote flippantly to Charles Dickens in December 1842: 'I am hammering away at my old Aztecs and have nearly knocked their capital about their ears'. [67] Declining Ángel's invitation to visit the Calderóns in Mexico, he wrote 'the only journey I shall make in the fair regions of Anahuac will be under the strong escort of some half-thousand Spanish *caballeros,* well preserved in stuffed cotton jackets and mail, with the gallant Cortés at their head'. [68]

In contrast to William Robertson, whose dry, rationalistic account of the conquest in the *History of America* (1777) leant heavily on the 'official' chronicle of Herrera, Prescott relied liberally 'on such gossiping chronicles as Bernal Díaz's' to enliven the narratives of Cortés and Gómara, and was indeed really the first important historian of the conquest so to do.[69] The unlettered foot-soldier Bernal Díaz, Prescott observed in the second volume, 'transfers the scenes of real life by a *sort of daguerreotype process*, if I may say so, to his pages . . . All the picturesque scenes and romantic incidents in the campaign are reflected in his pages as in a mirror' [my italics].[70] Prescott's enthusiasm for Bernal Díaz rather than Herrera is symptomatic of the romantic approach to historiography which he shared with such other members of the 'New England school' as George Bancroft, Francis Parkman and John Lothrop Motley. These historians sought to 'realize' the past by their literary manner and obsession with settings and costume, in the manner of Walter Scott's novels. Prescott's *Conquest of Mexico* employs the technique which Stephen Bann has called a 'rhetoric of evocation, in which objects, texts, and images all contribute to the materialization of the past'.[71] Bann points out that the effects which photography – in the form of the daguerreotype machine – first achieved around 1840

. . . had been sought after, through different techniques, in the previous half-century [by romantic historians like Prescott] . . . the techniques of photography, and subsequently cinematography . . . might be seen as the Utopia to which 19th century historical representation is valiantly striving.[72]

I want to argue that this 'rhetoric of evocation' is the historiographical equivalent of the appropriation and commodification of Mexico by the travel writers of the 'capitalist vanguard' discussed above, and one to which Fanny Calderón's subversive picturesque is profoundly antithetical.

Mary Louise Pratt has argued that Anglo-Saxon travellers in South America in the 1820s tend to figure themselves as 'conquerors', rather than 'discoverers' in the Humboldtian mould, and that 'the bits of nature they collected were samples of raw materials, not pieces of Nature's cosmic design'.[73] The 'capitalist vanguard' opened up commercial networks and imported northern technology to exploit Mexico's neglected silver mines, in exchange for exotic natural-historical and antiquarian objects which they exported to Europe and the USA in order to 'romanticize' Mexico in the eyes of metropolitan consumers of culture. This process of cultural 'exchange' is dramatically borne out by Fanny Calderón's male precursors in Mexico, often with amusingly literal force. Bullock in his *Six Months' Residence* is obsessed by collecting and preserving 'bits of Mexico' to display in the highly successful 'Mexican Exhibition' which he mounted at the Egyptian Hall in Soho in 1824. Like the South American traveller Charles Waterton, discussed by Stephen Bann,[74] Bullock was a keen ornithologist and taxidermist, having published in 1817 a paper entitled *A Concise and Easy Way of Preserving Subjects in Natural History*. Bullock was concerned that the exotic specimens in his collections should be as realistic as possible in order to 'recreate' Mexico in the metropolis according to the latest technologies of illusionistic representation (for the results, see illus. 2). During his unofficial commercial mission in Mexico, Bullock describes how he 'carefully preserved about two hundred specimens [of humming-birds] in the best possible manner, yet they are still but the shadow of what there were in life'.[75] As well as collecting and stuffing numerous species of animals such as 'armadillos, deers, parrots, currassow-birds, quans [*sic*], tiger-cats etc. etc.',[76] he made plaster casts of a wide variety of exotic fruit which he bought in the market, even trying to urge some of the bewildered indigenous inhabitants of Temascaltepec to accompany him to England to be put on show. He also bought an extensive collection of waxworks of the Mexican 'castas' or diverse ethnic groups which would familiarize the British public with a rather rigid version of the orders of Mexican society. With the permission of the Mexican authorities (desperate to encourage the influx of British capital) Bullock also made plaster-of-Paris casts of the so-called 'Aztec Calendar', the Coatlicue statue and the 'stone of sacrifices', as well as making off with several valuable codices and pre-Hispanic maps from the Boturini Collection in Mexico City.

Bullock's acquisitive mania was however small fry compared to the insatiable appetite of the US traveller and antiquarian John L. Stephens. Stephens's book *Incidents of Travel in Central America, Chiapas and*

Mexican Indians going to Market, from William Bullock,
*Six Months' Residence and Travels in Mexico, Containing Remarks on the
Present State of New Spain, Its Natural Productions, State of Society,
Manufactures, Trade, Agriculture, and Antiquities, etc* (London, 1824).

Yucatan, published in 1841, was sent by Prescott to Fanny as she left
Mexico for Cuba at the end of Ángel's diplomatic mission. *Incidents of
Travel* was illustrated by Frederick Catherwood's breathtaking engravings
of Mayan antiquities, the English artist having been equipped with a
sophisticated *camera obscura* which enabled a near-photographic precision of draughtsmanship. For Prescott, suspicious of what he called
'mushroom made-up antiquarians . . . of all humbugs the greatest',
Stephens's light-weight, anecdotal narrative was welcome precisely because
it didn't attempt to make hypotheses concerning Maya antiquity; he
found 'the real value of the work lies in the drawings and the simple
descriptions of the ruins'.[77] Whereas Prescott and Bullock were content
with collecting antiquarian objects or facsimiles of Mexican nature and
culture, Stephens actually *bought* the site of the Mayan city of Copán in
present-day Belize for 50 dollars, with the intention of removing it lock,

stock and barrel to the United States. He proclaimed proudly that his ambition was 'to buy Copán! remove the monuments of a by-gone people from the desolate region in which they were buried, set them up in the "great commercial emporium", and found an institution to be the nucleus of a great national museum of American antiquities!'[78]

By these standards, Prescott's desire for Mexican 'materiale' seems modest enough, and, confined to his Boston study, he was after all dependent upon appropriation at second hand. What role did he envisage for Fanny Calderón? Unfortunately, for all Bernal Díaz's 'daguerreotype' skills of description, Prescott found him rather insensible to the romantic background of the dramatic events which he had described. As Prescott ruefully admitted, 'the hearts of the stern conquerors were not very sensible to the beauties of nature'.[79] For this very reason, if he relied upon Ángel Calderón to send him historical documents, ethnographic objects like the 'Aztec skull' donated to the Harvard Medical School collection, or antiquarian curios like a piece of black lace from Cortés's shroud, Prescott relied upon Fanny for visual and picturesque documentation. His demands for picturesque description, as well as topographical, naturalistic and ethnographic details of Mexico to 'materialize' his romantic historiography, depended upon a gendered notion of superior female sensibility and observational skill, that, as the *Quarterly* article put it, 'there are peculiar powers inherent in ladies' eyes'. Such 'powers' filled women's travel accounts 'with those close and lively details which show not only that observing eyes have been at work, but one pair of bright eyes in particular'.[80] 'I wish you would tell me what kind of trees are found in the table land and in the valley', Prescott asked Fanny in a letter of 15 August 1840. 'In describing the march of the Spaniards I am desirous to know what was the appearance of the country through which they passed.'[81] A year later he begged for scenery, birds, trees etc. 'You see I want to dip my pencil in your colours – the colours of truth, gently touched with fancy, or at least feeling'.[82]

Maybe for the same reason Prescott sent the daguerreotype machine as a gift to Fanny rather than her husband, despite the fact that Ángel was something of an expert, having been engaged, according to Fanny, in 'translating [Fox Talbot's] *History of Photogenic Drawing* into pure Castilian' on board ship to Havana.[83] In her letter of 5 June 1840 thanking Prescott, Fanny promised to send him the first fruits of the new technology: 'I hope we shall be able to send you Chapultepec, correctly drawn by Nature herself. . .'[84] The precise realism of the daguerreotype image is signalled by the fact that Fanny (maybe not without a trace of irony) dubs

J. Clark, *Chapultepec*, an engraving from H. G. Ward, *Mexico* (London, 1829).

it simply 'Chapultepec' without even bothering to distinguish the copy from its original. And yet Fanny seems to have been less than happy with the new mimetic machine and its promise of yielding up nature's signature. On 20 November 1840, she described how she went with Ángel and some friends to Chapultepec park to 'take views with the daguerreotype, which Calderón had the pleasure of receiving some time ago from Boston, from our friend Mr Prescott'[85] (interesting that Ángel now seems to have appropriated Fanny's gift). In a repeat of her boredom at the mines at Real de Monte, Fanny rapidly lost interest in the face of eager male experimentation with the new toy; 'While they were working in the sun I, finding that the excessive heat had the effect of cooling my enthusiasm, established myself with a book under Montezuma's cypress, which felt very romantic'.[86] It is perhaps significant that no fruits of the afternoon's efforts at Chapultepec – or any other daguerreotypic sessions – survive among Prescott's papers, although there is a record of at least one of the Calderón images having reached him: appropriately enough, a botched representation of Cortés's tomb at the Hospital de Jesus.[87] By contrast, Mrs Henry G. Ward's picturesque evocation of Chapultepec was published in her husband's 1829 *Mexico*.

Despite the non-arrival of 'nature's drawing' from Chapultepec to supplement the half-blind historian's sense of Mexican place, Prescott made frequent use of Fanny's letters in his *Conquest*, citing 'one of the

most delightful of modern travellers'[88] at least five times. Appropriately
enough, one of the most striking of these citations refers to Fanny's
romantic evocation of Chapultepec as the former palace of the Aztec
emperor Moctezuma.[89] In her first account of Chapultepec in *Life in
Mexico*, Fanny employs the park as a symbol of historical continuity
between pre- and post-conquest Mexico, as well as between the colonial
and post-independence eras: 'Could these hoary cypresses speak, what
tales might they not disclose, standing there with their long gray beards
and outstretched venerable arms . . . already old when Montezuma was a
boy, and still vigorous in the days of Bustamante!'[90] In her evocation of
the pre-lapsarian idyll of Chapultepec before the irruption of the Europeans, she employs an 'orientalist' image of Moctezuma which would be
appropriated by Prescott in his reworking of the passage:[91]

There the last of the Aztec Emperors wandered with his dark-eyed harem. Under
the shade of these gigantic trees he rested, perhaps smoking his 'tobacco mingled
with amber' and fallen to sleep, his dreams unhaunted by visions of the stern
traveller from the far east, whose sails even then might be within sight of the
shore'. [92]

Fanny's Chapultepec past and present is now however haunted by another
historical figure, this time female as well as indigenous, that of the
enigmatic Malinche, Malintzin, Malinali, or 'Doña Marina', to use her
Christian baptismal name. Fernanda Núñez Becerra has recently pointed
out in her study of the changing historical interpretations of Malinche
that very little is really known about her life, the plurality of her names
symbolizing her fissured, hybrid identity.[93] It is however possible to
establish a few facts: 'Malinali' was presented to Cortés as a tribute slave
by the Maya lord of Potonchán in April 1817, apparently a native of
Coatzacoalcos, of noble birth, having been sold into slavery by her
mother after her father's death. The fact that she spoke both Chontal
Maya and Nahautl (the language of the Aztec empire) meant that she
provided the missing link in the interpretative chain which permitted
Cortés for the first time to communicate effectively with the Aztecs.[94] She
soon became Cortés's mistress, bearing him a son, Martín; before long
she was indispensable to the Spaniards, although the key role she played in
the diplomatic and strategic manoeuvring which brought them spectacular success against enormous odds earned her the invidious reputation of
having betrayed her own people. The fact that she was a woman with
powerful agency in the political sphere in indigenous Mexican society
where (according to the Florentine Codex) a woman 'was one who went

nowhere. Only the house was her abode'[95] furthered her alienation from her own people. Malinche was however doubtless aware that she had herself been twice betrayed by her people, once by her mother and again by the lord of Potonchán who had presented her as a slave to Cortés. The Spaniards seem to have been no more comfortable with La Malinche than the Potonchán Maya: after the conquest, when her services were no longer required, Cortés married her off to Don Juan Xaramillo so that he himself could elevate his social station by marrying into the high echelons of the Spanish aristocracy. Her fate thereafter is unknown, but she probably died in poverty and obscurity.

Although *criollo* historians like Clavigero sought to represent her as the first Mexican woman convert to Christianity and the symbol of Mexican *mestizaje,* her identity remains profoundly ambiguous. In post-independence Mexico, the term 'malinche' or 'malinchismo' was often employed rather as the term 'quisling' is used in English, a usage still current in today's Mexico. In a relevant recent essay Jean Franco has explored Malinche's currency in contemporary US Mexican–American women's (*chicana*) literature both as a symbol of the 'hegemony which replaces force, a contractually-based hegemony which functions on the basis of previous violence' and of the double crisis of separation from mother and from community accompanying the assimilative self-fashioning of many *chicana* women in US culture.[96]

Fanny Calderón's 'trembling', picturesque allusion to Moctezuma's court in Chapultepec park is suddenly disrupted by the uncanny apparition of La Malinche's ghost in present time. 'Tradition says that now the caves and tanks and woods are haunted by the shade of the conqueror's Indian love, the far-famed Doña Marina, but I think she would be afraid of meeting with the wrathful spirit of the Indian emperor'.[97] If Prescott's *Conquest of Mexico* is characterized by the author's strong identification with Cortés, Fanny's *Life in Mexico* shows an equivalent fascination with the historical legend of Doña Marina. In a subsequent passage of *Life in Mexico,* following Clavigero, Fanny describes the strikingly beautiful Marina as 'Cortés's Indian Egeria, the first Christian woman of the Mexican empire'[98] – doubtlessly alluding (giving the density of Byronic quotation throughout the book) to *Childe Harold,* Canto iv, stanza 115. In the light of the history of Malinche discussed above, the comparison with Byron's Egeria (the mythological object of the emperor Numa's 'nympholepsy of some fond despair')[99] seems rather an over-idealizing analogy for Cortés's *lengua*, his interpreter/mistress. But the Byronic allusion provides a clue to Fanny's powerful identification with Malinche, like her an undomesticated, travelling woman 'between cultures', like her 'married' to a Spaniard whose language she has adopted, and like her 'betraying' Mexico through her linguistic skills (in Fanny's case into the hands of the interventionist Anglo-Saxon readership of *Life in Mexico*).

Having skilfully guided Cortés through the diplomatic and strategic labyrinth of the conquest, Malinche is given away in marriage to another *conquistador* by her ungrateful lover, only to disappear into the obscurity of history. Fanny here imagines Malinche's remorseful, unrewarded and unquiet spirit haunting the groves of Chapultepec, shunned by the Spaniards and in turn shunning contact with the spectral embodiment of the people who have betrayed her and whom in turn she has betrayed. As Fernanda Becerra indicates, the 'tradition' of the ghost of Chapultepec seems never to have had a native Mexican currency, being most probably Fanny's romantic invention, although it would be taken up and given currency by Prescott in a celebrated passage of his *Conquest*.[100] Fanny's ghost in Chapultepec is a powerful symbol, not only for the tragic complexity of Mexican history but also for the life of the woman traveller whose narrative it haunts, a woman caught between cultures, whose gifts of observation and of tongue have been co-opted into the service of male conquerors, and whose interpretative acuity is unlikely to go rewarded by either side.

There is a sardonic, impatient note in Fanny's reply to Prescott's request for a portrait of Doña Marina in a letter of 19 September 1841. 'I never saw a picture of Doña Marina, and doubt there being one, but it will be easy to find out. They say she haunts the cave of Chapultepec, and at night bathes in the tank, so a spirited likeness might easily be caught'.[101] The turn of phrase makes it likely that, in addition to punning on the word 'spirited', Fanny is mocking Prescott by offering an erotic daguerreotype image of the bathing Marina for his delectation. There is perhaps a a hint here that she finds a touch of prurience in Prescott's historiographical obsession with materializing the past in all its nakedness; her 'spirited' likeness is also the likeness of a *spirit*. Curiously, the word 'spirited' stuck in Prescott's vocabulary in relation to Fanny's travel book: he used it at least twice to describe her descriptions and anecdotes in letters to Dickens in August and September of 1842, apparently oblivious to the spectral pun contained in the word.[102] Or had Prescott divined that Fanny's 'picturesque' narrative was haunted by the unresolved 'trembling' of the Mexican past in a manner quite distinct from his own official historiography, with its mania for verification and pictorial accuracy?

Prescott's enthusiasm for Fanny's ghost story ensured its inclusion in book 7, chapter 3, of the *Conquest,* in the context of his account of Malinche's marriage to Don Juan Xaramillo. Prescott here however filled the gap in the historical record, utterly suppressing the ambivalence and probable destitution which accompanied Malinche's later years.

She had estates assigned to her in her native province, where she probably passed the remainder of her days. From this time the name of Marina disappears from the page of history. But it has always been held in grateful remembrance by the Spaniards, for the important aid which she gave them in effecting the Conquest, and by the natives, for the kindness and sympathy which she showed them in their misfortunes. Many an Indian ballad commemorates the gentle virtues of Malinche – her Aztec epithet.[103]

As Fernanda Becerra points out, Prescott needed to invent this happy ending because he simply could not believe that such an important figure as Malinche could have been allowed to 'disappear' from the Spanish annals; he filled in the gap with a reference to a popular tradition that seems, in fact, to have been invented by Fanny Calderón.[104] For Prescott, Malinche becomes a tutelary deity for Mexico, symbol of a contractual hegemony which resolves the violence of conquest. The ambivalence of betrayal underlying Fanny's account of the unhappy ghost of Marina shying away from Moctezuma's spectre in Chapultepec park is completely suppressed in his version of the story:

Even now her spirit, if report be true, watches over the capital which she helped to win; and the peasant is occasionally startled by the apparition of an Indian princess, dimly seen through the evening shadows, as it flits among the groves and grottoes of the royal hill of Chapoltepec [*sic*].

In a footnote, Prescott cites *Life in Mexico*, chapter 8 (Fanny's passage cited above), adding: 'The fair author does not pretend to have been favoured with a sight of the apparition'.[105] This throw-away, half-joking remark (was this Prescott's rejoinder to Fanny's jibe about photographing the bathing spirit of Malinche?) maybe also contains a searching insight into Fanny's 'spirited' narrative, with its refusal to appropriate the abject indigenous counter-narrative of conquest into the terms of triumphalist Anglo-Saxon historicism. The unquiet spirit of La Malinche wandering in the groves of Chapultepec is the perfect metaphor for the haunting of Prescott's *Conquest of Mexico* by Fanny's picturesque travel narrative.

8

Partners: Guides and Sherpas in the Alps and Himalayas, 1850s–1950s

PETER H. HANSEN

Victorian mountaineers described their first ascents as the 'conquest' of the Alps. Leslie Stephen, a man of letters and the father of Virginia Woolf, made the first ascent of the Schreckhorn in 1861 because 'so long as Murray and Baedeker describe its wonders for the benefit of successive generations of tourists, its first conqueror may be carried down to posterity by clinging to its skirts'.[1] After nearly all the Alps were climbed in what later became known as the 'Golden Age' of mountaineering, Stephen predicted in 1868 that 'the pleasure of discovery in the Alps will be reckoned amongst extinct amusements'.

> When there is a railroad to Timbuctoo, and another through the central regions of Asia, our great-great-grandchildren will feel on a large scale the same regret for the old days, when the earth contained an apparently inexhaustible expanse of unknown regions, that the Alpine traveller now feels on a very diminutive scale.

Stephen suggested 'travelling will not cease', even though 'the glories of Columbus or of Livingstone will be no longer amongst the possible objects of ambition'.[2]

Like other writers in the nineteenth century, Stephen distinguished his 'travel' from ordinary 'tourism'.[3] To make this distinction, he described his travelling as a form of discovery and exploration, and his climbing as a form of conquest. But who was doing the conquering? Like 'travel' and 'exploration' in earlier periods or in other parts of the world, British climbers did not so much discover mountain summits as appropriate local knowledge to pursue goals which had meaning only in relation to their discourses of discovery. Local guides did the lion's share of the work by finding paths, carrying loads or cutting steps in the ice. Leslie Stephen was honest enough to admit how much he owed his guides.

I utterly repudiate the doctrine that Alpine travellers are or ought to be the heroes of Alpine adventures. The true way at least to describe all my Alpine ascents is that Michel or Anderegg or Lauener succeeded in performing a feat requiring skill, strength, and courage, the difficulty of which was much increased by the difficulty of taking with him his knapsack and his employer.[4]

Although many nineteenth-century mountaineers later climbed without guides in the Alps, they usually took Alpine guides with them when they travelled outside Europe. From the 1920s, however, British climbers in the Himalayas left behind their Swiss guides and hired local porters who later became famous climbers, the Sherpas.[5]

When Tenzing Norgay, a Sherpa, and Edmund Hillary, a New Zealand bee-keeper, reached the summit of Mount Everest in 1953, the 'conquest' of Everest was widely celebrated around the world. Since the news was released on the day of Queen Elizabeth II's coronation, the members of the British expedition were hailed as conquering heroes on their return to London. But the British were not the only ones to be so celebrated. Tenzing was received as a national hero in Nepal and India, and Hillary became an icon of a new national identity in New Zealand.[6] These multiple celebrations of the 'conquest' of Everest suggest the extent to which mountain climbing was made possible by the reciprocal relationship and dynamic dialogue between guides and climbers. From Stephen's language of 'conquest' and warm testimonial for his guides, to competing versions of the 'conquest' of Everest, climbers and guides in the Alps and Himalayas have been engaged in a partnership that enabled them both to reach the top. As Tenzing noted of his climb with Hillary: 'We were not leader and led. We were partners'.[7]

The partnership between climbers and guides exemplifies some of the dilemmas of 'travel' and 'tourism' since the nineteenth century. While travel has always confronted travellers with 'others', it has also created sites of transcultural exchange between hosts and guests.[8] The relationship British climbers enjoyed with their Alpine guides or Himalayan Sherpas sometimes resembled what Victor Turner has called 'communitas', a sense of egalitarian harmony and bonding that takes place between individuals who escape the social hierarchies of everyday life. On these occasions, many climbers – and even some of their guides or Sherpas – appear to be escaping themselves to become themselves, escaping the routines of home to construct new identities in nature and among the 'other'. On other occasions, however, mountaineering reinforced social hierarchies or exposed a range of competing discourses that could not be easily reconciled.[9] Stephen's language of 'conquest', for example, emphasized the privilege of his position and remained in tension with his intimate experiences with his guides.

This essay discusses two periods of dialogue and exchange in the Alps and Himalayas. Beginning in the 1850s, British men from the professional middle classes climbed the Alps to represent their masculinity and British power at a time when each appeared to be threatened. These climbers and Alpine guides enjoyed a warm friendship that became more formal and distant during the nineteenth century as mountaineers regulated the guides and tourists overran the Alps. In the Himalayas in the twentieth century, the paternalism that British climbers initially showed towards their Sherpa porters moved in the opposite direction, as coolies became colleagues. The divergent paths that climbers took with guides or Sherpas may be explained in part by very different political contexts: the Alps of European state-building and nationalism enabled Alpine guides to assert their own agency much earlier than Sherpas living on the border of the British Raj in the Himalayas. As a result, mountaineers could not experience with Sherpas the same relationship that they had once enjoyed with Alpine guides until Sherpas invented their identity as climbing 'tigers of the snow'. In the years since the 1950s, Sherpas and Western travellers have sustained cultural differences among one another. In the late twentieth century, travellers and tourists and mountaineers continue to face the ambiguities of 'travel' with local guides and 'other' cultures.

I

In the 1880s, members of the Alpine Club published *Pioneers of the Alps*, a collection of photographic portraits and biographical sketches of Swiss guides. In a photograph on the frontispiece, an anonymous British climber sits hunched over in a posture of exhaustion – elbows on knees, head on ice-axe, and face hidden under a hat. Roped to the climber and flanking him are two guides: one pours a drink from a flask with a steady hand while the other guide reaches for the wine. Like this image, the essays in *Pioneers of the Alps* commemorated 'those who first conquered the great peaks, opened out the mountain highways, and who may fairly be said to have made possible that sport which so many of us enjoy each year in the Alps – men who are, or have been in their day, undoubtedly great guides'.[10] British mountaineers had been unstinting in their praise of their guides since the first volumes of *Peaks, Passes, and Glaciers* in the 1850s and 1860s. The following passage from the *Alpine Journal* in 1863 illustrates the intense camaraderie that developed between guides and climbers:

Dangers and difficulties shared and the exchange of thoughts and opinions, which must result from days and sometimes weeks of companionship, wonderfully diminish, for the time, at least, the gulf that exists, socially, between them; while the courage, presence of mind, endurance and unselfishness which is so often displayed in behalf of the traveller, makes him feel that his advantages of birth and education do not weigh so very heavily against native worth.[11]

'It is difficult', wrote a contributor to *Pioneers of the Alps*, 'to make those outside the magic circle understand the peculiar relationship that rapidly springs up between the Herren and their guides'.[12] *Pioneers of the Alps* offered a nostalgic record of that 'peculiar relationship' at a time when it was threatened by the advance of mass tourism in the Alps in the 1880s. As guides increased in number to meet the rising demand from thousands of tourists, relations between guides and climbers in the Alps became more routinized, formal and distant.

The earliest Alpine guides were pathfinders – sources of local knowledge who showed the way over unfamiliar terrain.[13] Guides had been leading travellers through Alpine valleys for centuries and, by the early nineteenth century, mountain guides were available in a few Alpine resorts. After an accident on Mont Blanc in 1820 resulted in the deaths

'Alpine climber and guides', from C. D. Cunningham and W. de W. Abney, eds, *Pioneers of the Alps* (London, 1888).

of their comrades, local guides formed the Compagnie des Guides de Chamonix in 1821.[14] Elsewhere, guides were most often hired through hotels. Guides impressed travellers with their social graces and local knowledge. 'A good guide is generally a very intelligent man', wrote Alfred Wills in 1856, 'with a great love of nature and of adventure, often, with a considerable amount of acquired information, and with manners more like those of a gentleman than are to be found amongst men of any other class, in the same rank of society'. Attentive to the comforts of the traveller, the guide acts as 'a sort of personal servant, almost a valet'. Guides served as intermediaries with other communities. 'On arriving at a town or village, he knows, or will find out, where the best accommodation can be had, and will supply any other kind of local information you may desire.' The guide also performed the role of porter and interpreter: 'He will carry your traps, and think nothing of it, and point out to you a thousand objects of interest, which, but for him, you would have overlooked.'[15]

Alfred Wills's famous ascent of the Wetterhorn in 1854 suggests that his guides also shared his desire to conquer the mountain. When Wills decided to climb the Wetterhorn, he had been travelling with Auguste Balmat, one of Chamonix's most experienced guides. Balmat arranged to hire Auguste Simond, a strong Chamonix guide then in Interlaken, and Ulrich Lauener, 'the most renowned guide of the Oberland'. Lauener in turn procured ropes, crampons and supplies as well as the services of Peter Bohren, a Grindelwald guide. Lauener and Bohren insisted on bringing their own 'flagge', a piece of metal two feet by three feet in size which they intended to plant on the summit. As the group ascended the mountain, they were joined by two peasants carrying a fir tree. 'They turned out to be two chamois hunters, who had heard of our intended ascent, and resolved to be even with us, and plant their tree side by side with our "Flagge".' After confirming that 'they should not steal from us the distinction of being *the first* to scale the awful peak', Balmat allowed them to join the party. The flag and fir tree were duly planted on the summit by the local men. Although the significance of these actions to local politics is unclear, the ascent was celebrated in Grindelwald, not for Wills's role as 'Der Wetterhörner Herr', but for the heroism of the Grindelwald and Chamonix guides who cut through the final ice cornice to the summit. After Wills returned to England, Balmat's journey from 'Interlaken to Chamonix, along which route he was well known, was like a triumphal progress'.[16] The two peasants who joined them with the fir tree, Christian Almer and Ulrich Kaufmann, later became two of the most celebrated guides in the Alps.

The ascent of the Wetterhorn, 1854.

Relations between climbers and guides were reciprocal. After attempting to climb the Matterhorn with John Tyndall in 1860, Vaughan Hawkins wrote of their guide, Johann Josef Bennen:

A perfect nature's gentleman, he is to me the most delightful of companions; and though no 'theory' defines our reciprocal obligations as guide and employer, I am sure that no precipice will ever engulf me so long as Bennen is within reach, unless he goes into it also – an event which seems impossible – and I think I can say I would, according to the measure of my capacity, do the same by him.

During the same attempt on the Matterhorn, Tyndall told him: 'You are the Garibaldi of guides, Bennen', to which Bennen replied, 'Am I not?' ('Nicht wahr?').[17] In 1861 Bennen thanked Tyndall for his faith in him and

looked forward to serving him again: 'I will be always ready for you
and your friends and you have only to command'.[18] Although the
traveller who employed the guide usually stepped onto the summit first,
Tyndall insisted that Bennen take this honour during their first ascent
of the Weisshorn. Tyndall wrote of the moment when they neared the
summit:

The man who had been in the rear of our little party during the day here stepped
forward, and set his foot upon the ridge, with the apparent intention of going
to the top. His progress was arrested by a rather emphatic exclamation of 'Back!
– not you'. Johann Joseph Bennen – the best and bravest climber I have ever met –
had been my leader throughout. Him I ordered to the front, and he it was who
first planted a foot upon the summit of the Weisshorn.[19]

The ambiguities of leadership are evident in the shifts in Tyndall's language
from one sentence to the next: Bennen was 'my leader throughout. Him
I ordered to the front'. After this ascent, Tyndall wrote in Bennen's
Führerbuch: 'He is a man of approved courage, strength and caution. He
is also tender and kind. In short he bears much the same relation to the
common run of guides as a Wellington to an ordinary subaltern.'[20]

Although many mid-Victorian climbers described their favourite guides
as generals, they also gave them commands. Tyndall thought Bennen was
a Garibaldi or Wellington, and to other climbers Melchior Anderegg was
the 'Napoleon' of guides.[21] Yet the climber's deep respect for these elite
guides remained in tension with their attempts to regulate their conduct.
Tyndall's testimonial to Bennen, for example, was written in his *Führerbuch*. In these 'guide's books', each traveller wrote a brief evaluation of
the guide's performance which was then shown to prospective employers.
In the 1850s, these books were transformed from personal scrapbooks
into regulatory devices. In 1856, the Swiss government issued *Führerbücher* to guides in the Oberland, and they were renewed annually for
guides in good standing.[22] Only the most senior guides, who had already
made their reputation in the small world of climbers, refused to use such
books. At the age of 33, Franz Andermatten said in 1856: 'I'm too old for
those little books: if anyone doesn't know me or doesn't trust me, they
can take someone else'.[23] For the younger generation of guides, who came
of age after Alpine climbing had become popular, recommendations in
their book – even if the book was unofficial – were crucial to their prosperity. Consider how Josef Imboden of St Niklaus became a guide in the
mid-1850s:

I was never a porter, but when I was fifteen years old, and had saved twenty francs, I went and stayed at the Riffel, and asked gentlemen to take me as guide. They all asked me, 'where is your book, young man?' I showed them my book, but there was nothing written in it. The twenty francs were nearly spent when I persuaded an Englishman to let me take him up the Cima di Jazzi. He was pleased, and the next day I took him up Monte Rosa alone. We then went to Chamonix together, and afterwards he wrote a great deal in my book; since then I have never wanted a gentleman to guide.[24]

The rules governing guides and the use of *Führerbücher* varied from place to place. Christian Kluckner, who began leading climbs in 1874, was not officially registered as a guide in the Engadine until 1908.[25]

In Chamonix, guides regulated themselves, and the Alpine Club, founded in London in 1857, tried repeatedly to change their rules to favour the traveller instead of the guide. The Compagnie des Guides de Chamonix fixed the price of an ascent, the minimum number of guides, and the procedure for hiring guides in strict rotation. In 1858 the Alpine Club petitioned the government of the Kingdom of Piedmont and Sardinia to alter the rules in order to extend 'the regime of individual liberty.' Although the Chamonix rules were modified to accommodate experienced climbers, lax enforcement meant that these changes had to be reaffirmed by the French government after it annexed the region in 1860. In 1874, the Alpine Club successfully advised the French government to wrest control of the Compagnie des Guides from the guides themselves:

Nowhere in the Alps, except at Chamonix, is any restriction placed upon the free choice of a guide by the traveller; and they can conceive of no principle, except that of communism pure and simple, which can justify the deliberate suppression by law of the natural rewards of superior intelligence, manners, goodwill, vigour, or capacity.

The Alpine Club recommended a published register of guides compiled from employers' recommendations as a 'wholesome stimulus to competition, and offer to them the legimate rewards of superiority'.[26]

Yet as the number of tourists increased in the Alps, so too did the number of guides. In the 1780s Chamonix had been visited by 800 to 1,200 visitors annually. A century later, railways and steamships enabled nearly one million tourists of American, English, German or Russian nationality to visit Switzerland.[27] Many of these new visitors wanted to emulate the climbers of the Alpine Club. One tourist on Thomas Cook's first Swiss tour, for example, entitled her diary 'the Proceedings of the Junior United Alpine Club, 1863'.[28] Alpine Clubs were soon founded in

Switzerland (1863), Italy (1863), Austria (1869), Germany (1874) and
France (1874). These clubs improved access, built huts, offered insurance
and expanded the number of guides. Although it had been impossible to
find a single guide in the Pelvoux massif in 1872, for example, the French
Alpine Club noted with satisfaction that, as a result of its efforts, over 100
guides, porters or aspirant guides were available in the district in 1880.[29]
In 1884, an English climber noted that, while the Alpine Club had worked
for thirty years to regulate guides, now the guides were in the control of
local groups. 'We did all we could for the protection of travellers while
the duty lay on us. It has now passed into other hands'.[30] By the 1890s,
guides rules, regulations and fees were standardized by national clubs
dominated by local elites throughout the Alps.[31]

Some mountaineers began to climb without guides in response to the
increasing numbers of tourists and their new relationship with guides in
the Alps. The professionalization of Alpine guides led climbers to change
the language they used to describe themselves from the 'traveller' to the
'amateur'.[32] As tourists flooded the Alps, guideless climbers also searched
for an appropriate language to describe their position. Arthur Cust
defended his guideless ascent of the Matterhorn in 1876 by noting that,
while the number of climbers had increased, the number of good guides
remained steady. 'The competition between the old aristocracy of the
Alps, to use metaphorical language, and the moneyed upstarts has
resulted in a rise in prices.' Since thousands of people now climbed in
the Alps, 'the only way real mountaineers would be able to differentiate
themselves would be by banding together to go without guides'. Cust's
desire to climb without guides stemmed from his desire to escape tourists.
'What will be the feeling of genuine lovers of the Alps', Cust asked, 'when
hustled at every turn by creatures whose development has reversed
Darwin's process?'[33]

In similar language, A. F. Mummery highlighted the class distinctions
which had been erected in the Alps between climbers and guides. After
climbing the Aiguille des Charmoz without guides in 1892, Mummery
speculated about the changes in guides since the 1850s.

The guide of the 'Peaks, Passes and Glaciers' age was a friend and adviser; he led
the party and entered fully into all the fun and jollity of the expedition; on the
return to the little mountain inn, he was still, more or less, one of the party, and
the evening pipe could only be enjoyed in his company.

But, Mummery argued, times had changed:

The swarming of the tourist has brought with it the wretched distinctions of class, and the modern guide inhabits the guides' rooms and sees his Monsieur only when actually on an expedition. Cut off from the intercourse of the old days, the guide tends more and more to belong to the lackey tribe, and the ambitious tourist looks upon him much as his less aspiring brother regards a mule.[34]

Guides rushed through climbs and followed predictable routes, according to Mummery. 'The skill of the traveller counts for absolutely naught; the practised guide looks on him merely as luggage.'

By the early twentieth century guides were often treated like children or commodities. In *Mountain Craft*, a standard climbing handbook of 1920, Geoffrey Winthrop Young described the Alpine guide as 'hill-born, hill-bred – that is, a child, with a child's capacity for becoming much what we make him – a companion, a valet or a machine – and with a child's suspicion and shyness, which he hides under the appearance of professional reserve or formal politeness'. Young urged amateur climbers to get to know their guides as human beings: 'The better a man knows his child-guide, the more he will know how to manage him, so as to get the best out of his mountaineering precocity'.[35] In addition, as tourists travelled to mountain regions in other parts of the world, Swiss guides were exported with the other commodities of Alpine resorts. The Canadian Pacific Railway, for example, imported Swiss guides to promote tourism in the Canadian Rockies. Guides paraded in lederhosen and climbing gear through the streets of Canadian cities as they travelled to the mountains. In the Rockies, the railway built a mock Swiss village called Edelweiss, where guides lived in homes built in the style of Swiss chalets.[36]

Guides could turn the tables on their employers, even if their roles were only very rarely reversed. C. E. Mathews recalled the occasion when he led Melchior Anderegg, usually his guide in the Alps, to the top of Snowdon. 'I hesitated for a few seconds. Melchior instantly forged to the front and proffered his services, which I emphatically declined. "No," I said, "I am guide today, and you are the Herr".'[37] Guides' autobiographies from the early twentieth century show that they wanted to escape the social conventions that regulated mountaineering in the Alps. Conrad Kain, a guide who climbed in the Alps, New Zealand and Canada, often told the story of becoming a gentleman for a day by wearing a new Norfolk jacket and hiring a guide to climb the Gross Glockner. 'Seeing myself in this new suit, I thought here was my chance to travel as a tourist.' Kain remained incognito until he signed his recommendation in the book of his guide.[38] Guides had long fantasized about writing their own *Herrenbücher*, in which they could record their opinions of the

Herren who employed them: 'It is only reasonable that the guide, when invited by a stranger to convoy the latter up a difficult peak, should be entitled to some information about the aspirant in the shape of the candid opinions of his former guides.'[39] Christian Kluckner was one of the few guides to offer candid assessments of the abilities of his *Herren* in his autobiography.[40]

The most famous autobiography by an Alpine guide was written by Mattias Zurbriggen, whose climbs in the Alps, Himalayas, New Zealand and South America made him an international celebrity. Zurbriggen had worked as a shepherd, miner, construction worker, carriage driver, served in the Italian military, ran his own shop, joined a Swiss gentleman on a trip to North Africa, and considered emigrating to South America, before contacts with hoteliers resulted in work as a guide. Although he worked for several well-known climbers, he never left any doubt about who was in charge: 'The guide ought to act as captain of the vessel: however distinguished may be the persons who commit themselves to our charge it is for us alone to direct and govern'. Zurbriggen also required all his 'patrons' to prove themselves on lesser peaks before he would allow them to tackle big ones. When Martin Conway invited the guide to join his expedition to the Karakoram in 1891, Zurbriggen had already climbed with all the members of the party except Lieut. C. G. Bruce, a Gurkha officer. 'It being my custom to test the powers of any climber to whom I was going to act as guide, this led to Mr. Bruce's coming to Zermatt for a month.'[41] Zurbriggen led Conway, Bruce and others up Pioneer Peak on Baltoro Kangri, possibly a height record at the time. In India, Zurbriggen shared British prejudices towards the local population and he also acted like a Sahib.

Despite Zurbriggen's position of authority on the mountain, relations between employer and guide, even one of Zurbriggen's calibre, remained ambiguous. For several years Zurbriggen's main 'patron' was E. A. Fitz-Gerald, a wealthy adventurer. Before Zurbriggen could undertake employment with other climbers, he first had to obtain FitzGerald's consent. Yet Zurbriggen's ambitions and abilities surpassed those of FitzGerald. In 1894, they climbed together in New Zealand and, while FitzGerald rested, Zurbriggen made the second ascent of Mount Cook, the highest point in New Zealand. When they travelled to South America in 1896, FitzGerald fell ill and Zurbriggen went on alone to make the first ascent of Aconcagua, the highest peak in the Americas. Zurbriggen returned to a hero's welcome in South America, as well as in Europe after his return. He recorded the following events at the dinner hosted by the Swiss ambassador in Buenos Aires in his honour:

The champagne flowed freely, and cries of '*Evviva*' and '*Lebehoch*' alternated with those of '*Helvetius*', and '*Zurbriggen and the FitzGerald Expedition*'. I was afterwards invited by the *Schweizer Männerchor* to a large gathering where we had instrumental music, and there was a ball in honour of Aconguga and of the guide who had been the first to climb it.

In Argentina, German and Italian-language newspapers gave his ascent as much coverage as did newspapers in Europe. In later years Zurbriggen climbed primarily with Italian 'patrons' in the Alps and with Fanny Bullock Workman and her husband in the Himalayas. Zurbriggen's final ambition was to climb Mount Everest. 'I should like to ascend Mount Everest. Every great mountain has a good way, and I am sure that there is a good way up Mount Everest – the greatest of them all.'[42]

II

Swiss guides were not given the chance to climb Mount Everest until the 1950s. When British climbers went to Mount Everest, beginning in the 1920s, they refused to take Swiss climbers or guides with them because they wanted the expeditions to be 'all British'.[43] They rejected the Swiss partly because such large-scale expeditions of 'exploration', whether to the Antarctic or the Himalayas, had become expressions of British nationalism. In response, German, French, Italian and Swiss national expeditions were mounted from the 1930s into the 1950s. But the British also rejected the Swiss in the 1920s because Swiss guides had by then achieved parity if not superiority with the British as climbers. Thus, the British took to Everest not Alpine guides but local porters drawn from the 'hill tribes' of the Himalayas.

Since few climbing expeditions had taken place in the Himalayas before the 1920s, the earliest Everest expeditions hired their porters from among Tibetan, Bhotia and Sherpa labourers who lived in Darjeeling, India, the starting point for many expeditions.[44] Initially, the British did not distinguish between different ethnic groups but treated them all as 'coolies'. During the first Everest expedition in 1921, for example, George Mallory photographed 'coolies wearing snow shoes for the first time' while another British climber showed them the ropes. As porters learned the rudiments of climbing, established camps on Everest and made great personal sacrifices, the climbers soon developed a deep respect for their porters' strength and stamina. In 1922, as a large group of porters and climbers ascended to the North Col of Everest after a snowstorm, an avalanche struck the party and buried many of the porters. Although two

'Mr Bullock and coolies wearing snow shoes for the first time, July 10th' during
the first Mt Everest expedition (1921).

porters were dug out of the snow alive, seven died and remained buried
in the glacier's crevasses. T. H. Somervell, one of the British survivors,
regretted that only porters had been killed.

I remember well the thought gnawing at my brain.'Only Sherpas and Bhotias
killed – why, oh why could not one of us Britishers have shared their fate?' I would
gladly at that moment have been lying there dead in the snow, if only to give those
fine chaps who had survived the feeling that we shared their loss, as we had indeed
shared the risk.[45]

Such sacrifices raised the hopes of climbers that these porters would one
day develop skills that matched those of Alpine guides. Also in the 1920s,
the British began to single out Sherpas as the best high-altitude porters.
In 1924, for example, General C. G. Bruce, the Everest leader who had previously climbed in the Alps and Himalayas with Zurbriggen, compared
their Everest porters to Swiss guides.

We have tested, and found not wanting, a race of people who seem to be practically impervious to cold and fatigue and exposure, and in whom we also discovered, although as yet in an early stage of development, the seeds of those great
qualities which are so clearly distinguishable in the great pioneers of the Golden
Age of Alpine Exploration – cheerfulness under all conditions and a willingness
to undertake any task for employers in whom they have confidence.[46]

Everest climbers began to refer to the high-altitude porters as 'Tigers', and the French Olympic Committee awarded the Prix d'Alpinisme to several porters, along with the British members of the Everest expedition, during the Winter Olympics in Chamonix. But alongside such respect for the porters was an ambivalent paternalism. Lt.-Col. E. F. Norton, who succeeded Gen. Bruce as leader in 1924, wrote that the porters were 'singularly like a childish edition of the British soldier, many of whose virtues they share'.[47]

Although relations between British climbers and Sherpa porters were still governed by the conventions of British imperial rule in India, their paternalism began to evolve into a closer partnership. As porters assumed more responsibility in the Himalayas during the 1930s and 1940s on German, French and Swiss expeditions – countries whose climbers often carried fewer assumptions from the Raj in their rucksacks – the relationship between Sherpas and Sahibs was transformed. In the 1930s, the British struggled to describe the position of their porters – as coolies, guides, climbers or 'tigers' – and they regulated Himalayan porters much as they had attempted to regulate Swiss guides in the Alps.

During the Everest expeditions, Sherpas also constructed a heroic identity for themselves that inspired younger Sherpas to become climbers. In their autobiographies, for example, Ang Tharkay and Tenzing Norgay, two of the best known Sherpas of the 1950s, both said that they decided to become climbing porters after hearing about the Everest expedition from other Solu Khumbu porters. As Ang Tharkay recalled:

I was little more than 20 years old when I met one of my village comrades, Nim Tharkay, who was returning from the expedition with General Bruce, and came to see me at our home in Khunde, carrying all of his climbing equipment. He strutted about from house to house as if he had accomplished a remarkable feat. Being his junior, my imagination was fired by the extravagant descriptions he gave us of his adventures, so much so that I was not long in feeling a mad desire to follow his example and to seek to join an expedition in my turn.[48]

Tenzing Norgay heard similar stories from Sherpas who had been to Everest. Although priests told Tenzing of terrors which guarded the heights, Tenzing said that he knew men among his own people who had climbed on the other side of Chomolungma: 'What I wanted was to see for myself. This was the dream I have had for as long as I can remember'.[49] Ang Tharkay and Tenzing each left Solu Khumbu for Darjeeling around 1933 hoping to join the next Everest expedition.

Sherpas distinguished themselves on expeditions to Kangchenjunga,

Kamet, Everest and Nanga Parbat, sometimes literally carrying the
European climbers on their backs. By the early 1930s, Chettan and Lewa,
two Everest porters in the 1920s, were considered to be almost equal to
guides. Lewa had been one of the porters rescued from the avalanche on
Everest in 1922. Chettan, known familiarly as 'Satan', had been taught
to use an axe and rope on Everest in 1922 and later joined expeditions to
Nanda Devi, Garhwal and Kangchenjunga. When Frank Smythe choose
porters for an international expedition to Kangchenjunga in 1930, he
found them carrying tattered letters of recommendation from General
Bruce 'testifying to their courage and loyalty':

The men we had were all hard-bitten 'Tigers', as tough, hardy and weather-
beaten as the Old Guard of Napoleon. They were not merely porters, but genuine
mountaineers and adventurers, who enjoyed a tussle with a great mountain as
much as we did, and were as keen as we were to get to the top.[50]

The Kangchenjunga expedition was periodically strafed by avalanches,
one of which struck a climbing party and killed Chettan. Chettan's
obituary in a climbing journal harkened back to the partnerships with
early Alpine guides: 'He understood what mountaineering means to us
and shared our interests to the full. He was on the road to be a guide,
with all that word implies among mountaineers, which is that the servant
becomes a companion and a friend.'[51]

Lewa reached the summit of Kamet with Smythe in 1931. As they
walked to the base of the mountain, Lewa and the other Darjeeling
porters were by then so experienced and well paid that they hired their
own local porters to carry their loads to the mountain. 'In their own
estimation', Smythe wrote of the high-altitude porters, 'they were great
men specially picked to climb Kamet, and also selected by the Sahibs as
their personal servants. Strolling along like Sahibs, able to pay for substi-
tutes to carry their loads, their prestige in the valley would be enormously
enhanced.' But the prestige of the British climbers also rose as they gained
altitude: 'after the insolent stares of the "Congress Wallahs" of the lower
hills and plains, it was pleasant to be greeted with a respectful and
friendly "Salaam, Sahib" or "Salaam, Huzoor" from the villagers we met
on the path'. When, at last, Smythe and the first climbing party reached
the last few steps to the summit: 'We seized hold of Lewa and shoved him
on in front of us . . . And so he was first to tread the summit. It was the
least compliment we could pay to those splendid men, our porters, to
whom we owed the success of our expedition'.[52] Lewa lost several frost-
bitten toes during this ascent, yet served as Sirdar, head porter, for a

'Birnie being brought down from Camp II' during
the 1933 Everest expedition.

British expedition to Everest in 1933 and a German expedition to Nanga
Parbat in 1934.[53]

The deaths of many Sherpas during several German expeditions to
Nanga Parbat cemented the heroic self-image of the climbing Sherpa. In
1934, four Germans and six porters were killed during storms and
avalanches on Nanga Parbat. Fritz Bechtold did not exaggerate when he
wrote that many of the porters 'had done superhuman feats: no mere
porter-service, but comradeship in the purest sense of the word, loyalty
even to death'.[54] In the most famous story of such sacrifice, two porters,
Ang Tsering and Gaylay, were descending during a lull in the storm when
they found two of the German climbers weakened by fatigue. After one of
the Germans died in his sleep, the three survivors, including Willi Merkl,
the expedition leader, descended until Merkl again collapsed. Gaylay and

Ang Tsering dug an ice-cave for shelter where Gaylay chose to remain with the dying Merkl, even though he was still strong enough to descend with Ang Tsering. Gaylay died huddled next to Merkl. Ang Tsering was later given the Medal of Honour and the German Red Cross. In his auto-biography, Tenzing Norgay reported that among the Sherpas in Darjeeling in 1934, 'all the talk was of the German expedition of the past summer to Nanga Parbat'. Tenzing heard first-hand accounts from Dawa Thondup and Ang Tsering who told him how Gaylay had sacrificed himself to stay with Merkl: 'Even though I had not yet been on a mountain', wrote Tenzing, 'such a story made me, too, proud to be a Sherpa.'[55]

If such tragic events contributed to the Sherpa construction of a heroic identity as climbers, they also led to the regulation of porters by the British in India. The members of the Himalayan Club, founded in India in 1928, wanted to pay tribute to the porters who died on Nanga Parbat. When Joan Townend, wife of a member of the Indian Civil Service and the Himalayan Club's representative in Darjeeling, attempted to do so, she discovered that few details were known about the porters. As she and others compiled the porters' obituaries, they also began to develop rules and regulations to govern them. The Himalayan Club compiled a list of the porters and 'each Sherpa was to be issued with a "chit book" containing his photograph and wrapped up in a mackintosh case'.[56] At the end of each expedition, the leaders wrote recommendations in each 'chit book', which served the same purpose as the *Führerbuch* in the Alps.

For the next twenty years, all climbers in the Himalayas were depen-dent on the Himalayan Club in Darjeeling for the supply of porters. The club established recommended rates of pay, rations, disability com-pensation, examples of appropriate equipment, and so forth, in addition to publishing a list of porters in its journal with summaries of their character and ability compiled from their 'chit books'. In 1938 the Himalayan Club issued the first 'Tiger Badges' to Sherpas who reached the highest camps on Everest or accomplished similar feats on other peaks. While there was some dissatisfaction with the term 'Tiger', no suitable alternative was found:

'Climbers' is a term already used for Europeans of the party; 'guides' would give a false impression, for it is most undesirable that the porters should be looked upon as guide in the Swiss sense; and since the name 'Tiger' has been fairly con-stantly used since the Mount Everest expedition of 1924 for the picked porters who have gone high, it has been adopted as the best name put forward.[57]

Many porters earned this recognition, even if some Sherpas still received their tributes only posthumously. In 1937, for example, another seven Germans and nine Sherpas were killed on Nanga Parbat, and yet more Sherpas died on K2 a year later.[58]

By the time Himalayan climbing resumed after World War II, many Sherpas had internalized the desire to conquer the mountains. Ang Tharkay joined the first ascent of Annapurna with French climbers in 1950 and Tenzing Norgay 'conquered' Everest with Edmund Hillary in 1953. Tenzing's experience from the 1930s to the 1950s illustrates the rapid transition made by the Sherpas. Tenzing was born at Tsa-chu, Tibet, and grew up as a farmer and yak-herder in the shadow of Everest, or Chomolungma (Goddess-Mother of the World) as it was known locally. After leaving Nepal for Darjeeling to seek work as a porter, he joined seven Everest expeditions from 1935 to 1953. When Tenzing looked from Tibet into Nepal from the Lho La pass on Everest in 1938, he could almost see his hometown: 'Far below I could see yaks on the slopes near the Khumbu Glacier, and there was one man with them, and I wondered who he was'. Tenzing joined a Swiss party in Garhwal in 1947, and 'even though there was much language difficulty, I had felt truly close to them, and thought of them not as sahibs or employers, but as friends'. In 1950 he reached the summit of Nanda Devi East with a French expedition, and, in 1952, the Swiss Everest expedition made him a full member of the climbing team, 'the greatest honour that had ever been paid me'. Tenzing developed a close friendship with his climbing partner, Raymond Lambert, a famous Swiss guide. Although Tenzing and Lambert shared reputations as great guides, they only spoke a few words of each other's language. As Tenzing recalled, 'When things were good it was *ça va bien*! And when they weren't it was *ça va bien* just the same'.[59] During the Swiss expedition in 1952, Tenzing and Lambert reached within 800 feet of the summit, the highest elevation ever.

By 1953, Tenzing was one of the most experienced Himalayan climbers anywhere. 'In the beginning', Tenzing later noted, 'as novices, we were a little more than load-bearers – what in the East, for long ages, have been called coolies'. Although they still took pride in their ability to carry loads, Tenzing continued, 'Over the years we have learned much about the methods and skills of mountaineering, until we are now able to help other ways, such as in the finding of routes, the cutting of steps, the handling of ropes, the choosing of camp-sites'.[60] The Swiss recognized these skills and treated the Sherpas as equals. These experiences transformed the Sherpas' relationship with British climbers on Everest in 1953.

As the Darjeeling secretary of the Himalayan Club told Col. John Hunt, the expedition's leader: 'As Tenzing knows the route on Everest like the palm of his hand, he is the man to go'.[61] Hunt recognized the importance of Tenzing and recruited him as Sirdar, head porter, and a member of the climbing team. Tenzing also earned twice as much as he had been paid by the Swiss, equalling four times as much as had been usual before that.[62] Even ordinary porters earned a fortune compared to what they could earn in agricultural labour. 'Base camp porters made as much as seven times the daily wage of field workers and the high altitude porters who carried loads up onto the mountain itself were still better paid.'[63] After minor misunderstandings concerning housing and equipment at the start of the expedition, the British climbers and the Sherpa porters worked closely together and their teamwork enabled Hillary and Tenzing to reach the summit.

After the ascent, Tenzing, Hillary and Hunt became national heroes and global celebrities. When they returned from the summit, the world's

Edmund Hillary and Tenzing Norgay after the 1953 ascent of Everest.

press wanted to know who had 'conquered' the peak: did Hillary or Tenzing 'step on the summit first'? This question had not occurred to the climbers during the expedition, since they had reached the summit only through a team effort and shared in a feeling of 'communitas'. Yet Hillary's and Tenzing's ascent became a source of nationalist contention in Nepal, India, Britain and New Zealand. After a few newspapers reported that Tenzing had been first on top, the two climbers issued a joint statement that they had reached the summit 'almost together'.[64] This attempt to finesse the issue (Hillary had been first on the rope) maintained a useful ambiguity. Although they reached the summit together as partners, their experiences on the summit and their descriptions of the 'conquest' were remarkably different. On the summit, Tenzing buried an offering to the gods in the snow and thanked the mountain in a prayer: 'I am grateful, Chomolungma'. Hillary took photographs, urinated onto the peak and told another climber: 'We knocked the bastard off'.[65]

III

Since the first ascent of Everest in 1953, Sherpas have steadily assumed more responsibility and control over climbing expeditions. Tenzing became the head of the Himalayan Mountaineering Institute, established in Darjeeling in his honour, and turned the Sherpa Buddhist Association into a direct competitor to the Himalayan Club for the distribution of porters. In 1954, the Himalayan Club advised climbers to contact the Sherpas themselves for future expeditions:

As it was never the intention of the Club that the Hon. Local Secretary in Darjeeling should permanently be responsible for organising Sherpa porters for expeditions and as there are now Sherpa Sirdars able themselves to accept this responsibility, the Committee recommends that members should apply directly to the Sirdars.

By the 1970s, Sherpas no longer kept chit books, and Sherpas living in Nepal competed with Sherpas based in Darjeeling for control of the expedition market. Sherpas themselves owned a number of trekking and climbing agencies by the 1980s. By the late 1990s, individual Sherpas had climbed Everest upwards of ten times.[66]

By the late twentieth century, Sherpas had become accomplished climbers just as Alpine guides had been in the late nineteenth century. But relations between Sherpas and travellers have not followed the same pattern as in the Alps. Although friendships with guides still develop in the Alps, guides usually remain distant from their clients. Climbers and tourists hope to find guides who are friends and companions, yet the steadily increasing number of tourists makes this ideal ever more difficult to attain. According to a recent report on the guides of Chamonix:

The mountain guide has evolved from porter and humble servant to a highly trained, dedicated and superbly fit companion. Even so, one of Chamonix's top guides admits: 'Sometimes it's really just advanced babysitting.' ... The fact that today a tourist will commit himself to an ascent on Mont Blanc after only a cursory telephone conversation with his guide (Guide: 'Are you fit?' Client: 'How much does it cost?') is testimony to the progress that associations like the Compagnie des Guides have made in opening the peaks to the people.[67]

In the Alps, the response by many climbers/travellers to this 'opening up the peaks' by guides has been to climb without guides. Despite the increasing numbers of tourists in the Himalayas, climbers have not attempted to climb without Sherpas to the extent that they have done in the Alps.

On the contrary, one of the attractions of post-war mountaineering, trekking and adventure tourism in the Himalayas since the 1950s has been the contact between the tourist/climber and Sherpas or other indigenous peoples. The Catholic peasants of the Alps who became guides had also once been objects of fascination for British tourists. In consequence of the regulation of guides and the commercialization of tourism by the early twentieth century, British climbers came to see Swiss guides as less 'other' and perhaps more 'white' than they ever did with Sherpas. In the Himalayas, Western tourists and Sherpas have remained engaged in a complex process in which Sherpas attempt to retain the 'otherness' that the Western tourist and climber desires. In this process, the cultural practices and reciprocity of Sherpa Buddhism may be both the 'otherness' that travellers are looking for among Sherpas and the resource that has enabled Sherpas to assert their agency in this relationship. The climbers' desire to preserve such 'difference' may also be part of the wider phenomenon of 'ethnic' tourism around the world.[68]

Paradoxically, mountaineers have attempted to recover the friendship and sense of 'similarity' and 'communitas' that had once characterized their relationship with Alpine guides by developing collaborative relationships with Sherpas that preserve their cultural 'difference'. Recent deaths on Mount Everest in the 1990s have been controversial in large part because they were *guided* ascents with 'Western' guides. Fatal climbs with or by Sherpas do not appear to raise the same concerns. Yet these Western guides share with Sherpas in a broader legacy. On Everest in 1996, Rob Hall, a celebrated New Zealand guide, chose to stay near the summit and die with his client, just as Gaylay did on Nanga Parbat in 1934 and as several other Sherpas have continued to do in the years since.[69] To be sure, as the ascent of Everest becomes a 'guided' climb, in which travellers pay to be taken up Everest by either Western guides or local Sherpas, mountaineers in the Himalayas inevitably attempt to distinguish themselves from other tourists by climbing without guides or Sherpas. In many ways, such 'guideless' or 'Sherpaless' climbing is merely another response to the dilemma that climbers and travellers, and even anthropologists and historians, have faced since the nineteenth century: to experience cultural difference even as that difference is transformed by the traveller's presence.

9

The European Journey in
Postwar American Fiction and Film

KASIA BODDY

Connections between travel, travel writing and attempts to construct or define national, group or personal identities have, as the essays in this book demonstrate, a very long history. But since the Second World War, and even before, cultural commentators of all sorts have lamented what Lévi-Strauss famously termed 'an end to journeying'.[1] This lament, as the other essays here also show, is not unique to the last fifty years, but it has become increasingly prevalent. It is not that people don't travel anymore; rather, it is argued, travel as a significant transformative experience is no longer possible. There are two common explanations given for this loss of faith: the growth of mass tourism as a result of increasingly cheap air travel, and increasing global homogenization. The two phenomena are often considered to be linked, the strongest version arguing that the world has become homogenous because of mass tourism.

A typical example of the 'end to journeying' view can be found in Paul Fussell's book *Abroad: British Literary Travelling Between the Wars* (1980), where he contrasts the 1930s with the present and asserts that 'travel is now impossible and that tourism is all we have left'.[2] For Fussell travel and tourism are polar opposites. While travel is the preserve of elites, tourism is proletarian, catering to the lowest common denominator. Whereas travellers explore the wonders of the world, tourists go to designated sites – including what Fussell terms 'pseudo-places'.[3] The classic examples of such places are American – the Disneylands and Disney Worlds of this planet, destinations designed to fascinate and repulse cultured Europeans such as Baudrillard and Eco. But places like these exist wherever the tourist industry operates.[4] Furthermore, as the American humourist P. J. O'Rourke notes, 'many contemporary tourist attractions are not located in one special place the way tourist attractions used to be'. Whereas a previous generation could constitute 'a stately procession of like-minded individuals through half a dozen of the world's major principalities', today 'tourist attractions have no specific location' but 'pop up everywhere – that villainous cab driver with the all-consonant last name, for instance. He's waiting outside hotels from Sun City to the Seward Peninsula.'[5] To paraphrase the title of the 1960s film satire, the only way we can tell we're in Belgium is by knowing that this is Tuesday.[6]

The problem with modern or mass tourism for the elegiasts is its tendency to what Max Weber called 'rationalisation'. This is defined by a modern Weberian, George Ritzer, as 'the increasing effort to ensure predictability from one time or place to another. In a rational society people prefer to know what to expect in all settings and at all times'.[7] Ritzer re-names the phenomenon 'the McDonaldization of society'. What McDonalds have done to the global food industry, he argues, has become a model for many different kinds of commercial, social and cultural organization. Indeed McDonalds features as a common referent for American values, and McDonaldization is seen to be synonymous with Americanization in several of the texts that are considered here.[8]

When considered in relation to tourism, 'McDonaldization' results in what Paul Theroux calls 'Traveling as a Version of Being at Home'. 'Spain is Home-plus-Sunshine; India is Home-plus-Servants; Africa is Home-plus-Elephants-and-Lions; Ecuador is Home-plus-Volcanoes.' 'When a person says, in a foreign place, "I feel right at home here,"' writes Theroux, 'he is making a statement about the nature of travel, not the texture of the place he's in. I found it extremely pleasant to have a cheese-burger and a beer at the Inter-Continental Hotel in Kabul, Afghanistan; but I would have been a fool for thinking that this in any way represented a kind of Afghan experience.'[9] 'Travel as a Version of Being at Home' (tourism) is thus precisely an avoidance of the disruptive, revelatory experience that travel sought, or seeks, to achieve.

An extreme form of this is presented in Anne Tyler's 1985 novel *The Accidental Tourist*. It is the story of Macon Leary, a writer of guidebooks – 'chunky, passport-sized paperbacks. *Accidental Tourist in France. Accidental Tourist in Germany. In Belgium.* No author's name, just a logo: a winged armchair on the cover.'

Their concern was how to pretend they had never left home. What hotels in Madrid boasted king-sized Beauty-rest mattresses? What restaurants in Tokyo offered Sweet 'n' Low? Did Amsterdam have a McDonald's? Did Mexico City have a Taco Bell? Did any place in Rome serve Chef Boyardee ravioli? Other travellers hoped to discover distinctive local wines; Macon's readers searched for pasteurized and homogenized milk.[10]

Despite the increased prevalence of such tourists and the services they require, Paul Theroux maintains that there are genuine Afghan experiences, genuine travel experiences, still to be had. It is up to the few, the elite, to preserve the tradition, to affirm, he says 'that the world is still large and strange, and thank God, full of empty places that are nothing like home'.[11] And in the footsteps of Theroux we find what the anthropologist Dean MacCannell calls 'the anti-tourist', the wannabee traveller, catered for by Sunday supplement offers of 'exclusive' expeditions to Everest, or agencies specializing in 'independent travel'.[12] For most commentators, however, anti-tourism, even Theroux-like travel, is simply delusional. The modern traveller is 'chasing after the vestiges of a lost reality', writes Lévi-Strauss; 'we are all tourists now, and there is no escape', according to Fussell.[13]

TOURISTS AND PILGRIMS

If we accept the gloomy view that 'real' travel and varied destinations no longer exist, what then are the implications for our ideas of pilgrimage? The journey of the pilgrim has always been a journey with a definite destination and a definite purpose: the pilgrim wants to be transformed.[14] The tourist described above, on the other hand, has no specific destination in mind and does all he can to avoid any physical, far less psychic, disturbance. He seems antithetical to the traditional conception of a pilgrim. Yet what modern tourists do share with traditional pilgrims is a desire to encounter something that many others have also encountered, a desire for a communal experience. In his 1963 novel, V, Thomas Pynchon suggests that, for this reason, tourism forms 'the most absolute communion' possible in modern society. He imagines a country populated only by 'a breed called "tourists"':

Its landscape is one of inanimate monuments and buildings; near-inanimate barmen, taxi-drivers, bellhops, guides . . . More than this it is two-dimensional as is the Street, as the pages and maps of those little red handbooks . . . Tourism thus is supra-national, like the Catholic Church, and perhaps the most absolute communion we know on earth: for be its members American, German, Italian, whatever, the Tour Eiffel, Pyramids, and Campanile all evoke identical responses from them; their Bible is clearly written and does not admit of private interpretation; they share the same landscapes, suffer the same inconveniences; live by the same pellucid time-scale. They are the Street's own.[15]

While Pynchon's account of tourist 'communion' conforms to anthropological accounts of pilgrim 'communitas', a crucial facet of the traditional pilgrimage experience is abandoned in his scenario.[16] Pilgrimage no longer depends on going to specific places and seeing specific sights. It does not matter where tourists go, Pynchon suggests, or what they see; their experience will be identical in every situation.[17] Typical members of Pynchon's 'breed' are the figures depicted in Duane Hanson's super realist sculptures, *Tourists* and *Tourists II*. The figures are caricatures, 'Mr and Mrs Middle America on Vacation'[18]; dressed in the requisite gaudy clothes and carrying the requisite photographic equipment, they are looking up with typical tourist expressions of admiration. We do not see what they are looking at, as if Hanson is suggesting that the object of their gaze does not matter. Their response, we feel, will be the same wherever they are and whatever they see.[19] We might compare them with the sightseers depicted in, to take a typical nineteenth-century example,

Duane Hanson, *Tourists*, 1970.
Scottish National Gallery of Modern Art, Edinburgh.

David Roberts, *At Rome, Ruins of the Forum*, 1859.
Wolverhampton Art Gallery.

David Roberts's *At Rome, Ruins of the Forum* (1859). In this painting the figures are small and insignificant and the focus of interest squarely rests on the details of the Roman forum itself.[20] The shift in emphasis is also reflected in the titles of the two pieces. In Roberts's painting the important fact is to be 'at Rome'; in Hanson's sculpture the occasion is simply the pretext to observe the observers, the 'Tourists' themselves.

AN END TO TRAVEL WRITING?

Looking at Hanson's sculpture we see that changes in the experience of travel during the last hundred years have been accompanied by changes in ways of representing the experience of travel. I use the word 'accompanied' here, but others have gone much further and argued that there is a direct, even causal, relationship between changes in travel and changes in travel writing.

For Paul Fussell there is a crucial distinction to be made between the methods of the explorer, the traveller and the tourist. While 'all three make journeys', the explorer seeks the undiscovered, the traveller that which has been discovered by the mind working in history, the tourist that which has been discovered by entrepreneurship and prepared for him by the arts of mass publicity. The genuine traveller is, or used to be, in the middle between the two extremes. If the explorer moves toward the risks of the formless and the unknown, the tourist moves toward the security of pure cliché.[21]

The traveller mediates, for Fussell, between formlessness (a void that the explorer fills with new facts) and cliché (the only resource of the tourist). If we see this in terms of the analogy between writing and travelling, we might then think of explorers as the founders of our literary genres, travellers as those revisiting and modifying those genres, and tourists as weary postmodernists, who've given up the struggle and have accepted cliché as their only resource. 'Real' places are 'odd' and require 'interpretation' and 'real' writing.[22] 'Pseudo-places' only deserve the pseudo-responses of the third rate. For Fussell then, the 'end of travel' is intimately and inevitably associated with what he sees as the end of good writing.

The age of tourism, it is frequently noted, is also the age of mechanical reproductions of postcards and souvenirs. Collectors no longer capture the authentic 'aura' of a place through relics brought home, for those things gathered by modern tourists are, by Benjamin's definition, without aura.[23] If both the facts discovered by exploration and the transformative liminal experiences of travel are now thought to be impossible to find, then what stories can possibly be sent back by tourism? All one can do, many think, is send parodies of authentic experience in the fragmentary form of snapshots and messages designed to fit on (half) the back of a postcard.

Susan Sontag goes further and argues that photography and tourism are intimately linked, having developed 'in tandem'. Taking photographs is not about recording the strangeness of the world (whatever *National Geographic* might think); rather, she maintains, photographing some-thing makes it familiar and safe.[24] Tourist photographers seek neither originality nor verisimilitude in their snaps. They aspire instead to take pictures that resemble other images (the postcards that they send home) and provide 'indisputable evidence that the trip was made'. We cannot see what Hanson's 'tourist' is looking at, but we know that he will photograph it.

If it seems obvious that something is photographed because it is already a tourist attraction, one can also imagine a situation in which the very fact of being photographed creates the tourist attraction. This is precisely what novelist Don DeLillo does in his account of 'the most photographed barn in America'.

Soon the signs started appearing. THE MOST PHOTOGRAPHED BARN IN AMERICA. We counted five signs before we reached the site. There were forty cars and a tour bus in the makeshift lot. We walked along a cowpath to the slightly elevated spot set aside for viewing and photographing. All the people had cameras; some had tripods, telephoto lenses, filter kits. A man in a booth sold postcards and slides – pictures of the barn taken from the elevated spot.

The site is visited by two cultural historians, happy to play games with their signifiers and signifieds.

We listened to the incessant clicking of shutter release buttons, the rustling crank of levers that advanced the film.

'What was the barn like before it was photographed?' he said. 'What did it look like, how was it different from other barns, how was it similar to other barns? We can't answer these questions because we've read the signs, seen the people snapping the pictures. We can't get outside the aura. We're part of the aura.' . . .

He seemed immensely pleased by this.[25]

Jacques Derrida in turn plays with the implications of the postcard in his essay 'Envois', suggesting that he prefers the postcard to the letter (the traditional form of the traveller's communication) precisely because it is 'banal' – 'I prefer cards, one hundred cards or reproductions in the same envelope, rather than a single "true" letter . . . We have played the postcard against literature, inadmissible literature.'[26] The postcard 'plays against' traditional literature in several ways. First, as it is something that is un-ambiguously a reproduction, questions of originality need not arise in relation to the postcard. Secondly, its size limits what can be said and so inevitably the writer must reach for another to continue – perhaps ending up, as Derrida does, with 'one hundred cards in the same envelope'. Narrative progression is therefore necessarily disrupted. A letter can be as long as the writer wants it to be; at the very least the limits of the postcard force interruptions.

Two features of tourist photographs and postcards are important as models for contemporary writers: first, their status as products of 'mechanical reproduction' and hence their lack of originality; and, secondly, their brevity and unsuitability for long, linear narratives. The snapshot and the postcard therefore feature frequently in postmodern travel narratives. Lynne Tillman's 1992 novel *Motion Sickness*, for example, takes the postcard as its prime organizational feature. The story is told in a series of short segments labelled 'Paris', 'Istanbul', 'Amsterdam' etc, and each is represented by a short incident and image. Furthermore, the novel charts the protagonist's search for postcards, carefully chosen to send to her various friends. In the book's postscript she writes on the cards and spreads them out on her bed to form a bizarre collage of the cultural icons of Europe. She tears one up and then can't decide whether to send the others. 'I have no perfect person to send . . . [them] to, no ideal reader.'[27]

THE AMERICAN JOURNEY TO EUROPE

The American journey to Europe was never one of exploration. It didn't matter to most Americans that Europe was somewhere very well known and well documented, familiar, because for most travellers the very point of the journey was to fall into well-worn footsteps, to have the communal ritualized experience of pilgrimage. Many American travellers knew exactly what they were looking for, based on books they had read and paintings they had seen, and what they wanted was for reality to match up.

So, for example, Margaret Fuller records her initial disappointment on arriving in Genoa in the late 1840s:

The excessive beauty of Genoa is well known, and the impression upon the eye alone was corespondent with what I expected, but, alas! the weather is so cold I could not realise that I can actually touch those shores to which I had looked forward my whole life.

On arriving in Naples, however, she notes: 'Here at Naples I *have* at last found *my* Italy; I have passed through the Grotto of Pausillipo, visited Cuma, Baia and Capri – ascended Vesuvius, and found all familiar'.[28]

But many of the American travellers who went to Europe wanted more from the pilgrimage experience. They wanted to drink from the fount of European culture, but they also wanted to establish themselves as writers in the Romantic and post-Romantic period – in, that is, a period concerned with originality. As early as 1842 we find writers apologizing that they are 'travellers in climes so generally visited', that it is 'difficult to say what has not been said before'.[29] And so the search for new approaches began. Washington Irving presents this disingenuous apology for his sketches in 'The Author's Account of Himself':

As it is the fashion for modern tourists to travel pencil in hand and bring home their portfolios filled with sketches, I am disposed to get up a few for the entertainment of my friends. When, however, I look over the hints and memorandums I have taken down for the purpose, my heart almost fails me at finding how my idle humour has lead me aside from the great objects studied by every regular traveller who would make a book. I fear I shall give equal disappointment with an unlucky landscape painter, who had travelled on the continent, but, following the bent of his vagrant inclination, had sketched in nooks and corners and byplaces. His sketchbook was accordingly crowded with cottages and landscapes and obscure ruins, but he had neglected to paint St. Peter's, or the Coliseum; the cascade of Terni, or the bay of Naples; and had not a single glacier or volcano in his whole collection.[30]

There is no point in detailing familiar scenes, rather what is interesting are the 'nooks and corners and byplaces' that have been ignored by previous writers.

If, as Freud says, ' a great part of the pleasure of travel lies in the fulfilment of these early wishes [to run away from home] . . . and the essence of success was to have got further than one's father', a great part of the pleasure of travel writing, for Americans writing about Europe at any rate, lies in the possibility of establishing one's voice as distinct from that of the previous generation.[31] This is wonderfully dramatized in Herman Melville's *Redburn* (1849), published just ten years after the first of Karl Baedeker's famous series of guidebooks. Melville's narrator tells of how on his first voyage to England he studied his father's guidebooks but, on arriving at Liverpool, 'this precious book was next to useless. Yes, the thing that had guided the father could not guide the son. And I sat down on a shop step and gave loose to meditation'.

Here, now, oh Wellingborough, thought I, learn a lesson, and never forget it. This world, my boy, is a moving world . . . as your father's guide-book is no guide for you, neither would yours be a true to those who come after you. Guide-books, Wellingborough, are the least reliable books in all literature; and nearly all literature, in one sense, is made up of guide-books . . . Every age makes its own guide books, and the old ones are used for waste paper.[32]

New guidebooks, Wellingborough claims, need to be written because the world is 'a moving world'; what was true of one generation would not be true of the next. But by the late nineteenth and the early twentieth centuries, American writers were less interested in the idea of Europe as somewhere that changed and was unpredictable, like America itself. Instead Europe had become an ahistorical repository of culture, a museum, and what continued to change were its visitors.[33] So Pound's description in 1918 of Henry James as 'A Baedeker to a continent' does not provoke a call to follow in James's footsteps, nor a Melvillean anxiety about reflecting the 'moving world'.[34] What is important for Pound is that he and others 'make it new', rewrite the Baedeker. Writers such as Pound, Hemingway and Stein left America not to search for a cultural heritage in Europe but simply to find a place that was *not* America. While Henry James saw Rome, London and Paris as scenes for dramatic confrontation, Henry Miller valued Paris because he felt that 'of itself Paris initiates no dramas . . . Paris is simply an artificial stage'. 'I'm not an American anymore, nor a New Yorker, and even less a European, or a Parisian . . . I'm a neutral. [35]

*   *   *

In the American imagination Europe has traditionally functioned as a place of contrast; it was the place against which America defined itself, the place where Americans could conduct what Henry James termed the 'virtual quarrel of ours with our own country'.[36] Going to Europe was both a way of asserting one's difference from other Americans – as an artist or as an outsider because of one's race, sexuality or politics – and of asserting one's belonging to the class of Americans who go to Europe on a cultural pilgrimage.[37] Since the Second World War, however, there have been considerable changes in American–European relations and in the position of Europe in the American imagination. In the remainder of this essay I want to outline some of these and suggest some implications for writing in the period.

'EUROPE IS OVER'[38]

In 1945 Europe was seen as a collapsed civilization, saved only from complete self-destruction by the actions of its imperial successor, America, which then went on to help reconstruct it, largely in its own image.[39] As in the aftermath of the First World War, Europe was devastated economically as well as physically, while America experienced increased prosperity. The economic and cultural conditions that made it attractive for expatriates to settle in Europe in the 1920s – a strong dollar coupled with social conservatism at home – recurred in the 1950s. Yet some things had changed. By 1945 the cultural and economic strength, as well as the military prowess, of the United States were well established. Europe was now a place where American business ambitions could be fulfilled as well as rejected, and where Americans perceived themselves as both imitated and resented. Lynne Tillman writes in her 1980 story 'Weird Fucks' that it has become 'a universal truth' that 'Americans are hated in Europe'.[40]

When the narrator is caught trespassing in Rome she immediately takes advantage of this fact:

I point at my head and my chest, emphatically declaring, Stupido americana, stupido americana. I'm not at all sure of the agreement but I figure they'll get the point. And the point is that if I admit I'm an idiot, particularly an American idiot, Americans are hated in Europe, if I admit this, they may go easy on me.

If modernity was preoccupied with the problem of creating one's own new identity, postmodernity recognizes that one cannot escape the identities of nation. For the protagonist of Whit Stillman's comic film, *Barcelona* (1994), this has its advantages: 'one of the great things about getting involved with someone from another country', he says, 'you can't take it personally'.

What's really terrific is that when *we* act in ways which might objectively be considered incredibly obnoxious or annoying, . . . they don't get upset at all, they don't take it personally, they just assume it's some national characteristic.[41]

Not everyone, however, finds national stereotyping such a readily available excuse. When the narrator of Tillman's novel *Motion Sickness* is told by a Yugoslavian friend, '"You are like all Americans,"' she notes that, 'There is no way I can say to him, You are like all Yugoslavians, as I have no idea what all Yugoslavians are like'. Travelling in Europe does not provide a way of escaping her Americanness for it follows her everywhere in the assumptions of the people she meets – everything from her lack of history to her clean hair is put down to her nationality. You 'can't take the country out of the girl when the girl is out of the country'.[42]

Rather then fleeing corporate for bohemian life, the typical young American today is likely to be found running the Prague or Barcelona office branch of a multinational firm, and American fiction of the period can only find at most 'little differences' between Europe and America to comment upon. Consider for example the following exchange from Quentin Tarantino's 1994 film, *Pulp Fiction*:

VINCENT: . . . you know what the funniest thing about Europe is?
JULES: What?
VINCENT: It's the little differences. I mean, they got the same shit over there that we got here, but it's just, just, there it's a little different.
JULES: Example?
VINCENT: Well, you can walk into a movie theater and buy a beer. And I don't mean just, like, in no paper cup. And in Paris, you can buy a beer at McDonald's. And, you know what they call a Quarter-Pounder with Cheese in Paris?

JULES: They don't call it a Quarter-Pounder with Cheese?

VINCENT: No, man, they got the metric system there, they wouldn't know what the fuck a Quarter-Pounder is.

JULES: What'd they call it?

VINCENT: They call it a Royale with Cheese.

. . . .

JULES: What'd they call a Big Mac?

VINCENT: Well, Big Mac's a Big Mac, but they call it Le Big Mac.[43]

In *Pulp Fiction* the United States and Europe are distinguished solely in terms of the names of burgers; in *Barcelona*, anti-American feeling is blamed on the 'little differences' between burgers. Indeed one of the protagonists feels that it is the poor quality of the Spanish burger that gives America a bad name:

TED: Take hamburgers. Here 'hamburgesas' are really bad; it's known Americans like hamburgers – so again – we're idiots. They have no ideas how delicious hamburgers can be, and it's the ideal burger of memory we crave, not the disgusting burgers you get abroad.[44]

The film ends with the American protagonists duly married to their respective Spanish girlfriends whom they have taken back to an idealized New England and now feed 'ideal-burgers'.

More seriously, James Baldwin, who had left the United States in order to avoid becoming 'merely a Negro writer', wrote in a 1959 essay of his realization that 'there are no untroubled countries in this fearfully troubled world'. He felt that he might as well go home when 'an Algerian taxi-driver [told] him how it feels to be an Algerian in Paris'.[45] How could the writer conduct his quarrel with America from Europe if Europe was no different from what he had left behind?

THE OTHER EUROPE

For some writers, however, Europe did retain its differences from America. Indeed the main interest in Europe during the postwar period is really an interest in Europe as the site of the Holocaust. Most of this interest has come from Jewish–American writers, writers raised in the United States by families who have lived there for several generations, yet who locate their heritage in Europe.[46] The traditional American artist's feeling that 'life is elsewhere'[47] here bypasses western Europe and the traditional haunts of London, Paris and Rome for what Philip Roth terms the 'Other Europe'. It is only there that writers such as Roth, Malamud, Bellow and Ozick find 'real' subjects to distract them from the trivialities of personal

life that they see as the only subject available in America.[48] The other
Europe also provides these writers with an alternative, fruitful literary
tradition on which to draw, a tradition in which Babel, Kafka and
Bruno Schultz are central figures.[49] If the American identity is always,
as Henry James suggested, 'a complex fate', the European heritage of
these Jewish-American writers is even more complicated.[50] For example,
Bellow's Mr Sammler describes himself as 'doubly foreign, Polish-
Oxonian' while Malamud's Fidelman confronts his Jewish heritage while
pursuing a Jamesian one in stories such as 'The Lady of the Lake' and
'The Last Mohican'.[51]

The recent ending of the Cold War has also led to a re-kindling
of a different kind of American interest in eastern Europe. In particular
the last eight years have seen the growth of a sizeable American community in Prague. The attraction of the city for these Young-Americans-
in-Prague (sometimes referred to as YAPPIES) is both nostalgic and
thoroughly modern. On the one hand, living in Prague represents a
self-conscious attempt at the classic American Bohemian revolt. Indeed,
the editor-in-chief of the English language newspaper there, Alan Levy,
describes Prague as 'the Paris-of-the-twenties-in-the-nineties' – a place
where writers are still special and the modernist aura of 'kultura' still
present. 'I think I have found,' he writes, 'the kinder, gentler place that
George Bush once exhorted America to become.'[52] But most of the
Americans going to Prague are far from literary or 'political pilgrims'.[53]
Prague's appeal largely lies in its traditional sympathy to American culture
and values, and there are more Americans working for multinationals
there than writing poems.

*   *   *

With the exception of the postwar Jewish-American journey to Europe
(a topic deserving of a book in itself), the European journey is certainly less
important than it once was as a defining act for American writers. Within
American culture there has been an increasing awareness that the European heritage is only one of the many heritages of the United States, and
recently more attention has been paid to the sources of those others – for
example, African, Latin American, Chinese, Native American.[54] Furthermore, postwar American fiction has also tended to be preoccupied with
internal boundaries and distances, within cities, between races and classes.
So Macon Leary, the unwilling traveller in Anne Tyler's *The Accidental
Tourist*, finds that even he cannot escape the transformative experience of

travel. This does not occur on one of his trips around the world, however, but when he crosses the boundary from his middle-class neighbourhood in Baltimore to the working-class south side of the city.

Driving through the labyrinth of littered, cracked, dark streets in the south of the city, Macon wondered how Muriel could feel safe here. There were too many murky alleys and stairwells full of rubbish and doorways lined with tattered shreds of posters. The gridded shops with their ineptly lettered signs offered services that had a sleazy ring to them: CHECKS CASHED NO QUESTIONS, TINY BUBBA'S INCOME TAX, SAME DAY AUTO RECOLORING.[55]

While in Europe Macon remains forever unchanged, 'In the foreign country that was Singleton Street he was an entirely different person'.[56] The narrator of Paul Auster's *Moon Palace*, the not accidentally named Marco Stanley Fogg, has a similar experience in New York when he strays into Chinatown:

Chinatown was like a foreign country to me, and each time I walked out on the streets, I was overwhelmed by a sense of dislocation and confusion. This was America, but I could not understand what anyone said, could not penetrate the meanings of the things I saw . . . I did not have the feeling I had moved to another part of town. I had travelled halfway around the world to get where I was, and it stood to reason that nothing should be familiar to me anymore, not even myself.[57]

TRAVELLING CLICHÉS

If American writers had, from their earliest travels, had to struggle to rewrite the guidebook of Europe, by the late twentieth century there was an increasing sense that the whole project was exhausted and that parody was the only remaining resource. Parody is certainly the starting point for John Updike's story 'A Madman'. For the narrator of that story, 'England appeared to exist purely as a context for literature . . . I had studied this literature for four years and had been sent here to continue this study'. As he and his wife approach London by train:

The city overwhelmed our expectations. The Kiplingesque grandeur of Waterloo Station, the Eliotic despondency of the brick row in Chelsea where we spent the night in the flat of a vague friend, the Dickensian nightmare of fog and sweating pavement and besmirched cornices that surrounded us when we awoke – all this seemed too authentic to be real, too corroborative of literature to be solid. The taxi we took to Paddington Station had a high roof and an open side, which gave it to our eyes the shocked, cockeyed expression in an Agatha Christie melodrama. We wheeled past mansions by Galsworthy and parks by A. A. Milne;

we glimpsed a cobbled eighteenth-century alley, complete with hanging tavern boards where Dr. Johnson might have reeled and gasped the night he laughed so hard – the incident in Boswell so beautifully amplified in the essay by Beerbohm.[58]

As the Holy Land sites could operate as a kind of ahistorical doorway to God, so the sites of English literature traditionally operated as initiation points for 'passionate pilgrims' such as Hawthorne and James. Updike mocks this as his narrator moves so effortlessly from Agatha Christie to Dr Johnson. His London doesn't exist historically or even geographically; it is a city of words and preconceptions. In order to have what Theroux would see as a 'genuine travel experience', these must be left behind.[59]

Other writers are less hopeful about the possibility of having genuine experiences in the age of 'mechanical reproductions'. The European journey that Lynne Tillman's protagonist sets out on in *Motion Sickness* is also made up of texts and images. She spends much of her trip choosing postcards and reading Henry James in hotel bedrooms, but at the novel's end she is still in the hotel, still reading. Susan Sontag's short story 'Unguided Tour' also suggests that it is impossible to have a travel experience that is unburdened by the weight of previous generations of responses. Although trying hard 'to see the beautiful things' with an open mind – 'I haven't been everywhere but it's on my list' – the lovers in her story can only express themselves in the familiar clichés of travel and aesthetic response, and Sontag places these in quotation marks. 'Say to yourself fifty times a day: I am not a connoisseur, I am not a romantic wanderer, I am not a pilgrim.' But she does not provide an alternative.[60]

'THERE IS NO PROGRESS, THERE IS REPETITION'[61]

Travel writing, it seems, has reached an impasse in which the writer's characteristic response is either to repeat or to parody the experiences of previous generations. Yet not all writers are willing to go down these paths nor do they want to reject the relationship between travel and writing as exhausted. Rather than abandoning that relationship, they say, we simply need to redefine it.

Traditionally the travel narrative charted the progress of the traveller or explorer towards a specific destination, and often reported the return journey. The shape of the narrative was therefore linear or circular. Contemporary travellers, however, as we have seen, no longer experience their journeys as either linear or circular. 'Travelling', Calvino notes in his rewriting of *The Travels of Marco Polo*, 'you realize that differences are lost: each city takes to resembling all cities, places exchange their form, order, distances, a shapeless dust cloud invades the continents. Your atlas preserves the differences intact', but 'the places have mingled'.[62] While 'the atlas preserves the differences', new forms of travel narratives have developed and are structured according to principles of repetition rather than progress. Calvino imagines Polo's journey as 'shapeless' and without any definite objective, and his novel is therefore neither linear nor circular but consists of a series of many short and fabulous tales, containing many repetitions and minglings. The cities visited by Lynne Tillman's protagonists in 'Weird Fucks' and *Motion Sickness* are similarly inter-changeable and culturally confused. For example, when, in *Motion Sickness*, the narrator visits London, it is to go to 'a small French café on Moscow Road', where she talks with the Italian proprietor about the notion of an English summer. The novel begins and ends in Paris and, in between, she moves back and forth between many European and non-European cities. No pattern emerges, however, and there is no sense that Paris itself is particularly significant. According to Tillman, this 'lack of a scheme or plot', or 'reason for her to travel', frustrated many readers: 'some tried to find a reason, for some there was no reason to read on'.[63]

The notion of 'a trip without any objective' is contrasted by the French sociologist Jean Baudrillard with the fixed agenda of 'tourism': 'I reject the picturesque tourist round, the sights, even the landscapes (only their abstraction remains in the prism of the scorching heat). Nothing is further from pure travelling than tourism or holiday travel'.[64]

Baudrillard finds a 'pure travel' experience in the American desert and 'the equally desert-like banality of a metropolis – not at any stage regarded as places of pleasure or culture, but seen televisually as scenery, as scenarios'. He contrasts this with the tourist experience available in Europe which he considers as full of 'sights', of places of 'pleasure' and 'culture'. But this opposition between abstract American 'travel' (and travel writing) and the clichés of European 'tourism' (and travel writing) do not hold for American writers such as Sontag or Tillman. Their pro-tagonists are tourists – they see the 'sights' and buy postcards – yet their journeys are aimless and unstructured, the places they visit mere 'scenery' in their lives.[65]

ARMCHAIR TRAVEL

Although he believes that travel itself is now impossible, Lévi-Strauss argues that travel writing remains popular because it satisfies our weary nostalgia for a world of differences, even if these are not genuine.

Armchair travel in Paul Verhoeven's film *Total Recall* (1990).

I can understand the mad passion for travel books and their deceptiveness. They create the illusion of something which no longer exists but still should exist, if we are to have any hope of avoiding the overwhelming conclusion that the history of the past twenty thousand years is irrevocable.[66]

Complementing the desire to travel but feel 'at home', then, is the desire to stay at home but experience 'different' cultures vicariously through our reading or television viewing. 'For most people', says a character in Don DeLillo's *White Noise*, 'there are only two places in the world. Where they live and their TV set.'[67] While bookstores offer shelves labelled 'the armchair traveller', this desire reached its apotheosis in the travel service offered by Rekall, Inc. in Paul Verhoeven's 1990 film *Total Recall*.[68] The film is set in the year 2084 when Mars has become a colony of the earth. Construction worker Doug Quaid has no time to visit the colony so he goes to Rekall, a 'travel' service which specializes in implanting artificial memories of 'vacations' into its customers' brains. The customer reclines in a high-tech chair and enjoys all the pleasures of a 'vacation' at an accelerated rate, without any of the usual fuss. Quaid thus purchases the memory of a trip to Mars, and included in his package is Rekall's special 'Ego Trip', which allows the customer to travel as another person. Quaid chooses to be a secret agent, and the story goes on from there.

Travel without the inconvenience of ever having to leave your desk is also a popular metaphor in the language of computing – Microsoft advertisements ask, 'Where would you like to go today?' and suggest that its software has created the kind of global village Malcolm McLuhan imagined television would. The Internet in turn is described as a 'World Wide Web' or as 'cyberspace', which the novelist William Gibson describes as 'a consensual hallucination experienced daily by billions of legitimate operators, in every nation'.[69] As we become citizens of cyberspace, Gibson suggests, our national affiliations become less important to us and physical travel is redundant. The only frontiers existing in this brave new world are economic and technical: 'travellers' are those who can afford the requisite gadgets and know how to use them.

FICTIVE NATIONS AND NATIONAL FICTIONS

If imaginary journeys are now popular, so too are imaginary destinations. If the world is no longer able to provide sufficiently unfamiliar destinations, then the writer must simply invent his own. Post-Renaissance travel writing was empirically driven – the writer described the world in which he had travelled – and from this the novel was born. In rejecting the possibility of travel, the postmodern writer is also rejecting the representational ambitions of traditional travel and fiction writing. 'World-making', long the preserve of the science-fiction genre, is now a reputable part of mainstream contemporary literature.[70] But rather than leaving the world behind, much of this fiction prefers to explore the tension between real and imagined places. If, for example, in *Slaughterhouse Five* (1969), Kurt Vonnegut cannot find peace in war-torn Dresden, then why not invent Tralfamadore? The writer's aim, as William Gass, puts it, is 'to take apart the world where you have very little control, and replace it with language over which you can have control. Destroy and then repair'.[71]

Alternatively the writer can explore the way that a 'real' country is constructed through language and signs. When American novelists Saul Bellow and Walter Abish wrote about Africa as a 'fictive' continent, neither had ever travelled there. Henderson notes in Bellow's novel, *Henderson the Rain King* (1959), that 'the world is a mind' and all travel essentially 'mental travel'. Indeed, he says, 'what we call reality is nothing but pedantry'.[72] For Walter Abish, however, travel is not so much mental or mythical as literary and lexical. Parodying novels of tortuous journeys into the continent, his first novel, *Alphabetical Africa* (1974), charts 'a journey of literary hardship' through the alphabet.[73] The first chapter contains only words beginning with the letter 'A'; a new letter is introduced with each chapter until half way through the book, when the process is reversed. The novel makes no attempt to represent 'Africa', rather it creates a self-sufficient system, a 'geography of the imagination'.[74] The borders of 'Africa' (and Germany and Mexico in subsequent novels) are nothing more than the constraints imposed by the novel's system.[75]

The value of travel for modernists such as Pound and Stein was that it enabled the writer to step outside the borders of his or her own cultural and national identity in order to create language and literature afresh. For postmodernist writers such as Abish, Tillman and Sontag there is no 'stepping outside' of these boundaries. The most that can be done is to explore the construction of a (national, mythical, semiotic and linguistic) system and observe it in relationship to other such systems. 'Here [in America],' Walter Abish maintains, 'I know what is familiar, and I don't feel as free to break away from it.' Yet, he goes on, 'I tend to establish or reestablish the familiar in what is foreign, allowing the familiar to determine the subsequent defamiliarization. The result is a tension, a sense of *unbehagen* [sic], a discomfort'.[76]

Constructing a system and observing the discomfort of one's relation to it is also Roland Barthes's strategy in *Empire of Signs* (1970). The essay begins by relating this procedure to 'world-making':

If I want to imagine a fictive nation, I can give it an invented name, treat it declaratively as a novelistic object, create a new Garabagne, so as to compromise no real country by my fantasy (though there is then that fantasy itself I compromise by the signs of literature). I can also – though in no way claiming to represent or to analyze reality itself (these being the major gestures of Western discourse) – isolate somewhere in the world (*faraway*) a certain number of features (a term employed in linguistics), and out of these features deliberately form a system. It is this system which I shall call: Japan.[77]

Barthes is not concerned to show the real Japan beyond 'Japan', the system that he isolates; rather he simply considers its interactions with other (particularly his own) 'national fiction'. The postmodern travel 'dream', as he defines it, is not therefore to experience new realities but to observe our own 'reality' as it encounters others:

... to know a foreign (alien) language and yet not to understand it: to perceive the difference in it without ever being recuperated by the superficial sociality of discourse, communication or vulgarity; to know, positively refracted in a new language, the impossibility of our own; to learn the systematics of the inconceivable; to undo our own 'reality' under the effect of other formulations, other syntaxes; ... in a word, to descend into the untranslatable, to experience its shock without ever muffling it.[78]

National identity cannot simply be left behind and viewed from a safe distance (as the modernists had hoped); instead we carry it with us and observe it, and ourselves, 'under the effect of other formulations'. Tillman compares her characters to nation states defined by boundaries continually 'in dispute', shifting 'like ones do after a war when countries lose or gain upon having won or lost',[79] while her prose emulates the carefulness and self-awareness of someone using a second language as a way of, as Barthes puts it, 'undoing' their own reality, or as she says, of 'inconveniencing the majority language'. 'It will probably be my fate', says the narrator of *Motion Sickness,* 'not to learn other languages but to speak my own as if I were a foreigner.'[80]

In the last fifty years our expectations of journeys, destinations and travellers have all undergone considerable changes. In response to these changes new forms of writing about travel have developed, writing that challenges traditional ways of thinking about what travel, and travel narratives, constitute. Despite the protestations of Lévi-Strauss, Fussell and Theroux, it seems premature to announce the end of either travel or travel writing.

10

Per ardua ad astra: *Authorial Choice and the Narrative of Interstellar Travel*

EDWARD JAMES

Stories of loss and frustration have surfaced again and again in the American science-fiction magazines since the Challenger disaster of 28 January 1986. American science fiction had for decades functioned as one element of the propaganda drive for space travel, and since the Apollo mission in particular there had been close links between NASA and some science-fiction writers. The interrelationship between NASA and the science-fiction (sf) world is deeper and more complex than a mere public relations exercise, however. Constance Penley, for instance, has recently shown some of the ways that NASA and *Star Trek* together have helped to shape the American imagination.[1] The American imagination, however, has taken what it needed from the space programme, and no more. It was not the loss of Challenger that was so depressing and frustrating for supporters of the space programme so much as the reaction of the American public, who seemed to regard the space programme as worthwhile only if no astronauts ever lost their lives. For many at NASA and in the science-fiction community, on the other hand, the space programme was the playing out of an essential aspect of the American Dream: the opening up of the frontier. 'Space, the final frontier', as Patrick Stewart intoned during the credits of each episode of *Star Trek: The Next Generation* between 1987 and 1994. 'These are the voyages of the Starship Enterprise. Its continuing mission: to explore new worlds, to seek out new life and new civilizations, to boldly go where no one has gone before.' Numerous sf stories have explored the idea that without the constant expansion of humanity, and the continual extension of scientific knowledge, comes stagnation and decline.

One of the more recent stories inspired by Challenger, and by the twenty-fifth anniversary of the Apollo landing, is 'Abandon in Place',[2] by Jerry Oltion, a writer more associated with hard-edged technological science fiction. Some time in the near future Neil Armstrong dies, and on the following dawn a ghost Saturn V launches itself from the Cape. For the astronaut who witnessed it, the first Saturn launching for thirty years, it evoked memories of a golden age.

Nowadays, the shuttle astronauts seemed more like appliance repairmen than intrepid explorers. Rick had convinced himself that the shuttle was doing some valuable science, but now, after seeing a Saturn V launch only two weeks earlier, he realized that science wasn't what had thrilled him when he'd watched them as a kid, and it wasn't why he was here now. He was in space because he wanted to explore it, and this – barely two hundred miles off the ground – was the farthest into it he could get. (p. 109).

The next time a ghost Saturn V solidified on the launch-pad, Rick was on it. Contrary to Mission Control orders, he joins up with two orbiting Shuttle astronauts and heads off to the Moon. They rename the ship *The Spirit of Hope* and speculate about its origins.

What if it's the ghost of your entire space program? When Neil Armstrong died, so did the dreams of space enthusiasts all over your nation, maybe all over the world. It reminded them that you had once gone to the Moon, but no longer could. Maybe the unfulfilled dreams of all those people created this spaceship. [. . .] (p. 131)
   What, you think I'm channelling the combined angst of all the trekkies and fourteen-year-old would-be astronauts in the world?' (p. 132)

Two of them land on the Moon and then make a rendezvous with the orbiter to return to Earth. Its Japanese pilot continues to speculate about the nature of the ghost: she decides that it is Rick who embodies the spirit of exploration:

Every time someone goes into space, your nation's spirit flies with them. When *Apollo 1* killed its crew, your nation faltered for two years before going on, and when the *Challenger* blew up it took three more. When the Soviets' Moon rocket blew up in 1969, they completely scrapped their lunar program and shifted to space stations. [. . .] Every astronaut who's ever flown has had your ability, and your responsibility; yours is just more obvious than most, made physical by the same power that created this ship. (p. 153)

When they all return to Earth, we may assume, the space programme will be kickstarted into action again. Their mission had been watched by millions all over the world, which caused them constant worry: 'the biggest catastrophe with *Challenger*, in terms of the space program as a whole, was not that it blew up, but that millions of people *watched* it blow up' (p. 129). Despite this, the interest of the fickle American TV audience could not be relied upon. 'People were interested again? After years of shuttle flights, the astronauts taping science shows that were only broadcast on the educational channels after they ran out of cooking and painting programs, that was hard to believe.' (p. 128)

Oltion's story is fantasy, not science fiction: his ghost spaceships materializing from the unexpressed spirit of the American nation are pure hokum. But the story illustrates some interesting points. It was very clear in the years after Challenger, but apparent long before that, that the space programme flourished only as long as it was seen to be playing an important role in the emotional life of the American people, whether in terms of competition with the Soviet Union or for some more imaginative reason. Oltion expresses a common view among the space fraternity: that the urge to explore is innate in the human, and particularly the American, spirit. But he also recognizes that the *majority* of Americans are only enthused by the exceptional: the Moon landing, the Apollo 13 drama, perhaps the Pathfinder landing on Mars – or the ghost Saturn V mission. It may be, ironically, that the imagined yearning of Americans, or some Americans, for the 'High Frontier' is more satisfied by *Star Trek* and other works of the science-fictional imagination than it is by the often routine and poorly explained, and sometimes bungling, actuality of NASA's space programme. For some, perhaps, the totally fantastic means of transport described by Oltion – the ghost Saturn V – is no more and no less comprehensible than the various engineering solutions that have been devised for space exploration. Indeed, as we shall see in what follows, the imaginary exploration of the galaxy conducted by science-fiction writers frequently uses the rationalized equivalents of the ghost Saturn V: various fantastic means of defeating the perceived laws of physics which may in reality condemn us to imprisonment within the solar system.

*   *   *

Imaginary travel has been a staple of science fiction ever since the time of Jules Verne, the first commercial writer of science fiction (even though he wrote all his novels before the phrase 'science fiction' was invented). Verne's series of over sixty novels was publicized as 'Voyages extraordinaires': they were fantastic travel narratives. Occasionally Verne used means of transport that were perfectly familiar, such as the balloons in *Five Weeks in a Balloon* or *Around the World in Eighty Days*, or the Amazon raft in *La Jangada*; sometimes he would merely perfect vehicles that were already known, like the submarine of *Twenty Thousand Leagues under the Sea*. But he also invented means of transport: the cannon shell, shot to the Moon in *Voyage to the Moon*; a steam-engine in the form of an elephant, pulling two houses, 'sortes de bungalows roulants', in *La Maison à Vapeur*; a dirigible, as in *Clipper of the Clouds*; even a comet, in *Hector Servadac (Off On a Comet)*. Most of Verne's vehicles were as comfortable as the Victorian drawing-room in which his readers sat, as he took them on an educational Cook's Tour of the universe.[3]

Travel narratives are among the several ancestors of science fiction, along with satirical and utopian literature. Imaginary travel stories have had a history as long as genuine travel narratives: longer, if one admits the *Epic of Gilgamesh* and the *Odyssey* to the genre. At times readers have confused the real and the imaginary: Marco Polo, after all, appeared just as fantastic as Sir John Mandeville, and an early reader of Sir Thomas More's *Utopia* was said to be surprised at the admiring reaction to the book, since all More had done was write down what some traveller had told him.[4] Later stories of imaginary travel to unknown corners of the Earth – a genre which survived well into the twentieth century – often tried for as much verisimilitude as possible, in the manner of later science fiction, and often had the same didactic purpose as Verne's 'Voyages'.[5]

The most common form of nineteenth-century travel narrative which used imaginary destinations, in the manner of later science fiction, were the dozens of stories of the discovery of lost races in the far corners of the earth. H. Rider Haggard's *Allan Quatermain* (1897), with its kingdom of Hellenized Persians in the heart of Africa, is probably the best known today, but it is only one of the stories in which English or American explorers come across the descendants of Greeks, Romans, Vikings, the Ten Tribes of Israel or the survivors of drowned Atlantis.[6] Oddly enough, although many nineteenth-century scientists believed in the possibility or probability of life on other planets, there were relatively few stories of travel to contact alien life-forms in the solar system or beyond: it was in the late nineteenth century, when many scientists had abandoned the idea that life was likely elsewhere within the solar system, that writers of fiction started to imagine the possibility of finding it.[7] It was also only at the very beginning of the twentieth century, in Robert W. Cole's *The Struggle for Empire* (1900), that travelling beyond the solar system to the stars (without the help of angels or other occult means) was contemplated by novelists.

Travel of some sort has been a frequent element in twentieth-century science fiction. Sometimes this is simply travel through exotic scenery on an alien planet, occasionally with reference back to classic explorers' narratives, as in the epic sea journey in Robert Silverberg's *Majipoor Chronicles* (1982) or the gruelling journey across the ice in Ursula K. Le Guin's *The Left Hand of Darkness* (1969). But in the last two or three decades it is mostly only in fantasy novels, of the post-Tolkien kind, where the voyage on a planet's surface is the central plot element; in these cases a map is often provided for the convenience of the reader, if not the protagonists. In modern fantasy, travel is a means by which the hero or heroine, or both, grow up or discover themselves; usually they meet with one adventure after another on their travels, often over several volumes, before reaching their goal. Plot is subordinated to landscape and to the need to test the protagonists in different ways. The common motif of travel in the typically pseudo-medieval setting of the post-Tolkien heroic fantasy, with its clichetized trappings and stereotyped dangers, has been the target for the recent parody by Diana Wynne Jones, *The Tough Guide to Fantasyland* (1996).

In science fiction the preeminent means of transport is not the horse (or dragon) of fantasy, but the space ship. In the 1970s, in particular, it was the custom for sf book covers in Britain to carry a picture of a space ship as a generic indicator, regardless of whether the action in the book ever moved off the surface of a planet or concerned a pre-industrial society centuries away from developing heavier-than-air flight. Travel through space is the stereotypical form of travel in science fiction, although travel through time, whether on the surrogate bicycle of H. G. Wells's Time Traveller or in some less easily imaginable device, is also common: a number of science-fiction anthologies unite these two themes in a title such as *Travels through Space and Time*.[8]

Most science-fiction stories that are actually concerned with the process of travel deal with travel to the Moon, to the planets and to the asteroids. Travel within the solar system is easily imaginable, since the destinations are known and the means of travel are fairly certain (even if methods of propulsion may vary according to time and authorial preference). Authors found it relatively easy, if they wished, to present a tale of interplanetary travel with up-to-date scientific support. Since well before the Apollo programme of the late 1960s, interplanetary travel has been the focus of scientific and technological analysis as well as of the imaginative investigations of sf writers, while knowledge of the planets themselves has been increasing throughout the twentieth century. For many science-fiction writers, indeed, the plausible depiction of inter-planetary travel was part of a mission to propagandize a particular vision of the future which regarded such expansion as essential for humanity's spiritual and physical survival. The response of the United States to the Challenger disaster in 1986 briefly set back those ambitions, as we have seen, but President Bush's pledge in 1990 to put Americans on Mars by the third decade of the twenty-first century revived them again and was responsible for a flurry of Mars novels in the 1990s.

Interstellar travel, the subject of this paper, is very much more problematical for the science-fiction writer. Indeed, there is a basic conflict between the desire for scientific plausibility, an ideal to which most sf writers have paid lip-service since the 1930s, and the desire of writers to get their protagonists among the stars. First of all, we must place this in historical context, looking at the way the theme has waxed and waned within the history of science fiction during this century. Secondly, we shall look in more detail at the ways science-fiction writers have dealt with the laws of physics, 'the cold equations', to use the title of a celebrated story.[9]

Interstellar travel was a topic that such authors as Verne and Wells shunned. Wells, who pioneered so many of the themes of modern science fiction, never sent his human characters further than the Moon. Those writers who did, in the early years of the century and the early years of the American science fiction magazines, did so without much thought about the technological problems: they just wanted to put their protagonists in new exotic locations, and the more easily they could do this, the better. E. E. 'Doc' Smith, for instance, one of the best-known early writers of interstellar epic, treated interstellar distances with great insouciance in all his novels. In his very first novel, *The Skylark of Space*, his genius scientist hero Seaton made friends with Crane, 'the multi-millionaire explorer–archaeologist–sportsman',[10] and, after becoming national doubles tennis champions, they put together a spaceship in Crane's back yard. On their maiden voyage they soon gained velocity, rather more easily than they had anticipated, and they began to wonder where they were:

> 'This object-compass still works – let's see how far we are away from home.'
> They took a reading and both men figured the distance.
> 'What do you make it, Mart? I'm afraid to tell you my result.'
> 'Forty-six point twenty-seven light centuries. Check?'
> 'Check. We're up the well-known creek without a paddle. . .' (pp. 80–81)

Smith's contemporary Edmond Hamilton had an equally cavalier attitude to distance in his stories, though he does at least recognize the difficulties of interstellar travel at our current state of knowledge. In an early sequence of stories he situated the development of his star-drive one hundred thousand years in the future and described how, before that, humans had been restricted to the Eight Planets (this was written before the discovery of Pluto).[11]

Even when science-fiction writers became aware of the implications of Einstein's theories for travel at speeds faster than light, they treated the problem of interstellar travel in a very similar fashion to Smith or Hamilton, as if it were no more difficult than sailing across the Atlantic.[12] Although the characters in the early stories of John W. Campbell, later to become science fiction's most influential editor, did acknowledge the prohibition of faster-than-light travel – 'look, teacher, a man named Einstein said that the velocity of light was tops over two hundred years ago'[13] – they found a way round it which enabled them to travel from star to star in minutes. Even so, travelling to a neighbouring galaxy in a few hours (on their maiden voyage in the new spaceship, *The Ancient Mariner*) seemed unbearably boring:

The men found little to do as they passed at high speed through the vast realm of space. The chronometer pointed out the hours with exasperating slowness. The six hours that were to elapse before the first stop seemed like as many days. They had thought of this trip as a wonderful adventure in itself, but the soundless continued monotony was depressing.[14]

During the 1930s and 1940s science-fiction writers adopted variations on the means Campbell had utilized to get round Einstein, and rapid travel from star to star became a familiar trope which sf writers rarely needed to explain. Typically, the punctilious Isaac Asimov feels the need to do so very early on in his influential 'Foundation' series: indeed, on the second page of text. The protagonist, Gaal Dornick, had only travelled in interplanetary space before:

. . . but space travel was all one whether one travelled half a million miles, or as many light years.

He had steeled himself just a little for the Jump through hyperspace, a phenomenon one did not experience in simple interplanetary trips. The Jump remained, and would probably remain for ever, the only practical method of travelling between the stars. Travel through ordinary space could proceed at no rate more rapid than that of ordinary light (a bit of scientific knowledge that belonged among the new items known since the forgotten dawn of human history), and that would have meant years of travel between even the nearest of inhabited systems. Through hyperspace, that unimaginable region that was neither space nor time, matter nor energy, something nor nothing, one could traverse the length of the Galaxy in the intervals between two neighbouring instants of time.[15]

Hyperspace, space warp, the Jump, and other such phrases were normal currency by the 1950s, and by then most sf writers were prepared to set many of their stories in a future in which the stars had been reached and their planets colonized (though there were few who followed Asimov in the 'Foundation' series in imagining that humans would settle twenty-five million suns – and not meet a single intelligent alien race). By the 1950s, indeed, a 'consensus cosmogony' had emerged: an agreed framework for the future history of humanity. It was identified and mapped by Donald A. Wollheim.

Are science-fiction writers wrong in utilizing a framework which is subject to such close definition? Not really. There is only a limited number of general possibilities open to human conjecture. When all the many highly inventive minds of science-fiction writers find themselves falling again and again into similar patterns, we must perforce say that this does seem to be what all our mental computers state as the shape of the future.[16]

Rather more pertinently, this framework allowed writers, particularly writers of short stories, to save time and space. They did not need laboriously to fill in the background: all they needed to do was to drop some hints, and the experienced reader would be able to slot it into his or her perception of the consensus cosmogony. Wollheim counts eight stages in the science-fictional future:

1. The initial exploration of the solar system; the stories of colonization and economic exploitation of the solar system, and of the breakaway of the colonies from Earth (often along the lines of the American War of Independence).
2. The first flights to the stars, with some of the same problems (or potential plot-lines).
3. The rise of the Galactic Empire, and its contact with alien empires.
4. The Galactic Empire in full bloom; exploration and adventure still takes place, especially on the Rim.
5. The Decline and Fall of the Galactic Empire, first sketched by Isaac Asimov in the 'Foundation' series, closely following Gibbon's *Decline and Fall of the Roman Empire*.[17]
6. The inevitable interregnum, or Dark Ages, with worlds reverting to conditions of barbarism: again writers were able to adapt scenarios drawn from our own real history.
7. The rise of a permanent Galactic Civilization, with the restoration of civilization to lapsed worlds and the exploration of the rest of the universe.
8. What Wollheim calls the Challenge to God: the effort to solve the last secrets of the universe, and the end of time and/or the beginning of a new universe.

This framework was used by many writers in the 1950s and still continues to be an unspoken background to many stories. The early beginnings of space flight from Sputnik to Apollo did little to change the framework; after all, it was easy to fit real history into stage 1. Stages 2 to 8 all not only assumed interstellar travel, but interstellar travel that was, if not instantaneous, then many times faster than light.

Those who wanted to write about interstellar travel had to think about three problems above all.

Firstly, how were they to make a journey through absolute nothingness interesting? It is difficult enough even in narratives of travel between the planets in our own solar system. There it has become almost a cliché that a journey will be punctuated by crises such as meteor showers or solar flares: both the two major novels of space exploration of the early 1990s, Ben Bova's *Mars* (1992) and Kim Stanley Robinson's *Red Mars* (1992), decided to introduce a solar flare (producing life-threatening gamma radiation) to liven up the tedium of the several months' travel between Earth and Mars. But there is a severe limit to the amount of external interest that a writer can manufacture for a journey through interstellar space. Meteor showers are unlikely; solar flares will be of no importance. Many writers have been willing to invent similar crises in interstellar space, like the 'energy clouds' and 'time-loop distortions' resorted to by the scriptwriters of *Star Trek: The Next Generation*.[18] In the absence of a manufactured crisis, the length of the journey clearly makes a difference to the narrative demands, as we shall see. If it is measured in months, the writer might concentrate on the interpersonal problems arising when a small group of people live together in a claustrophobic environment; if it is measured in centuries, the narrative is likely to focus upon social change and conflict within the community of space travellers. But the solution found by most writers has been to minimize the length of the journey: to make it almost instantaneous, as in Asimov's 'Foundation' series, or at least to measure it in days rather than years or centuries. If the journey itself is not to take over the narrative, it must be as speedy as possible.

Secondly, how are authors to react to the immensity of the universe? Distances are made palatable by thinking of them in light-minutes or light-years, but this only hides the reality of the distances. Light takes 8 minutes to reach the Earth from the Sun; it takes 4.3 years for the Sun's light to reach the nearest other star. In 1973, the Pioneer probe to Jupiter, travelling at 14 kilometres a second, some 36,000 miles per hour, reached its destination in 21 months. If it had been aimed in the right direction, it would take it a further 80,000 years to get to the nearest star – which happens to be a star almost certainly deprived of planets.[19] Authors have reacted in two ways to these immense distances. There are those for whom the frisson of awe, the consciousness of the sublime, what science-fiction readers have come to call 'the sense of wonder', is at the heart of science fiction and who thus emphasize the difficulties or dangers of interstellar travel. There are others who want to make the universe seem approachable: to minimize the distance and the dangers, to make an interstellar voyage seem as predictable and exciting as a train journey. The astrophysicist and science-fiction writer Gregory Benford has suggested that it is fear of the infinite which persuades some writers to postulate faster-than-light travel, but that it subverts the true nature of the universe, as well as depriving the science-fiction addict of his or her fix of the sense of wonder: 'Going to the stars becomes very much like taking the stellar subway; you don't even have to look at the view. Collapsing the true scale of the universe this way robs it of significance and power.'[20]

But he somewhat undermines his case by admitting that 'domesticating the infinite' does allow the science-fiction writer to populate the universe and to make it a setting for human adventure. The sf community is not made up of those who react in different ways to fear of the infinite, according to their psychological makeup. Apart from anything else, the writing of science fiction is not as serious for some as it is, say, for Professor Benford. Even those who realize the immensity of the universe may want to write a story about interstellar warfare which must, in order for the plot to work, minimize the distances between the stars.

The third and most difficult problem of all relates to the science in science fiction. Any author who wishes his or her protagonists to travel to the stars has to have some response to the challenge of Einsteinian physics. If mass increases to infinity as speed approaches the speed of light, then approaching the speed of light is impossible. If subjective speed slows down as one approaches the speed of light, then outward trips can be made at less than the speed of light, but on a return trip to Earth the traveller will find his world has aged far more than the travellers. A trip made at 99.99 per cent of the speed of light will travel a light-year in five subjective days; if the traveller then returned to Earth, in another subjective five days, humans on Earth would be over two years older. In terms of travelling between the inhabitable planets of stars, which are going to be very much more than one light-year apart, the time-lapse will be much more significant; more pertinently, the energy needed to reach this speed will be enormous, since at near light-speed the ship's mass will have increased over seventy times. In addition, the acceleration needed to reach such speeds, which might be possible for unmanned probes, would put intolerable pressures upon the human organism.

There are a number of ways in which science-fiction authors might respond to Einstein. They could say, to begin with, that Einstein's calculations were wrong, or that he was only describing a phenomenon local to this part of space. This has *not* been a popular solution, and there are only a few examples in the post-war period. Science-fiction writers like to maintain the pretence that their literature does not contradict accepted scientific theories, and there have been few scientists since Einstein who have seriously questioned his conclusions. For that reason, most of the solutions along these lines are playful, postulating a non-Einsteinian (or even non-Euclidian) universe, or suggesting that the solar system has been placed artificially in an Einsteinian pocket of the universe in order to quarantine the unruly species of *Homo sapiens* and prevent it from making contact with galactic civilization.

Secondly, the writer might agree that Einstein is right, and that there is no way to exceed the speed of light. There are literary consequences, however. It may mean that he or she decides never to write a story of interstellar travel. Or the story of the voyage may become the main theme of the story or novel, either because the voyage itself will be very long, travelling at well below light-speed, or because the time-dilation effects of sub-light-speed are themselves so striking that the effects of that time dilation is likely to be a major theme. We thus have stories like Robert F. Young's 'Cousins',[21] where a man returns from the stars and falls in love with his own great-granddaughter, or James White's 'Nuisance Value',[22] in which a middle-aged man meets his young father on his return from the first trip into interstellar space.

There are two ways of dealing with very long voyages between the stars that will last far beyond the life-span of individual humans: suspended animation or generation ships. The former assumes either that computers and/or robots will tend the rows of sleeping or frozen crew members until their destination approaches and they are woken up (or defrosted), or else that crew members are woken up in shifts in order to carry out those duties. Stories will either skip over the journey, using suspended animation simply as a device to get the characters to the planet on which the action of the story will develop, or they will concentrate on problems arising from the suspended-animation method itself, such as upon relations among the active crew. Some writers have imagined that suspended animation, like generation ships, will be the first means of interstellar travel but will soon be replaced by some form of faster-than-light travel.

A. E. Van Vogt's 'Far Centaurus' ends with the crew in suspended animation arriving at their stellar destination five hundred years later to find a welcome party made up of the Earthmen who had invented faster-than-light drive after the pioneer ship had left Earth. A variant is found in Gregory Benford's 'Redeemer', where the faster-than-light ship catches up with the ship with its frozen crew in order to remove, at gun point, valuable genetic material that is needed back home in a war-torn solar system.[23]

The generation ship story, on the other hand, is normally less about the actual voyage than about the social development of the community living on board ship. A generation ship, by definition, is a large ship containing a large enough population for viable survival without the problems that might be caused by too much inbreeding: since it is normally intended to colonize a planet, it will also contain genes and seeds from earth fauna and flora, making it even more like a latter-day ark. The 'space-ark' was first suggested by J. D. Bernal, in his classic scientific essay *The World, The Flesh, and the Devil* (1929), and first appeared in fiction in Laurence Manning's 'The Living Galaxy' (*Wonder Stories*, September 1934), but the science-fiction story against which others measure themselves and to which others make reference is Robert A. Heinlein's 'Common Sense'.[24] In this story, as in others (such as *Non-Stop* [1958] by Brian W. Aldiss, *Seed of Light* [1959] by Edmund Cooper and *Captive Universe* [1969] by Harry Harrison), the purpose of the journey has been forgotten, or cloaked in religious mythology; the plot revolves around the dramatic results of the revelation of the truth about their place in the universe. As such, these stories are 'about' conceptual breakthrough: a metaphor for the kind of intellectual revolution associated with such names as Copernicus or Darwin and couched, as so often in science fiction, in terms of scientific truth versus religious obscurantism.[25] The journey which these people are taking is irrelevant to the story: these stories are not about learning through travel – unless by analogy with human beings on earth, who travel through space as the sun circles the galactic core. As if to make the point, in Jerry Oltion's story 'Frame of Reference'[26] the conceptual breakthrough is that the generation ship is not travelling through space at all, as all on board had thought: it is buried underground, on Earth, forming a self-contained environment in which the remnants of humanity might live out a nuclear winter.

Finally, the science-fiction writer could use the suggestions of other physicists to get around Einstein or simply adopt a device which would seem to solve the problem and enable humans to travel rapidly from star system to star system. This has been the most popular solution, mainly because it offers authors the chance to imagine galactic empires and galactic wars and to meet a whole host of alien races. Faster-than-light travel does have the effect of domesticating the universe. It shrinks the galaxy and allows the writer to imagine galactic conflict to be not unlike global conflict on Earth. Sometimes the author can very deliberately translate past historical events into the future, vastly expanding the astronomical scale. Thus, as we have seen, Isaac Asimov's 'Foundation' series began as a galactic version of the decline and fall of the Roman empire; David Weber's much more recent 'Honor Harrington' novels mirror the world of Horatio Nelson (and Horatio Hornblower) on a galactic scale, even to the extent of space-navy battle tactics being like Nelson's tactics with the addition of the third dimension.[27] Such stories would be impossible if the authors believed in the strict operation of Einsteinian principles.

Without faster-than-light travel, galactic empires could not be created. Galactic *civilizations* might be possible, however, if faster-than-light communication – rather than faster-than-light travel – could be developed. Thus, in Ursula K. Le Guin's 'Hainish' sequence of stories and novels, the 'ansible' is a device which allows such communication. In *The Dispossessed* (1974), one of the very few sf novels to focus on the intellectual process of theoretical physics, Le Guin depicts the physicist Shevek in the course of developing the principles of instantaneous communication, which will break through the walls of Einsteinian space. As so often in the community of science fiction, the idea was borrowed by other writers, who began to use Le Guin's term 'ansible'.

The most common forms of faster-than-light travel avoid Einstein without actually denying him. They are referred to by various terms and are sometimes confused with each other: authors delight in offering their own variant explanation of the method. Hyperspace (or overspace or subspace) refers normally to another form of space in the universe, which operates according to different laws from normal space (or 'realspace') and where a journey of several light-years might be undertaken in a few hours. The space warp drive,[28] on the other hand, is usually described as warping real space or exploiting its irregularities, in order to jump from one part of normal space to another, occasionally instantaneously. The eponymous boy hero of Robert A. Heinlein's *Starman Jones* (1953) explained it by folding up a girl's scarf, just as space is folded:

You can't go faster than light, not in our space. If you do, you burst out of it. But if you do it where space is folded back and congruent, you pop right back into our own space again – but a long way off. How far depends on how it's folded. [. . .] We've been gunning at twenty-four gee ever since we left the atmosphere. We don't feel it of course because we are carried inside a discontinuity field at an artificial one gravity. . . [. . .] But we're getting up close to the speed of light, up against the Einstein Wall; pretty soon we'll be squeezed through like a watermelon seed between your finger and thumb and we'll come out near Theta Centauri fifty-eight light years away. [. . .][29]

Inventing one piece of science, as the above extract suggests, may involve inventing more than one: as Heinlein knows, there is no way at which one can accelerate at a practicable rate towards near light-speed without inventing something like artificial gravity, to protect human tissue from otherwise intolerable forces.[30]

Hyperspace or one of its variants has been one of the most enduring devices of science-fiction writers, allowing them to explore and colonize the galaxy without violating scientific laws too obviously. Since it is as yet an unknown, they have been able to describe it in very different ways. Occasionally hyperspace is itself populated by aliens; sometimes interaction with other human travellers is possible while in hyperspace. But in most cases sf writers seem to think that human senses can detect little or nothing in hyperspace: a journey through hyperspace is the equivalent of a railway journey through a tunnel. Navigation in hyperspace may thus be a real problem and might require particular gifts. Frederik Pohl suggested that a blind person might have the knack; others have suggested that only particular races might have the ability, that the experience might be mentally damaging, or that transportation might be possible only in particular circumstances – like during sexual orgasm, according to Norman Spinrad's *The Void Captain's Tale* (1983).[31]

Some, at least, of these many variants were based on the suggestions of theoretical physicists in the generations after Einstein. Work from the late 1960s onwards by such theoretical physicists as Stephen Hawking on the theoretical properties of black holes actually turned the analogy of hyperspace travel being like a tunnel into something approaching a reality for sf writers: black holes might create irregularities in the structure of the universe that might make them gateways to elsewhere in the universe. The 'tunnel' that a black hole might open up was called a 'wormhole' by theoretical physicists, and by the late 1970s many sf writers were imagining that our galaxy was riddled through, Gruyère-like, with wormholes: established short-cuts from one part of visible space to another. New plot-lines were called for. A spaceship with a hyperspace drive could enter hyperspace at any point, but wormholes exist at random fixed points, control of which would immediately become vital for commercial and military purposes. One of the prime functions of David Weber's Royal Manticoran Navy, in the 'Honor Harrington' series mentioned above, is to secure and defend these strategically important but rare natural phenomena.

The most recent suggestion emanating from theoretical physicists to be adopted by science-fiction writers has been the 'tachyon': a theoretical particle which not only may travel faster than light but may even travel in time. Tachyons were first picked up by Gregory Benford in his novel *Timescape* (1980), but tachyon drives soon made their appearance. The mere mention of the word was enough to give the new fictional concept scientific value, even if the explanations were little different from those in earlier forms of fictional travel.

Any other forms of faster-than-light travel are, most sf writers think, closer to fantasy than to science. Some writers have speculated upon the possibility of the human mind having the power to move the body to the stars. This is what got John Carter to Mars in Edgar Rice Burroughs's classic *A Princess of Mars* (1912). John W. Campbell's superhumans moved whole spaceships this way in his story 'Forgetfulness'.[32] In the year that story was published, 1937, Campbell became the influential editor of *Astounding*, the leading American sf magazine, and in the 1950s, when a few scientists became convinced of the potential of extrasensory perception and the potential of telekinesis and teleporting, Campbell for a while pushed his writers in this direction. The British writer John Brunner, for instance, published 'Listen! The Stars!' in Campbell's magazine, depicting a UN special agent who uncovered a group of people in England who were teaching people the knack of using their minds to go to the stars.[33] The most celebrated treatment of teleportation was in Alfred Bester's *Tiger! Tiger!*, where the author's tongue-in-cheek attitude towards this mode of transport is suggested by the name of its discoverer, Charles Fort Jaunte. (Charles Fort, whose name is still celebrated in the increasingly popular journal *Fortean Times*, made his reputation by the study of everything that orthodox science rejected.) In this novel 'jaunting' is at first restricted to the earth's surface; it is the novel's tormented protagonist, Gulliver Foyle, who discovers how to jaunt to the stars, 'up the geodesic lines of space-time to an Elsewhere and an Elsewhen'.[34]

More commonly found as a means of instantaneous travel through the galaxy, though probably equally based upon wish-fulfilment, is the matter transmitter or transporter. In most cases, this involves the scanning of the human body, its transmission as electronic data and its reconstitution at the desired arrival point. Normally it makes travel mundane: a question, at its extreme, of stepping through a doorway on one world and stepping out of it again on another. A good writer might make the very mundaneity of it something to wonder at, as in the last story of Harry Harrison's *One Step from Earth*, in which, tens of thousands of years in the future, wealthy descendants of Earth humans will build their houses so that each doorway is a matter transmitter and each room built on a different planet or worldlet, so that in walking through their house they travel though the galaxy.[35] Despite the oft-quoted phrase from Arthur C. Clarke – 'any sufficiently advanced science will be indistinguishable from magic' – many sf writers consider matter transmission, particularly across vast distances, to be, effectively, magic: cheating on their obligation to be as scientifically plausible as possible. It has been estimated that the computing capacity required to scan and transmit one human exceeds the computing capacity of the entire Earth in the mid-1990s. Nevertheless, sf writers have continued to play with the idea and, in particular, with some of its plot possibilities. What would happen if the transmitted data never arrives at its destination, or if it is distorted in the process of transmission? Joe Patrouch's story 'The Attenuated Man', where the first transmission to Mars ends in near disaster because the settings had been wrong, suggests that such transmission may have deeper spiritual or metaphysical problems. 'Transmats turn people into energy and broadcast them from place to place. Whenever we Transmat, we willfully turn ourselves from thinking, sentient human beings into nonthinking, nonexperiencing bursts of energy. Transmats dehumanize.'[36]

What about the ethical problems which may be inherent in the system? The human body is scanned prior to transmission as electronic data and then, apparently, disintegrated: murdered. What if the original body was not destroyed as the scanned data was transmitted? Lee Robinson's story 'One Way from New York'[37] concentrates on the man whose job it is to 'quiesce' (i.e. murder) passengers at one end of the transmission process: he deliberately keeps one man, a senator, so that an influential person would be made personally aware of the ethical and legal problems inherent in the system. Without 'quiescing', each time a transmission is made the traveller is cloned and the human population increases by one. A 'well-travelled' person may thus feel that he or she has never left home, yet his or her copies may be scattered across the galaxy, or might even copy themselves in order to visit the original back home.

Matter transmission is, like most of the means of avoiding Einstein, a way of allowing the author to develop interstellar plots. There is no better example of its convenience as an imaginary device than in the television programme *Star Trek*. When orbiting a planet, the crew members of *USS Enterprise* can go to the transporter room and beam down onto the surface. This device was the result of the realization, early on in the shooting of the first season of the series in 1966, that filming numerous sequences showing model shuttle-ships landing on different planetary surfaces would be extremely expensive. The transporter, however scientifically implausible, offered a cheap alternative, as well as offering the possibility of plot twists when the transporter malfunctioned. In 'The Enemy Within', for instance, the malfunction creates two Captain Kirks, one compassionate and vacillating, and the other amoral and aggressive.[38] Transporting offered similar potential for plot development for the crew of the British television series *Blake's 7* (1978–81), who had to wear a communications bracelet in order to be transported and who had a startling propensity for losing their bracelets while on hostile planets. Like *Star Trek*, *Blake's 7* offers a sop towards scientific plausibility. Both series maintain that matter transportation is only possible over relatively short distances, as from an orbiting spaceship to the planet below. It cannot be used over a greater distance because of the problems of transmitting data clearly and quickly to the right spot. It is interesting how fictitious science develops its own laws, which can hold true from story to story and from author to author: the idea that a spaceship cannot go into hyperspace too close to a star is another example of a widely diffused concept that has no more and no less scientific validity than hyperspace itself.

For greater distances *Star Trek* engineers rely on the warp drive, which makes everything seem as close as the next country, the next state. 'Warp Factor Ten, Mr Sulu'; and the next day, apparently, we are dozens of light-years away. It was interesting that in the last season of the second series, in *Star Trek: The Next Generation*, it is discovered that the warp drive causes malformation of the 'very fabric of space and time': the Federation is threatened with destruction if their faster-than-light travel becomes impossible or too dangerous to use.[39] It is a metaphor, of course, aimed at *Star Trek*'s fellow inhabitants of Los Angeles; the pollution caused by the automobile threatens the city which the automobile has made possible. Luckily for the Federation, wormholes have been discovered by the time of *Star Trek: Deep Space 9*, the second spin-off from the original series. And in *StarTrek: Voyager* the immensity of the universe is acknowledged for almost the first time: the USS *Voyager* is lost, thousands of light-years from Earth, and at the time of writing is spending the rest of the series trying to get back.

Space-warps and hyperspace expose the contradictions at the heart of science fiction. Sf writers still often ascribe to the convention that the science they use should be plausible. Some writers certainly do believe that travelling faster than light may one day be a possibility, and they are supported in this by a few theoretical physicists. But others recognize that in fact sf writers are frequently dealing with imaginary devices – whether time machines, telepathy or star-drives – which are plot devices: ways of playing with intriguing 'what-ifs'. One of the more thoughtful writers of science fiction, Brian Stableford, muses: 'Given that much of the machinery in sf is really disguised magic, and that the 'explanations' of its workings are fake, it is not easy to see why some fakes pass muster and others don't. . .'[40]

His answer is that it depends on the audience: that the average viewer of sf films or television series, for instance, is capable of accepting scientific nonsense that would be scorned by skilled science fiction readers,[41] while the readers of a science-oriented sf magazine like *Analog* would expect rather more care with the fakery.

Stableford also notes that personal experience plays a part. His scientific training was in biology, and he finds the cavalier attitude of most sf writers towards genetic engineering positively distressing. But he himself is prepared to play with the laws of physics.

I like to tell stories which require a galactic community of worlds, so that I can indulge my taste for building unusual Earthlike ecospheres. This requires space-ships which travel faster than light (though I am perfectly prepared to believe that in reality faster-than-light travel is quite impossible) and in order to make this plausible I am only too happy to woffle [*sic*] about 'hyperspace', shoring up that rather old-hat item of jargon with 'wormholes' borrowed from the black hole theorists, and equipping my starships with 'stressers' which are supposed to make said wormholes (and also supposed to make my jargon sound that important little bit different from other people's).[42]

He adds the comment, addressed to would-be writers, that near-future science fiction requires a great deal of homework and research; far-future adventures just require the judicious employment of jargon. One can compare what a conscientious sf writer has to do now to write about Mars by juxtaposing Arthur C. Clarke's *The Sands of Mars* (1951) with Kim Stanley Robinson's Mars trilogy (*Red Mars*, 1992; *Green Mars*, 1993; *Blue Mars*, 1996). Robinson has to take into account the massive amount of data about the surface of Mars which has been recovered by the Mariner and Viking programmes, and his homework at times threatens to stop the plot. So far the writer about interstellar travel has a very much easier time.

There are some science-fiction writers today who eschew Wollheim's consensus cosmogony, for various reasons: because it results in recursive sf, which is in debate with itself and not with the real world; because it has become tarnished by being associated with too much unthinking adventure fiction; because it has become escapist, ignoring the problems of Earth's near future and propagating the expansionist views of the space lobbyists in a world which is no longer receptive to them. Some writers who indulge in interstellar fiction now do it ironically, like the British writers Iain M. Banks and Colin Greenland, rather than with the kind of serious intent that many writers were able to bring to it in the 1950s and 1960s.

Yet interstellar travel is still a popular theme, and not just for those writers who don't want to do their homework, or who want exotic settings for their adventures in the subgenre of interstellar sf known as 'space opera'. The space lobbyists are still significant, particularly in the United States, and have an influence outside their own circle upon the thinking of science-fiction writers. Their thinking conforms with significant areas of the American myth, as we have seen, above all in the concept of the frontier. Without the frontier, there is stagnation. By the late twentieth century the only frontier left is 'the high frontier' or 'the final Frontier': space. The *Analog* editor's blurb for Joe Haldeman's story from the bicentennial year of 1976, 'Tricentennial', read: 'The basic choice of all life forms is: expansion or stagnation'. In that story a starship is sent out in 2076: because of time dilation, the crew are only seventeen years older when they reach the stars, but on Earth it is AD 5000. But Earth is dead, the victim of some environmental catastrophe, and the millennium went without celebration: 'No fireworks were planned, for lack of audience, for lack of planners: bacteria just don't care. May Day too would be ignored.'[43] In the 'real world', space lobbyists may well conflict with environmentalists, for the latter would regard the expenditure of huge quantities of valuable mineral resources in the 'conquest of space' as wholly unnecessary; nor would many think that the kind of 'terraforming' of other planets described by space scientists or in science-fiction books such as Robinson's 'Mars' trilogy was at all ethical. Yet a long-term form of environmentalism is at least one strand of the space lobbyists' rhetoric: the solar system is not sufficient as a permanent home for the human species. The assumption that humanity *must* expand beyond the solar system leads to the idea that, barring the catastrophes that sf writers are so good at, humanity *will* so expand.

If in the mind of a space lobbyist the solar system is too small for the human race, the solar system is also much too small for the science-fiction writer. NASA's discovery in the summer of 1996 of bacteria in an ancient Martian meteorite would, if confirmed, suggest that there may be life in the solar system other than on Earth, but it is not easy to write an exciting novel about bacteria. The mysteries of the solar system are gradually being demystified by scientists; travelling in imagination to the stars becomes still more necessary. Jack McDevitt well captures the feelings of sf writers and readers about the romance of the infinite spaces beyond the solar system in his short story 'To Hell with the Stars', written in the immediate wake of the Challenger disaster.[44] A boy asks his father why men never went to the stars, as they did in the books of Bradbury and Clarke, a thousand years before. The man points out that even at present-day speeds it would take almost twenty thousand years to reach the stars. It would not make economic sense, and no one would volunteer for a twenty-thousand year trip: 'the payoff is so far down the road that, in reality, there *is* no payoff.' The boy pointed out how disappointed they would have been: 'Who would have?' 'Benford. Robinson. Sheffield.' His father retorted that humans now live in a near-utopia, with no war or hunger; if you could ask one of these old writers 'whether he would have settled for this kind of world, he'd have been delighted. Any sensible man would. He'd have said *to hell with the stars!*'. The boy could not agree, and, the story concludes, his dreams would prevail:

While Will Cutler stared through the plexidome at the slowly awakening stars, thousands of others were also discovering Willis and Swanwick and Tiptree and Sturgeon. They lived in a dozen cities across Will's native Venus. And they played on the cool green hills of Earth and farmed the rich Martian lowlands; they clung to remote shelters among the asteroids, and watched the skies from silver towers beneath the great crystal hemispheres of Io and Titan and Miranda.

The ancient summons flickered across the worlds, insubstantial, seductive, irresistible. The old dreamers were bound, once again, for the stars.

References

Introduction

1 Richard Burton, *Narrative of a Pilgrimage to El Medinah and Meccah* (London, 1893; original version, 1855), vol. II, p. 161.

2 On Burton's journey to Mecca, see T. J. Assad, *Three Victorian Travellers* (London, 1964), pp. 9–52; B. Farnwell, *Burton* (London, 1988), pp. 63–97; F. McLynn, *Burton: Snow upon the Desert* (London, 1990), pp. 72–87.

3 Badia dedicated his book to Louis XVIII, but the publication was in fact commissioned by Napoleon. On his return to Spain in 1808 Badia found the French in power and his boss – the former prime minister Godoy – in disgrace. Like many would-be reformers, Badia worked for the Napoleonic regime and fled to France when it collapsed in 1812. For a detailed account, see the edition of Ali Bey's *Viajes por Marruecos* by S. Barberá (Madrid, 1984), pp. 9–109.

4 In a series of appendices to later editions of his *Narrative of a Pilgrimage* (vol. II, app. IV–VI), Burton included discussions of the recorded trips to Mecca by Ludovico de Varthema (1503), Joseph Pitts (1680) and Giovanni Finati (1814): all 'authentic' but variously tainted with 'credulity', 'prejudice and bigotry' or 'ignorance'.

5 See Varthema, *Itinerario* (Milan, 1929, ed. P. Giudici, from the original edition of 1510), pp. 123–5. Burton reviews Varthema's description of unicorns, concluding: 'They might, therefore, possibly have been African antelopes, which a *lusus naturae* had deprived of their second horn. But the suspicion of fable remains' (Burton, *Narrative of a Pilgrimage*, vol. II, p. 337).

6 On romantic exoticism as an 'urge to transcend the familiar', see R. Cardinal, 'Romantic Travel', in *Rewriting the Self: Histories from the Renaissance to the Present*, ed. R. Porter (London, 1997), pp. 135–55.

7 Burton, *Narrative of a Pilgrimage*, vol. I, p. 2.

8 On Burton's Orientalism, see E. Said, *Orientalism* (London, 1978), pp. 194–7. On his sexuality and sexual interests in an exotic context, see R. Kabbani, *Imperial Fictions: Europe's Myths of Orient*, 2nd edn (London, 1994), pp. 45–66.

9 Said, *Orientalism*, p. 169. See in general his account of the theme of 'Pilgrims and Pilgrimages, British and French' at pp. 166–97.

10 *Ibid.*, p. 169.

11 See for instance the interesting text by Mirzâ Mohammad Hosayn Farâhâni describing a pilgrimage to Mecca in *A Shi'ite Pilgrimage to Mecca, 1885–1886*, ed. H. Farmayan and E. L. Daniel (Austin, TX), 1990.

12 S. Sontag, 'Model Destinations', *Times Literary Supplement* (22 June 1984), pp. 699–700.

13 C. Lévi-Strauss, *Tristes Tropiques* (Harmondsworth, 1976), pp. 50–51. (original French version: Paris, 1955).

14 For an introduction to Chinese travel writing, see R. Strassberg, *Inscribed Landscapes* (Berkeley and Los Angeles, 1994). On Islam, see for instance D. Eickelman and J. Piscatori (eds), *Muslim Travellers: Pilgrimage, Migration and the Religious Imagination* (London, 1990).

15 The translation is by S. McKenna, with slight adaptations.

16 Generally on Odysseus the traveller, see P. Pucci, *Odysseus Polytropos* (Ithaca and London, 1987), pp. 127–54; S. Goldhill, *The Poet's Voice* (Cambridge, 1991), pp. 1–68. A particularly useful theoretical and bibliographic introduction to Homer is I. Morris and B. Powell (eds), *A New Companion to Homer* (Leiden, 1997).

17 Porphyry, *On the Cave of the Nymphs,* 34 (translated by R. Lamberton, with some adaptations). See further F. Buffière, *Les mythes d'Homère et la pensée grecque* (Paris, 1956), pp. 419–37; R. Lamberton, *Homer the Theologian* (Berkeley and Los Angeles, 1986), pp. 108–33; and R. Lamberton, 'The Neoplatonists and the Spiritualization of Homer', in *Homer's Ancient Readers*, ed. R. Lamberton and J. J. Keaney (Princeton, 1992), pp. 115–33, esp. pp. 126–30.

18 See for instance, Basil, *Ad adulescentes* 4, and Fulgentius, *Fabulae secundum Philosophiam moraliter expositae*, 11.8. See also the discussion in H. Rahner, *Greek Myths and Christian Mystery* (London, 1963), pp. 328–86.

19 See Clement, *Protrepticus,* 12, and Hippolytus, *Elenchus,* 8. 13.1–3. Again Rahner in *Greek Myths*, pp. 329–86, offers a very useful discussion.

20 For a traditional presentation of the third-century crisis see S. Williams, *Diocletian and the Roman Recovery* (London, 1985), pp. 15–23, and L. de Blois, 'Emperor and Empire in the Works of Greek-speaking Authors of the Third Century A.D.', *Aufstieg und Niedergang der Römischen Welt*, II.34.4, pp. 3391–443, esp. pp. 3394–9 with bibliography; for the synopsis of a long overdue revisionist view, see A. Cameron, *The Later Roman Empire (AD 284–430)* (London, 1993).

21 On the religious context of the Roman empire at this period, a good introduction is J. North, 'The Development of Religious Pluralism', in *The Jews among Pagans and Christians*, ed. J. Lieu, J. North and T. Rajak (London, 1992), pp. 174–93. On the rise of new religions (so called 'Oriental' cults), see R. Turcan, *The Cults of the Roman Empire* (Oxford, 1996).

22 On the growth of universalism in the Roman empire, see G. Fowden, *Empire to Commonwealth: Consequences of Monotheism in Late Antiquity* (Princeton, 1993), pp. 37–60.

23 On travel in the Roman empire see, for instance, L. Casson, *Travel in the Ancient World* (London, 1974), pp. 229–329 and E. D. Hunt, 'Travel, Tourism and Piety in the Roman Empire', *Echos du monde classique*, XXVIII (1984), pp. 391–417. Unsurpassed as a collection and discussion of the sources is L. Friedländer, *Darstellungen aus der Sittengeschichte Roms*, vol. I (Leipzig, 1921–3), pp. 318–490. For good overviews of the world as conceived by ancient Greeks and Romans, see J. S. Romm, *The Edges of the Earth in Ancient Thought* (Princeton, 1992); C. Jacob, *Géographie et ethnographie en Grèce ancienne* (Paris, 1991); and F. Hartog, *Mémoire d'Ulysse: Récits sur la frontière en Grèce ancienne* (Paris, 1996).

24 Monographs on Pausanias include C. Habicht, *Pausanias' Guide to Ancient Greece* (Berkeley and Los Angeles, 1985), and K. Arafat, *Pausanias' Greece* (Cambridge, 1996). Other important discussions include J. Elsner, 'Pausanias: A Greek Pilgrim in the Roman World', *Past and Present*, 135 (1992), pp. 3–29; S. Alcock, 'Landscapes of Memory and the Authority of Pausanias', in *Pausanias Historien*, Entretiens Fondation Hardt 41 (Geneva, 1996), pp. 241–67; S. Swain, *Hellenism and Empire* (Oxford, 1996), pp. 330–56.

25 On Aelius Aristides, see P. Cox Miller, *Dreams in Late Antiquity* (Princeton, 1994), pp. 106–83, 184–204, and Swain, *Hellenism and Empire*, pp. 254–97.

26 On Lucian's *Syrian Goddess* see R. Oden, *Studies in Lucian's 'De Syria Dea'* (Missoula, MT, 1977); Swain, *Hellenism and Empire*, pp. 304–8; and J. Elsner, 'Describing Self in the Language of Other: Pseudo (?) Lucian at the Temple of Hire', in *'All is Greece to the Wise': Literature and Identity in the Second Sophistic*, ed. S. Goldhill (Cambridge, forthcoming).

27 On issues of 'resistance' within the empire, see G. Woolf, 'Becoming Roman, Staying Greek', *Proceedings of the Cambridge Philological Society*, XL (1994), pp. 116–43, and J. Elsner, 'The Origins of the Icon: Pilgrimage, Religion and Visual Culture in the Roman East as "Resistance" to the Centre', in *The Early Roman Empire in the East*, ed. S. Alcock (Oxford, 1997), pp. 178–99.

28 An elegant discussion of the *Anacharsis* is R. Bracht Branham, *Unruly Eloquence: Lucian and the Comedy of Traditions* (Cambridge, MA, 1989), pp. 82–104.

29 Lucian, *Anacharsis*, 18 (translated by A. M. Harmon).

30 On Favorinus, see M. Gleason, *Making Men: Sophists and Self-Presentation in Ancient Rome* (Princeton, 1992), pp. 3–20, and generally on Lucian, see Swain, *Hellenism and Empire*, pp. 298–329, with bibliography.

31 Lucian, *A True Story*, 4.

32 On the *Life of Apollonius* and its relation to travel, see especially J. Elsner, 'Hagiographic Geography: Travel and Allegory in the *Life of Apollonius of Tyana*', *Journal of Hellenic Studies*, 117 (1997), pp. 22–37, with further bibliography.

33 Philostratus, *Life of Apollonius*, VIII.15 (translated by F. C. Conybeare).

34 *Ibid.*, VIII.19.

35 *Ibid.*, VIII.15.

36 *Ibid.*, VIII.30.

37 On travel in the novels, see A. Billault, *La création romanesque* (Paris, 1991), pp. 191–243; and on the allegorical function of the travel theme, R. Beck, 'Mystery Religions, Aretalogy and the Ancient Novel', in *The Novel in the Ancient World*, ed. G. Schmeling (Leiden, 1996), pp. 31–50, esp. pp. 149–50.

38 On the *Acts of the Apostles* and its various contexts, see the six-volume commentary edited by B. W. Winter, *The Book of Acts in Its First Century Setting* (Carlisle, 1993–).

39 On Paul and his travels in the *Acts*, see L. Alexander, '"In Journeyings Often": Voyaging in the Acts of the Apostles and in Greek Romance', in *Luke's Literary Achievement*, ed. L. M. Tuckett (Sheffield, 1995), pp. 17–49; and D. Marguerat, 'Voyages et voyageurs dans le livre des Actes et culture Gréco-Romaine', *Revue d'histoire et de philosophie religieuses*, 78 (1998), pp. 33–59, with bibliography. On the *Acts* as fiction in the tradition of the ancient novels, see R. I. Pervo, *Profit with Delight: The Literary Genre of the Acts of the Apostles* (Philadelphia, PA, 1987). For other Christian novels of the second and third centuries (the apocryphal *Acts*), see J. Perkins, 'The Social World of the *Acts of Peter*', in *The Search for the Ancient Novel*, ed. J. Tatum (Baltimore and London, 1994), pp. 296–307, and R. Pervo, 'Early Christian Fiction', in *Greek Fiction*, ed. J. R. Morgan and R. Stoneman (London, 1994), pp. 239–54. For the interesting parallel of Christ with Apollonius, see M. Smith, *Jesus the Magician* (New York, 1978), pp. 84–91, 94–140, and H. C. Kee, *Medicine, Miracle and Magic in the New Testament* (Cambridge, 1986), pp. 84–6. For the parallel of Paul with Apollonius, see Elsner, 'Hagiographic Geography', p. 35.

40 Philostratus, *Life of Apollonius*, I.3.

41 See Eusebius, *Contra Hieroclem*.

42 See G. S. Kirk, J. E. Raven and M. Schofield, *The Pre-Socratic Philosophers*, 2nd edn (Cambridge, 1983), fr. 16, p. 169.

43 *Ibid.*, fr. 15, p. 169.

44 On Gilgamesh in relation to the traditions of the Graeco-Roman epic, see T. van

Nortwick, *Somewhere I Have Never Travelled: The Second Self and the Hero's Journey in Ancient Epic* (Oxford, 1996), pp. 8–38.

45 On Herodotean autopsy, see A. K. Armayor, *Herodotus' Autopsy of the Fayoum* (Amsterdam, 1985); F. Hartog, *The Mirror of Herodotus* (Berkeley and Los Angeles, 1988), pp. 260–309; and D. Fehling, *Herodotus and His Sources* (Leeds, 1989), pp. 100–4, 115–17, 240–3. See also J. Redfield, 'Herodotus the Tourist', *Classical Philology*, 80 (1985), pp. 97–118; Hartog, *Mirror of Herodotus*; J. Gould, *Herodotus* (London, 1989), pp. 86–109; and D. Fehling, 'The Art of Herodotus and the Margins of the World', in *Travel Fact and Travel Fiction*, ed. Z. von Martels (Leiden, 1994), pp. 1–15.

46 See especially Plutarch (writing in Greek at the end of the first century AD) in his *Malice of Herodotus*; also, more playfully perhaps, Lucian in *A True Story*, 2.31 and *Lover of Lies*, 2.

47 On such competition (and its relation to rationality) see G. E. R. Lloyd, *The Revolutions of Wisdom* (Berkeley and Los Angeles, 1987), pp. 91–108, and, for the Roman period, T. Barton, *Power and Knowledge: Astrology, Physiognomics and Medicine under the Roman Empire* (Ann Arbor, 1994), pp. 13–14.

48 Lucian, *Lover of Lies*, 32–9.

49 On Strabo, see R. French, *Ancient Natural History* (London, 1994), pp. 114–48, and K. Clarke, 'In Search of the Author of Strabo's Geography', *Journal of Roman Studies*, 87 (1997), pp. 92–110, with bibliography.

50 On Pliny, see M. Beagon, *Roman Nature: The Thought of Pliny the Elder* (Oxford, 1992), and French, *Ancient Natural History*, pp. 196–255, with further bibliography.

51 On Pausanias as an empirical collector of myths, see P. Veyne, *Did the Greeks Believe in Their Myths?* (Chicago and London, 1988), pp. 3, 95–102; on his collection of rituals, see J. Elsner, 'Image and Ritual: Reflections on the Graeco-Roman Appreciation of Art', *Classical Quarterly*, XLVI (1996), pp. 515–31.

52 One other inheritance from Antiquity was the non-religious model of Alexander, the traveller as conqueror. See R. Stoneman, *The Legends of Alexander the Great* (London, 1994).

53 For some interesting reflections see J. Z. Smith, *To Take Place* (Chicago and London, 1987), especially pp. 74–95, and R. A. Markus, 'How On Earth Could Places Become Holy? Origins of the Idea of Holy Places', *Journal of Early Christian Studies*, II (1994), pp. 257–71.

54 The literature on the Christianization of Palestine and the rise of pilgrimage is vast. On the Holy Land specifically see, e.g., P. W. L. Walker, *Holy City, Holy Places?* (Oxford, 1990); R. L. Wilken, *The Land Called Holy* (New Haven and London, 1992); and J. E. Taylor, *Christians and the Holy Places* (Oxford, 1993). On pilgrims and pilgrimage, see B. Kötting, *Peregrinatio Religiosa* (Regensburg, 1950); E. D. Hunt, *Holy Land Pilgrimage in the Roman Empire* (Oxford, 1982); and P. Maraval, *Lieux saints et pèlerinages d'Orient* (Paris, 1985).

55 On the Bordeaux Pilgrim (whose text is known as the *Itinerarium Burdigalense*), see especially L. Douglass, 'A New Look at the Itinerarium Burdigalense', *Journal of Early Christian Studies*, IV (1996), pp. 312–33, and G. Bowman, 'Mapping History: Redemption, Eschatology and Topography in the Itinerarium Burdigalense', in *Jerusalem: Its Sanctity and Centrality to Judaism, Christianity and Islam*, ed. Lee I. Levine (New York and Jerusalem, 1998), both with further bibliography.

56 *Itinerarium Burdigalense*, 588, translated by J. Wilkinson.

57 On the issue of Jewish holy places see J. Wilkinson, 'Jewish Holy Places and the Origins of Christian Pilgrimage', in *The Blessings of Pilgrimage*, ed. R. Ousterhout (Urbana and Chicago, 1990), pp. 41–53; Taylor, *Christians and the Holy Places*, pp. 318–31.

58 On Egeria, see J. Wilkinson, *Egeria's Travels* (London, 1971); M. B. Campbell, *The Witness and the Other World* (Ithaca and London, 1988), pp. 20–33; A. Palmer, 'Egeria the Voyager', in *Travel Fact and Travel Fiction*, ed. Z. von Martels, pp. 39–53, with bibliography. On the rise of liturgy in the Holy Land, see J. Baldovin, *The Urban Character of Christian Worship* (Rome, 1987), pp. 55–104.

59 On the cult of the saints and their relics, see especially H. Delehaye, *Les origines du culte des martys* (Brussels, 1912), and *Sanctus: essai sur le culte des saints dans l'antiquité* (Brussels, 1927); also P. Brown, *The Cult of the Saints* (London, 1981).

60 *Itinerarium Egeriae*, 22.2–23.6, translated by J. Wilkinson.

61 *Ibid.*, 23.7–10.

62 For holy persons as the goal of pilgrimage, see *Itinerarium Egeriae*, 17.1: 'God also moved me with a desire to go to Syrian Mesopotamia. The holy monks there are said to be so numerous and of so indescribably excellent a life that I wanted to pay them a visit.'

63 *Ibid.*, 17.1.

64 The quote is from Valerius's letter 1a. On the letter of Valerius, see Wilkinson, *Egeria's Travels*, pp. 174–8; H. Sivan, 'Who Was Egeria? Piety and Pilgrimage in the Age of Gratian', *Harvard Theological Review*, 81 (1988), pp. 59–72, esp. pp. 59–63.

65 Valerius's letter 3.

66 Valerius's letter 4a.

67 Anglo-Saxon Chronicle for 891 (according to MSS A and F; 892 according to MSS C and D). Here we use J. O'Meara's translation from *The Voyage of St Brendan* (Gerrards Cross, 1978), p. ix.

68 On *The Voyage of St Brendan*, see the versions by O'Meara (1978) and by J. F. Webb and D. H. Farmer in *The Age of Bede* (Harmondsworth, 1983), pp. 211–46. For a good account of the background, see T. Charles-Edwards, 'The Social Background to Irish "Peregrinatio"', *Celtica*, XI (1976), pp. 43–59. For a critical discussion, see R. A. Bartoli, *La 'Navigatio sancti Brendani' e la sua fortuna nella cultura romanza dell' età mezzo* (Fasano, 1993).

69 See the interesting sixth-century interpretation by Fulgentius in L. Whitbread, *Fulgentius the Mythographer* (Ohio, 1971), and the twelfth-century commentary by Bernardus Silvestris in E. Schreiber and J. Maresca, *Commentary on the First Six Books of Virgil's 'Aeneid' by Bernardus Silvestris* (Nebraska, 1979).

70 'Vitae Willibaldi et Winnebaldi, auctore sanctimoniali Heidenheimensi', ed. O. Holder-Egger, in *Monumenta Germaniae Historia. Scriptorum*, vol. XV, part 1, p. 87.

71 Very large pilgrimages are recorded, for instance, for the years 1033 and 1064.

72 See Georges Duby, *Medieval Art. The Making of the Christian West 980–1140* (Geneva, 1966), especially pp. 171–207.

73 This is also true of local shrines. See Robert Worth Frank, 'Pilgrimage and Sacral Power', in *Journeys toward God. Pilgrimage and Crusade*, ed. B. N. Sargent-Baur (Kalamazoo, 1992), p. 31.

74 As discussed by Béatrice Dansette in 'Les relations du pèlerinage Outre-Mer: des origines à l'age d'or', in *Croisades et pèlerinages. Récits, chroniques et voyages en terre sainte, XIIe–XVIe siècle*, ed. Daniel Régier-Bohler (Paris, 1997), pp. 881–92.

75 Dorothea R. French, 'Journeys to the Centre of the Earth: Medieval and Renaissance Pilgrimages to Mount Calvary', in *Journeys toward God*, pp. 61–4.

76 J. Wilkinson, *Jerusalem Pilgrimage 1099–1185* (London, 1988), p. 260. Dorothea French (in *Journeys toward God*, p. 66) seems to identify the navel of the world with a rent on the rock upon which the cross was said to have been fixed, on Mount Calvary. There was also below the site of the cross a split cleft on the rock where Christ's blood was said to have fallen, touching the skull of Adam (who was also buried below). However, the navel of the world was usually described as a separate hole (albeit under

the same dome at the Church of the Holy Sepulchre). See the map in Wilkinson, *Jerusalem Pilgrimage*, p. 35.

77 Liudprand of Cremona, *The Embassy to Constantinople and Other Writings*, trans. F. A. Wright, ed. J. J. Norwich (London, 1993).

78 Robert the Monk in his *Historia Hyerosolymitana*: see E. Peters, *The First Crusade: The Chronicle of Robert the Monk and Other Source Materials* (Philadelphia, 1971), p. 4.

79 See Marcus Bull, *Knightly Piety and the Lay Response to the First Crusade* (Oxford, 1993).

80 Guibert of Nogent, *Dei gesta per francos*, I, 1.64–73, ed. R. B. C. Huygens, in *Corpus Christianorum* 127a (Turnholt, 1996), p. 87, translated by Bull in *Knightly Piety*, p. 3, with adaptations.

81 William of Tyre, *Chronicon* XXI, 7, ed. R. B. C. Huygens, in *Corpus Christianorum* 63a (Turnholt, 1986), pp. 969–70.

82 Chrétien de Troyes, *Arthurian Romances*, trans. D. D. R. Owen (London, 1987), p. 417.

83 A passage in the *roman* solves the puzzle by explaining (through a hermit) that the Grail is used to take the Eucharist to the sick king's father, whilst the lance is clearly the one Longinus used to pierce the body of Christ during his passion – the most important crusading relic. It is also made clear that Perceval's failing was a religious one, and he is accordingly subjected to harsh penance in order to meditate upon Christ's passion (Chrétien de Troyes 1987, pp. 458–9). However, this passage, of clumsy construction, is understood by many as an interpolation. This is not implausible, because it appears in the second half of the *roman* concerning the adventures of Gawain. It seems that at his death Chrétien was working on two separate works, which an editor put together. The editor might have been tempted to add this passage, but it seems more consistent with his lack of further interventions that he was using Chrétien's drafted notes.

84 For a lucid exposition of this interpretation see the introduction by Mart'n de Riquer to his edition of Chrétien de Troyes, *Li contes del graal: El cuento del Grial* (Barcelona, 1984). We have also used the English translation by D. D. R. Owen in Chrétien de Troyes, *Arthurian Romances*. There have been many attempts to trace the theme of the Grail back to Celtic oral traditions, and Chrétien mentions a book given to him by Philip of Flanders as basis for his work. However, whilst the British Celtic *setting* is an obvious inspiration for the whole Arthurian cycle, the existence of actual Celtic *sources* is a more dubious proposition. For example a Welsh version of the story of Perceval, the *Peredur* which appears in the *Mabinogion*, is a thirteenth-century composition derived from Chrétien, rather than the other way round. For the Grail and its evolution see Jean Frappier, *Chrétien de Troyes et le mythe du Graal. Étude sur le Perceval ou le conte du Graal* (Paris, 1972), and D. D. R. Owen, *The Evolution of the Grail Legend* (Edinburgh, 1968). More generally, see Roger S. Loomis, *The Development of Arthurian Romance* (London, 1963).

85 See E. Gilson, 'La Mystique de la grace dans la *Quête du Saint Graal*', in his *Les idées et les lettres* (Paris, 1932).

86 Courtly love was first developed by Provençal troubadours but was codified more explicitly in a treatise by Andreas Capellanus, a contemporary of Chrétien at the court of Marie of Champagne at Troyes. What characterized this love, uniquely, was the emphasis on a rigid social hierarchy, which made the woman almost inaccessible, but also the power of this impossible love to improve the lover's soul.

87 V. Cirlot, ed., *Les Cançons de l'amor de Lluny de Jaufré Rudel* (Barcelona, 1996), p. 76.

88 For a more detailed account of the topics raised in this section, see the first five chapters of J.-P. Rubiés, *Travel and Ethnology in the Renaissance: South India through European Eyes* (forthcoming).

89 From 'La Vita Nuova', trans. D. G. Rossetti, in *The Portable Dante*, ed. P. Milano (Harmondsworth, 1977), pp. 616–18.

90 Dante Alighieri, *The Divine Comedy. Inferno*, Italian text with prose translation and comment by J. D. Sinclair (New York, 1939), pp. 325–7.

91 For a general historical context see J. R. S. Philips, *The Medieval Expansion of Europe* (Oxford, 1988).

92 The best edition is still Anastasius van den Wyngaert, *Sinica Franciscana. Volumen I. Itinera et relationes fratrum minorum saeculi XIII et XIV* (Karachi, 1929). In English see Peter Jackson (ed.), *The Mission of Friar William of Rubruck*, Hakluyt Society (London, 1990), although for Carpini's narrative one still needs to refer to C. Dawson (ed.), *The Mongol Mission. Narratives and Letters of the Franciscan Missionaries in Mongolia and China in the Thirteenth and Fourteenth Centuries* (London, 1955). Juan Gil, *En demanda de Gran Khan. Viajes a Mongolia en el siglo XIII* (Madrid, 1993), is a comprehensive Spanish edition of these and related writings.

93 Jackson, *The Mission of Friar William*, p. 59.

94 *Ibid.*, p. 71.

95 For Francis of Assisi as missionary see Benjamin Kedar, *Crusade and Mission. European Approaches towards the Muslims* (Princeton, 1984), pp. 119–24. For Ignatius see John O'Malley, *The First Jesuits* (Cambridge, MA, 1993), chapters 1 and 2, as well as the concise biography by Philip Caraman, *Ignatius Loyola* (London, 1990).

96 From the *Phantasticus*, as translated by Anthony Bonner in *Doctor Illuminatus. A Ramon Llull Reader* (Princeton, 1993), p. 41. Bonner's anthology (based on a more extended edition – *Selected Works of Ramon Llull* [Princeton, 1985]) is by far the best introduction to Ramon Llull in English.

97 Ramon Llull, *Llibre de meravelles*, ed. M. Gustà and J. Molas (Barcelona, 1980), which follows one of the best manuscripts of the Catalan original. For a discussion of this book see also Anthony Bonner and Lola Badia, *Ramon Llull. Vida, pensament i obra literària* (Barcelona, 1988), pp. 135–8.

98 For a careful discussion of Gerald of Wales as ethnographer in Wales and Ireland, in the context of the twelfth-century Renaissance, see Robert Bartlett, *Gerald of Wales 1146–1223* (Oxford, 1982). European peripheries in the high Middle Ages were of course also the first 'other' of feudal Latin Christendom.

99 Marco Polo, *The Travels*, trans. and ed. Ronald Latham (Harmondsworth, 1958), p. 33. This is a good English translation, but for a critical edition and analysis of the manuscripts see L. F. Benedetto, *Il Milione* (Florence, 1928), and for an English translation which distinguishes different variants see A. C. Moule and P. Pelliott, *Marco Polo. The Description of the World* (London, 1938).

100 *The Travels*, pp. 260–62.

101 Within the literature on Marco Polo, Leonardo Olschki's *L'Asia di Marco Polo* (Venice, 1957) remains fundamental. For the reception of the *Divisament* as a book of traditional marvels (not to be confused with authorial intentions) see R. Wittkower, 'Marco Polo and the Pictorial Tradition of the Marvels of the East', in *Oriente Poliano. Studi e conferenze . . . in occasione del VII centenario della nascita di Marco Polo* (Rome, 1957).

102 On Mandeville see especially Malcolm Letts, *Sir John Mandeville: The Man and his Book* (London, 1949); Josephine W. Bennett, *The Rediscovery of Sir John Mandeville* (New York, 1954); M. C. Seymour, *Sir John Mandeville* (Aldershot, 1993); Mary B. Campbell, *The Witness and the Other World: Exotic European Travel Writing, 400–1600* (Ithaca, 1988), chapter 4; Christiane Deluz, *Le livre de Jehan de Mandeville: une 'geographie' au XIVe siècle* (Louvain, 1988); Iain Macleod Higgins, *Writing East. The 'Travels' of Sir John Mandeville* (Philadelphia, 1997).

103 M. Letts (ed.), *Mandeville's Travels, Texts and Translations*, Hakluyt Society (London, 1953), II, pp. 220–31. Letts prints the French manuscript from the Bibliothèque Nationale, ms.fr. 4,515 (from *c.* 1371), which represents a 'Continental' version that is probably closer to the authorial text than the Anglo-Norman French and English variants mainly found in England.

104 For a discussion of variants, see Higgins 1997.

105 On the general theme of post-medieval pilgrimage to Rome, see W. Williams, *'The Undiscovered Country': Pilgrimage and Narrative in the French Renaissance* (Oxford, 1998).

106 For a discussion of the subject, with reference to Mandeville, see Christian K. Zacher, *Curiosity and Pilgrimage. The Literature of Discovery in Fourteenth-Century England* (Baltimore, 1974).

107 A. Lanza and M. Troncarelli (eds), *Pellegrini Scrittori. Viaggatori Toscani del Trecento in Terrasanta* (Florence, 1990), pp. 224–5.

108 *Itinerarium Symonis Semeonis ab Hybernia ad Terram Sanctam*, with English translation, in *Scriptores Latini Hiberniae*, vol. IV, ed. M. Esposito (Dublin, 1960).

109 Christiane Deluz (ed.), *Liber de quibusdam ultramarinis partibus de Guillaume de Boldensele* (Paris, 1972); Ludolph of Sudheim, *De itinere Terrae Sanctae*, ed. F. Deycks (Stuttgart, 1851). For an analysis of this literature see B. Dansette, 'Les pèlerinages en Terre Sainte aux XIV et XV siècles: étude sur les aspects originaux et édition d'une relation anonyme', PhD thesis, University of Paris–Sorbonne, 1977.

110 Thus von Harff did not simply follow the substance of Mandeville; he followed the model. See Malcolm Letts (ed.), *The Pilgrimage of Arnold von Harff*, Hakluyt Society (London, 1946). The manuscript was written in a German dialect from the Lower Rhine.

111 We have used the modern English translation: Geoffrey Chaucer, *The Canterbury Tales*, trans. Nevill Coghill (Harmondsworth, 1951), p. 40 (from the 'General Prologue', vv. 773–6). The original reads:

> And wel I woot as ye goon by the waye
> Ye shapen you to talen and to playe,
> For trewely, confort ne mirthe is noon
> To ride by the waye domb as stoon.

112 Erasmus devoted one of his Latin *Colloquies* (1518, with new editions in 1522 and 1526) to a satirical exposé of devotional journeys as meaningless actions from a strictly evangelical Christian viewpoint. See C. R. Thompson, *The Colloquies of Erasmus* (Chicago, 1965).

113 J. R. R. Tolkien and E. V. Gordon, *Sir Gawain and the Green Knight*, 2nd edn, rev. N. Davies (Oxford, 1967).

114 For the text we have used *Le petit Jehan de Saintré*, ed. M. Eusebi (Paris, 1993), and *Curial e Güelfa*, ed. M. Gustà and G. E. Sansone (Barcelona, 1979). It is worth speculating that these two novels actually emerged from a similar cultural moment, the Humanist influence in the Angevin and Aragonese courts, in a specific context of interaction – the contest for Naples between René of Anjou (whom la Sale served) and Alfonso of Aragon (whom the Catalan author of the *Curial* is likely to have served, since he shows a knowledge of Italy and Italian literature). Both la Sale and the author of the *Curial* offer strong evidence of the fresh reception of the themes of classical mythology within a chivalric tradition. On la Sale see F. Desonay, *Antoine de la Sale, aventureux et pédagogue. Essai de bibliographie critique* (Liège and Paris, 1940); on his use of historical setting see M. de Riquer, 'El episodio barcelonés del *Jehan de Saintré* y Juan de Calabria en Barcelona', in *Mélanges offertes à Jean Frappier*, II (Paris, 1969), pp. 957–67; on the limits of his narrative realism, which

captures human tragedy but on the whole follows the conventionalized style of medieval chronicles, see E. Auerbach, *Mimesis. The Representation of Reality in Western Literature* (Princeton, 1953), chapter 10. On the *Curial*, at an introductory level, see Martín de Riquer, 'La novel.la cavalleresca', in *Història de la literatura catalana*, vol. II (Barcelona, 1965).

115 Antoine de la Sale, *Le Paradis de la Reine Sibylle*, ed. F. Desonay (Paris, 1930). For further comment see J. Demers, 'La quête de l'anti-Graal ou un récit fantastique: "le paradis de la reine Sibylle"', in *Le Moyen Age*, LXXXIII (Brussels, 1977), pp. 169–92.

116 La Sale, 1930, p. 15.

117 The links between chivalry and the early modern literature of discovery are stressed – perhaps with some exaggeration – by Jennifer Goodman in *Chivalry and Exploration, 1298–1630* (Woodbridge, 1998).

118 Miguel de Cervantes, *El ingenioso hidalgo don Quijote de la Mancha*, ed. J. J. Allen (Madrid, 1981), I, p. 556.

119 For a discussion of the theme of travel in Cervantes, see A. Vilanova, *Erasmo y Cervantes* (Barcelona, 1989), esp. pp. 326–409.

120 *Embajada a Tamorlán*, ed. Francisco López Estrada (Madrid, 1943). *Le Voyage d'Outremer de Bertrandon de la Broquière*, ed. C. Schefer (Paris, 1892).

121 Poggio Bracciolini, *Historia de varietate fortunae*, ed. O. Merisalo (Helsinki, 1993). Ramusio's collection has been edited by Marica Milanesi in *Navigazione e Viaggi*, 6 vols (Turin, 1978–).

122 George Sandys, *Relation of a Journey Begun An.Dom. 1610*, 2nd edn (London, 1615); Pietro della Valle, *Viaggi di Pietro della Valle il pellegrino*, 4 vols: 'La Turchia', 'La Persia' (I and II), 'L'India' (Rome, 1658–63). For a discussion of Sandys's pilgrimage narrative see J. Haynes, *The Humanist as Traveller. George Sandys' 'Relation of a Journey Begun An.Dom. 1610'* (London and Toronto, 1986).

123 On this subject see Anthony Pagden, *Lords of All the World. Ideologies of Empire in Spain, Britain and France c. 1500–c. 1800* (New Haven and London, 1995); David Armitage (ed.), *Theories of Empire, 1450–1800: An Expanding World* (Aldershot, 1998).

124 J.-P. Rubiés, 'New Worlds and Renaissance Ethnology', *History and Anthropology*, VI (1993), pp. 157–97.

125 Henry Peacham, *The Compleat Gentleman, Fashioning him Absolute in the Most Necessary and Commendable Qualities concerning Minde or Bodie that may be Required in a Noble Gentleman* (London, 1622), p. 200 (with modernized spelling). Peacham was a Master of Arts from Trinity College, Cambridge.

126 For a discussion of the figure of the traveller in the eighteenth century, see M.-N. Bourget, 'The Explorer', in *Enlightenment Portraits*, ed. M. Vovelle (Chicago and London, 1997), pp. 257–315.

127 See C. A. Bayly, *Imperial Meridian. The British Empire and the World, 1780–1830* (London and New York, 1989). For an introduction to the earlier phases of European colonialism see J. H. Parry, *The Age of Reconnaissance. Discovery, Exploration and Settlement, 1450–1650* (London, 1963), and J. H. Parry, *Trade and Dominion. European Overseas Empires in the Eighteenth Century* (London, 1971).

128 Bernard Smith, *European Vision and the South Pacific*, 2nd edn (New Haven and London, 1985), p. 99.

129 A. Pagden, *European Encounters with the New World* (New Haven and London, 1993), p. 114. Humboldt's *Cosmos* – his life-time work, a universal traveller's vision of the physical world which was both scientific and romantic – was published in 1846–58 in its English translation from the German original.

130 Dea Birkett and Sarah Wheeler, *Amazonian* (Harmondsworth, 1998), pp. vii–xii.

131 Said, *Orientalism*, p. 170.

132 As noted in Cardinal, 'Romantic Travel', in *Rewriting the Self* (see note 6 above).

133 The theme of Tenzing's role in the conquest of Everest has been subject to a subtle debate, with Gordon T. Stewart and Peter Hansen offering different interpretations of the extent to which the Tibetan Sherpa's celebrity challenged 'an imperial master narrative'. Hansen suggests a less dichotomous analysis. See P. Hansen and G. Stewart, 'Tenzing's Two Wrist-Watches: The Conquest of Everest and Late Imperial Culture, 1921–1953: Comment', *Past and Present*, 157 (1997), pp. 159–90.

134 Joseph Conrad, 'Geography and Some Explorers', in *Late Essays*, ed. R. Curle (London, 1926). Quoted in Felix Driver, 'Stanley and His Critics: Geography, Exploration and Empire', *Past and Present*, 133 (1991), pp. 134–66.

135 On the controversies surrounding Stanley, see Driver, 'Stanley and His Critics'. Stanley's appeal to British nationalism as the ideology which sustained imperial annexations is evident, for example, in the preface to the second edition of his *Through the Dark Continent* (London, 1899), pp. xi–xxv, reflecting on the growth of German influence since the first edition (1879).

136 For a close study of the relationship between autobiography and fictional recreation in this and other novels by Conrad, see Norman Sherry, *Conrad's Western World* (Cambridge, 1971).

137 J. Conrad, *Heart of Darkness*, ed. Paul O'Prey (Harmondsworth, 1973), p. 112.

138 A. E. Van Vogt, *The Voyage of the Space Beagle* (1950). The book was a 'fix-up' of previously published stories and has proved very popular with readers. We have used the British Panther edition (St Albans, 1959).

139 For a succinct account see Edward James, *Science Fiction in the 20th Century* (Oxford, 1994), pp. 70-71, 158-9.

1 *Jesús Carrillo: From Mt Ventoux to Mt Masaya*

  1 Petrarch's letter *Ad Dyonisium de Burgo Sancti Sepulcri* is included in Francisci Petrarca, *Epistolae Familiares*, IV, i. I use the Venetian edition of 1492. I will not explore here the veracity of Petrarch's account, although G. Billanovich has convincingly demonstrated that it was probably written a few years after its ostensible date. See 'Il Petrarca e il Ventoso', in *Italia medioevale e umanistica*, IX (1966), p. 397.

  2 See Billanovich (1966) and B. Martinelli's 'Del Petrarca e il Ventoso', in *Studi in Onore di Alberto Chiari* (Brescia, 1973), II, pp. 767–834.

  3 See Pierre Courcelle, *Les Confessions de Saint Augustin dans la tradition Littéraire. Antecedents et Postérité* (Paris, 1963), pp. 339–44; and, especially, the detailed comparative analysis of the two texts made by Evelyne Luciani in *Les Confessions de Saint Augustine dans les lettres de Pétrarque* (Paris, 1982), pp. 65–81.

  4 This connection was originally pointed out by A. von Martin in 'Petrarca und Augustin', *Archiv für Kulturgeschichte*, XVIII (1928), p. 59.

  5 *Epistolae Familiares,* IV, i, fol. 50r:

  > [. . .] nondum enim in portu sum, ut securus preteritarum meminerim procellarum. Tempus forsam veniet, quando eodem quo gesta sunt ordine universa percurram, prefatus illud Augustini tui: 'Recordari volo transactas feditates meas et carnales corruptiones anime mee, non quod eas amem, sed ut amam te'. Michi quidem multum adhuc ambigui molestique negotii superest.

  The English translation is by Hans Nachod in 'Petrarca: Ascent of Mont Ventoux', included in *The Renaissance Philosophy of Man*, ed. E. Cassirer, P. O. Kristeller and J. H. Randall, pp. 36–46 (p. 42).

  6 Robert M. Durling, 'The Ascent of Mt. Ventoux and the Crisis of Allegory', *Italian Quarterly*, XVIII/69 (1974), pp. 7–28.

7 Robert M. Durling had earlier explored the ambivalence of Petrarch's approach to allegory in poetry in 'Giovane donne sotto un verde lauro', *Modern Language Notes*, LXXXVI/1 (1971), pp. 1–21. Durling's argument was developed by John Frecero in 'The Fig Tree and the Laurel: Petrarch Poetics', *Diacritics*, 5 (1975), pp. 34–40; and Thomas M. Greene traced the crisis of the allegorical interpretation of history in Petrarch's new humanist hermeneutics in 'Petrarch and the Humanist Hermeneutic', in *Italian Literature: Roots and Branches*, ed. G. Rimanelli and K. J. Atchity (New Haven, 1976), later republished in a revised version in T. M. Greene's *The Light in Troy. Imitation and Discovery in Renaissance Poetry* (New Haven, 1982), pp. 81–104.

8 See Durling (1974), p. 24.

9 On this topic, see Richard Turner, *The Vision of Landscape in Renaissance Italy* (Princeton, 1966).

10 The relationship between the development of perspective in the Renaissance and the rise of modern subjectivity has been discussed in different terms by William W. Ivins, Jr, *On the Rationalization of Sight: with an Examination of Three Renaissance Texts on Perspective* (New York, 1973); Norman Bryson in the introduction to his *Word and Image: French Painting of the Ancient Regime* (Cambridge, 1981); John White, *The Birth and Rebirth of Pictorial Space* (Cambridge, MA, 1987); Michael Kubovy, *The Psychology of Perspective and Renaissance Art* (Cambridge, 1986); Martin Jay in 'Scopic Regimes of Modernity', in *Vision and Visuality,* ed. Hal Foster (Seattle, 1988), pp. 29–51, and *Downcast Eyes. The Denigration of Vision in Twentieth-century French Thought* (Berkeley, 1993), ch. 1; and by Louis Marin in 'Topic and Figures of Enunciation; It is Myself that I Paint', in *Vision and Textuality*, ed. Stephen Melville and Bill Readings (Durham, 1995), pp. 195–215.

11 On the ambivalence of Petrarch's attitude and its philosophical foundations in classical philosophy, see Charles Trinkaus, 'Petrarch and the Tradition of a Double Consciousness', chapter 2 of *The Poet as Philosopher and the Formation of Renaissance Consciousness* (New Haven, 1979), pp. 27–51.

12 See Aldo S. Bernardo, *Petrarch, Scipio and the 'Africa'. The Birth of Humanism's Dream* (Westport, 1978).

13 For a study of Petrarch as traveller, see A. Sacchetto, *Il pellegrino viandante. Itinerari italiani ed europei di Francesco Petrarca* (Florence, 1985). See also the first section of chapter III, 'Voyages', in Evelyne Luciani (1982), pp. 111–26.

14 'Fateor iuvenile mihi studium fuisse ut homerici caminis sententiam, mores hominum multorum urbisque conspicerem novas terras, altissimas montes, laudatus lacus, abditas fontes, insignia flumina variosque locorum situs curiosissime contemplarer', *Familiares*, XV, iv, as quoted in Evelyne Luciani (1982), pp. 113, 116.

15 Fernández de Oviedo's account occupies chapter V of book XLII of his *Historia General y Natural de las Indias*. This passage, together with parts II and III and a new version of part I, remained unpublished until José Amador de los Ríos made an edition of the extant manuscripts in 1851–5 *(Historia General y Natural de las Indias, islas y tierra firme del mar Océano, por el capitán Gonzalo Fernández de Oviedo y Valdés, primer cronista del Nuevo Mundo*, 4 vols, Madrid). Amador's version was later republished by Juan Pérez de Tudela y Bueso *(Biblioteca de Autores Españoles*, vols 118–22, Madrid, 1959), which is the edition that I have used for this article (IV, pp. 390–98) and to which I shall refer here as *Historia*. Amador de Los Ríos recorded this passage from a sixteenth-century copy of Oviedo's lost original manuscript made by Andrés and Antonio Gascó, which is today preserved in the Library of the Royal Palace in Madrid (MS. II-3042).

16 For a standard biography of Gonzalo Fernández de Oviedo, see Juan Pérez de Tudela's 'Vida y Escritos de Gonzalo Fernández de Oviedo', the introduction to the edition of the *Historia General y Natural de las Indias*, 5 vols (Madrid, 1959), pp. I–CLXXV.

17 'Multis iter hoc annis in animo fuerat; ab infantia enim his in locis, ut nosti, fato res hominum versante, versatus sum; mons autem hic late undique conspectus, fere semper in oculis est', *Familiares*, IV, i, fol. 48v, Nachod, p. 36 (adapted).

18 '[...] sola videndi insignem loci altitudinem, cupiditate ductus, ascendi', *Familiares*, IV, i, fol. 48v, Nachod, p. 36.

19 A summary of the *relación* was copied in the late eighteenth century by Juan Bautista Muñoz when preparing his *Historia del Nuevo Mundo* (Library of the Academy of History, Muñoz Collection, A/81), fol. 129v. For a brief but accurate definition of *relación* and the other types of narrative related to the Spanish conquest of America, see Walter D. Mignolo's 'Cartas, crónicas y relaciones del descubrimiento y de la conquista' in *Historia de la Literatura Hispanoamericana*, I (Madrid, 1982), pp. 57–116.

20 See Roland Greene, 'Petrarchism among the Discourses of Imperialism', in *America in European Consciousness (1493–1750)*, ed. Karen O. Kupperman (Chapel Hill, 1995), pp. 133–66; on Oviedo, see especially pp. 155–8.

21 Roland Greene (1995), p. 135.

22 See my chapter entitled 'The Representation of American Nature' in my unpublished PhD dissertation, 'The Representation of the Natural World in the Early Chronicles of America: the *Historia General y Natural de las Indias* by Gonzalo Fernández de Oviedo', University of Cambridge, 1997. Among Fernández de Oviedo's extensive literary productions there are two works particularly interesting in this respect: the *Batallas y Quinquágenas* (*c.* 1535–52) – a collection of more than two hundred biographical dialogues which includes the ekphrases of the jewellery and works of art owned by Spanish gentlemen; and the *Quinquágenas de los muy famosos reyes* ... (1556), which consists of the gloss and paraphrasis of poems composed by Oviedo himself.

23 Durling (1974), p. 7.

24 *Historia*, book VI, ch. XV, vol. I, p. 177:

> En conclusión, yo confieso que no habrá pintor que lo pinte, por lo que he dicho; pero leído ésto a par del pájaro, se me figura que he dicho algo, y así lo he escrito: mirándole, y dando gracias a Dios que estas aves crió. Para mi yo la tengo por la más extremada en su plumaje o gentileza de todas las que yo he visto y de que más me he admirado. Ella es de tal artífice y mano hecha, que se puede y debe creer que no se le acabó el arte en ésta. Ni sus obras puede pintor ni escultor ni orador expresar tan al natural, ni perfectamente dar a entender ingenio humano como ellas son.

25 Augustine, *Soliloquia*, II, vi, 10, *Patrologia Latina*, XXXII, p. 903. The image seduces by its resemblance to reality, but it is false for it cannot be grasped and has no life.

26 'Así es como don Hugo lo dize, porque en la verdad muy sin comparación es mejor lo natural que lo artificial y la diferencia es como del muerto al bivo y quanto de la verdad a la mentira y quanto de la su obra [...]', Gonzalo Fernández de Oviedo, *Batallas y Quinquágenas, Batalla II, Quinquágena II, diálogo XXXVIII* (University of Salamanca Library, MS. 359), fol. 935v. Oviedo made the same point in the Quinquágenas: 'Ni todos los pintores famosos del mundo nunca supieran dar tal tez a sus ymágines femeniles de aquellos que contrahizieron sus pinceles que se ygualase con la tez natural de aquellos que quisiesen ymitar ni que dexase de por su pintura cosa muerta'. *Qinquágena I, estancia IX* (National Library of Madrid, MS. 2217), fol. 30v. Unfortunately the manuscript does not include the actual drawing of this 'invención'. Orviedo uses this word, 'invención', which has clear literary connotations, because he reserved the word 'impresa' for the figures used by knights in tournaments. Cardona would die in 1503 at the orders of Gonzalo Fernández de Córdoba during the Spanish conquest of Naples.

27 See Mauda Bregoli-Russo, *L'impresa come ritratto del Rinascimento* (Naples, 1990), pp. 120–33. Lucian's dialogue is the *Imagines*.

28 See Robert M. Durling (1971) and John Frecero (1975).

29 On the Petrarchan language of desire expressed through the theme of the fragmented female body and the presence of the image of the beloved in the heart of the male lover see, especially, Nancy Vickers, 'Diana Described: Scattered Women and Scattered Rhyme', *Critical Inquiry*, VIII/2 (Winter 1981), pp. 265–79. For the influence of this Petrarchan topos on Renaissance readings of female portraits, see Mary Rogers, 'Sonnets on female portraits from Renaissance North Italy', *Word and Image,* II/4 (Oct.–Dec. 1986), pp. 291–306.

30 See especially John Frecero (1975) and T. M. Greene (1976).

31 *Batallas, Batalla II, Quinquágena II, diálogo XXXVIII* (University of Salamanca Library, MS. 359), fol. 935v:

> Riyéndome yo un día con él sobre estos retratos y pinturas y mirándolas diziendo esta figura lo paresce más que aquella y aquella que la otra, le pregunté qué acordaba de hazer de aquellas gentes o mujeres insensibles y don Hugo me respondió con un gran sospiro y dixo: 'sabe Dios quanto querría yo más la biva que las pintadas, pero gran delito sería tocar en éstas ni que se dexassen de estimar pues por imitar lo que está dentro de mi ánima'.

32 See Christian K. Zacher, *Curiosity and Pilgrimage. The Literature of Discovery in Fourteenth-century England* (Baltimore, 1976), pp. 23–7; also Christopher S. Wood, 'Curious Pictures and the Art of Description', *Word and Image*, II/4 (Oct.–Dec. 1995), pp. 332–52, 338.

33 'Aquel matiz o sombra que está en las puntas de estas hojas debuxadas aveys de entender que es lo que tienen como morado', *Historia*, book XI, ch. V (Seville, 1535), fol. XCVIIIr.

34 On the mermen, see *Historia*, book XXIII, chapter V, vol. II, pp. 360-63.

35 The second and third parts of the *Historia General y Natural*, and a whole new version of part I, were drafted after the first Seville edition of 1535 and took Oviedo fourteen years to complete. The extant original manuscripts of this projected new edition – today at the Huntington Library in Los Angeles and the Academy of History in Madrid – show numerous corrections and additions, analysis of which allows the reconstruction of an outline chronology. For the evolution of the text, see the second chapter of my unpublished PhD dissertation.

36 *Historia General y Natural de las Indias* (Seville, 1535), fol. LXXXIXv.

37 *Historia*, book IX, ch. XI, vol. I, p. 289.

38 *Ibid.*, p. 290.

39 *Vara* is a traditional unit of measure which corresponds to 0.835 metres.

40 *Ibid.*, p. 290:

> [...] el cual árbol yo lo medí por mis manos con un hilo de cabuya, e tenía de circuito en el pie treinta e tres varas de medir, que son ciento e treinta e dos palmos; e porque estaba orilla del rio no se podía medir por lo más bajo, cerca de las raices, e sería sin dubda más de otras tres varas más gorda: que los unos e los otros palmos, bien medido, tengo que en todo serían treinta e seis varas, que tienen ciento e cuarenta e cuatro palmos de vara.

41 *Historia*, book XLII, chapter V, p. 391.

42 Library of the Academy of History, Muñoz Collection, A/81, fols 129v and 139r.

43 *Historia*, book XLII, chapters VI–XI, vol. IV, pp. 398–413.

44 On Oviedo's family background, see José de la Peña Cámara, 'Contribuciones documentales y críticas para una biografía de Gonzalo Fernández de Oviedo', *Revista de Indias*, 69–70 (1957), pp. 603–705 (pp. 631–40).

45 The same formula can be found in the *relaciones* sent by Oviedo in 1537 to the Council which Juan Bautista Muñoz copied from the archive of Simancas (Library of the Academy of History, Muñoz Collection, A/81), fols 1r–6v and 16r–18v.
46 *Historia*, book XLII, chapter V, vol. IV, p. 396.

> Digo que en la hondura e última parte que yo vi deste pozo había un fuego líquido como agua, o la materia que ello es, estaba más que vivas brasas encendida su color e, si se puede decir, muy más fogosa materia parescía que fuego alguno puede ser; la cual todo el suelo e parte inferior del pozo ocupaba y estaba hirviendo, no en todo, pero en partes, mudándose el hervor de un lugar a otro e resurgía un bullir o borbollar sin cesar de un cabo a otro. Y en aquellas partes donde aquel hervor no había (o cesaba), luego se cubría de una tela o tez de napa encima como horura o requebrada e mostraba por aquellas quebraduras de aquella tela o napa ser todo fuego líquido como agua lo de debajo; e así por todo el circuito del pozo. E de cuando en cuando, toda aquella materia se levantaba para suso con gran ímpetu e lanzaba muchas gotas para arriba, las cuales se tornaban a caer en la misma materia o fuego, que a la estimación de mi vista más de un estado subían.

47 *Historia*, book XLII, chapter V, vol. IV, p. 396.

> Digo más, que yo arrojé algunas piedras e también las hice tirar al negro porque era mancebo e rescio, e nunca jamás pude ver adonde paraban o daban, sino que, salidas de la mano hacia el pozo, parescía que se iban enarcando e se metían debajo de donde hombre estaba mirando; en fin, que ninguna se vido adonde paró, lo que notoriamente mostraba la mucha altura que hay hasta la plaza.

48 > Sacaron de lo bajo del bolcán tierra i piedra y en 15 de Mayo en la ciudad de Leon ante el dicho governador se echaron a fundir despues de moldes en un crisol. Los oficiales plateros digeron no ser metal alguna, sino piedras que ard'an como ascuas por tener cantidad de piedra y salitre. Uno de los que asistieron a la esperiencia fue Pedro de los Ríos, tesorero.

Library of the Academy of History, Muñoz Collection, A/81, fol. 129v.

49 *Historia*, book XLII, ch. VI (Library of the Royal Palace of Madrid, MS. II-3042), fol. 65r. Andrés Gascó, inquisitor and teacher in Seville, received the manuscripts which Oviedo had left in Seville in 1549. Gascó was ordered to send the original manuscripts back to the Council, but he and his nephew Antonio made a copy before taking them to the Casa de Contratación. The three volumes of this copy are today in the Colombina Library in Seville and in the Library of the Royal Palace in Madrid. See Klaus Wagner, 'Legajos y otras aficiones del inquisidor Andrés Gascó', *Boletín de la Real Academia de la Historia*, CLXXVI (1979), pp. 149–55.
50 '[. . .] estuve más de dos horas, e aún cuasi hasta las diez del día de Sancta Ana gloriosa, mirando lo que he dicho', *Historia*, book XLII, ch. VI, vol. IV, p. 397.
51 '[. . .] e debujando la forma deste monte con papel, como aquí lo he puesto', *ibid.*
52 For notions of evidence in early modern Europe see, especially, Lorraine Daston, 'Marvelous Facts and Miraculous Evidence in Early Modern Europe', in *Questions of Evidence, Proof, Practice, and Persuasion across the Disciplines*, ed. J. Chandler, A. I. Davidson and H. Harootunian (Chicago, 1994), pp. 243–75.
53 'Combinable mobile' is the term used by Bruno Latour to designate conveyors of information capable of transferring empirical data into abstract and infinitely extensible networks; see his *Science in Action. How to Follow Scientists and Engineers Through Society* (Milton Keynes, 1987), pp. 223–8.
54 These illustrations are contained in the manuscripts of books VII, IX and XI today in the Huntington Library MSS 177, 2 vols). For a detailed analysis of the illustrations

included in Oviedo's manuscripts, see the final section of my PhD dissertation. The *perorica* is a medicinal herb which I have been unable to identify. According to Oviedo, it grew in Central America and was used by the Indians to heal injuries.

55 *Historia General y Natural de las Indias*, book XI (Huntington Library, MS. 177, vol. II).

56 Roland Greene (1995), p. 153.

57 Prester John was a mythical Christian king who was believed to reign in the remote Orient. This belief is possibly related to the existence of Nestorian khans in central Asia in the thirteenth century, and afterwards of a Christian Monophysite kingdom in Abyssinia. The first mention of his realm occurs in Otto Freising's chronicle about the middle of the twelfth century. Portuguese sailors sought out this Christian kingdom during their exploration of Africa. See Rudolf Wittkower's famous article 'Marvels of the East: a Study in the History of Monsters', included in *Allegory and the Migration of Symbols* (London, 1977), pp. 45–76 (pp. 60–61).

58 No reference to these mountains can be found either in classical geographies (Herodotus, Strabo, Pomponius Mela, Pliny) or in medieval travel accounts such as Marco Polo's. There is a Mt Colupo in the region of Anofagasta on the northern coast of Chile, famous for its rich mines of copper, to which Oviedo may well refer in this passage.

59 Meotides is the classical denomination of the Azov Sea in Middle Asia.

60 También dezía Tales Milesio que lo más veloz o ligero y puesta cosa es el intelecto del ombre, pero, a mi parescer, que dixera mejor la mente y pensamiento. Porque muchas cosas el entendimiento del hombre no acepta ni entiende sino despacio o tarde o nunca, y la memoria o el pensamiento es el que en un momento discurre por toda parte, de forma que, a mi parescer, ninguna cosa ay más veloz y presto, porque en proviso esta desde donde yo agora estoi en estas Indias y va al Preste Joan de las Indias o a los montes Colupios y buelve, en continente, hasta la Nueva España y México y desde allí, en un instante, va al lago Meótides y buelve hasta el lago del Enderi y Ara en la provincia y gobernación de Nicaragua.

Quinquágenas, Quinquágena II, estancia I (National Library of Madrid, MS. 2218), fol. 4.

61 On the theme of the *Somnium Scipionis* in Juan Luis Vives see D. Baker Smith, 'Juan Luis Vives and the *Somnium Scipionis*', in *Classical Influences in European Culture 1500–1700*, ed. R. R. Bolgar (Cambridge, 1976), pp. 239–54. Also see Louis Swift, '*Somnium Vivis y Sueño de Escipión*', in *Homenaje a Luis Vives* (Madrid, 1977). The introduction to the English translation of Vives's text by Edward V. George provides a good insight into the circumstances of the production of the different versions of the *Somnium*: see Juan Luis Vives, *Somnium et Vigilia in Somnium Scipionis* (Greenwood, 1989). Juan de Maldonado's *Somnium* was published as part of his Quaedam opuscula (Burgos, 1541). Menéndez y Pelayo provided a first study of Maldonado's work in *Bibliografía hispano-latina clásica* (Santander, 1950), III, pp. 164–77. More recently the *Somnium* has attracted the attention of Miguel Avila, who translated Maldonado's work in *Sueños ficticios y lucha ideológica en el Siglo de Oro* (Madrid, 1980).

62 In this regard I follow Durling's allusion to Angus Fletcher's discussion of allegory in *Allegory. The Theory of a Literary Mode* (NY, 1963); Durling (1974), p. 21.

2 Joan-Pau Rubiés: Futility in the New World

1 Alejo Carpentier, *El reino de este mundo/Los pasos perdidos*, 'Narrativa Completa', I (Barcelona, 1995), p. 16. Unless otherwise indicated, all translations in this article are mine.

2 Christopher Columbus, *Journal of the First Voyage (diario del primer viaje)*, edited and translated by B. W. Ife (Warminster, 1990). Among many examples:

> Last night [23 October] at midnight I weighed anchor from the island of Isabela [. . .] to go to the island of Cuba which I hear from these people is very large and very busy and where there are gold and spices and great ships and merchants [. . .] this I am doing because I think that if it is as all the Indians of these islands and those I have on the ships say it is, in sign language because I do not understand the tongue, then it is the island of Cipangu of which so many marvellous tales are told. On the globes which I have seen and on the world maps Cipangu is in this area (p. 55).

Columbus's open confession that he learnt so many particulars through sign language, implausible as it appears, is not evidence of an absurd reasoning but rather reveals the primacy of his hypothesis that the islands discovered by him were the Far East (without this assumption the Spanish ships would not have travelled there in the first place). From that hypothesis, what follows is in fact a logical argument, in which Marco Polo and the late medieval maps of the world (rather than the signs of the Indians in response to repeated questioning) supply 'Cipangu', with its desired 'ships and merchants' as well as the gold and spices. The authority of this and many other assumptions would of course be dispelled by experience – but not all, crucially, since the Spanish did find a land populated by gentile idolators (of course according to the Christian definition) and, what is perhaps more decisive, gold and silver in abundance. In the light of the reality of many a disillusionment, Columbus's exaggerated reluctance to depart from his assumptions only serves to highlight the fact that assumptions such as these were necessarily the cultural backbone of the enterprise of discovery and conquest.

3 Among the more recent treatments of the theme see especially: Beatriz Pastor, *Discursos narrativos de la conquista de América* (2nd rev. edn, Hanover, NH, 1988), translated into English as *The Armature of Conquest. Spanish accounts of the discovery of America, 1492–1589)* (Stanford, 1992); Juan Gil, *Mitos y utopías del descubrimiento*, 3 vols (Madrid, 1989); Stephen Greenblatt, *Marvellous Possessions. The Wonder of the New World* (Oxford, 1991); Anthony Grafton, *New Worlds, Ancient Texts. The power of tradition and the shock of discovery* (Cambridge, MA, 1992); Anthony Pagden, *European Encounters with the New World from Renaissance to Romanticism* (New Haven and London, 1993); Wolfgang Hease and Meyer Reinhold (eds), *The Classical Tradition and the Americas*, I (Berlin and New York, 1994). For the myth of Eldorado in particular, see also Demetrio Ramos Pérez, *El mito del Dorado: su génesis y proceso* (Caracas, 1973). For the English experience, Mary Fuller, *Voyages in Print. English Travel to America, 1576–1624* (Cambridge, 1995). For the French perspective see the various works by Frank Lestringant, among them, in English, *Mapping the Renaissance World* (Cambridge, 1994). Among earlier general treatments of the mythical dimension of the mental world of the Spanish conquerors, see especially Enrique de Gandía, *Historia crítica de los mitos de la conquista* (Buenos Aires, 1929) and Irving A. Leonard, *Books of the Brave* (Cambridge, MA, 1949).

4 Galeotto Cei, *Viaggio e relazione delle Indie (1539-1553)*, ed. Francesco Surdichi (Roma, 1992), p. 57. The report of the Amazons was given by a Dominican who accompanied Orellana, Gaspar de Carvajal, and was inserted by Gonzalo Fernández Oviedo (who, like Galeotto Cei, was in Santo Domingo when the survivors arrived) in his monumental history of the Indies. There is another version of Carvajal's account. See José Toribio Medina, *The Discovery of the Amazon* (New York, 1934), pp. 167–235, 383–448. (Toribio Medina edits the sources of Orellana's expedition. The English version edited by H. C. Heaton is based on the original Spanish edition of

1894, but more complete.) It appears from a close reading of the text that the elaborate description of the civilization of the Amazons, obtained from a 'very intelligent' Indian prisoner who did not speak any language known to the Spanish, except for an improvised list of words, was actually a confirmation of reports heard by the Spanish near Quito, much before they set out along the river (*ibid*., p. 222). Orellana's discovery of the Amazon was an accidental offshoot from Gonzalo Pizarro's expedition, which left from Quito in 1541 in search of gold and cinnamon trees east of the Andes. The story of the original expedition, prompted by indigenous reports, is itself a memorable disaster. After the failure of Gonzalo Pizarro (brother of the conqueror of Peru) to find anything valuable in 'the land of cinnamon', with all his Indians slaves dead, his horses and dogs eaten up, and his Spanish followers hungry, sick and disillusioned in the jungle, his lieutenant, Orellana, had volunteered to travel down the unknown river where they had ended up, in order to find supplies. He took the only boat but did not return to meet up with his companions. Since the event there has been a lively debate about whether Orellana had betrayed Pizarro in order to fulfil his own ambition, or whether he could not return upstream because of the current and the lack of food, as he claimed.

5 Although in this article I shall focus on travel accounts and on chronicles of conquest and discovery which reflect upon an experience of travel, ultimately the whole colonial conquest involves a kind of massive experience of travel – hence the recurrence of the metaphor. For this reason, the three elements that I have outlined – imperial projection, personal social strategy and scientific construction – also appear in other forms of discourse of conquest, from administrative material (like the *Relaciones geográficas* compiled by the Council of the Indies under Philip II) to personal correspondence or even poetry. The case of the epic poem *La Araucana* by Alonso de Ercilla (1589–90), on the conquest of Chile, is particularly remarkable for the complexity of the readings that it suggests, and it has merited a great deal of comment in the last few years (as in Pastor 1992, ch. 5). This poem thus functions as a literary recreation of a chronicle of the wars between Indians and Spanish and is to some extent based on personal experience. However, exceptionally, the recourse to literary models and conventions, classical and Renaissance, manages to multiply, rather than falsify, the significance of the historical events. Thus, while the obvious models are Virgil, Lucan and Ariosto, the key theme is the relationship between Indians and Spaniards, with the native resistance reaching unprecedented heroic dimensions which reflect on both the achievements and the shortcomings of the conquerors. Both the idea of travel and the idea of a new geographical vision are made explicit in the poem by the poet's own intervention (for instance in the exploration of the Chilean coastline towards the Strait of Magellan).

6 Among recent treatments of the literature of discovery from this perspective, that by Pastor (1992) is clearly outstanding, despite some exaggerations. The critical literature is of course vast. For a general survey of the chronicles of discovery and conquest see Francisco Esteve Barba, *Historiografía indiana* (Madrid, 1964). This is however now quite outdated owing to the enormous advances of the last 30 years (the 1992 edition of the same work failed to remedy this, despite its declared intention to the contrary).

7 Gonzalo Fernández de Oviedo, *Historia general y natural de las Indias*, ed. Juan Pérez de Tudela, 5 vols (Madrid, 1959). This edition follows the text established by José Amador de los Ríos in 1851–5. Considering that only the first part was published by Oviedo (Seville, 1535, 2nd edn Salamanca, 1547), a proper modern critical edition of this absolutely fundamental work is long overdue.

8 The Renaissance in Spain and Portugal, as in other parts of Europe, was based on the selective adaptation of themes and genres first developed in Italy and ultimately

inspired by classical models. The peculiar circumstances of that contact (essentially, the growing Spanish political overlordship over much of Italy from the beginning of the century) and the selective bias of the Spanish social and political system (severely Catholic, and very much inspired by the crusading values of a frontier society) conditioned the formation of a distinct Hispanic Renaissance. We might characterize it by the continuing dominance of medieval social and religious ideologies, which explains the limited impact of critical humanism, the failure of an Erasmian spiritual leadership, and above all the strength of chivalric traditions and religious institutions. As apparent signs of modernity it is important to mention the precocious development of a linguistic and monarchic nationalism, fulfilling with splendid results the Renaissance ideal of combining arms and letters, often in support of an enthusiastic but contradictory imperialism. Not least among these contradictions was the assimilation of the Kingdom of Castile, a well-defined legal entity, into Spain as a whole, with its different kingdoms only united in the persons of the monarchs, alongside many other European territories. From a political perspective the distinctiveness of the New World colonies was their full integration within the legal structure of Castile, quite apart from the Holy Roman Empire proper, or even the Habsburg monarchy as a European-wide system of government. In the literature of conquest more often than not the conquerors appear as 'Spanish' rather than 'Castilian', although the participation of people from the Crown of Aragon (Catalonia, Aragon, Valencia, Majorca, Sardinia) was obviously limited, in theory and in practice. An attempt to define globally this Hispanic Renaissance, from an optimistic premise, is provided by José Antonio Maravall, 'La diversificación de modelos de Renacimiento: el Renacimiento francés y el Renacimiento Español', in *Estudios de Historia del pensamiento Español,* II (Madrid, 1984), pp. 123–92.

9 Gonzalo Fernández de Oviedo, *Sumario de la natural historia de la Indias* (Toledo, 1526), ch. 2. Oviedo wrote this brief overview of the ethnography, flora and fauna of the Caribbean islands and the southern mainland for Charles V while on a visit to the court after a bitter experience in the conquest of the mainland (*Tierra Firme*), in the gulf of Darién and Panama. There his own ambitions as conqueror–settler in a number of official capacities had twice been thwarted by the governor, Pedrarías Dávila, whom Oviedo (at this stage posing as defender of the Indians) duly accused of cruel and tyrannical rule. After confronting an Indian rebellion and escaping an assassination attempt in the town of Santa María Antigua by Spanish settlers (who among other things disliked his restrictive rule concerning sexual and political liaisons with Indians), Oviedo had had to leave the New World in 1523. In these circumstances he was not yet able to acknowledge the full significance of Cortés's conquest of Mexico (1519–21), although he was already engaged in the composition of his general history of the Indies. After another attempt in Central America (Nicaragua and Panama), from 1533 Oviedo would make *Española* [Hispaniola] his American base, as captain (*alcaide*) of the fortress of Santo Domingo. His historical research was a personal undertaking which derived from his activities as an adventurous courtier.

10 Oviedo 1959, IV, p. 298.

11 *Ibid.*, pp. 300-01:

> Así quiero decir que tan a escuras vienen muchos a estas Indias como los sobreescriptos que he dicho, sin entender ni saber a dónde van [. . .] casi nunca sus Majestades ponen su hacienda y dinero en estos nuevos descubrimientos, excepto papel e palabras buenas [. . .] e despachado de la corte, viénese a Sevilla con menos dineros de los que querría; y en tanto que un atambor por una parte, e un fraile o dos, e algunos clérigos que luego se le allegan so color de la conversión de los Indios, por otras vias andan trastornando sesos e

References

prometiendo la riqueza de aquellos que ninguna cosa saben, entiende el capitán en tomar cambios y en comprar navíos cansados y viejos [. . .] entienden en hablar a los pobres compañeros e atraerlos a dos cosas: la una que presten al capitán dineros sobre las esperanzas vanas [. . .] La otra cosa es que de diez en diez, e más o menos compañeros, los hacen obligar a mancomunarse para pagar a cierto tiempo cada diez o doce ducados o pesos de oro del flete donde van y de la comida [. . .] como el viaje es largo e la vida corta, e las ocasiones para perderla innumerables, todos los más que acá vienen es de asiento e para no tornar a su tierra, y muy al revés de lo que en España se les figuró . . .

12 The distance from success to disaster was in fact very small, because not even the greatest conquests brought the expected results. For instance, and to return to the expedition that led to the discovery of the Amazon river (see note 4 above), the fact that Gonzalo Pizarro had obtained the governorship of the province of Quito, only recently conquered, to use it immediately as a base from which to look for wealth further afield reveals a common pattern underlying the rapid process of conquest. Essentially, the Spanish were not interested in the systematic exploitation of the existing agrarian economy and the creation of new trading routes and industries, but rather in the rapid acquisition of wealth, preferably gold or perhaps spices. They often settled for *encomiendas* of Indians (a source of forced labour and tribute) only when it became obvious that nothing better could be obtained elsewhere. Even in Mexico and Peru the wealth that could be plundered was quite limited and could not satisfy the aspirations of more than a few leaders. Orellana himself was one of the conquerors of Peru and a relative of the Pizarros who as a reward for his services had been given the province of La Culata (in modern Ecuador) to conquer and settle. Things were even more difficult for the common soldier. Characteristically, one of the participants in the conquest of Mexico, the chronicler Bernal Díaz del Castillo, confessed that after his initial disappointment with the spoils of the fall of Tenochtitlan he missed a number of opportunities to settle in Mexico, always in the hope of better rewards. He ended up in Guatemala, not very happily. See Bernal Díaz del Castillo, *Historia verdadera de la conquista de la Nueva España*, ed. Miguel León Portilla, 2 vols (Madrid, 1984), ch. 157 (II, pp. 120–8).

13 This journey has generated a great deal of literature and a number of attempts to reconstruct the itinerary from the Gulf of Mexico (beginning west of Galveston Bay) to somewhere near El Paso (modern New Mexico frontier – see map). Among these, perhaps the dominant hypothesis is that Cabeza de Vaca and his companions essentially crossed modern Texas, as was clearly put forth by Cleve Hallenbeck, *Alvar Núñez Cabeza de Vaca; the Journey and Route of the First European to Cross the Continent of North America, 1534–36* (Glendale, CA, 1940). However, the traditional interpretation put forward in 1918 by H. Davenport and J. K. Wells, in which the journey took place south of the Río Grande rather than along and across the Colorado and Pecos rivers, continues to find strong defenders, such as Alex D. Krieger. His views are supported by Donald E. Chipman, 'In Search of Cabeza de Vaca's Route Across Texas: an Historiographical Survey', *The Southwestern Historical Quarterly*, 91 (1987), pp. 127–48. The most useful biography of Cabeza de Vaca is still Morris Bishop's *The Odyssey of Cabeza de Vaca* (New York, 1933), well documented but to a large extent a paraphrase of the conqueror's own writings.

14 The second edition, *La relación y comentarios del governador Álvar Núñez Cabeza de Vaca, de lo acaescido en las dos jornadas que hizo a las Indias* (Valladolid, 1555), actually includes two works, the *Relación* of the journey from Florida to California and the *Comentarios* on Cabeza de Vaca's experience in Paraguay. It is also probably the only edition supervised by the author, which may explain some of the small differences

between this and the 1542 Zamora edition of the *Relación*, discussed in the critical edition by Enrique Pupo-Walker (ed.), *Los Naufragios* (Madrid, 1992). I quote from the text of the 1555 edition, as established by Manuel Serrano y Sanz in his *Relación de los naufragios y comentarios de Álvar Núñez Cabeza de Vaca*, in vol. v of *Colección de libros y documentos referentes a la historia de América* (Madrid, 1906). I have compared this with a copy of the 1555 version now held in the British Library. Serrano y Sanz also published a number of further documents concerning Cabeza de Vaca's experiences in Paraguay (*ibid.*, vol. vi). Ramusio's Italian version, in his *Delle navigationi et viaggi*, iii (Venice, 1556), was also based on the 1555 text. In English, a more recent version is *Castaways*, ed. E. Pupo-Walker and trans. Frances López-Morillas (Berkeley and Los Angeles, 1993). Oviedo's version, which at the time remained unpublished with much of his *Historia*, is a separate document, based on the official report prepared by Cabeza de Vaca and his companions and sent to the Royal Court of Santo Domingo during the latter's return trip to Spain in 1539 (Oviedo, iv, pp. 281–318). Careful reading of Oviedo's statements suggests that he actually conflated this joint report with the printed version of Cabeza de Vaca's account (1542) and his oral testimony in 1547. Thus: 'fueron a España a dar relación a Su Majestad, *viva voce*, de las cosas que aquí se dirán, alargándome a su información, e acortando algunas superfluas palabras que duplicadamente dicen' (*ibid.*, p. 287); 'Esta relación sacó el cronista de la carta que estos hidalgos enviaron a la Real Audiencia que reside en esta cibdad de sancto Domingo [. . .] Todo esto lo que es dicho en esta relación, lo había fecho imprimir este caballero. . .' (pp. 314–5). Thus Oviedo's text, while keeping the substance of Cabeza de Vaca's account, logically gives more emphasis to the point of view of Andrés Dorantes and Alonso del Castillo (especially when they were separated from the former) and curiously attributes to Dorantes a leadership role that Cabeza de Vaca tends to assume in his account. There is no reason to suppose that Oviedo's account is always more accurate because he used different sources – as he put it, 'yo tengo por buena la relación de los tres, e por más clara que estotra que el uno sólo hace e hizo imprimir' (p. 315). It is very likely that Cabeza de Vaca initially wrote his report for the emperor on the occasion of his journey to Spain to explain his adventures and discoveries in 1537–40.

15   The Indians, seeing the disaster which had struck us and the disaster we were now in, with so much misery and misfortune, sat down with us, and with the great grief and compassion they felt on seeing us in that sorry state, they all began to weep loudly, and so sincerely, that they could be heard from a long distance. This lasted half an hour.

(Cabeza de Vaca 1906, pp. 48–9.) This episode occurs in what is now Galveston Island, and the Indians were Karankawas. The weeping of the Indians was probably a ritual form of weeping, perhaps friendly, but in any case not entirely identical with Christian compassion. For Cabeza de Vaca, however, it was an instantly recognizable sign, of course according to European conventions of suffering and misfortune, and thus a bond of humanity that deepened his awareness of a miserable condition. However, this literary construction of compassion did not imply the equality of humans and Indians – Indians were still more brutish – but rather the descent of the Spanish to a lower condition: 'to see these men, who are so lacking in reason and so crude, like animals, weeping on our behalf, made me and others in the group even more desperate and more aware of our unhappy condition' (*ibid.*).

16 *Ibid.*, p. 52:

    . . . five Christians who were staying in a camp on the coast came to such straits that they ate each other until only one was left [. . .] the Indians were so disturbed by this event, and there was among them such anger, that I do not doubt that they would have killed the men, had they seen this when it began to happen, and then all of us would have been in great trouble.

Afterwards the Indians of the island were hit by an epidemic but, despite the fact that they considered that the Spanish might be the cause (through some kind of magic power, we are made to understand), they did not kill the few survivors, considering, according to Cabeza de Vaca, that if they were so powerful, their companions would not have died too.

17 The precariousness of the conditions of life in the coastal regions was compounded, it seems, by the local custom observed by Cabeza de Vaca of fasting after the death of a relative. In the circumstances of the epidemic brought by the Spaniards, this made things worse, as Cabeza de Vaca duly observes (*ibid.*, p. 55).

18 A particularly revealing passage describes some peculiar cooking habits 'so that it may be seen and known how diverse and peculiar are the devices and techniques of *human men*' – that is, 'para que se vea y se conozca quán diversos y estraños son los ingenios e industrias de los *hombres humanos*' (my italics – see *ibid.*, p. 116). Obviously, here the adjective is logically redundant and points towards the fact that it is a part of human nature, as opposed to animal or other, to create skills and techniques.

19 This is particularly difficult to detect because so much of what we know about the Indians of these areas in this period relies on Cabeza de Vaca's own account. He certainly spent many years there and could have developed a cultural insight, but we only know the little that he lets us discover. On the other hand, the tradition of describing native customs in reports of discovery and conquest was pervasive enough, and official enough, to create clear standards of empirical plausibility.

20 *Ibid.*, pp. 59–60. This lonely life was not however without its dangers, the cold winter and lack of food being the most important ones, as the narrative goes on to explain.

21 For these identifications see Pupo-Walker (ed.) in Cabeza de Vaca 1993, pp. 133–7.

22 Cabeza de Vaca 1906, chapters 20ff. As indicated earlier, the itinerary of this progress is the more controversial part of the *relación*, with such authors as Alex Krieger defending a journey south-east towards Mexico and then (from a point near modern Monterrey) north-west from the Mexican side of the Río Grande. In the more conventional view, the Spanish crossed Texas from the Brazos and Colorado rivers to the Pecos river. The rest of the journey, towards the Pacific coast and the south alongside it, is less controversial.

23 This is, for instance, the interpretation followed by Tzvetan Todorov, *La conquête de l'Amérique. La question de l'autre* (Paris, 1982). Todorov depicts the Aztecs as unable to relate to their invaders as humans relate to humans, having recourse instead to the catastrophic model of a men–gods relationship. This would be the result of two alternative models of communication, Indian and Spanish, based on a natural as opposed to an anthropological focus: that is, Europeans related to people, Indians related to the world. This interpretation of the first encounter sustains a radical relativism which is theoretically unsatisfactory (how do cultures change, if they are to be described as completely self-contained systems of communication?). Moreover, Todorov's distinction is hardly borne out by the evidence. Cortés's success as a manipulator of Indian perceptions and fears can be seen as the result of his command of relative rather than exclusive skills, both technological and linguistic. His manipulation of people through religious symbols, charismatic leadership, linguistic acquisition, diplomatic dissimulation, opportunistic alliances and flexible military tactics is to be set alongside the Aztec ability to create an empire in Mexico in the first place. A common ground between Europeans and Indians as 'culturally capable beings' was surely necessary, a common ground that may be

defined as the capacity to learn and use skills or language-games and that ultimately makes the emergence of a syncretic cultural system possible, rather than a complete substitution.

24 Cabeza de Vaca 1906, ch. 28, p. 101:

> ... and here began a new custom, which is that although they [the Indians] received us very well, those [other Indians] who came with us started to inflict great damage upon them, taking their property and plundering their houses and leaving them with nothing [. . .] we were afraid that this behaviour would cause disorders and violence among them, but were not in a position to stop it or punish anyone, and had to accept it until we gained more authority.

Later, ch. 30, p. 110:

> Here began another way of receiving us, as far as their plundering each other is concerned, because those who came out to meet us in the way with some things for us and for our companions were not robbed, but after we arrived at their houses, they themselves offered everything they had. . .

And so on. (This last sentence is of difficult interpretation and should be translated differently if one assumes – as I have not – that the preposition 'a' in the original is a mistake: 'los que salían de los caminos a traernos alguna cosa *a* los que con nosotros venían no los robavan').

25 *Ibid.*, ch. 30.

26 Among the critical interpretations of the journey of Álvar Núñez Cabeza de Vaca, two are outstanding for their subtlety and congenial to the argument of this article: Pastor 1992, ch. 3; and Rolena Adorno, 'The Negotiation of Fear in Cabeza de Vaca's *Naufragios*', *Representations*, 33 (1991), pp. 163–99. See also Jacques Lafaye, 'Les miracles d'Álvar Núñez Cabeza de Vaca, 1527–1536', *Bulletin Hispanique*, 64 (1962), pp. 136–53. Beatriz Pastor is particularly insightful in placing the analysis of Cabeza de Vaca's narrative in the context of the theme of failure. Her emphasis on 'the first ever account to present an anthropological view of the American native' is perhaps exaggerated. On the other hand, Rolena Adorno develops with remarkable perception the theme of mutual fear as a driving force in the relationship between European and Indian, although her interpretation of Cabeza de Vaca's ultimate position in the theme of religious belief and conversion is less convincing and perhaps too concerned with questioning the obviously simplistic providentialism of Oviedo's rendering.

27 This part of the journey has been analysed from an archaeological perspective by Daniel T. Reff, *Disease, Depopulation and Culture Change in Northwestern New Spain, 1518–1764* (Salt Lake City, 1991), pp. 43–68.

28 The Amazons were an ancient theme, described for instance by Herodotus and Diodorus, who locate these kingdoms of famous breastless women warriors in both Scythia and Ethiopia, but also in the past. They remained alive as part of the mythical geography of the Indian Ocean throughout the Middle Ages (it is for this reason that the 'male and female islands' are reported by Marco Polo, possibly from Arabic sources) and then appeared in a number of places in the New World, from Brazil and Paraguay through Yacatan to north-western Mexico. The transmission of the theme was both textual and oral: that is, it was at the same time an erudite and a popular myth. As Frank Lestringant has noted, 'loin d'infirmer la science traditionelle, la découverte du Nouveau Monde vient très exactement la compléter. A chaque continent ses Amazones. . .' (in Andre Thévet, *Les singularités de la France antarctique. Le Brésil des cannibales au XVIe siècle*, ed. F. Lestringant, Paris, 1983, p. 33). Beyond their obvious significance as an anxious projection of male desire, by associating the female gender with political and military power in a kind of transcultural castration

myth, in the conquest of America the Amazons were also invariably an indication of further wealth ahead, a sign of a strange civilization which would confirm the validity of the hopes for some wonderful discovery that fuelled the Europeans.

29 These events are difficult to reconstruct because all the sources are, in one way or another, part of a debate between opposing participants and often carry legal connotations. In the opposition to Cabeza de Vaca it is possible to identify a Basque faction of 'old conquerors', led by Domingo Martínez de Irala (Cabeza de Vaca was Andalusian, and his arrival with the title of governor curtailed the power which Irala had acquired on the ground). Irala, with his muddled rebellion and his well-documented harem of Indian women, is a perfect example of the dramatic divergence of the life of the conqueror in Paraguay and the official ideology of conquest. His conflict with Cabeza de Vaca is, to some extent, a conflict of '(abusive) practical arrangements' with '(idealistic) official policy', although it would be wrong to assume that only the disorderly conqueror-settlers were moved by dreams of wealth untold. For an attempt to clarify these events see Enrique de Gandía, *Historia de la conquista de Río de la Plata y del Paraguay* (Buenos Aires, 1931). Gandía supports the general validity of the information contained in the *Comentarios*. The difficulty of reaching a balanced judgement is illustrated by the first *criollo* historian of Paraguay, Ruy Díaz de Guzmán (*c.* 1560–1629), whose confused account of this conflict in his *Anales del descubrimiento, población y conquista de las provincias del Río de la Plata* (1612) is an attempt to save the public image of both Irala and Cabeza de Vaca. This fusion of perspectives is more than coincidental: Guzmán's paternal grandmother was Cabeza de Vaca's sister (Guzmán's father was therefore Andalusian and in fact one of Cabeza de Vaca's men), while his maternal grandparents were Martínez de Irala and an Indian. The very existence of the chronicler was an indirect product of the defeat of Cabeza de Vaca: his father was then forced to settle in Paraguay and, by marrying him to one of his *mestizo* daughters, Irala secured his fidelity. Ruy Díaz de Guzmán was also a failed conqueror with modest resources.

30 Ulrico Schmidel, *Relatos de la conquista del Río de la Plata y Paraguay, 1534–1554*, ed. Klaus Wagner (Madrid, 1989), ch. 44, p. 86. This narrative is quite explicit about the fact that the conquerors were often given young women as a present by Indian lords, that their main use was sexual and that, short of finding gold or silver, taking slaves was one of the main aims of plunder. Schmidel in fact explains that when enslaving Indians he was particularly careful to pick young ones, especially females (*ibid.*, p. 88). He also explains that quite often innocent Indians were attacked, not only the enemies of the Spanish. The conditions in Paraguay, a remote area in the middle of the southern American continent, well populated by Indians but without many other obvious resources, made the tendency towards polygamous concubinage a regular phenomenon.

31 *Ibid.*, chapters 38–40.

32 Eventually, after having expelled Cabeza de Vaca from his governorship (1544–5), Martínez de Irala (with Schmidel among his men) would lead an expedition north and west of Asunción towards the frontiers of Peru (1548), where they found Spanish-speaking Indians. He was however forced to turn back by Pedro la Gasca, the king's representative (who had just finished suppressing a rebellion by Gonzalo Pizarro, the young brother of the conqueror, against the previous viceroy's implementation of the 1542 New Laws, which limited the conquerors's rights and attempted to protect the Indians against abusive exploitation). Irala and his men could have claimed possession of the fabulous silver mines of Potosí if they had arrived a few years earlier (Potosí was only settled in 1545). As Schmidel commented, if they had arrived in time to join Pizarro's rebellion (1544–8), they would have done it too.

33 For this expedition see Emiliano Jos, *La expedición de Ursúa a el Dorado y la rebelión de Lope de Aguirre* (Huesca, 1927). Among the relatively many sources of the expedition

see in particular the narrative by Francisco Vázquez, 'Relación de todo lo que sucedió en la jornada de Amagua y Dorado. . .'. I have consulted the edition by Javier Ortiz de la Tabla, *El Dorado. Crónica de la expedición de Pedro de Ursúa y Lope de Aguirre* (Madrid, 1987).

34 See Francisco Vázquez (1987), pp. 136–43 (for this and the following quotations).

35 *Ibid.*, pp. 142–3.

36 *Ibid.*

37 In this context *peregrino* should not be translated as 'pilgrim', because there is no religious significance attached to the word. 'Traveller', even 'wanderer', come closer to the Latin root *peregrinator*, and sixteenth-century Humanists would write treatises on travel as *De peregrinatione*. They were also aware that 'this word *peregrinatio*, travel, descends from the word *peragrare*, to wander, which signifies to travel in strange and foreign countries, to wander in places as well unknown as known out of a man's own country or citie. . .' (from Jerome Turler, *The traveiler* [London, 1575], ch. 1, translated from the Latin original of 1574. I have modernized spellings. Turler was a German Humanist, and his was the first significant Renaissance treatise on the subject).

38 *Ibid.*, p. 106. Vázquez calls these Indian women 'cien piezas ladinas cristianas', an expression which reveals the contradiction between their status as sexual objects and their status as Spanish-speaking Christians. The implication is that the Indian could never *really* have the rights of the Spanish, but that higher and lower categories of value and respect existed nevertheless. Aguirre's 'tyranny' was therefore his lack of regard for these categories, his indiscriminate cruelty, both towards the Indian women, who would be eaten by the 'Caribs', it was assumed, and towards the Spanish who protested this loss and were killed for it.

39 Aguirre's rebellion has also been analysed with brilliance as a 'discourse of rebellion' by Beatriz Pator (1992, pp. 188–204). Pator insists that Aguirre's behaviour, cruel and rebellious, was not an expression of madness but rather an expression of the true nature of conquest, which institutionalized violence and the abuse of power. His tragedy was that he failed to understand his own marginalization from a medieval order in which he believed but which was in fact in crisis. His rebellion was therefore an act of nostalgia. I am less convinced that we should analyse this 'reactionary nostalgia' as a 'transition toward a baroque consciousness' (p. 203).

40 The narrative of the travels of Galeotto Cei was only published in 1992, from a Tuscan manuscript kept in the British Library (see note 4 above). This edition by Francesco Surdich represents an important addition to the sources on the conquest, because, besides his special perspective as a foreigner and trader, Galeotto Cei is also interesting for a large number of original observations.

41 As indicated in the dedicatory preface to 'messer Bartolomeo Delbene', another Florentine merchant whose family was developing interests in the exploitation of the silver of Potosí (Cei 1992, p. 1 and iv–v).

42 *Ibid.*, p. 1 (in the translation I have rearranged the text slightly to make it more coherent).

43 *Ibid.*, pp. 1, 9, 5.

44 *Ibid.*, pp. 8–9, 124.

45 *Ibid.*, p. 45, concerning the foundation of Tocuio in 1545.

46 *Ibid.*, p. 42.

47 *Ibid.*, p. 37. There is very little in all these details that is not essentially accurate.

48 *Ibid.*, pp. 89–90, for a description of the devastation brought about by slavery, only partially tolerated by the kings on the basis of reports of cannibalism, sodomy and aggression, and how the laws that limited this practice were circumvented, so that by the time the kings changed the law it was too late. Cei also suggests that an additional reason for the tolerance of slavery was lack of economic alternatives for the colonists.

49 *Ibid.*, p. 99. Gonzalo Fernández de Oviedo shared a similar scepticism about conversions. The official view was of course that they would all be converted and gradually civilized under Spanish supervision.

50 *Ibid.*, pp. 79, 84.

51 I have consulted Alonso de Andrade, *Varones ilustres en santidad, letras y zelo de las almas de la Compañia de Jesús* (Madrid, 1666), v, pp. 759–83. Andrade explains clearly that the text had been sent around as a rare inspirational example of how God calls men to his service in strange ways. Andrade was therefore in the business of sustaining the marvellous interpretation suggested by Acosta, but betrayed his own misgivings by explaining that this example showed how God used 'strange ways' to call men to a religious vocation, admirable ways which 'many times seem contrary to actual sainthood' (p. 760). From another manuscript, Francisco Mateos prepared his edition in *Obras del padre José de Acosta* (Madrid, 1954), pp. 304–20. I have used this for my quotations. José-Juan Arrom recently prepared a new edition restoring Andrade's text: *Peregrinación de Bartolomé Lorenzo* (Lima, 1982).

52 Late in his life, between 1553 and 1555, Ignatius dictated his reminiscences to his secretary Luis Gonçalves da Camara at the instigation of Father Jeroni Nadal – perhaps the key organizer of the Society in its formative period. It was circulated extensively among the Jesuit houses, in manuscript form, until the writing of a more polished biography of the founder of the Society was entrusted to Pedro de Ribadeneira after 1567. For a recent and reliable English edition see Saint Ignatius of Loyola, *Personal Writings*, ed. Joseph A. Munitiz and Philip Endean (Harmondsworth, 1996), pp. 3–64. It must be noted however that the practice preceded Ignatius. Thus, Cosme de Torres, the Valencian Jesuit who sustained the mission of Japan over twenty years after the departure of Francis Xavier in 1551, similarly recounted his life to his brothers in Valencia and Goa as a spiritual pilgrimage leading to his missionary vocation. This letter was written from Yamaguchi, apparently at Francis Xavier's request, in September 1551. See Juan Ruiz Medina (ed.), *Documentos del Japón 1547–1557*, in Monumenta Historica Societatis Iesu, 137 (Rome, 1990), pp. 219–30. We may even wonder whether Torres influenced Nadal and Ignatius, since he wrote an earlier letter to Rome (which Ignatius is known to have answered) sketching his conversion and entry to the Order in 1549 (*ibid.*, pp. 92–101). The root was Augustinian; as Torres wrote, 'the creature cannot rest until he finds his creator' (*ibid.*, p. 94). There existed also medieval models of autobiographical spirituality – Ramon Llull's *Vita Coaetania* (1311) may have been known by Nadal and Torres – and the very structure of the spiritual exercises that all Jesuit fathers undertook when they entered the Society in order to 'overcome the self' promoted this kind of literature.

53 For the interpretation of Acosta's account the most important contribution (and the only one of which I am aware) is the introduction of the edition prepared by José-Juan Arrom (1982). He argues that the text is not an autobiography but rather a fictionalized account of a spiritual journey, created by Acosta on the basis of a number of literary models. My argument here is that the text is indeed an attempt to suggest a spiritual journey, but that it follows quite closely the original story told by Lorenzo, and that this prevents Acosta from eliminating the true voice of the traveller, which is neither entirely fictional nor conventionally Christian.

54 Acosta 1954, p. 305.

55 *Ibid.*, p. 309.

56 *Ibid.*, p. 311.

57 *Ibid.*

58 *Ibid.*, p. 312.

59 *Ibid.*, p. 313.

60 *Ibid.*, p. 314.
61 *Ibid.*, p. 318.
62 Oviedo 1959, IV, pp. 366–75.
63 On Acosta much has been written. See especially Anthony Pagden, *The Fall of Natural Man. The American Indian and the Origins of Comparative Ethnology*, 2nd edn (Cambridge, 1986), pp. 146–97.

3 *Wes Williams: 'Rubbing up against others'*

1 Michel de Montaigne, 'On Vanity', *Essays*, p. 747. References to the *Essays* and the *Travel Journal* are to Donald Frame's translation, *Complete Works of Montaigne* (London, 1957); subsequent page references are given in the text. I have occasionally adapted the translation to my reading of the French. Translations of other texts are mine unless otherwise indicated.
2 Desiderius Erasmus, *Peregrinatio religionis ergo* (Basel, 1526). Not one Renaissance French translation of the Erasmus texts I shall be using survives.
3 Desiderius Erasmus, *Enchiridion* (Basel, 1515) fol. vv. The entire fifth section is a powerful meditation on the relative values of relics and scripture, and on pilgrimage as ritual and as reading.
4 François Rabelais, *Gargantua* [1534], ed. R. Calder and M. A. Screech (Geneva, 1970), p. 256. In fact the King quotes Luther, not Paul, but Rabelais delights in obscuring matters. For more on this, see my 'Salad Days: Revisiting pilgrimage in the Sixteenth Century', *Michigan Romance Studies* [MRS], xv (1995), pp. 151–76.
5 Jean Calvin, 'Advertissement tresutile du grand proffit qui reviendroit à la Chrestienté, s'il se faisoit inventoire de tous les corps sainctz, et reliques. . .' [1543], in F. Higman (ed.), *Three French Treatises* (London, 1970), pp. 47–97. For more on this in relation to Rabelais, see my '"Marchandises peregrines": Renaissance Pilgrimage and the Occupation of Literature', *Paragraph*, 18 (1995), pp. 132–47.
6 For more on this debate and its background see Christian Zacher, *Curiosity and Pilgrimage: The Literature of Discovery in Fourteenth Century England* (Baltimore and London, 1976), and J. Céard (ed.), *La curiosité à la Renaissance* (Paris, 1986). Secular arts of travel were elaborated at much the same time and in very similar terms to the pilgrim handbooks; I return to them below.
7 Much useful recent criticism has elucidated the literary and diplomatic politics of the journey; see for instance Warren Boutcher, '"Le moyen de voir ce Senecque ecrit à la main": Montaigne's *Journal de Voyage* and the Politics of *Science* and *Faveur* in the Vatican Library', *MRS*, xv (1995), pp. 177–215.
8 In the *Essays* Montaigne experiments with a kind of comparative religion on a number of occasions, most directly in 'On Cannibals'; relativism is more fully addressed in the 'Apology for Raymond Sebond'. Nowhere does he fully embrace the idea that faith is entirely a function of place: 'other witnesses, similar promises and threats' are cited alongside 'another region' as things which might 'imprint on us . . . contrary belief' (p. 325). The aphorism is added in his own later revision of the argument.
9 It is important to note that the *Journal* was never prepared for publication – unlike the meticulously, obsessively altered *Essays*. In reading it we are trespassing, crowding out what can seem at times to be a very private house. Some readers wish the journal had never been found, never brought to print. To such, Montaigne the pilgrim traveller seems wholly unrepresentative both of the Renaissance – which they would have him epitomize – and of himself as revealed by the *Essays*. The journal was first discovered in the 1770s and its first readers, Grimm and Diderot, found the philosopher they thought they recognized in the *Essays* to be embarrassingly conventional in his devotions, an old-fangled pilgrim. They, and many readers since, have also found him too

curiously concerned with the details of the movements of his own body, and with those of the saints and locals he met.

10 For other readings of this punning process in relation to inheritance, the body, its maintenance and cure see Terence Cave, *The Cornucopian Text: Problems of Writing in the French Renaissance* (Oxford, 1979), pp. 147–50, Antoine Compagnon, *Nous, Michel de Montaigne* (Paris, 1980), pp. 170–93, Irma Majer, 'Montaigne's Cure: Stones and Roman Ruins', in *Modern Languages Notes*, 97 (1982), pp. 958–74, and Georges van den Abeele, *Travel as Metaphor: From Montaigne to Rousseau* (Minneapolis and Oxford, 1992), pp. 1–38.

11 Contrast this to Montaigne's praise in 'On Vanity' of the man who displayed his weekly bowel movements in chamber-pots as a way of 'making his life known' (p. 721).

12 Henri de Castela, *La Guide et adresse pour ceux qui veulent faire le S. Voyage de Hierusalem* (Paris, 1604), fol. 4v.

13 Much has been written about this guide literature in recent years. For a useful synthesis see J.-P. Rubiés, 'Instructions for Travellers: Teaching the Eye to See', *History and Anthropology*, ix/2–3 (1996), pp. 139–90. On Lipsius, see Norman Doiron, *L'Art de voyager: le déplacement à l'époque classique* (Paris, 1995), pp. 17–32. For more on the development of the pilgrim guidebooks in relation to those of the Protestant north, see my forthcoming *'The Undiscovered Country': Pilgrimage and Narrative in the French Renaissance* (Oxford).

14 Nicole Huen, *Le Grant Voyage de Jherusalem* (Paris, 1517) fol. vv.

15 The model of pilgrimage as 'controlled liminality' was pioneered by Victor and Edith Turner in *Image and Pilgrimage in Christian Culture: Anthropological Perspectives* (New York, 1978). It underscores much of Peter Brown's work on pilgrimage, notably, *The Cult of the Saints* (Chicago, 1981).

16 The letter was first published by Morel in Paris, in 1551, in a Latin translation; it then went through many editions and Latin re-translations for the next fifty years before being translated into French in 1604. The French translation is now lost, but other texts from the debate survive. See Pierre Maraval, 'Un controverse sur les pèlerinages autour d'un texte patristique', in *Revue d'Histoire et de Philosophie Religieuses*, 66 (1986), pp. 131–46, and '"Le jargon des errans": Arguments against Pilgrimage', in my forthcoming *'The Undiscovered Country'*.

17 Gregory of Nyssa, *Select Writings and Letters* (*Select Library of Nicene and Post-Nicene Fathers*, ii, 5), ed. W. Moore and H. A. Wilson (Oxford, 1893), pp. 382–3.

18 For a careful reading of some of these encounters which has inspired my own thoughts here, see Terence Cave, 'Le récit Montaignien: un voyage sans repentir', in his *Préhistoires: textes troublés du seizième siècle* (Paris, forthcoming).

19 The analogy is not perfect: English is, today, an Indian language, whereas French did not have the same status in early modern Rome. From the perspective of the visiting traveller, however, the shock of being addressed in what one (mistakenly) takes to be one's own language echoes across time and place.

20 See Mary McKinley, 'Le Vagabond: Montaigne à cheval et les errances romanesques des Essais', in *Montaigne: espace, voyage, écriture*, ed. Z. Samaras (Paris, 1995), pp. 113–24.

21 Montaigne, having witnessed and recorded in detail a Lutheran marriage ceremony, asks the minister in Kempten for a copy of the new confession, published just the year before. 'But,' the *Journal* notes, 'it is not in Latin.' (p. 895)

22 Travel writing often appears to be the 'raw' material which is then cooked in the books of fiction, poetry, epic, romance, essay . . . but Montaigne tries hard *not* to figure 'being a writer' as a profession akin to that of priest or doctor.

23 Seamus Heaney, from 'Wheels within Wheels', in *Seeing Things* (London, 1991), p. 46.

24 Marteau, who will go on to become a leading member of the Ligue and right-hand

man to the Duc de Guise, will also, in 1588, come to Montaigne's assistance when he is held in the Bastille. See Montaigne, *Oeuvres complètes*, ed. A. Thibaudet and M. Rat (Paris, 1962), p. 1410, n. 29.

25 The Uncanny comes into play 'when the distinction between imagination and reality is effaced . . . or when a symbol takes over the full functions of the thing it symbolises'. Sigmund Freud [trans. A. Strachey], 'The Uncanny', in *Art and Literature* (Harmondsworth, 1985), p. 367.

26 See Ian Maclean, '"Le païs au delà": Montaigne and philosophical speculation', in *Montaigne*, ed. I. D. Macfarlane and I. Maclean (Oxford, 1982), pp. 101–32.

4 *Peter Burke: The Philosopher as Traveller*

1 This paper was first presented to the 1988 meeting of the UK South Asia Social Anthropology Group, 'Orientalism and the History of the Anthropology of South Asia' but has been extensively revised for this book. My thanks to the editors for their constructive criticisms of an earlier draft.

2 Cf. Joan-Pau Rubiés, 'Christianity and Civilization in Sixteenth-Century Ethnological Discourse', in *Shifting Cultures: Interaction and Discourse in the Expansion of Europe*, ed. Henriette Bugge and Joan-Pau Rubiés (Münster, 1995), pp. 45–6, citing Bernier alongside George Sandys and Pietro della Valle.

3 Paul Hazard, *La crise de la conscience européenne, 1680–1715* (1935); translated as *The European Mind* (London, 1953).

4 Edward Said, *Orientalism* (London, 1978); Ronald Inden, 'Orientalist Constructions of India', *Modern Asian Studies*, 20 (1986), pp. 401–46.

5 Said (1978), p. 8.

6 *Ibid.*, p. 3.

7 Lewis D. Wurgraft, *The Imperial Imagination* (Middletown, 1983), pp. 7–8.

8 Théodore Morison, 'Un Français à la cour du Grand Mogol', *Revue Historique*, 156 (1927), pp. 83–97; René Pintard, *Les libertins érudits dans la première moitié du 17e siècle* (Paris, 1943; revised edn Geneva and Paris, 1983), pp. 328–9, 384–6, 409–12; John S. Spink, *French Free Thought* (London, 1960), pp. 106–8; Joseph Pineau, 'Bernier l'Angevin, voyageur', in *Les Angevins de la littérature*, ed. Georges Cesbron (Angers, 1979), pp. 119–31.

9 'la capacité rare de se débarrasser des préjugés de son milieu et de son éducation et d'entrer en sympathie avec la civilisation étrangère au milieu de laquelle il se trouvait'. Morison (1927), p. 84.

10 'Lettre à Colbert', in Bernier, *Voyage dans les Etats du grand Mogol*, ed. France Bhattacharya (Paris, 1981), p. 175. For convenience, Bernier's three famous letters will be cited in this edition.

11 'Lettre à Chapelain', in Bhattacharya, p. 247. On interactions between Western and local knowledge, cf. Christopher Bayly, *Empire and Information* (Cambridge, 1996), and Bernard S. Cohn, *Colonisation and its Forms of Knowledge* (Princeton, 1996), especially p. 16.

12 General survey in Donald Lach and Edwin J. Van Kley, *Asia in the Making of Europe*, vol. 3: *A Century of Advance* (Chicago, 1993), pp. 601–837.

13 Nicolao Manucci, *Storia del Mogor or Mogul India* (English trans., 4 vols, Calcutta, 1907–8, which is the first unabridged edition); Angelo Legrenzi, *Il Pellegrino nell'Asia* (Venice, 1705). On them, see Alessandro Grossato, *Navigatori e viaggiatori veneti sulla rotta per l'India* (Florence, 1994), chs 5, 6.

14 Heinrich Roth, *Relatio Regni Mogor* (Aschaffenburg, 1665).

15 Abraham Rogier, *De open-deure tot de verborgen heydendom* (1651).

16 The most thorough study – Meera Nanda, *European Travel Accounts during the*

Reigns of Shajahan and Aurangzeb (Kurukshetra, 1994), pp. 2–11 – adds Peter Mundy, Sir Thomas Herbert, John Marshall, Thomas Bowrey, Streynsham Master, Sir William Hedges and Sir William Norris. In her *India Inscribed: European and British Writing on India 1600–1800* (Delhi, 1995), Kate Telscher adds William Finch and Nicholas Withington.

17 Pierre Du Jarric, *Histoire des Indes Orientales* (Paris, 1608); Johannes de Laet, *De imperio magni Mogolis* (Leiden, 1631).

18 François Pyrard de Laval, *Voyage* (2 vols, Paris, 1611); François La Boullaye le Gouz, *Voyages et Observations* (Paris, 1653); Jean-Baptiste Tavernier, *Six Voyages* (s. l., 1676); Jean de Thévenot, *Voyages* (1664–84; 3rd edn, 5 vols, Amsterdam, 1727), v; Barthélemy Carré, *Voyage* (Paris, 1699: Eng. trans. London, 1947). Cf. Nanda, pp. 12–18.

19 Jean Chardin, *Journal de Voyage en Perse et aux Indes Orientales*, 2nd edn (Amsterdam, 1686), preface.

20 Abraham Rogier, *La porte ouverte pour parvenir à la connaissance du paganisme caché* (Amsterdam, 1670).

21 François Bernier, *Histoire de la dernière révolution des états du Grand Mogor* (2 vols, Paris, 1670).

22 Karl-Heinz Bender, *Revolutionen* (Munich, 1977), especially pp. 51–78; Gabriel Naudé, *Considérations politiques sur les coups d'état* (1639: ed. Louis Marin, Paris, 1990).

23 Bhattacharya, pp. 201, 234, 260. On della Valle, see Rubiés.

24 Bhattacharya, p. 226.

25 Pintard (1943); Spink (1960); Antoine Adam (ed.), *Les libertins au 17e siècle* (Paris, 1964); Tullio Gregory (ed.), *Ricerche su letteratura libertina e letteratura clandestina nel '600* (Florence, 1981), especially pp. 3–48.

26 On 'atheist', see Lucien Febvre, *Le problème de l'incroyance au 16e siècle: la religion de Rabelais* (Paris, 1942), pp. 138–41.

27 Norman Cohn, *Europe's Inner Demons* (London, 1975), pp. 1–59.

28 Hans Blumenberg, *The Legitimacy of the Modern Age* (1966: Eng. trans., Cambridge, MA, 1983), part 3; idem, *Der Prozess der theoretischen Neugierde* (Frankfurt, 1988); Lorraine Daston, 'Curiosity in Early Modern Science', *Word and Image*, 11 (1995), pp. 391–404.

29 Bernier (1670), p. 1.

30 Jean Chapelain, *Lettres*, II (Paris, 1883), pp. 167–8.

31 Rupert Hall and Marie B. Hall (eds), *The Correspondence of Henry Oldenburg*, VII (Madison, 1970), pp. 85–7.

32 François Bernier, *Abregé de la philosophie de Gassendi* (1675–7; 7 vols, Lyon, 1678); Spink (1960), pp. 85–102; Richard H. Popkin, *History of Scepticism from Erasmus to Spinoza* (Berkeley, 1979), pp. 99–109, 141–6.

33 Pintard (1943), pp. 334–48.

34 Joan-Pau Rubiés, 'Hugo Grotius's Dissertation on the Origin of the American Peoples and Comparative Methods', *Journal of the History of Ideas*, 52 (1991), pp. 221–44.

35 Harcourt Brown, *Scientific Organizations in Seventeenth-Century France* (Baltimore, 1934), pp. 66–134.

36 Chapelain (1883), p. 171; cf. pp. 166, 221, 640.

37 *Ibid.*, pp. 166–72. Cf. Adam Olearius, *Orientalische Reise* (Schleswig, 1645–7); Martino Martini, *De bello tartarico* (Amsterdam, 1655). A French translation of Olearius was available by 1659 and one of Martini by 1667.

38 Chapelain (1883), p. 663.

39 Eamon O'Flaherty, 'Relativism and Criticism in 17th-Century French Thought', PhD thesis, University of Cambridge, 1987, especially pp. 5–12; cf. Zachary S. Schiffman,

On the Threshold of Modernity: Relativism in the French Renaissance (Baltimore, 1991), especially pp. xi–xii.

40 John Ovington, *A Voyage to Surat* (London, 1692), pp. 339–40.

41 Peter Burke, *Montaigne* (Oxford, 1981), especially chapters 3 and 7.

42 'Plutarque veut que les petites choses ne soient pas toujours à négliger. . .': Bhattacharya, p. 206.

43 Montaigne, *Essays*, Book 1, ch. 31; Book 2, ch. 12.

44 Pierre Macherey, *Pour une théorie de la production littéraire* (Paris, 1966); Jacques Derrida, 'Plato's Pharmacy', in his *Dissemination* (1972: Eng. trans. Chicago, 1982), chapter 1.

45 Bhattacharya, pp. 177–8

46 Bhattacharya, p. 237.

47 'Lorsque ce chariot de triomphe infernale roule . . . il se trouve des personnes si folles et si éperdues de fausses croyances et superstitions qu'ils se jettent. . .': Bhattacharya, p. 230.

48 *Ibid.*, p. 240.

49 *Ibid.*, p. 210.

50 *Ibid.*, p. 226.

51 *Ibid.*, p. 195.

52 Cf. Sylvia Murr, 'Le politique "au Mogol" selon Bernier: appareil conceptual, rhétorique stratégique, philosophic morale', in Jacques Pouchepadass and Henri Stern (eds), *De la royauté à l'état dans le monde Indien* (Paris, 1990), pp. 239-302. My thanks to Nicholas Dew for the reference.

53 Chapelain (1883), p. 663.

54 F. Bernier, 'Mémoire sur l'établissement du commerce dans les Indes', *Mémoires de la société nationale d'agriculture, sciences et arts d'Angers* (1884), pp. 11–37. My thanks to Nicholas Dew for drawing my attention to this edition.

55 Bhattacharaya, pp. 143–76.

56 On these 'trois états', see Bhattacharya, p. 170: cf. Jean-Baptiste Tavernier, *Six Voyages* (Paris, 1676), introduction.

57 'ont tous osté ce Mien et ce Tien a l'esgard des fonds de terre et de la propriété des possessions': Bhattacharaya, pp. 170–01.

58 Richard Koebner, 'Despot', *Journal of the Warburg and Courtauld Institutes*, 14 (1951); Melvin Richter, 'Despotism', *Dictionary of the History of Ideas*, ed. Philip Wiener (4 vols, New York, 1973), II, pp. 1–18.

59 Jean Bodin, *Six Livres de la République* (Paris, 1576), Book 2, chapter 2.

60 Lucette Valensi, *Venise et la Sublime Porte: la naissance du despote* (Paris, 1987), especially pp. 97ff.

61 Thomas Roe, *Embassy to the Court of the Great Mogul*, ed. W. Foster (2 vols, London, 1899), I, pp. 110–11, 120.

62 Louis XIV, *Mémoires*, ed. Jean Longnon (Paris, 1978), p. 203.

63 Murr, 'Le politique', p. 277.

64 Spink (1960), pp. 106–8.

65 F. Bernier, 'Introduction à la lecture de Confucius', *Journal des Savants* (1688). Cf. Virgile Pinot, *La Chine et la formation de l'esprit philosophique en France 1640–1740* (Paris, 1932), pp. 376–84; B. Guy, *The Image of China before and after Voltaire* (Geneva, 1963), pp. 132ff.

66 *Ibid.*, p. 249.

67 Bhattacharya, p. 227; cf. Pierre Bayle, *Lettre sur la comète* (1682), and Hazard (1935).

68 Mark Goldie, 'Priestcraft and the Birth of Whiggism', in *Political Discourse in Early Modern Britain*, ed. N. Phillipson and Q. Skinner (Cambridge, 1993), pp. 209–31; Justin Champion, *The Pillars of Priestcraft Shaken* (Cambridge, 1992).

69 François Bernier, 'Mémoire sur le quiétisme des Indes', *Journal des Savants* (September 1688).

70 On Fryer, see Nanda (1994), p. 7; John Dryden, *Works*, ed. Vinton A. Dearing, vol. 12 (Berkeley and Los Angeles, 1994), pp. 385, 411–41. Cf. Telscher, *India Inscribed*, pp. 60-61.

71 Elisabeth Labrousse, *Pierre Bayle* (2 vols, The Hague, 1964), ii, p. 16n.

72 Edward Terry, *A Voyage to East-India* (London, 1655).

73 Montesquieu, *Lettres Persanes* (1721).

74 Muriel Dodds, *Les récits de voyage sources de l'Esprit des Loix de Montesquieu* (Paris, 1929), pp. 81–4.

75 Françoise Weil, 'Montesquieu et le despotisme', *Actes Congrès Montesquieu* (Bordeaux, 1956), pp. 191–215.

5 Melissa Calaresu: Looking for Virgil's Tomb

I dedicate this article to the memory of my father, Franco Romano Calaresu, who understood the dangers of leaving home.

1 On the history of this traditional proverb, the origin of which Benedetto Croce dates from the fourteenth century, see Croce, 'Il "paradiso abitato da diavoli"', in *Uomini e cose della vecchia Italia* (2 vols, Bari, 1927), i, pp. 68–86.

2 Pietro Napoli-Signorelli, *Vicende della coltura nelle Due Sicilie, o sia Storia ragionata della loro legislazione e polizia, delle lettere, del commercio, delle arti, e degli spettacoli dalle colonie straniere insino a noi* (5 vols, Naples, 1784–6), v, p. 494, fn. 1.

3 De Seta, 'Grand Tour: The Lure of Italy in the Eighteenth Century', in *Grand Tour: The Lure of Italy in the Eighteenth Century*, exhibition catalogue by A. Wilton and I. Bignamini (eds): Tate Gallery, London; Palazzo delle Esposizioni, Rome (London, 1996), p. 15. For a similar interpretation, see also C. De Seta, 'L'Italia nello specchio del "Grand Tour"', *Il paesaggio*, ed. C. De Seta, Annali 5 of *Storia d'Italia* (Turin, 1982), pp. 207–63 and, for a later illustrated version of this chapter, see De Seta, *L'Italia nel Grand Tour da Montaigne a Goethe* (Naples, 1992).

4 Ilaria Bignamini has suggested alternative ways of looking at the material on the Grand Tour, including the consideration of the different and competing identities within the Grand Tourist (Bignamini, 'Grand Tour: Open Issues', in *Grand Tour*, exh. cat. by Wilton and Bignamini [eds], p. 32).

5 For a classic study of the publishing networks of eighteenth-century Europe, see R. Darnton, *The Business of Enlightenment: A Publishing History of the 'Encyclopédie' 1775–1800* (Cambridge, MA, 1979). Despite his contribution of this earlier work to our understanding of the variety and breadth of enlightened culture, Darnton later denied that breadth in a recent review article in 'George Washington's False Teeth', *New York Review of Books*, 27 March 1997, pp. 34–8.

6 For an attempt to establish Freemasonry as a unifying force in eighteenth-century Europe, see M. C. Jacob, *Living the Enlightenment: Freemasonry and Politics in Eighteenth-Century Europe* (Oxford, 1991). For another study of enlightenment and Freemasonry, with less emphasis on northwestern Europe and for later in the century, see Giuseppe Giarrizzo, *Massoneria e illuminismo nell'Europa del Settecento* (Naples, 1994).

7 There is extensive literature on the Grand Tour, with particular focus on British travellers. See, for example, C. Hibbert, *The Grand Tour* (London, 1987) and Jeremy Black, *The British Abroad: The Grand Tour in the Eighteenth Century* (Stroud/New York, 1992).

8 Elisabeth Chevallier notes that guidebook writers had no qualms in including descriptions of sites which they had not seen, and they were less interested in providing an

original account of their travels than a traditional itinerary. While her useful introduction highlights the German traveller to Italy in the eighteenth century, she also provides some general observations on the changing conceptions of travel to the end of the century, in F.-J. Meyer, *Les Tableaux d'Italie [Darstellungen aus Italien, 1792]* (Naples, 1980), p. XVI.

9   For the most recent treatment of the role of Italy in the itinerary of the Grand Tour (again with particular emphasis on British travellers), see the catalogue for the 1996 Tate Gallery exhibition cited in note 3 above.

10 On the effect of the Grand Tour on the study and collecting of classical sculpture, see F. Haskell and N. Penny, *Taste and the Antique: The Lure of Classical Sculpture 1500–1900* (New Haven/London, 1981), pp. 74–8.

11 Herculaneum and Pompeii were continuously excavated by the Bourbon government from 1739 and 1755 respectively. De Seta places particular importance on the discovery of the cities in the creation of a cosmopolitan culture in eighteenth-century Europe (De Seta, 'L'Italia nello specchio del "Grand Tour"', p. 208). A museum near the royal palace of Portici was established for the display of the objects found at Herculaneum. Travellers were particularly fascinated by the cabinets containing the charred remains of everyday life in the city. For the fullest account of the Bourbon excavations, see C. C. Parslow, *Discovering Antiquity: Karl Weber and the Excavation at Herculaneum, Pompeii, and Stabiae* (Cambridge, 1995). For French Travellers' accounts of the Portici museum, see Chantal Grell, *Herculanum et Pompéi dans les récits des voyageurs français du XVIIIe siècle* (Naples, 1982), pp. 123–39. For a series of short articles on antiquity and French travellers, in particular in the eighteenth century, see Parts One and Three on Naples and Rome in E. and R. Chevalier, *Iter Italicum: Les voyageurs français à la découverte de l'Italie ancienne* (Paris/Geneva, 1984).

12 *Voyage pittoresque ou Description des royaumes de Naples et de Sicile* (5 vols, Paris, 1781–5) remains the most important visual record of the Grand Tour in southern Italy and had enormous influence after its publication in France. Saint-Non directed the publication and promotion of the work; it was Dominique Vivant-Denon who travelled to the Kingdom of Naples with a group of French artists and wrote the text. For a discussion of the *Voyage pittoresque*, see De Seta, 'L'Italia nello specchio del "Grand Tour"', pp. 238–44.

13 For French travellers' interest in (and often disdain of) the painting and architecture of Naples, see Anthony Blunt, 'Naples as seen by French Travellers 1630–1780', in F. Haskell, A. Levi and R. Shackleton (eds), *The Artist and the Writer in France: Essays in Honour of Jean Seznec* (Oxford, 1974), pp. 12–14. On the foreign reception of the work of a contemporary Neapolitan painter, see Rodney Palmer, 'Francesco Solimena's Frescoes in the Sacristy of S. Paolo Maggiore, Naples: Patronage, Iconography, Reception', in *Regnum Dei (Collectanea Theatina)*, 119 (1993), pp. 80–100. Saint-Non's work includes descriptions and engravings of paintings from Neapolitan churches and palaces (Saint-Non, *Voyage pittoresque*, I, pp. 95–120).

14 While Venice had been the Italian city which had attracted the most foreign visitors in the early part of the century, Naples, after Rome, had become the most popular city to visit by the end of the century. This change of 'axis' was due in part to the popularity of the excavations of Herculaneum and Pompeii, but also to a change in taste which marks the beginning of a turning point as the Grand Tour begins to go further south within Europe and further afield in search of new and more exotic destinations (De Seta, 'L'Italia nello specchio del "Grand Tour"', pp. 217 and 223). On the Kingdom of Naples as the 'frontier' of the Grand Tour, see Atanasio Mozzillo, *La frontiera del Grand Tour: Viaggi e viaggiatori nel Mezzogiorno borbonico* (Naples, 1992).

15 See, for example, Joseph-Jérôme Lefrançais de Lalande's *Voyage du'un François en*

Italie Fait dans les Années 1765 & 1766. Contenant l'Histoire et les Anecdotes les plus singulières d'Italie, et sa description, les Moeurs, les Usages, le Gouvernement. . . (8 vols, Paris/Venice, 1769), VI, pp. 114–15. For the continuity of the theatrical metaphor in descriptions of Naples from the seventeenth century to the present, see Peter Burke, 'The Virgin of the Carmine and the Revolt of Masaniello', *Past and Present*, 99 (1983), pp. 3–21.

16 See note 15 above. A second edition was published, with a new title and with additions and corrections, as *Voyage en Italie* (6 vols, Paris, 1786).

17 On Lalande, see H. Monod-Cassidy, 'Un astronome-philosophe, Jérôme de Lalande', *Studies on Voltaire and the Eighteenth Century*, 56 (1967), pp. 907–30, and L. L. Bongie, 'J.-J. Lalande: standard clichés and the private man', *Studies on Voltaire and the Eighteenth Century*, 245 (1986), pp. 373–402.

18 Chevalier writes that Lalande's guide had a particular place among the many guides published in the eighteenth century for its 'richesse incomparable par l'étendue et la précision de l'information' (R. Chevalier, 'Lecture de Virgile par un scientifique du XVIIIe siècle. J. de Lalande dans son *Voyage d'un François en Italie. . .*', in E. and R. Chevalier, *Iter Italicum: Les voyageurs français à la découverte de l'Italie ancienne* (Paris, 1984), p. 406).

19 Lalande notes the counterfeit editions published in Yverdon and Liège in the second edition, in *Voyage en Italie* (Yverdon, 1787), I, p. xxii.

20 On the 'collective' nature of earlier eighteenth-century travel accounts, see Elizabeth Chevalier's introduction to F.-J. L. Meyer, *Les Tableaux d'Italie*, pp. XXIII–XXIV.

21 For example, Giovanni Botero wrote: 'The Neapolitans are most doubted for revolt, by reason of the instabilities of that people, alwaies desirous of change and novelties'. (*Relations of the Most Famous Kingdoms and Commonweales Through the World: Discoursing of their Situations, Strengths, Greatness and Policies. Enlarged, according to moderne Observation* [London, 1616], p. 153).

22 An account of the revolt often accompanied descriptions of the character of the Neapolitan people in guidebooks. For example, in Saint-Non's *Voyage*, the section on the customs of Neapolitans is followed by a section on Masaniello and the revolt which includes a plate entitled 'Mazanielle haranguant le peuple de Naples'(Saint-Non, *Voyage pittoresque*, I, pp. 242–8 and pl. 103).

23 For example, the paintings, etchings and watercolours of Pietro Fabris – the British genre painter resident in Naples and etcher for William Hamilton's book on the volcanic activity around the Bay of Naples, *Campi Phlegraei* (Naples, 1776) – shift between caricatures of the happy Neapolitan peasant and more realistic (and unusual) depictions of street life. Fabris' collection of etchings, *Raccolta di varii vestimenti ed arti nel Regno di Napoli* (Naples, 1773), has been reprinted, with an introductory essay, as P. Fabris, *Raccolta*, ed. F. Mancini (Naples, 1985). On the contemporary depiction of Neapolitans, see also *Vases and Volcanoes: Sir William Hamilton and his collection*, exhibition catalogue by Ian Jenkins and Kim Sloan, British Museum, London (London, 1996), pp. 241–51. There does not yet exist an integrated study of the depiction of the poor in Neapolitan landscape painting such as exists for English painting in the same period: J. Barrell, *The Dark Side of the Landscape: The Depiction of the Poor in English Painting 1730–1840* (Cambridge, 1980). On eighteenth-century views of Naples, see *In the Shadow of Vesuvius: Views of Naples from Baroque to Romanticism 1631–1830*, exhibition catalogue, Accademia Italiana delle Arti e delle Arti Applicate (Naples, 1990).

24 On this change of emphasis, see Venturi's account of the image of Italy in Europe, 'L'Italia fuori dell'Italia', in *Storia d'Italia*, III (Turin, 1973), pp. 1055–9. Pilati's work was first published in 1767 as *Di una riforma d'Italia, ossia dei mezzi di riformare i più cattivi costumi e le più perniciose leggi d'Italia* and translated into French in 1769

(Venturi, 'L'Italia fuori d'Italia', pp. 1046–7). Another work by Ange Goudar, although less widely read, dealt with similar themes as Pilati's and was published anonymously as *Naples. Ce qu'il faut faire pour rendre ce royaume florissant ou L'on trait des avantages que le gouvernement peut retirer de sa fertilité, de l'abondance de ses denrées, des facilités pour perfectionner les arts: de sa position favorable pour s'emparer des premiers branches du Commerce Étranger* (Amsterdam, 1769).

25 On the important role of Swiss publishing houses as an arena for the publication and exchange of books and journals for both French and Italian writers, see Venturi, 'L'Italia fuori d'Italia', pp. 1045–6.

26 Claudia Petraccone estimates a population of between 300,000 and 350,000 at mid-century and more than 400,000 by the end of the eighteenth century in *Napoli dal cinquecento all'ottocento: Problemi di storia demografica e sociale* (Naples, 1974), pp. 137–9.

27 Abbé [Jérôme] Richard, *Description historique et critique de l'Italie, ou Nouveaux Mémoires Sur l'Etat actuel de son Gouvernement, des Sciences, des Arts, du Commerce, de la Population et de l'Histoire Naturelle* (6 vols, Dijon, 1766), IV, pp. 203–63. There was a second edition in 1770.

28 *Ibid.*, IV, pp. 231–2.

29 These 'devils' are not of much interest to Richard and he recommends that the traveller should not let them get in the way of their enjoyment of paradise: 'car on oublie les vices du peuple pour jouir des beautés et de la douceur du climat qu'il habite' (*ibid.*, IV, pp. 232–3).

30 Lalande, *Voyage*, VI, pp. 334–5.

31 Saint-Non, *Voyage pittoresque*, I, p. 236–7.

32 Lalande writes: 'La multitude de gens oisifs dans le bas peuple doit contribuer, aussi bien que l'ardeur du climat, à rendre fort communs le libertinage, et les maladies qui en sont la suite.' (Lalande, *Voyage*, VI, p. 337).

33 Lalande, *Voyage*, VI, pp. 346–9. This moral corruption includes selling their wives and daughters as prostitutes, in Richard, *Description*, IV, p. 232.

34 Lalande, *Voyage*, VI, pp. 280–85. See Saint-Non's depiction of the San Gennaro ceremony, in his *Voyage pittoresque*, I, pl. 33 and pp. 73–4, and Fabris's less dramatic depiction of the religious devotion of the Neapolitan poor in Fabris, *Raccolta*, ed. Mancini, pl. 32.

35 Saint-Non describes the pillage of the *cuccagna* with an accompanying engraving (Saint-Non, *Voyage*, I, pl. 102 and pp. 249–52). Another contemporary painter, Antonio Joli, painted several *cuccagna* scenes for the tourist market; see, for example, *In the Shadow of Vesuvius*, exh. cat., p. 46.

36 R. Mercier, 'La théorie des climats des "Réflexions critiques" a "L'Esprit des lois"', *Revue d'Histoire Littéraire de la France*, 53 (1953), esp. pp. 27–37.

37 On the laws and climate, see Montesquieu, *Spirit of the Laws*, ed. A. Cohler, B. Miller and H. Stone (Cambridge, 1989), Books 14–19. On an earlier work on climate by Montesquieu and the *Spirit of the Laws*, see R. Mercier, 'La théorie des climats', pp. 170–74.

38 Montesquieu, *Spirit of the Laws*, Book 14, ch. I, p. 231.

39 See J. N. Shklar, *Montesquieu* (Oxford, 1987), pp. 93–5. Mercier sees Montesquieu's understanding of climate and political change as slightly more flexible, in Mercier, 'La théorie des climats', p. 172.

40 Montesquieu's travel journal was not discovered and published until the late nineteenth century, as *Voyages de Montesquieu*, ed. A. de Montesquieu (2 vols, Bordeaux, 1896).

41 On his first day in Naples, he wrote: 'Il me semble que ceux qui cherchent les beaux ouvrages de l'art ne doivent pas quitter Rome. A Naples, il me paroît qu'il est plus facile de se gâter le goût que de se le former' (*ibid.*, II, p. 6).

42 *Ibid.*, pp. 20–21.

43 *Ibid.*, pp. 18–20 and 22–3.

44 *Ibid.*, p. 20. For this information, he may have read Giannone's *Civil History of Naples* (*ibid.*, p. 23).

45 For his description of the *lazzaroni*, see *ibid.*, p. 13.

46 'Le peuple de Naples, où tant de gens n'ont rien, est plus peuple qu'un autre' (*ibid.*, p. 23).

47 Lalande, for instance, makes this connection and suggests that, in the case of the Kingdom of Naples, 'to change the taste (*goût*) of a nation, and go against its nature (*et en forcer le naturel*), one needs a clear and rigorously applied project and Prince at its head' (Lalande, *Voyage*, VI, p. 334).

48 Cited in note 12 above.

49 Saint-Non begins: 'Plus qu'on voyagé et plus on trouvera que les hommes se ressemblent dans tous les pays: ils n'ont et ne peuvent avoir de différence entre eux, que quelques nuances qu'ils tiennent du climat qu'ils habitent, des Loix qui les gouvernent'. He continues: 'Quoique le climat n'influe pas directement sur la nature de l'homme, il influe tellement sur le caractère, qu'elle en est modifée par contre-coup' (Saint-Non, *Voyage*, I, p. 236).

50 *Ibid.*, pp. 236–7.

51 Richard, *Description*, IV, pp. 224–6. Lalande also describes the opulent and luxurious life of the nobility (Lalande, *Voyage*, VI, pp. 338–9). After his description of the lifestyle of the nobility, Saint-Non makes the comparison that 'Ce même goût pour le répresentation, ce manque absolu d'ordre & d'economie qui ruine les Grands, on le trouve répandu dans les dernières classes du Peuple'(Saint-Non, *Voyage*, I, p. 225, fn. 1).

52 Lalande, *Voyage*, VI, pp. 363–4. Although not making this connection to climate and perhaps more respectful than Lalande to the intellectual traditions of Naples, Richard characterizes scholarship in Naples as one of 'useless digressions and misplaced erudition' (Richard, *Description*, IV, pp. 242–3).

53 For an overview of the reform movement in Naples, see Franco Venturi, 'The Enlightenment in Southern Italy', in Venturi, *Italy and the Enlightenment*, ed. S. Woolf and trans. S. Corsi (London, 1972), pp. 198–224. There is as yet no monograph on the late Neapolitan Enlightenment in any language. For a series of comprehensive introductory essays as well as extracts of reformers' writings, see Franco Venturi, *Riformatori napoletani*, vol. V of *Illuministi italiani* (Milan/Naples, 1962).

54 On the famine of 1763–4 and the ensuing debate among Neapolitan reformers on the problems of maintaining such a populated city, see Petraccone, *Napoli dal cinquecento all'ottocento*, pp. 163–83. On the Italian famines, see also Franco Venturi, *Settecento riformatore*, V(I), (Turin, 1987), ch. II.

55 For a discussion of Genovesi's life and writings, including a useful bibliography and extracts, see Venturi, *Riformatori napoletani*, pp. 3–330. For a more recent account of Genovesi and his place in the historiography of the Neapolitan Enlightenment, see also Giuseppe Galasso, 'Genovesi: il pensiero economico', in *La filosofia in soccorso de' governi: La cultura napoletana del settecento* (Naples, 1989), pp. 401–29.

56 On these themes, see, in particular, chapter 5 of my doctoral dissertation, 'Political culture in late eighteenth-century Naples: The writings of Francesco Mario Pagano', Cambridge University, 1994, which is currently being prepared for publication.

57 Ferdinando Galiani began his career with the publication of *Della moneta* in 1751 in Naples. He was later to become the secretary to the Neapolitan ambassador in Paris and friend to many *philosophes* such as Diderot. He also wrote *Dialogues sur le commerce des blés* (Paris, 1770). For a comprehensive introduction to Galiani's life and writings, see *Opere di Ferdinando Galiani*, ed. F. Diaz and L. Guerci, vol. VI of *Illuministi italiani* (Milan/Naples, 1975). On Galiani's relationship with Diderot, see R. Davison, *Diderot et Galiani: étude d'une amitié philosophique* (Oxford, 1985).

58 Galiani to Antonio Cocchi (Naples, 20 February 1753), in *Opere di Ferdinando Galiani*, pp. 832–3.

59 On travellers to Naples, see Robert Shackleton's suggestive essay, 'Travel and the Enlightenment: Naples as a Specimen', in D. Gilson and M. Smith (eds), *Essays on Montesquieu and on the Enlightenment* (Oxford, 1988), pp. 437–46. On studying the Italian response to travellers, see Bignamini, 'The Grand Tour: Open Issues', in *Grand Tour*, exh. cat. by Wilton and Bignamini (eds), pp. 31–6. For several references to Neapolitan reactions, see also N. Cortese, 'Aspetti e visioni della Napoli del Settecento', in *Napoli Nobilissima*, n.s. II (1921), pp. 104–8 and 152–8.

60 M. L. Pratt, *Imperial Eyes: Travel Writing and Transculturation* (London, 1992), p. 7.

61 As Pratt herself recognizes: *ibid.*, p. 10.

62 For the only complete account of Torcia's life and writings, see A. M. Rao's recent article, 'Un "letterato faticatore" nell'Europa del settecento: Michele Torcia (1736–1808)', *Rivista storica italiana*, 108 (1995), pp. 647–726.

63 For example, Torcia wrote an outline of the political state of Europe, entitled *Sbozzo politico di Europa* (Florence, 1775), and also translated and annotated an account of the commercial activities of the English government by George Grenville as *Stato presente della Nazione inglese* (2 vols, Naples, 1775) (Rao, 'Michele Torcia', pp. 666 and 657).

64 On Torcia's stay in Holland and then between 1767 and 1768 in London, see Rao, 'Michele Torcia', pp. 649–53. Torcia had studied under Antonio Genovesi and corresponded with him during his time away from Naples, providing his mentor with news of new books published in Holland and London (*ibid.*, pp. 649–50).

65 *Ibid.*, pp. 665–6.

66 [Michele Torcia], *Appendice contenente una breva difesa della nostra nazione contro le incolpe attribuitele da alcuni scrittori esteri* (Naples, 1783). This work was published separately as well as together with his *Sbozzo al commercio di Amsterdam*, republished in the same year (Rao, 'Michele Torcia', p. 694).

67 Torcia, 'Note del traduttore', in Grenville, *Stato presente*, pp. XCVIII–C, cited in Rao, 'Michele Torcia', p. 660, fn. 63.

68 Torcia, for example, criticizes Lalande's use of climate to interpret national differences in his *Appendice*, pp. 52–3. See also his comments in *ibid.*, pp. 101–2 and p. 101, fn.(a). An exception was D'Argenson who had understood well the role of the history of bad government in encouraging bad customs in Naples and whom he cites in *ibid.*, p. 53, fn.(a).

69 *Ibid.*, p. 45.

70 Torcia rejects this with equally absurd explanations of a particular illness in Apulia which achieves the same effect and of untended farmer's children mutilated by wild animals (Torcia, *Appendice*, pp. 50–51).

71 Torcia accuses Lalande of having copied this from an English account, in his *Appendice*, p. 52.

72 *Ibid.*, p. 52.

73 Torcia, 'Note del traduttore', in Grenville, *Stato presente*, pp. CXIX–CXX, cited in Rao, 'Michele Torcia', p. 664, fn. 77.

74 *Ibid.*, p. 104.

75 See, for example, Torcia's defence of the contribution of Neapolitan jurists in *Appendice*, p. 61.

76 The full title of Napoli-Signorelli's *Vicende della coltura nelle Due Sicilie* is cited in note 2 above. On the eighteenth century, see *Vicende*, V, pp. 445–572, and his *Supplimento alle Vicende della coltura delle Due Sicilie* (Naples, 1791), VII, pp. 199–205.

77 The most recent study of Napoli-Signorelli's life and works is that by C. G. Mininni, *Pietro Napoli Signorelli* (Città di Castello, 1914). Neglect of Napoli-Signorelli in

Italian historiography stems, in part, from the fact that his works have never been
clearly associated with the reform movement at the end of the century and that he
managed to escape execution, unlike many of his contemporaries, by the Bourbon
government after the failure of the revolution of 1799.

78 As an expression of this cultural revival, see, for instance, Ferdinando Galiani's book,
Del dialetto napoletano [1789], ed. E. Malato (Rome, 1970).

79 Napoli-Signorelli also questioned Lalande's methods, writing:

> Ma se un valentuomo qual è Mr. de la Lande è caduto ne' difetti de' Misson, de
> Sharp, de Grosley e dell'ultimo meschino Sherlock, quando potremo sperare
> che de'oltramonti esca un *Viaggio d'Italia* giudizioso, storico, imparziale, e
> spogliato delle favole de' locandieri ciecamente addotate?' (Napoli-Signorelli,
> *Vicende*, v, pp. 494–5.)

80 *Ibid.*, p. 494.

81 N. Cortese, *Eruditi e giornali letterari nella Napoli del Settecento* (Naples, 1921),
p. 100. Defending Italian poetry against French accusations of plagiarism – an
ongoing debate from the seventeenth century – Vespasiano also criticized Lalande's
recently published *Voyage* in 'Lettre sur un fait de Poesie Italienne, addressée à MM.
les Auteurs du Journal des Scavans; par M. Vispasiani', *Journal des Scavans*, XLI (11),
October 1769, pp. 135–43. In an earlier number, there is a review of Lalande's *Voyage*
in *Journal des Scavans*, XLI (10) (September 1769), pp. 289–92. On the facing page of
this review there is an advertisement for the Amsterdam edition of 1769 of Pilati's
book on the reform of Italy, which links clearly contemporary interest in travel to, as
well as reform in, Italy.

82 On the *Scelta miscellanea*, see Cortese, *Eruditi e giornali*, pp. 97–103.

83 'Articolo I. Lettera al Signor de la Lande della Accademia delle Scienze ec.', *Scelta
miscellanea*, May 1784 (n. v), p. 273.

84 For the passage by Lalande, see note 52 above.

85 'Lettera II. Al Signor de la Lande della Accademia delle Scienza ec.', *Scelta miscellanea*,
June 1784 (n. vi), pp. 358–9.

86 'Continuazione della seconda lettera scritta a M. de la Lande dal Signor Vespasiano',
in *Scelta miscellanea*, July 1784 (n. vii), fn.(a), pp. 432–3.

87 'Lettera II', in *Scelta miscellanea*, June 1784 (n. vi), pp. 360–61.

88 'Articolo I', *Scelta miscellanea*, May 1784 (n. v), p. 283.

89 To the charge that Neapolitans write little that one could actually read (a common
criticism of the rhetorical style and digressions of Italian works in general), Torcia
responds similarly of Montesquieu's intellectual debt to Vico (Torcia, *Appendice*,
p. 61).

90 In Venice, Montesquieu wrote: 'Acheter à Naples: Principi d'una nova [sic] Scienza di
Joan Batista [sic] Vico, Napoli.' (Montesquieu, *Voyages*, p. 65). For the lingering
authority of this accusation of plagiarism, see Croce, *Bibliographia vichiana*, ed.
F. Nicolini (Naples, 1947), i, pp. 283–94.

91 *Scelta miscellanea*, May 1794 (n. v), pp. 273–4, fn. (a).

92 Lalande notes in the preface of the second edition the advice which he received from
Italians as well as French residents in Italy and French travellers to Italy. He listed their
names according to each city. Vespasiano's name appears in the list for Naples along
with Torcia's (Lalande, *Voyage en Italie* (Yverdon, 1787), p. xxviii).

93 The only other comparable occasion was Misson's inclusion of the protests of a
reader in Naples to his characterization of the Neapolitan people as 'very wicked' in a
footnote to a later edition of his work. Misson writes: 'I must say here that a Person of
Distinction wrote to me from Naples, in 1705, to desire I would strike out that Article,
in the next edition of the Book, assuring me that it gave the world a false Idea

of the People of Naples'. Misson, however, is reluctant to believe his reader and refuses to do so (Misson, *A New Voyage to Italy* (London, 1739), vol. I (Pt. II), p. 426, fn.). Of course, this exchange took place by private letter and not through the public forum of a literary journal, as in the case of Vespasiano.

94 A Neapolitan publisher and book-shop owner complained about the article on Naples and warned the publisher of the Italian edition of the *Encyclopédie* that these articles would have 'to be re-written in order to avoid alienating [his] customers' (R. Darnton, *The Business of Enlightenment*, p. 314.). The article on Naples included the usual references to the ancient reputation of the city as a place of pleasure noting an inescapable continuity with the present day: 'Les Napolitains étoient autrefois ce qu'ils sont aujourd'hui, épris de l'amour du repos & de la volupté' (*Encyclopédie ou Dictionnaire raisonné des sciences, des arts, et des métiers* (Neuchâtel, 1765), vol. 11, p. 17). Napoli-Signorelli also protested against the inaccuracies of the article in *Vicende*, I, pp. 179–80.

95 In the rewriting of ancient history, in the same period, with native traditions at the centre, see my article 'Images of Rome in Late Eighteenth-Century Neapolitan Historiography', *Journal of the History of Ideas* (1997), pp. 641–61.

96 *Nuova descrizione storica e geographica delle Sicilie* (4 vols, Naples, 1786–90). There is a manuscript, which was not published during Galanti's lifetime, entitled *Viaggio in Calabria*, which despite its title is similar in organization to his *Descrizione*. This journal has now been published as *Viaggio in Calabria (1792)*, ed. A. Placanica (Naples, 1981).

97 For an introduction to Galanti and his works, see Venturi, *Riformatori napoletani*, pp. 941–83. On his extensive publishing projects, see Maria Luisa Perna, 'Giuseppe Maria Galanti Editore', in *Miscellanea Walter Maturi* (Turin, 1966), pp. 221–58.

98 On the *Descrizione* and feudal reform, see Giuseppe Galasso, 'L'ultimo feudalismo meridionale nell'analisi di Giuseppe Maria Galanti', in *Giuseppe Maria Galanti nella cultura del settecento meridionale* (Naples, 1984), pp. 27–66.

99 In the first edition, Lalande notes that going any farther south than Salerno was not part of his plan (Lalande, *Voyage d'un François*, p. xlii). Although certainly not meant as a practical guidebook, the last three volumes of Richard de Saint-Non's richly engraved description of the Kingdom of the Two Sicilies include the less travelled southern provinces outside of Naples and the island of Sicily: see Saint-Non, *Voyage Pittoresque*, vols 3–5.

100 Galanti, *Breve descrizione di Napoli e del suo Contorno: Da servire di appendice alla Descrizione geografica e politica delle Sicilia* (Naples, 1792).

101 'Avvertimento degli Editori', *ibid.*, pp. v–vi. Saint-Non's *Voyages pittoresque* is also mentioned as particularly inexact. See also Napoli-Signorelli's criticism of Lalande's methods cited above in note 79.

102 'Infatti per opera del clima gli abitanti in ogni età sono dedicati all'ozio e a' divertimenti, ed inclinati agli eccitamenti di allegria e di piacere.' (Galanti, *Breve descrizione*, p. 5). A similar depiction of the *lazzaroni* appears later in the guidebook (*ibid.*, pp. 267–9).

103 See, for instance, *ibid.*, pp. 14–16.

104 Torcia published a very conventional guidebook, despite his earlier criticisms of Lalande, as *Breve cenno di un giro per le province meridionali ed orientali del Regno di Napoli . . . per uso di un Cavaliere Spagnolo* (Naples, 1795). Torcia had already published an earlier book for the tourist market, a parallel French–Italian account of an eruption of Vesuvius, as *Relation de la dernière éruption du Vesuve Arrivée au mois d'Août de cette anneé 1779* (Naples, 1779).

105 Galanti, *Breve descrizione*, p. 14.

106 *Ibid.*, p. 190.

107 See the long section on Science and Letters in *ibid.*, pp. 191–234.

108 'L'aspetto morale di un paese, ch'è quanto dire i costumi, sono quelli che forse più interessano uno spettatore. Essi sono l'opera così delle leggi costituzioali che del clima.' (*ibid.*, p. 265)

109 The passage quoted in note 108 above precedes a section on the customs of Neapolitans which repeats (with a few corrections) the usual stereotypes of the *lazzaroni* and the link with the mild climate which was found in contemporary guidebooks (*ibid.*, pp. 267–9).

110 Galanti writes: 'Lalande intanto pretende, che Parigi abbia oggi il primato nella coltura delle belle arti sull'Italia e sopra l'Europa intera. Vuole che fino la presente scuola francese possa sostenere il paragone colle nostre celebri antichi scuole. Il giudizio sembra essere troppo *patriottico*.' [his italics] (*ibid.*, 253).

111 Herder's reflections on travelling to France from Riga in 1769 show the complexities of recognizing national cultural differences within a cosmopolitan culture dominated by the French, in 'Journal of My Voyage in the Year 1769', in *J. G. Herder on Social and Political Culture*, trans. and ed. F. M. Barnard (Cambridge, 1969), especially Part III, pp. 86–113. On Romantic travel, see the article by Roger Cardinal in *Rewriting the Self: Histories from the Renaissance to the Present*, ed. R. Porter (London, 1997), pp. 135–55.

6 *Michael T. Bravo: Precision and Curiosity in Scientific Travel*

1 C. L. Batten Jr., 'Literary Responses to the Eighteenth Century Voyages', in D. Howse (ed.), *Background to Discovery: Pacific Exploration from Dampier to Cook* (Berkeley and Los Angeles, 1990), pp. 128–59. Quoted material from p. 154.

2 D. Diderot, *Supplement to the Voyage of Bougainville*, translated from French (*Supplement au Voyage de Bougainville*). An excellent study of cultural appropriation and 'Otherness' in the eighteenth century is contained in A. Pagden, *European Encounters with the New World*. . . (New Haven, 1993).

3 The standard guide to sources on Banks is H. B. Carter, *Sir Joseph Banks (1743–1820): A Guide to Biographical and Bibliographical Sources* (London, 1987). Classic biographies of Banks include H. C. Cameron, *Sir Joseph Banks: the Autocrat of Philosophers* (London, 1952) and H. B. Carter, *Sir Joseph Banks, 1743–1820* (London, 1988). An important reassessment of Banks's role in the eighteenth-century intellectual sphere is J. Gascoigne, *Joseph Banks and the English Enlightenment: Useful Knowledge and Polite Culture* (Cambridge, 1994). For some discussion of his work in the context of botany and empire, see D. P. Miller and P. H. Reill (eds), *Visions of Empire: Voyages, Botany, and Representations of Nature* (Cambridge, 1996). A more specific account of his work in relation to the imperial dimension of Kew Gardens is R. Drayton, *Nature's Government* (New Haven, forthcoming).

4 An excellent example of an institutional and intellectual history of precision in eighteenth-century France as it affected engineering and architecture is A. Picon, *French Architects and Engineers in the Age of Enlightenment* (Cambridge, 1992), translated from the French by Martin Thom.

5 Simon Schaffer has developed this theme much more fully in his study of disciplining observers at the Royal Greenwich Observatory under George Airy in the early nineteenth century. See S. Schaffer, 'Astronomers Mark Time: Discipline and the Personal Equation', *Science in Context*, II (1988), pp. 115–45.

6 Simon Schaffer made this point when he contrasted Joseph Banks's endorsement of slavery and control over his draftsmen and engravers with his Linnean contemporary William Fothergill, a dissenting Quaker concerned with practical moral rectitude

and committed to abolitionist values. In his *Travels*, Bartram gives a prominent place to Amerindian manners and political organization proffered as a useful model for other societies, alongside his botanical illustrations of the vegetable tribes: see S. Schaffer, 'Visions of Empire: Afterword', in D. P. Miller and P. H. Reill (eds), *Visions of Empire: Voyages, Botany, and Representations of Nature* (Cambridge, 1996), pp. 335–52; W. Bartram, *Travels through North and South Carolina, Georgia, East and West Florida* (London, 1792).

7 An excellent study of science, tourism and travel literature in this period is to be found in R. Hamblyn, 'Landscape and the Contours of Knowledge: The Literature and the Sciences of the Earth in Eighteenth-Century Britain', PhD dissertation, Cambridge, 1994. The classic study of the aesthetics of Cook and Pacific exploration is B. Smith, *European Vision and the South Pacific, 1768–1850: A Study in the History of Art and Ideas* (1st edn Oxford, 1960; 2nd edn New Haven, 1985). The best treatment of aesthetics, precision and travel for the period 1800–20 is M. Dettelbach, 'Romanticism and Administration: Mining, Galvanism and Oversight in Alexander von Humboldt's Global Physics', PhD dissertation, Cambridge, 1992.

8 T. Kuhn, *The Structure of Scientific Revolutions*, 2nd edn (Chicago, 1970).

9 C. R. Markham, *Major James Rennell and the Rise of Modern English Geography* (London, 1895), pp. 77–81.

10 I have borrowed the term 'imagined community' loosely from the revised and extended version of B. Anderson, *Imagined Communities: Reflections on the Origin and Spread of Nationalism* (London, 1991).

11 The term 'openness' captures Rennell's utilitarian sentiments very well. Rennell and other democrats of his time linked transparency of knowledge to the foundations for a reformed, democratic state.

12 J.-P. Rubiés, 'Instructions for Travellers: Teaching the Eye to See', *History and Anthropology*, 9 (1996), p. 142.

13 *Ibid.*, p. 140.

14 *Ibid.*, pp. 139–42.

15 Smith 1985, p. 8.

16 To what extent these river surveys were actually an effective instrument for the Company's subsequent revenue surveys, and to what extent their value lay in the rhetoric of utility, is tied up in the wider political questions concerning the Company Directors' loss of control, the Company's difficulty in disengaging its commitments from regional politics, and the accumulation of the massive balance of payments deficit. Chris Bayly and Matthew Edney have each made comprehensive studies of the social history of the Indian surveys and the racial politics of information-gathering, respectively, in India. See C. A. Bayly, *Empire and Information: Intelligence Gathering and Social Communication in India, 1780–1870* (Cambridge, 1997); M. Edney, *Mapping an Empire: The Geographic Construction of British India, 1765–1843* (Chicago, 1997). I am especially grateful to Chris Bayly for sharing unpublished essays on the cultural politics of science in India and to Matthew Edney for allowing me to read large sections of his book while still at proofs stage. A beautifully crafted and researched copy of the *Bengal Atlas* has been prepared: A. S. Cook (ed.), *Major James Rennell and a Bengal Atlas, 1780 and 1781* (London, 1976). There are useful references to Rennell in Z. Baber, *The Science of Empire: Scientific Knowledge, Civilization and Colonial Rule in India* (Albany, New York, 1996).

17 This account revises Harlow's portrayal of the 'Second British Empire' as a period of relatively benign neo-mercantilism. Bayly, Majeed (1992) and others have stressed the growth of colonial administration, the development of Orientalist scholarship and mythography by William Jones as a vehicle of legal reform and the creation of the learned Asiatic societies, the removal of indigenous leaders from positions of power

and the importance of empire as a theatre for the growth of nationalism. See C. A. Bayly, *Imperial Meridian: The British Empire and the World 1780–1830* (London, 1989), pp. 8–9; V. Harlow, *The Founding of the Second British Empire, 1763–1793* (London, 1952). See also Edney (n. 20); J. Majeed, *Ungoverned Imaginings: James Mill's the History of British India and Orientalism* (Oxford, 1992); J. Rendall, 'Scottish Orientalism: from Robertson to James Mill', *Historical Journal*, 25 (1982), 43–69.

18 Vicziany has shown that the botanical travels in Mysore of Francis Buchanan, a Scottish surgeon, were performed as part of a wider survey for the benefit and patronage of Lord Wellesley, in need of evidence to justify his invasion. These studies and others illustrate very well how precisely conducted surveys and studies were employed for different purposes in the service of the colonizing project. See M. Vicziany, 'Imperialism, Botany and Statistics in Early Nineteenth-Century India: The Surveys of Francis Buchanan (1762–1829)', *Modern Asian Studies*, 20 (1986), pp. 625–60, P3.

19 Bodleian Library, Oxford. Rennell manuscripts, Box 6.

20 *Ibid.*

21 See Edney (1996), (n. 20).

22 J. Gascoigne, in *Joseph Banks and the English Enlightenment: Useful Knowledge and Polite Culture* (Cambridge, 1994), provides a rounded and incisive discussion of Banks, focusing broadly on different aspects of his intellectual world. H. Carter's biography, *Sir Joseph Banks, 1743–1820* (London, 1988), is wide-ranging and voluminous. Banks, though a great patron of travel in many forms, wrote comparatively little on the subject and published even less, and consequently relatively little has been said about his views on travel literature. However, his own library's holdings of travel literature, now housed in the British Library, are very extensive and deserve further study.

23 J. Majeed, *Ungoverned Imaginings: James Mill's the History of British India and Orientalism* (Oxford, 1992), pp. 11–46. The principal source on Henry Thomas Colebrooke is the biography by T. E. Colebrooke, *The Life of H. T. Colebrooke* (London, 1873).

24 Markham (London, 1895; pp. 106–21, 171–92) points out the extent of Rennell's reliance on his classically-trained friends in the chapters dealing with his Oriental geography. Also relevant is Markham 1895, pp. 122–45. Of Rennell's several published books in this area, his mostly widely recognized was J. Rennell, *The Geographical System of Herodotus Examined and Explained, by a Comparison with Those of Other Ancient Authors, and with Modern Geography* (London, 1800).

25 The most recent popular account of Harrison as scientific hero is D. Sobel, *Longitude: the true story of a lone genius who solved the greatest scientific problem of his time* (London, 1995). A more rigorous account, but in the same heroic vein, is W. S. Laycock, *The Lost Science of John "Longitude" Harrison* (Brant Wright Associates, 1976). A better account of the fight between Harrison and Maskelyne, the Astronomer Royal who championed astronomical methods, is given in D. Howse, *Greenwich Time: and the Discovery of the Longitude* (Oxford, 1980). All of the above fail to pay much attention to the imperial context.

26 Markham 1895, p. 9.

27 Jan Golinski (in Wise 1995, pp. 86–7) gives an example of this in his study of Nicholson's precision chemistry (also in the late eighteenth century). To endorse a measurement as 'sufficiently exact' by showing only one decimal place implied 'a vision of the community of experimenters in which resources were to be as accessible as possible'.

Though Rennell was less the religious dissenter and less ardent a political reformer than Priestley, he nonetheless wished the establishment institutions of his day to be more inclusive, with scientific merit as the arbiter of eligibility. Priestley and

Rennell also illustrate how differently dissent could be displayed in the context of Unitarianism in England itself and in that of Company politics in India, distanced from the metropolis. Rennell's political views, which, according to Markham, were democratic, anti-corruption and free thinking in regard to religious dogma, were consistent with his commitment to provide transferable, reliable information for the management of the empire.

28 T. Richards, *The Imperial Archive: Knowledge and the Fantasy of Empire* (London and New York, 1993).

29 The term 'anti-conquest' was coined by Marie-Louise Pratt, who construes this absence in terms of visualization and imagination. For example, she writes (Pratt 1992, p. 59):

> As with his predecessors, Barrow's account by and large separates Africans from Africa (and Europeans from Africans) by relegating the latter to objectified ethnographic portraits set off from the narrative of the journey . . . Visual details are interspersed with technical and classificatory information. The travellers are chiefly present as a kind of collective moving eye on which the sights/sites register; as agents their presence is very reduced.

30 A further study could look at the relationship between cartographic memoirs and memoirs in other sciences such as mineralogy, botany or zoology.

31 J. Rennell, 'On the Rate of Travelling, as Performed by Camels; and its Application, as a Scale, to the Purposes of Geography', *Philosophical Transactions*, 81 (1791), pp. 129–45.

32 *Ibid.*, pp. 140–41.

33 *Ibid.*, p. 130.

34 *Ibid.*, p. 132.

35 *Ibid.*, p. 131.

36 British Library, Add. MS 32,439, fol. 355. James Rennell to Joseph Banks.

7 Nigel Leask: 'The Ghost in Chapultepec'

1 In this the *Political Essay* was quite distinct from Humboldt's monumental South American travelogue, the unfinished *Personal Narrative of Travels to the Equinoctial Regions of the New Continent* (translated into English between 1814 and 1826 by Helen María Williams), which did not deal with Mexico at all. See my essay 'Helen María Williams, Alexander von Humboldt and the Discourse of Romantic Travel', forthcoming in *Women and the Public Sphere*, ed. Warburton, Grant, Eger *et al.* (Manchester University Press).

2 Barbara María Stafford, *Voyage into Substance: Art, Science, Nature, and the Illustrated Travel Account 1760–1840* (Cambridge, MA, and London, 1984), particularly p. 442; Charles Batten, *Pleasureable Instruction: Form and Convention in 18th Century Travel Literature* (Berkeley, Los Angeles, London, 1978), *passim.*

3 Mary Louise Pratt, *Imperial Eyes: Travel Writing and Transculturation* (London and New York, 1992), p. 146.

4 William Bullock, *Six Months' Residence and Travels in Mexico, Containing Remarks on the Present State of New Spain, Its Natural Productions, State of Society, Manufactures, Trade, Agriculture, and Antiquities, etc.* (London, 1824), p. 130.

5 *Mexico, by Henry Ward, Esq. His Majesty's Charge d'Affaires in that Country during the Years 1825, 1826, and part of 1827. Second Edition, enlarged, with an account of the Mining Companies, and of the Political Events in that Republic, to the Present Day,* 2 vols (London, 1829), II, pp. 17, 37.

6 *The Correspondence of William Hickling Prescott 1833–47*, transcribed and edited by Roger Wolcott (Cambridge, MA, 1925), April 31st 1842, p. 315.

7 *Blackwood's Edinburgh Magazine* (1828), quoted in Pratt, p. 170.

8 *Quarterly Review*, LXXVI (June and Sept. 1845), p. 99.

9 When he does make an appearance, Fanny tends to be impatient with his scholarly obsessions: 'Calderón indulged his botanical and geological propensities, occasionally to the great detriment of his companions, as we were anxious to arrive at some resting place before the sun became insupportable'. *Life in Mexico: The Letters of Fanny Calderón de la Barca, with new material from the author's private journal*, edited and annotated by Howard T. Fisher and Marion Hall Fisher (New York, 1966), p. 396; hereafter referred to as *Life*.

10 Pratt, pp. 158–9.

11 Quoted in Antonello Gerbi, *La Disputa del Nuevo Mundo: Historia de una Polémica 1750–1900* [original text published in Italian in 1955, Spanish translation in 1982] (Mexico, 1982), p. 597. English edn: *The Dispute of the New World* (Pittsburgh, 1973).

12 Fanny Calderón, *Life*, p. 109.

13 *Ibid.*, pp. 449–50.

14 *Ibid.*, p. 133.

15 *Ibid.*, p. 137.

16 *Ibid.*, p. 133.

17 *Ibid.*, p. 444.

18 *Ibid.*, p. 445.

19 Alexander von Humboldt, *Political Essay on the Kingdom of New Spain*, translated from the original French by John Black (London, 1811), p. 172.

20 See Fanny Calderón, *Life*, pp. 420–21, for a character sketch of Carlos Bustamante.

21 Quoted by David Brading in *The First America: The Spanish Monarchy, Creole Patriots, and the Liberal State 1492–1867* (Cambridge, 1991), pp. 634–5.

22 Brading, pp. 641–2; Anthony Pagden, 'Identity Formation in Spanish America', in *Colonial Identity in the Atlantic World*, ed. Nicholas Canny and Antony Pagden (Princeton, 1993), pp. 66–8.

23 Fernanda Núñez Becerra, *La Malinche: De la Historia al Mito* (Mexico, Instituto Nacional de Antropología e Historia, 1996), p. 79.

24 Quoted in Brading, p. 630.

25 William Hickling Prescott, *The Conquest of Mexico*, 2 vols (Everyman's Library, London, n.d.), I, p. 35.

26 Whilst the Mexican translation of Prescott's *Conquest of Mexico* was welcomed by *criollo* intellectuals as a break with the triumphalist tradition of Spanish historiography, José Fernando Ramírez criticized Prescott's over-use of such terms as 'savage' and 'barbarian' to describe the Aztec armies as well as his marked Protestant bias. Cf. Fernanda Núñez Bercerra, *La Malinche*, pp. 48–50, and Brading, p. 634.

27 *Quarterly Review*, LXXVI (June–Sept. 1845), p. 116.

28 In this light it is interesting that Fanny invoked the sibylline authority of another undomesticated and cosmopolitan woman writer, Germaine De Staël, to authorize her excursions over the boundaries of allowable female discourse. As a prelude to her detailed political commentary on the Mexican *pronunciamiento* of July 1840 Fanny cited Madame De Staël's sarcastic objection to the ban on women writing about politics (*Life*, p. 315):

> when a woman's head is about to be cut off, it is natural she should ask: *Why?* . . . when bullets are whizzing about our ears, and shells falling within a few yards of us, it ought to be considered extremely natural, and quite feminine, to inquire into the cause of such phenomena.

29 *Life*, p. 329.

30 *Life*, p. 450.

31 Brading, p. 642.

32 *Life*, p. 470.
33 Pratt, p. 160.
34 *Life*, p. 364.
35 *Life*, p. 69.
36 Sara Suleri, *The Rhetoric of British India* (London, 1992), p. 76.
37 *Life*, p. 175.
38 *Life*, p. 239.
39 *Life*, p. 240.
40 *Ibid.*
41 The conventional notion of picturesque disinterestedness – as Elizabeth Bohls has recently argued, a discourse designed 'to display and reinforce master' by naturalizing ideologies of landownership – is thus reinflected here by Fanny's intervention as a female aesthetic subject and, through her 'colonial' situation, its ideological meaning reversed. Elizabeth Bohls, *Woman Travel Writers and the Language of Aesthetics 1716–1818* (Cambridge, 1995), p. 87.
42 Quoted in Malcolm Andrews, *The Search for the Picturesque: Landscape Aesthetics and Tourism in Britain 1760–1800* (Aldershot, 1989), p. 58.
43 Prescott's *Correspondence*, p. 127.
44 *Life*, p. 216.
45 Pratt, p. 149.
46 *Life*, p. 335.
47 *Ibid.*
48 *Life*, p. 216.
49 *Life*, p. 335.
50 *Life*, p. 194.
51 Alan Liu, *Wordsworth: the Sense of History* (Stanford, 1990), p. 120.
52 Bernal Díaz del Castillo, *The Conquest of New Spain*, translated with an introduction by J. M. Cohen (Harmondsworth, 1963), p. 214.
53 Bullock, p. 123.
54 Ward, II, p. 35.
55 *Ibid.*, II, p. 39.
56 *Life*, p. 87.
57 *Life*, pp. 87–8.
58 *Madoc*, Part II, book xxiv, *Southey's Poetical Works, Complete in One Volume* (London, n.d.), p. 408.
59 *Life*, p. 88.
60 Prescott, *Conquest*, II, p. 79.
61 *Ibid.*, I, p. 23.
62 *Ibid.*, I, p. 87.
63 For example, at I, pp. 83, 270, 336; II, p. 223.
64 Hugh Thomas, *The Conquest of Mexico* (London, 1993), p. xiv.
65 Brading, p. 643.
66 *Correspondence*, p. 115.
67 *Correspondence*, p. 329.
68 *Correspondence*, p. 120.
69 Brading, p. 631; 54.
70 Prescott, II, p. 161.
71 Stephen Bann, 'The Sense of the Past: Image, Text and Object in the Formation of Historical Consciousness in 19th century Britain', in *The New Historicism*, ed. H. Aram Veeser (London, 1989), p. 74.
72 *Ibid.*, p. 111.
73 Pratt, p. 148.

74 Stephen Bann (ed.), 'Introduction', in *Frankenstein, Creation and Monstrosity* (London, 1994), pp. 7–13.
75 Bullock, *Six Months' Residence*, p. 272.
76 *Ibid.*, p. 483.
77 *Correspondence*, p. 239.
78 John L. Stephens, *Incidents of Travel in Central America, Chiapas & Yucatan* (1841; London, 1988), p. 57.
79 Prescott, *Conquest*, I, p. 211.
80 *Quarterly Review*, LXXVI (June–Sept. 1845), p. 98.
81 *Correspondence*, p. 150.
82 *Correspondence*, p. 240.
83 *Life*, p. 12.
84 *Correspondence*, p. 128.
85 *Life*, p. 357.
86 *Life*, p. 357.
87 *Life*, p. 748, note 3, and *Correspondence*, pp. 116–17, 122, 128.
88 *Conquest*, I, p. 212.
89 *Conquest*, II, p. 327, but see also I, p. 367, where Prescott builds on Fanny's description of Chapultepec without citing her.
90 *Life*, p. 114.
91 *Conquest*, I, p. 367.
92 *Life*, p. 114.
93 Fernanda Núñez Becerra, *La Malinche*, pp. 21–41.
94 Thomas, *Conquest of Mexico*, p. 173.
95 Quoted in *ibid.*, p. 173.
96 Jean Franco, 'La Malinche y el Primer Mundo', in Margo Glanz (ed.), *La Malinche sus Padres y sus Hijos* (UNAM, Mexico, 1994), pp. 157–8 (whence the quote); 165.
97 *Life*, p. 114.
98 *Life*, p. 401.
99 *Byron's Poetical Works*, p. 242.
100 Becerra, p. 107; Prescott, *Conquest*, II, p. 327.
101 *Correspondence*, p. 251.
102 *Correspondence*, pp. 315, 329.
103 *Conquest*, II, p. 327.
104 Becerra, pp. 106–7.
105 *Conquest*, II, p. 327.

8 Peter H. Hansen: Partners

This article was made possible by fellowships from the National Endowment for the Humanities and Clare Hall, Cambridge. I am grateful for helpful comments at the Anthropology of Travel conference in Cambridge and from Jas Elsner, Sherry Ortner and Joan-Pau Rubiés.

1 Leslie Stephen, *The Playground of Europe* (London, 1871), pp. 73–4.
2 Leslie Stephen, 'Alpine Climbing', in *British Sports and Pastimes*, ed. Anthony Trollope (London, 1868), pp. 274–5.
3 See James Buzard, *The Beaten Path: European Tourism, Literature, and the Ways to Culture, 1800-1918* (Oxford, 1993), and Peter H. Hansen, 'Albert Smith, the Alpine Club, and the Invention of Mountaineering in Mid-Victorian Britain', *Journal of British Studies* XXXIV (1995), pp. 300–24.
4 Stephen, *Playground of Europe*, p. 76.
5 See Peter H. Hansen, 'Vertical Boundaries, National Identities: British Mountain-

eering on the Frontiers of Europe and the Empire, 1868–1914', *Journal of Imperial and Commonwealth History*, XXIV (1996), pp. 48–71, and Peter H. Hansen, 'The Dancing Lamas of Everest: Cinema, Orientalism, and Anglo-Tibetan Relations in the 1920s', *American Historical Review*, CI (1996), pp. 712–47.

6 See Peter H. Hansen, 'Tenzing's Two Wrist-Watches: the Conquest of Everest and Late Imperial Culture, 1921–1953: Comment', *Past and Present*, 157 (1997), pp. 159–77, Peter H. Hansen's unpublished essay, 'Confetti of Empire: the Conquest of Everest in Nepal, India, Britain and New Zealand', as well as the television programme 'Hillary and Tenzing: Everest and After', broadcast on BBC2, 18 June 1997.

7 Tenzing Norgay, *Man of Everest: the Autobiography of Tenzing told to James Ramsay Ullman* (London, 1955), p. 266.

8 See Valene Smith (ed.), *Hosts and Guests: the Anthropology of Tourism,* 2nd edn (Philadelphia, 1989), Mary Louise Pratt, *Imperial Eyes: Travel Writing and Trans-culturation* (London, 1992), and James Clifford, *Routes: Travel and Translation in the Late Twentieth Century* (Cambridge, MA, 1997).

9 Victor Turner and Edith Turner, *Image and Pilgrimage in Christian Culture* (Oxford, 1978), and John Eade and Michael J. Sallnow (eds), *Contesting the Sacred: The Anthropology of Christian Pilgrimage* (London, 1991), p. 5.

10 C. D. Cunningham and W. de W. Abney (eds), *Pioneers of the Alps* (London, 1888), p. iii. See also Francis Gribble, 'Mountaineering as a Profession', *Idler*, XXIII (1903), pp. 131–7, Louis Spiro, *Guides de Montagnes* (Lausanne, 1928), Carl Egger, *Pionere der Alpen: 30 Lebensbilder der Grossen Schweizer Bergführer von Melchior Anderegg bis Franz Lochmatter, 1827–1933* (Zurich, 1946), and Ronald W. Clark, *The Early Alpine Guides* (London, 1949).

11 *Alpine Journal*, I (1863), p. 44.

12 Cunningham and Abney, *Pioneers of the Alps*, p. 89.

13 See Erik Cohen, 'The Tourist Guide: the Origins, Structure and Dynamics of a Role', *Annals of Tourism Research*, XII(1985), pp. 5–29.

14 See Daniel Chaubet, *Histoire de la Compagnie des Guides de Chamonix* (Mont-mélian, 1994).

15 Alfred Wills, *Wanderings Among the High Alps* (London, 1856), p. 330.

16 Wills, *Wanderings Among the High Alps*, pp. 269, 277, 290–01, 311.

17 F. Vaughan Hawkins, 'Partial Ascent of the Matterhorn', in *Vacation Tourists and Notes on Travel in 1860*, ed. Francis Galton (London,1861), p. 291.

18 Joseph Bennen to John Tyndall, 21 July 1861, B48, Alpine Club Archives, London.

19 *Athenaeum* (14 December 1861), p. 808.

20 John Tyndall in J. J. Bennen, *Führerbuch*, 3 September [1861], K15/12, Alpine Club Archives, London.

21 *Alpine Journal*, XXIX (1915), pp. 68, 72.

22 See *Reglement für die Bergführer und Träger*, 12 May 1856, in surviving *Führerbücher* such as *A Facsimile of Christian Almer's Führerbuch, 1856–1894* (London, 1896). Other *Führerbücher* are held in the Alpine Club, London, the Swiss Alpine Club collection, Zurich, the Museo Nazionale della Montagne, Turin, and in microfilm M421–2, British Library, London.

23 Quoted in Clark, *Early Alpine Guides*, p. 41.

24 Quoted in Cunningham and Abney, *Pioneers of the Alps*, pp. 97–8.

25 Christian Kluckner, *Adventures of an Alpine Guide* (London, 1932), pp. 10–11.

26 For the Chamonix rules, see Chaubet, *Histoire de la Compagnie de Guides de Chamonix*, and C. E. Mathews, *Annals of Mont Blanc* (London, 1898), pp. 248–60. For the Alpine Club petitions, see John Ball, to Marquis d'Azeglio, n.d. [1858], AC3S 1, Alpine Club Archives, London, and *Alpine Journal*, VI (1874), pp. 425–6.

27 Michael G. Mullhall, *Mullhall's Dictionary of Statistics* (London, 1884), p. 453.

28 See Jemima Morrell, *Miss Jemima's Swiss Journal: the First Conducted Tour of Switzerland* (London, 1963).

29 'Organisation des compagnies de guides', *Annuaire du Club Alpin Français*, VII (1880), p. 604.

30 C. D. Cunningham, 'The Decline of Chamonix as a Mountaineering Centre', *Alpine Journal*, XI (1884), pp. 459–71.

31 See Dominique Lejeune, *Les 'alpinistes' en France à la fin du XIXe et au début du XXe siècle (vers 1875–1919)* (Paris, 1988), and Rainer Armstädter, *Der Alpinismus: Kultur, Organisation, Politik* (Vienna, 1996).

32 Compare F. C. Grove, 'Comparative Skill of Travellers and Guides', *Alpine Journal*, V (1872), pp. 87–95, and C. T. Dent, 'Amateurs and Professional Guides of the Present Day', *Alpine Journal*, XII (1886), pp. 289–300.

33 Arthur Cust, 'The Matterhorn Without Guides', *Alpine Journal*, VIII (1877), pp. 244–7.

34 A. F. Mummery, *My Climbs in the Alps and Caucasus* (London, 1895), pp. 110–11.

35 G. W. Young, *Mountain Craft* (London, 1920), pp. 125, 128, 136–7.

36 See John Marsh, 'The Rocky and Selkirk Mountains and the Swiss Connection, 1885–1914', *Annals of Tourism Research*, XII (1985), p. 428, and Beat Nobs, *Vom Eiger in die Rockies: Berner Oberlander Bergführer im Dienste der Canadian Pacific Railway* (Berne, 1987).

37 *Alpine Journal*, XXIX (1915), pp. 58–9.

38 'The Millionaire Guide', in Conrad Kain, *Where Clouds Can Go* (New York, 1935), pp. 427–42.

39 *Alpine Journal*, XX (1900), p. 150.

40 Christian Kluckner, *Erinnerungen eines Bergführers* (Zurich, 1930) and *Adventures of an Alpine Guide* (London, 1932).

41 Mattias Zurbriggen, *From the Alps to the Andes: Being the Autobiography of a Mountain Guide* (London, 1899), pp. 38, 41, 50, and Felice Benuzzi, *Mattias Zurbriggen, Guida Alpina: Le sue imprese, i suoi uomini, i suoi monti* (Turin, 1987).

42 Zurbriggen, *From the Alps to the Andes*, p. 260. He committed suicide in 1917.

43 On the exclusion of Swiss climbers, see Unsworth, *Everest,* pp. 22, 38, and Alan Hankinson, *Geoffrey Winthrop Young* (London, 1995), p. 227.

44 Dane Kennedy, *The Magic Mountains: Hill Stations of the British Raj* (Berkeley, 1996), Sherry Ortner, *High Religion: A Cultural and Political History of Sherpa Buddhism* (Princeton, 1989).

45 T. H. Somervell, *After Everest* (London, 1936), p. 64.

46 C. G. Bruce, 'Third Everest Expedition', *Times* (28 January 1924).

47 E. F. Norton, *The Fight for Everest: 1924* (London, 1925), p. 39.

48 Ang Tharkay, *Mémoires d'un Sherpa* (Paris, 1954), p. 47.

49 Tenzing Norgay, *Man of Everest*, pp. 39–40, 42.

50 F. S. Smythe, *The Kangchenjunga Adventure* (London, 1930), pp. 97, 341–2.

51 T. G. Longstaff, 'In Memoriam, Chettan', *Himalayan Journal*, III (1931), p. 117. See also Kenneth Mason, *Abode of Snow* (London, 1955), pp. 187–8, and Smythe, *Kanchenjunga Adventure*, pp. 254–6.

52 F. S. Smythe, *Kamet Conquered* (London, 1932), pp. 96, 205.

53 Mason, *Abode of Snow*, p. 202.

54 Fritz Bechtold, *Nanga Parbat Adventure: a Himalayan Expedition* (London, 1935), p. 51.

55 Tenzing, *Man of Everest*, p. 51. On Ang Tsering, see Champak Chatterjee, 'Ang Tsering', *Himalayan Journal*, LII (1996), pp. 186–90.

56 See *Himalayan Journal*, XXV (1976–8), p. 17. On these Sherpas, see *Himalayan Journal*, VII (1935), pp. 159–60; VIII (1936), pp. 175–6; VIII (1936), p. 179; IX (1937), pp. 198–202, XII (1940), pp. 155–6; XVI (1950–51), pp. 132–3.

57 *Himalayan Journal*, XII (1940), p. 141; XI (1939), p. 217; XVI (1950–51), pp. 121–33; and XXVII (1966), pp. 188–9.

58 For the obituaries of these Sherpas, see *Himalayan Journal*, X (1938), pp. 189–92; and XII (1940), pp. 134–6.

59 Tenzing, *Man of Everest*, pp. 60, 35, 50, 72, 111, 197, 208, 205; and Tashi Tenzing interview.

60 Tenzing, *Man of Everest*, p. 140.

61 Henderson to Hunt, 2 January 1953, telegram; EE/68/Himalayan Club file, Royal Geographical Society Archives, London. See also Tenzing, *Man of Everest*, p. 222.

62 Tenzing, *Man of Everest*, p. 227. Also EE/68/Himalayan Club file, RGS Archives.

63 Stanley F. Stevens, *Claiming the High Ground* (Berkeley, 1993), p. 359.

64 See Hansen, 'Confetti of Empire', and Hansen, 'Tenzing's Two Wrist-Watches'.

65 See Tenzing, *Man of Everest*, pp. 270, 315; Unsworth, *Everest*, p. 337; 'Hillary and Tenzing: Everest and After'; and Edmund Hillary interview.

66 *Himalayan Journal*, XVIII (1954), pp. 191–2; James F. Fisher, *Sherpas: Reflections on Change in Himalayan Nepal* (Berkeley, 1990), p. 117; and Vijay Jung Thapa, 'Lords of Everest,' *India Today*, XXII (7 July 1997), pp. 54–6.

67 *Independent on Sunday* (24 March 1991), p. 46.

68 See Vincanne Adams, *Tigers of the Snow and Other Virtual Sherpas: an Ethnography of Himalayan Encounters* (Princeton, 1996), Vincanne Adams, 'Dreams of a Final Sherpa', *American Anthropologist*, XCIX (1997), pp. 85–98, Sherry Ortner, *Making Gender: the Politics and Erotics of Culture* (Boston, 1996), pp. 181–212, Sherry Ortner, 'Thick Resistance: Death and the Cultural Construction of Agency in Himalayan Mountaineering', *Representations*, 59 (1997), pp. 135–62, and Pierre L. van den Berghe, *The Quest for the Other: Ethnic Tourism in San Christobal, Mexico* (Seattle, 1994).

69 See Jon Krakauer, *Into Thin Air* (New York, 1997).

9 Kasia Boddy: The European Journey in Postwar American Fiction and Film

1 The title of the first section of *Tristes Tropiques* (Paris, 1955), translated by John and Doreen Weightman (London, 1973).

2 Paul Fussell, *Abroad: British Literary Travelling Between the Wars* (Oxford, 1980), p. 41.

3 Fussell is drawing on Daniel Boorstin's concept of 'pseudo events'. See *The Image: A Guide to Pseudo-Events in America* (Harmondsworth, 1963). Boorstin writes that, 'while an "adventure" was originally "that which happens without design; chance, hap, luck", now in common usage it is primarily a contrived experience that somebody is trying to sell us' (p. 86).

4 See Jean Baudrillard's seminal discussion on the re-creation of France's prehistoric Lascaux caves in *Simulations*, trans. Philip Beitchmann (New York, 1983). See also *America*, trans. Chris Turner (London, 1988), and 'Simulacra and Simulations', in *Selected Writings*, ed. Mark Poster (London, 1988), and Umberto Eco, 'Travels in Hyperreality' (1975), in *Faith in Fakes*, trans. William Weaver (London, 1986), pp. 3–58.

5 P. J. O'Rourke, 'The Innocents Abroad, updated', in *Holidays in Hell* (London, 1989), pp. 15–21 (p. 19).

6 *If It's Tuesday, It Must Be Belgium* (1969), directed by Mel Stuart.

7 George Ritzer, *The McDonaldization of Society* (Thousand Oaks and London, 1993), p. 83.

8 Other brand names are also ubiquitous. Some talk of 'Coca-colonization', while Boorstin quotes Conrad Hilton as saying that each of the hotels in his chain is 'a little America', *Image*, p. 106.

9 Paul Theroux, 'Stranger on a Train: The Pleasures of Railways' (1976), in *Sunrise with Seamonsters* (Harmondsworth, 1986), pp. 126–35 (p. 133).

10 Anne Tyler, *The Accidental Tourist* (1985) (London, 1995), p. 10. In 1996 McDonalds's advertisements in London showed a picture of a hamburger accompanied by the slogan, 'A Taste of Home', in all the main tourist languages.

11 'Stranger on a Train', p. 135.

12 Dean MacCannell, *The Tourist: A New Theory of the Leisure Class* (New York, 1976). For a discussion of the fine line between 'mass' and 'alternative' tourists, see David Zurick, *Errant Journeys: Adventure Travel in a Modern Age* (Austin, TX, 1995).

13 *Tristes Tropiques*, p. 43; *Abroad*, p. 49.

14 For an idealized view of such transformation drawing on anthropological notions of initiation, ritual and liminality see Victor Turner and Edith Turner, *Image and Pilgrimage in Christian Culture: Anthropological Perspectives* (Oxford, 1978).

15 Thomas Pynchon, *V* (1963) (London, 1975), pp. 408–9.

16 Victor and Edith Turner argue that the phenomenon of pilgrimage, particularly religious pilgrimage, has increased in recent times because:

> . . . it has become an implicit critique of the life-style characteristic of the encompassing social structure. Its emphasis on transcendental, rather than mundane, ends and means; its generation of communitas; its search for the roots of ancient, almost vanishing virtues as the underpinnings of social life, even in its structured expressions – all have contributed to the dramatic resurgence of pilgrimage.

Image and Pilgrimage in Christian Culture: Anthropological Perspectives, p. 38. For a critical discussion of Turner's notion of communitas see John Eade and Michael J. Sallnow (eds), *Contesting the Scene: The Anthropology of Christian Pilgrimage* (London, 1991). In their introduction (pp. 1–29), Eade and Sallnow argue that, 'a recurrent theme throughout the [pilgrimage] literature is the maintenance and, in many cases, the reinforcement of social boundaries and distinctions in the pilgrimage context, rather than their attenuation or dissolution' (p. 5).

17 For a different view on the relationship between tourism and pilgrimage see Zygmunt Bauman, 'From Pilgrim to Tourist – or a short history of identity', in *Questions of Cultural Identity*, ed. Stuart Hall and Paul du Gay (London, 1996), pp. 18–36.

18 Martin H. Bush, *Duane Hanson* (Wichita, 1976), p. 38. For a discussion of Hanson's sculptures as examples of what he calls 'hyperrealism', see Fredric Jameson, 'The Cultural Logic of Late Capitalism', in *Postmodernism, or, The Cultural Logic of Late Capitalism* (London, 1991).

> Your moment of doubt and hesitation as to the breadth and warmth of these polyester figures . . . tends to return upon the real human beings moving about you in the museum and to transform them also for the briefest instant into so many dead and flesh-coloured simulacra in their own right. (p. 34)

19 While Pynchon argues that identical lowest common denominator responses arise from and are fundamental to tourism, Roland Barthes finds infinitely open responses to be provoked by a particular tourist sight, the Eiffel Tower. 'The Eiffel Tour', in *The Barthes Reader*, ed. Susan Sontag (London, 1982), pp. 236–50.

20 The painting, which is held in Wolverhampton Art Gallery, is reproduced and discussed in Michael Liversidge and Catherine Edwards (eds), *Imagining Rome: British Artists and Rome in the Nineteenth Century* (London, 1996), p. 100.

21 *Abroad*, p. 39. See Cora Kaplan's discussion of these 'levels of virtue' in *Questions of Travel: Postmodern Discourses of Displacement* (Durham, NC, 1996), p. 56.

22 *Abroad*, p. 43.

23 Walter Benjamin, 'The Work of Art in the Age of Mechanical Reproduction', in *Illuminations*, ed. Hannah Arendt, trans. Harry Zohn (New York, 1969), pp. 217–51 (p. 221).

24 Susan Sontag, *On Photography* (Harmondsworth, 1979), p. 9.

25 Don DeLillo, *White Noise* (London, 1985), pp. 12–13. A similar preference for signifier over signified is found in Italo Calvino's *Invisible Cities* when Marco Polo notes that in the city of Muarila, 'If the traveler does not wish to disappoint the inhabitants, he must praise the postcard city [the city as it used to be] and prefer it to the present one . . .': *Invisible Cities*, trans. William Weaver (London, 1974), p. 26.

26 Jacques Derrida, 'Envois' in *The Postcard: From Socrates to Freud and Beyond*, trans. Alan Bass (Chicago, 1987), pp. 11, 9. While usually considered a philosophical essay, the piece has, perhaps more accurately, been described by Allan Megill as a 'brilliantly funny epistolary novel'. See *Prophets of Extremity: Nietzsche, Heidegger, Foucault, Derrida* (Berkeley and Los Angeles, 1985), p. 267. For an account of the role of the letter, and other genres, within travel writing, see Percy G. Adams, *Travel Literature and the Evolution of the Novel* (Lexington, 1983), p. 43.

27 *Motion Sickness*, p. 70. Looking at her postcard collection Tillman's protagonist thinks of 'that scene in *The Discreet Charm of the Bourgeoisie* when the dinner guests look at tourist postcards as if they're pornography'. There is nothing new to say about either sex or the 'sights' (p. 12). See also Naomi Schor's scholarly-cum-autobiographical essay on collecting postcards of *belle époque* Paris, 'Collecting Paris', in John Elsner and Roger Cardinal (eds), *The Cultures of Collecting* (London, 1994), pp. 252–74.

28 Margaret Fuller, *These Sad but Glorious Days: Dispatches from Europe, 1846–1850*, ed. Larry Reynolds and Susan Belasco Smith (New York, 1992), pp. 129–30, quoted in William W. Stowe, *Going Abroad: European Travel in Nineteenth-Century American Culture* (Princeton, NJ, 1994), p. 25.

29 Lydia Sigourney, preface to *Pleasant Memories of Pleasant Lands* (1842), quoted in Stowe, *Going Abroad*, p.12.

30 Washington Irving, *The Sketch Book of Geoffrey Crayon, Gent.* (1820) (New York, 1961), p. 15.

31 Sigmund Freud, 'A Disturbance of Memory on the Acropolis: An Open Letter to Romain Rolland on the Occasion of his Seventieth Birthday' (1936), in *The Standard Edition of the Complete Psychological Works of Sigmund Freud*, XXII, trans. James Strachey (London, 1964), pp. 237–48 (p. 247).

32 Herman Melville, *Redburn* (1849), (New York, 1983), pp. 171–2.

33 For a satirical view of the packaging of Europe as an American museum, see Mark Twain, *The Innocents Abroad* (1869). See also Henry James's portrayal of Gilbert Osmond in *The Portrait of a Lady* (1881) and Orson Welles's *Citizen Kane* (1940) for an exploration of the considerable dangers involved in American art collecting in Europe.

34 Ezra Pound, 'Henry James', *Little Review*, Aug. 1918, reprinted in T. S. Eliot (ed.), *The Literary Essays of Ezra Pound* (London, 1954), pp. 295–338 (p. 295).

35 Henry Miller, *Tropic of Cancer* (1934) (London, 1965), pp. 35, 157. There has been an enormous amount written about the American expatriate experience in Paris. Two useful recent studies are J. Gerald Kennedy, *Imagining Paris: Exile, Writing and American Identity* (New Haven, 1993), and Jean Méral, *Paris in American Literature*, trans. Laurette Long (Chapel Hill, 1989).

36 Henry James, *Roderick Hudson* (1876) (Harmondsworth, 1986), p. 69.

37 See, for example, Thorstein Veblen's seminal work on the importance of the European journey as a mark of conspicuous consumption and leisure in *The Theory of the Leisure Class* (1899).

38 John Hollander, 'Late August on the Lido' (1958), in *A Crackling of Thorns* (New

Haven, 1958), quoted in Robert von Hallberg's excellent essay, 'Tourism and Postwar Poetry', in Michael Kowalewski (ed.), *Temperamental Journeys: Essays on the Modern Literature of Travel* (Athens, GA, 1992), pp. 126–52. Von Hallberg notes that 'the theme of the rise and fall of empires is a subject that comes up often' in the 'tourist poetry' of the period. It is also an important theme in Thomas Pynchon's *Gravity's Rainbow* (1973), which describes the movement of displaced people in the wastelands of Europe at the end of the Second World War. 'The Nationalities are on the move. It is a great frontierless streaming out of here.' (London, 1973), p. 549.

39 In *Rise to Globalism: American Foreign Policy since 1938*, Stephen E. Ambrose writes that 'Americans who wanted to bring the blessings of democracy, capitalism, and stability to everyone meant just what they said – the whole world, in their view, should be a reflection of the United States'. The Pelican History of the United States, VIII (Harmondsworth, 1971), p. 21.

40 Lynne Tillman, *Absence Makes the Heart* (London, 1990), p. 16. In his study of anti-Americanism, Paul Hollander, however, argues that 'the anti-Americanism in Western Europe . . . has not been generally speaking, the attitude of majorities but rather of substantial minorities and especially of important elite groups'. *Anti-Americanism: Critiques at Home and Abroad, 1965–1990* (Oxford, 1992), p. 369. During the Vietnam war, however, anti-Americanism was common even in Paris, one of the more America-phile cities of Europe. See, for example, Mary McCarthy's *Birds of America* (Harmondsworth, 1972).

41 Whit Stillman, *Barcelona* (London, 1994), p. 150.

42 *Motion Sickness*, pp. 106, 161, 189.

43 Quentin Tarantino, *Pulp Fiction* (1994). Quoted from the screenplay (1994), pp. 14–15.

44 *Barcelona*, p. 58.

45 James Baldwin, 'The Discovery of What It Means to Be an American', in *Nobody Knows My Name* (New York, 1962), pp. 3–12 (p. 9).

46 Bryan Cheyette adopts Salman Rushdie's notion of the 'imaginary homeland' for his essay, 'Philip Roth and Clive Sinclair: Representations of an "Imaginary Homeland" in Postwar British-Jewish and American-Jewish Literature', in Ann Massa and Alistair Stead (eds), *Forked Tongues?: Comparing Twentieth-Century British and American Literature* (London, 1994), pp. 355–73.

47 I am using Milan Kundera's phrase. *Life is Elsewhere* (London, 1986).

48 Roth edited a series for Penguin Books entitled 'Writers from the Other Europe'. Roth also finds a fruitful subject in English anti-Semitism. 'England's made a Jew of me in only eight weeks, which, on reflection, might be the least painful method.' *The Counterlife* (Harmondsworth, 1988), p. 328. See also *Deception* (1990).

49 Cynthia Ozick's *The Messiah of Stockholm* (1987) is a rewriting of Schultz's *The Messiah*, and Philip Roth's *Zuckerman Bound* (1989) ends with a search for Schultz's lost papers. Meanwhile *The Ghost Writer* (1979) is a fantasy about Anne Frank.

50 Henry James, Letter to Charles Eliot Norton, 4th February 1872, in Leon Edel (ed.), *Henry James: Letters*, I (London, 1974), p. 274.

51 Saul Bellow, *Mr Sammler's Planet* (Harmondsworth, 1971), p. 35; Bernard Malamud, *The Magic Barrel* (London, 1960), pp. 105–33, 155–82.

52 Alan Levy, 'Preface', in Scott H. Rogers (ed.), *Bohemian Verses: An Anthology of Contemporary English Language Writings from Prague* (Prague, 1993), pp. xix–xxxvii (p. xxxvi).

53 I am using Paul Hollander's term from his account of communist pilgrimages, *Political Pilgrims: Travels of Western Intellectuals to the Soviet Union, China and Cuba, 1928–1978* (Oxford, 1981). The modern Yappies have no interest in either politics or pilgrimage.

54 Robert Young, for example, argues that the 'problematic of the place of Western

culture in relation to non-Western cultures' is definitive of postmodernism: *White Mythologies: Writing History and the West* (London, 1990), p. 19.

55 *The Accidental Tourist*, p. 196.

56 *Ibid.*, p. 210.

57 Paul Auster, *Moon Palace* (Harmondsworth, 1989), p. 230. Fogg's uncle believes his name – evoking Marco Polo, the African explorer Stanley and Phileas Fogg – proved that travel 'was in [his] blood' (p. 6). Fogg's experience in Chinatown recalls Henry James's reaction on returning to New York in 1904 after twenty years away:

> I think indeed that the simplest account of the action of Ellis Island on the spirit of any sensitive citizen who may have happened to 'look in' is that he comes back from his visit not at all the same person that he went. He has eaten of the tree of knowledge, and the taste will be for ever in his mouth.

> *The American Scene* (1907) (Harmondsworth, 1994), p. 66.

58 John Updike, 'A Madman', in *Forty Stories* (Harmondsworth, 1987), pp. 187–96 (p. 187).

59 A similar lesson is learnt by Alison Lurie's protagonist in her novel *Foreign Affairs*. Before visiting England she felt it had been 'slowly and lovingly shaped and furnished out of her favourite books, from Beatrix Potter to Anthony Powell'. The books may be different from those listed by Updike's narrator, but her conviction that 'she could literally walk into the country of her mind' is the same as his. She too must learn that 'the real thing' is something else. *Foreign Affairs* (London, 1986), p. 15.

60 Susan Sontag, 'Unguided Tour' (1978), in *A Susan Sontag Reader* (Harmondsworth, 1983), pp. 371–81 (pp. 374, 381, 371). See Sontag's essay on Lévi-Strauss, 'The Anthropologist as Hero', in *Against Interpretation* (New York, 1966), pp. 69–81.

61 *Motion Sickness*, p. 107. In his parody, *The Great American Novel* (New York, 1980), William Carlos Williams linked the form of the novel with the idea of progress – 'if there is progress then there must be a novel' – only to add, 'there cannot be a novel. There can only be pyramids of words, tombs' (p. 9). Tillman's protagonist says of the Great American Novel that 'no woman I've ever known has ever used that phrase, one that's ridiculous to me' (p. 14).

62 *Invisible Cities*, pp. 127, 141.

63 Lynne Tillman, 'Telling Tales', *Critical Quarterly*, XXXVII/4 (Winter 1995), reprinted in *The Broad Picture: Essays* (London, 1997), pp. 134–44 (p. 142).

64 *America*, p. 9. See also *Cool Memories*, pp. 168–9.

65 This sense of a mixed-up European cultural identity is reflected in Richard Linklater's film *Before Sunrise* (1995). In many ways a conventional story of a brief encounter between a boy and girl on their travels, the film is interesting for several reasons. The boy is American and has been visiting Madrid. She is Parisian but has been visiting her grandmother in Budapest. Vienna, where they have their night of romance, is simply a scenic backdrop for their rather banal encounter. Linklater has said that the film was conceived 'with an unnamed European city in mind', while its producer Anna Waler-McBay described Vienna as 'like a European Austin [Texas]'. Quoted in Howard Feinstein, 'Stars and Tripe', *Guardian*, Tabloid, 6 April 1995, pp. 8–9.

66 *Tristes Tropiques*, p. 38.

67 *White Noise*, p. 66.

68 The film is based on Philip K. Dick's short story, 'We Can Remember It for You Wholesale', in *The Collected Stories of Philip K. Dick*, V (London, 1991).

69 William Gibson, *Neuromancer* (1984) (London, 1986), p. 67.

70 The phrase 'worldmaking' is now commonly used by postmodern theorists and writers. It was first used by the philosopher Nelson Goodman in *Ways of Worldmaking* (Indianapolis, 1978) and has subsequently been adapted to suit very different purposes.

The relationship between science fiction and postmodernism is discussed by, among others, Brian McHale in *Constructing Postmodernism* (London, 1992).

71 'A Debate: William Gass and John Gardner', in Tom LeClair and Larry McCaffery, *Anything Can Happen: Interviews with Contemporary American Novelists* (Urbana, IL, 1983), pp. 20–31 (p. 27).

72 Saul Bellow, *Henderson the Rain King* (1959) (Harmondsworth, 1966), p. 157.

73 John Updike, 'Through a Continent, Darkly', in *Picked-Up Pieces* (New York, 1975), pp. 343–51.

74 The phrase comes from the title essay in Guy Davenport's *The Geography of the Imagination: Forty Essays* (San Francisco, 1981), pp. 3–15.

75 On Germany, see 'The English Garden', in *In the Future Perfect* (London, 1975), and *How German Is It* (London, 1980). On Mexico, see *Eclipse Fever* (London, 1993).

76 Sylvère Lotringer, 'Walter Abish: Wie Deutsch Ist Es', *Semiotext(e)*, IV/2 (1982), pp. 160–78 (p. 161).

77 Roland Barthes, *Empire of Signs*, trans. Richard Howard (New York, 1982), p. 3.

78 *Ibid.*, p. 6.

79 *Absence Makes the Heart*, pp. 66, 105.

80 Lynne Tillman, 'Critical Fiction/Critical Self', in Philomena Mariani (ed.), *Critical Fictions: The Politics of Imaginative Writing* (Seattle, 1991), p. 99, reprinted in *The Broad Picture*, pp. 18–25 (p. 21). *Motion Sickness*, p. 51.

10 *Edward James:* Per ardua ad astra

1 C. Penley, *NASA/Trek: Popular Science and Sex in America* (London, 1997).

2 *Magazine of Fantasy and Science Fiction* (December 1996), pp. 100–58.

3 A point made by Arthur B. Evans in an unpublished paper given at the 'Utopies' conference at the Maison d'Ailleurs in Yverdon-les-Bains, Switzerland, in 1990. The quotation is from *La Maison à Vapeur* in the Livre de Poche Jules Verne series (Paris, 1968), p. 70. Although Verne was one of the creators of science fiction, this paper will concentrate exclusively on the Anglo-American brand of science fiction that has been dominant throughout the world, above all since 1945.

4 In the introduction to a book of More's epigrams, 1518, cited by Paul Turner in the introduction to his translation of *Utopia* (Harmondsworth, 1961), p. 10.

5 See Philip Babcock Gove, *The Imaginary Voyage in Prose Fiction. A History of its Criticism and a Guide for its Study, with an Annotated Check List of 215 Imaginary Voyages from 1700 to 1800* (New York, 1941); a more recent study is that of Paul Baines, '"Able Mechanick": The Life and Adventures of Peter Wilkins and the Eighteenth-Century Fantastic Voyage', in David Seed (ed.), *Anticipations: Essays on Early Science Fiction and its Precursors* (Liverpool, 1995), pp. 1–25.

6 See Everett F. Bleiler, *Science-Fiction: The Early Years. A Full Description of More than 3,000 Science-Fiction Stories from Earliest Times to the Appearance of the Genre Magazines in 1930* (Kent, OH, 1990), pp. 896–8. A numerical study of Bleiler's data is to be found in Edward James, 'Science Fiction by Gaslight: An Introduction to English-Language Science Fiction in the Nineteenth Century', in Seed (ed.), *Anticipations*, pp. 26–45.

7 This has been discussed in Michael J. Crowe, *The Extraterrestrial Life Debate, 1750–1900: The Idea of a Plurality of Worlds from Kant to Lowell* (Cambridge, 1986).

8 E.g. Groff Conklin (ed.), *Seven Trips Through Time and Space* (New York, 1968); Damon Knight (ed.), *First Flight: Maiden Voyages in Space and Time* (New York, 1963); and – the most influential of all sf anthologies – R. J. Healy and J. F. McComas (eds), *Adventures in Time and Space* (New York, 1946). Chapter 3 of Gary K. Wolfe's

The Known and the Unknown: The Iconography of Science Fiction (Kent, OH, 1979) is an excellent introduction to the 'icon of the spaceship'.

9   Tom Godwin, 'The Cold Equations', first published in *Astounding Science Fiction* (August 1954) and frequently anthologized, as in R. Silverberg (ed.), *The Science Fiction Hall of Fame* (New York, 1971). It has been a touchstone for the approach of the hard-headed sf writer who wants to show 'society's institutionalized delusions set against the overwhelmingly, absolutely neutral point of view of the universe': G. Benford, 'Teaching Science Fiction: Unique Challenges', *Science-Fiction Studies*, 6 (1979), p. 250. J. Huntington's masterly deconstruction of the story in *Rationalizing Genius: Ideological Stategies in the Classic American Science Fiction Short Story* (New Brunswick, 1989), pp. 79–85, shows how 'the rhetoric of science' may be a 'sop to reason, allowing the reader to indulge in a fantasy which may be entirely irrational'. The debate about the reading of this story is a very live issue: see the debate in the *New York Review of Science Fiction*, 64 (December 1993) (John Kessel), 66 (February 1994) (Taras Wolansky, Brian Stableford, David Stewart Zink, Gordon Van Gelder), 58 (April 1994) (Sherry Coldsmith, Darrell Schweitzer, Catherine Mintz, Donald G. Keller), 69 (May 1994) (John Kessel), 71 (July 1994) (Sam Moskowitz) and 72 (August 1994) (Mark W. Tiedemann).

10 *The Skylark of Space* was serialized in *Amazing Stories* between August and October 1928 but was begun in 1915. He wrote it initially together with Mrs Lee Hawkins Garby, who allegedly helped with the romantic passages. The quotation is from the revised edition of 1958 (Digit Books, London), p. 11.

11 This is true at least for 'Crashing Suns' (*Weird Tales*, August–September 1928); the six stories featuring the Interstellar Patrol, beginning with 'The Sun-Stealers' (*Weird Tales*, February 1929), although set equally far into the future, are in a somewhat different future. All seven were reprinted together as *Outside the Universe* (1964) and *Crashing Suns* (1965). See Bleiler, *Science-Fiction*, pp. 334–7, and Clute and Nicholls (eds), *Encyclopedia*, p. 538.

12 The readers of *Amazing* were not necessarily happy with this. *Amazing* in April 1929 published three letters complaining about the shoddy science in Smith's *The Skylark of Space*: in answer to one from C. N. Cook, the editor Hugo Gernsback, a great missionary for the cause of science, excused Smith (and himself) by saying 'A considerable latitude must be allowed to a writer of interplanetary stories' (p. 82).

13 'Islands of Space' first appeared in *Amazing Stories Quarterly* (Spring 1931) and was published in book form in 1957; the edition cited is the Ace paperback (New York: no date given, but apparently 1966), p. 9.

14 *Ibid.*, p. 59.

15 Isaac Asimov, *Foundation* (1942; printed in book form 1951), cited from the Panther edition (London, 1960), p. 3.

16 Donald A. Wollheim, *The Universe Makers: Science Fiction Today* (New York, 1971; cited from the Gollancz edition, London, 1972), p. 42.

17 The sequence began as a series of linked stories in *Astounding Science Fiction*, with 'Foundation' (May, 1942); they were collected as *Foundation* (1951), *Foundation and Empire* (1952) and *Second Foundation* (1953). Between 1988 and his death in 1992 he wrote a number of other 'Foundation' novels; currently Greg Bear, Gregory Benford and David Brin are writing more.

18 'Lonely Among Us', first season, air-date November 2 1987 (energy cloud); 'We'll Always Have Paris', first season, air-date May 2 1988 (time-loop); 'Time Squared', second season, air-date April 3 1989 (energy whirlpool creating time-loop); and so on.

19 These figures are taken from Peter Nicholls (ed.), *The Science in Science Fiction* (London, 1982), p. 10.

20 Gregory Benford, 'Pascal's Terror', *Foundation: The Review of Science Fiction*, 42 (Spring 1988), p. 19.

21 Published in *Analog*, April 1986, pp. 76–86.

22 Published in *Analog*, October 1975, pp. 102–21.

23 Van Vogt, first published in *Astounding* (January 1944), and collected in Van Vogt, *Destination: Universe!* (1952; UK, 1960); Benford, published in *Analog* (April 1979), pp. 132–9.

24 Bernal's priority is suggested by A. C. Clarke, *The Challenge of the Spaceship* (New York, 1961), p. 59; on Bernal's booklet (published by Kegan Paul in 1929), see M. Hammerton, 'An (Almost) Forgotten Masterpiece', *Foundation: The Review of Science Fiction*, 49 (Summer, 1990), pp. 48–55. 'Universe' was first published in *Astounding Science Fiction* (May 1941); together with its sequel 'Common Sense' (*Astounding*, October 1941) it was published in book form as *Orphans of the Sky* (New York, 1964).

25 The term 'conceptual breakthrough' was introduced to science-fiction criticism by Clute and Nicholls in *The Encyclopedia of Science Fiction*: see pp. 254–7.

26 Published in *Analog* (January 1984), pp. 94–123.

27 The series currently comprises: *On Basilisk Station* (New York, 1993); *The Honor of the Queen* (1993); *The Short Victorious War* (1994); *Field of Dishonor* (1994); *Flag in Exile* (1995); *Honor Among Enemies* (1996); and *In Enemy Hands* (1997).

28 According to Clute and Nicholls (pp. 607 and 1142), 'hyperspace' and 'space warp' may have both been first used by John W. Campbell Jr in his 1931 story *Islands of Space*; but according to Clute and Nicholls (p. 420) 'hyperspace' did not appear until Campbell's *The Mightiest Machine* (1934).

29 Quoted from pp. 77–8 of the Puffin edition (Harmondsworth, 1966). John Clute and Peter Nicholls (eds), *The Encyclopedia of Science Fiction* (London, 1993), describe this as 'a particularly clear account' (p. 607). Clute and Nicholls's authoritative reference work discusses the faster-than-light motif under 'faster than light', 'hyperspace', 'space-warp': see also 'generation ships', 'space flight', 'spaceships' and 'suspended animation'.

30 Leigh Brackett, in *The Starmen* (London, 1954), imagines a race (the Vardda), who are genetically bred to stand the strain of acceleration and who thus control starflight in the galaxy. Similar stories which imagine starflight to be a restricted ability are mentioned in the following paragraph.

31 Frederik Pohl, 'The Mapmakers', first published in *Galaxy* (July 1955) and collected in Pohl, *Alternating Currents* (Harmondsworth, 1960), pp. 78–113; Frank Herbert's *Dune* series beginning in 1965 had a specialized Spacing Guild; Cordwainer Smith's 'Instrumentality' series, beginning with 'Scanners Die in Vain' (*Fantasy Book*, 6 [1950]; then in *The Best of Cordwainer Smith* [New York, 1975], reprinted as *The Rediscovery of Man* [London, 1988], pp. 1–39), has hyperspace navigators, 'scanners', who suffer a functional loss of part of their brains.

32 'Forgetfulness' was published as by Don A. Stuart in *Astounding* (June 1937) and republished several times, as in Campbell, *Cloak of Aesir* (New York, 1972).

33 Published in *Analog* (July 1962) (British edition November 1962, pp. 10–52); in book form as *Listen! The Stars!* in 1963; and in an expanded version as *The Stardroppers* in 1972.

34 Alfred Bester, *Tiger! Tiger!* (UK, 1956; revised version in US as *The Stars My Destination*; quoted here from the Science Fiction Book Club edition, London, 1958), p. 229.

35 Harry Harrison, 'A Tale of the Ending', in *One Step from Earth* (1970).

36 Published in *The Magazine of Fantasy and Science Fiction* (March 1979), pp. 32–40, citation from p. 33.

37 Published in *Analog* (July 1979), pp. 155–68.

38 'The Enemy Within' was the fifth episode of the first season, first aired on 6 October 1966; the script was by science-fiction writer Richard Matheson.

39 'Force of Nature', episode 161 of *Star Trek: The Next Generation*, was first aired on 13 November 1993.

40 Brian Stableford, *The Way to Write Science Fiction* (London, 1989), p. 47.

41 For some of the scientific lunacies of the most ubiquitous series, see Lawrence Krauss, *The Physics of Star Trek* (London, 1996). Concentration on the *physical* sciences, however, does gloss over some even more extreme lunacies, such as the idea that the crew of *USS Voyager* can travel 70,000 light years across the galaxy and still communicate instantaneously with aliens who, judging from their lip movements, are speaking English.

42 Stableford, pp. 47–8.

43 Published in *Analog* (July 1976), pp. 10–29; quotations from pp. 10 and 29.

44 Published in *Isaac Asimov's Science Fiction Magazine* (December 1987), pp. 18–23.

Select Bibliography

This bibliography is offered as a starting point for readers interested in developing their understanding of the subject. It would of course be vain to attempt to be comprehensive in a subject spanning the whole of the Western tradition. We have therefore limited ourselves to a selected list of books or significant journal articles which raise general issues and which discuss a variety of sources, avoiding as a rule both collections of sources or monographic treatments of single texts or single travellers, however important those might be.

Adams, P. G., *Travellers and Travel Liars 1600–1800* (Berkeley, 1962)

Augustinos, O., *French Odysseys: Greece in French Travel Literature from the Renaissance to the Romantic Era* (Baltimore, 1994)

Beer, G., *Open Fields: Science and Cultural Encounter* (Oxford, 1996)

Bourguet, M.-N., 'The Explorer', in *Enlightenment Portraits*, ed. M. Vovelle (Chicago and London, 1997)

Brotton, J., *Trading Territories: Mapping in the Early Modern World* (London, 1997)

Cairns, H. A. C., *Prelude to Imperialism: British Reactions to Central African Society 1840–1890* (London, 1965)

Campbell, M., *The Witness and the Other World: Exotic European Travel Writing, 1400–1600* (Ithaca and London, 1988)

Casson, L., *Travel in the Ancient World* (London, 1974)

Céard, J. and J. C. Margolin, *Voyager à la Renaissance*, Actes du colloque de Tours 1983 (Paris, 1987)

Clifford, J., *The Predicament of Culture: Twentieth-Century Ethnography, Literature and Art* (Cambridge, MA, 1988)

Curtin, P., *The Image of Africa: British Ideas in Action, 1780–1850* (London, 1965)

Elliot, J. H., *The Old World and the New 1492–1650* (Cambridge, 1970)

Fuller, M., *Voyages in Print: English Travel to America, 1576–1624* (Cambridge, 1995)

Goodman, J. R., *Chivalry and Exploration 1298–1630* (Woodbridge, 1998)

Greenblatt, S., ed., *New World Encounters* (Berkeley, 1993)

Hartog, F., *The Mirror of Herodotus: The Representation of the Other in the Writing of History* (Berkeley, 1988)

Helms, M., *Ulysses's Sail: An Ethnographic Odyssey of Power, Knowledge and Geographical Distance* (Princeton, 1988)

Hopkirk, P., *Trespassers on the Roof of the World. The Race for Lhasa* (Oxford, 1982)

Hulme, P., *Colonial Encounters: Europe and the Native Caribbean 1492–1797* (London, 1986)

——, ed., *Writing Travels*, vol. I of *Studies in Travel Writing* (Spring 1997)

Jardine, N., J. A. Secord and E. C. Spary, eds, *Cultures of Natural History* (Cambridge, 1996)

Kupperman, K. O., ed., *America in European Consciousness 1493–1750* (Chapel Hill and London, 1995)

Lach, D. F., *Asia in the Making of Europe*, 3 vols (Chicago and London, 1965–93)

Leask, N., *British Romantic Writers and the East: Anxieties of Empire* (Cambridge, 1992)

Leonard, I. A., *Colonial Travelers in Latin America* (New York, 1972)

Lestringant, F., *Mapping the Renaissance World: The Geographical Imagination in the Age of Discovery* (Cambridge, 1994)

Maczak, A., *Travel in Early Modern Europe* (Cambridge, 1995)

Marshall, P. J. and G. Williams, *The Great Map of Mankind: British Perceptions of the World in the Age of Enlightenment* (London, 1982)

Martels, Z. von, *Travel Fact and Travel Fiction: Studies in Fiction, Literary Tradition, Scholarly Discovery and Observation in Travel Writing* (Leiden, 1994)

Mitter, P., *Much Maligned Monsters: History of European Reactions to Indian Art* (Oxford, 1977)

Ohler, N., *The Medieval Traveller* (Woodbridge, 1989)

Pagden, A., *European Encounters with the New World* (New Haven and London, 1993)

Pastor Bodmer, B., *The Armature of Conquest: Spanish Accounts of the Discovery of America 1492–1589* (Stanford, 1992)

Penrose, B., *Travel and Discovery in the Renaissance 1420–1620* (Cambridge, MA, 1952)

Pratt, M. L., *Imperial Eyes: Travel Writing and Transculturation* (London and New York, 1992)

Riffenburgh, B., *The Myth of the Explorer. The Press, Sensationalism and Geographical Discovery* (Oxford, 1994)

Romm, J., *The Edges of the Earth in Ancient Thought: Geography, Exploration and Fiction* (Princeton, 1992)

Rotberg, R., *Africa and its Explorers: Motives, Methods and Impact* (Cambridge, 1970)

Rubiés, J. P., 'New Worlds and Renaissance Ethnology', *History and Anthropology*, VI/2–3 (1993), pp. 157–97

Said, E., *Orientalism* (New York, 1978)

Salmon, C., ed., *Récits de voyages asiatiques: Genres, mentalités, conception de l'espace* (Paris, 1996)

Sargent-Baur, B. N., ed., *Journeys toward God: Pilgrimage and Crusade* (Kalamazoo, 1992)

Schwartz, S. B., *Implicit Understandings: Observing, Reporting and Reflecting on the Encounters between Europeans and Other Peoples in the Early Modern Era* (Cambridge, 1994)

Smith, B., *European Vision and the South Pacific* (New Haven and London, 1985)

Stafford, B., *Voyage into Substance: Art, Sciences and the Illustrated Travel Account, 1760–1840* (Cambridge, MA, 1984)

Stagl, J., *A History of Curiosity: The Theory of Travel 1550–1800* (Chur, 1995)

Stagl, J. and C. Pinney, eds, *From Travel Literature to Ethnography*, *History and Anthropology*, IX/2–4 (1996)

Stoye, J., *English Travellers Abroad 1604–1667* (London, 1952)

Teltscher, K., *India Inscribed: European and British Writing on India 1600–1800* (Delhi, 1995)

Todorov, T., *La conquête de l'Amerique: La question de l'autre* (Paris, 1982)

Turner, V. and E. Turner, *Image and Pilgrimage in Christian Culture: Anthropological Perspectives* (Oxford, 1978)

Youngs, T., *Travellers in Africa: British Travelogues 1850–1900* (Manchester, 1994)

Acknowledgements

Many of the subjects in this book were discussed in the congenial surroundings of a small-group colloquium consisting of most of the contributors and a few others – working from the perspectives of various disciplines – on the understanding of travel literature. We would like to offer particular thanks to all of the colloquium participants, both the contributors to this book and Glenn Bowman, Michael Harbsmeier, Elisa Sampson and Antje Stannek. Held at Sidney Sussex College, Cambridge, the colloquium was supported financially by the Courtauld Institute and the Department of History at the University of Reading. At different times, Stephen Bann, Edward James and Anthony Pagden offered valuable readings and comments. We owe special gratitude to Sorcha Carey for her help with the index, and to Kasia Boddy and Melissa Calaresu for hosting everyone so warmly in Cambridge.

J.E. and J.-P.R.

Photographic Acknowledgements

The editors and publisher wish to express their thanks to the following authors or sources of illustrative material and to offer their gratitude for permission to reproduce it:

British Film Institute, London: p. 248; British Library Reproductions, by permission of The British Library: p. 159; Canal Plus: p. 248; Courtauld Institute of Art, London (Conway Library): p. viii; Mrs Wesla Hanson: p. 235; Harvard University: pp. 213, 215; courtesy of the Chief Librarian, The Huntington Library, San Marino, CA: p. 72; courtesy of the Director, Library of the Palacio Real, Madrid: p. 69; Royal Geographical Society: pp. 222, 225, 228; Scottish National Gallery of Modern Art, Edinburgh: p. 235; Service Bibliographique & Historique de l'Armée de Terre: the front cover; the Syndics of Cambridge University Library: pp. 139, 143, 145, 147, 148, 188, 203, 205; the University of Manchester: p. 171; the University of Reading Library: p. 42; and Wolverhampton Art Gallery/Eardley Lewis: p. 236.

Index